GOOD NEWS!

THE LIFE AND TEACHINGS OF JESUS

THE FOUR GOSPELS IN A SINGLE ACCOUNT

Translated & Blended by Charlie Webster

Copyright 2016 by Charlie Webster
First Edition – March 2016 (Electronic)
Second Edition – June 2016 (Paperback)

ISBN-13: 9781530819157

All rights reserved.
Quotations of material in this book may be used freely as long as the source of those quotations is clearly identified and the quotations do not change the meaning of the words in the context of this book.

For further information on this book or the translator, visit

www.NewCenturyMinistries.com

SO WHY A NEW TRANSLATION OF THE GOSPELS?

This is a new translation providing a blend of everything from all four Gospels in conversational English. If you're interested in more details, see Why a New Translation? in the Glossary. Otherwise, just enjoy!

Statement of Rights: Anyone who wishes to use excerpts from this translation of the Gospels may do so without written permission provided that the source of such excerpts is identified.

Table of Contents

Chapter 1 – Two Birth Announcements and John's Birth	9
Chapter 2 – Two More Birth Announcements and Jesus' Birth	11
Chapter 3 – Jesus' Childhood	12
Chapter 4 – Jesus Is God with Us	14
Chapter 5 – The Ministry of John the Immerser	15
Chapter 6 – A Preview of Things to Come	17
Chapter 7 – The Wilderness Temptation	18
Chapter 8 – Getting Started	18
Chapter 9 – Teaching about Growing Up Spiritually – Part 1	22
Chapter 10 – Teaching about Growing Up Spiritually – Part 2	26
Chapter 11 – Teaching about Growing Up Spiritually – Part 3	27
Chapter 12 – The Great Physician	29
Chapter 13 – Warnings about Selfish Pride and Worldly Focus	31
Chapter 14 – The Twelve Disciples	34
Chapter 15 – A Trip to Jerusalem	35
Chapter 16 – Back to Galilee	36
Chapter 17 – Some Additional Teaching	39
Chapter 18 – Stories about Seeds that Jesus Used	43
Chapter 19 – Other Stories Illustrating the Kingdom	46
Chapter 20 – Stories about Wealth that Jesus Used	46
Chapter 21 – More Stories that Jesus Used	49
Chapter 22 – About Forgiveness and Christian Love	51
Chapter 23 – A Trip to Judea	52
Chapter 24 – Returning to Galilee	55
Chapter 25 – John the Immerser's Ministry Ends	57
Chapter 26 – The Bread of Life-Part 1	58
Chapter 27 – The Bread of Life-Part 2	61
Chapter 28 – A Feast in Jerusalem	63
Chapter 29 – Beginning Preparations for the End	65
Chapter 30 – The Greatest and the Least	65
Chapter 31 – A Changing Ministry	67
Chapter 32 – To Jerusalem for the Feast of Tents	69
Chapter 33 – Teaching in the Temple – Part 1	71
Chapter 34 – Teaching in the Temple – Part 2	73
Chapter 35 – Encamped along the Jordan	75
Chapter 36 – A Trip to Bethany	78
Chapter 37 – The Final Trip from Galilee to Jerusalem	79
Chapter 38 – Jesus Enters Jerusalem	82
Chapter 39 – Teaching in the Temple Again – Part 1	85
Chapter 40 – Teaching in the Temple Again – Part 2	87
Chapter 41 – Questions about the End	90
Chapter 42 – Passover Preparations and the Meal	93

Chapter 43 – After Supper in Jerusalem ... 96
Chapter 44 – On the Way to the Garden ... 98
Chapter 45 – The Lord's Prayer ... 100
Chapter 46 – In the Garden ... 102
Chapter 47 – Three Jewish Examinations and Peter's Denial ... 104
Chapter 48 – Trials Before Pilate and Herod ... 106
Chapter 49 – The Crucifixion and Burial ... 109
Chapter 50 – Resurrection Events ... 112
Chapter 51 – Jesus Is Alive and Appears to Followers ... 114
Chapter 52 – Appearances in Galilee ... 116
Chapter 53 – Final Events ... 118

GLOSSARY

Abraham ... 121
Agent / Angel ... 121
Andrew the Disciple ... 121
Anointing Jesus ... 121
Augustus Caesar ... 122
Baptize / Immerse ... 122
Bar-Abbas ... 124
Belief / Faith / Trust ... 124
Bethabara ... 125
Bethlehem ... 125
Bethsaida ... 126
Biblical Chronology ... 126
Biblical Judges ... 128
Biblical Names ... 128
Birth and Childhood of Jesus – Events ... 128
Birth of Jesus – The Date ... 131
Caesar ... 133
Capernaum ... 133
Christ / Messiah ... 134
Christian Love / Caring Love ... 134
Common Gender ... 135
Crucifixion Events and Issues ... 136
　1. Crucifixion Timing Issues ... 136
　2. Jesus' Trials ... 139
　3. Jesus' Crucifixion ... 142
　4. Jesus' Resurrection ... 145
Cursing, Swearing, and Profanity ... 147
Dining Customs ... 148
Disciples, Apostles, Messengers, and Missionaries ... 148
Elijah ... 150
Evil Spirits, Unclean Spirits, and Demons ... 150
Faith ... 151

A Fig Tree Cursed	151
Forgiveness	151
Genealogy of Jesus	152
Gentiles / Nations	154
The Gospels	155
1. John's Gospel	155
2. Luke's Gospel	156
3. Mark's Gospel	156
4. Matthew's Gospel	157
The Great Commission	158
Heaven / Sky	158
Hell	159
Herod	159
Herod's Temple	160
High Priest	161
Immediately / Quickly	161
In the Name of	161
Isaiah	161
Disciples Named James	161
Jericho	162
Jerusalem	162
Jesus and Divorce	162
Jesus and Temptation	163
Jesus and the Law	164
Jesus as the Logic	164
Jewish Elders	165
Jewish Feasts	165
Jewish Marriage Customs	166
Jews and Samaritans	167
John the Disciple	167
John the Immerser	167
Joseph-Father of Jesus	168
Men Named Judas	168
Judea and Galilee	169
Judeans / Jewish Authorities	169
Lamb of God	170
The Languages of the New Testament	170
The Law of Moses	170
Lawyers	171
Lazarus	171
Levites	172
Mary Magdalene	172
Mary-Mother of Jesus	172
Matthew / Levi	173

Maturity / Perfection	174
Miracles	174
Money in the Bible	175
Moses	176
Nathanael	177
Nazareth	177
Nicodemus	178
Peter the Disciple	178
Pharisees	178
Pilate	178
Poetry in the Bible	179
The Pool of Healing	179
Preaching / Proclaiming	179
Priests / Chief Priests	179
Prophecies that the Christ would replace Judaism	180
Prophecies and Fulfillments	180
The Prophet	181
Repentance	181
Sabbath	181
Romans and Jews	180
Sabbath	182
Sacred Writings	182
Sadducees	184
Satan / Devil	184
Scribes	184
Servants / Slaves	185
Sin / Rebellion	185
Son of Man and Son of God	186
Sons and Fathers in Biblical Thinking	187
Supreme Court	187
Tax Collectors and "Sinners"	188
Team / Church	188
Theophilus	188
Third Person Commands	189
Triumphal Entry	189
Unforgivable Sin	189
"The Whole World"	190
Why a New Translation?	190
Wind, Breath, and Spirit	191
Priests Named Zechariah	191

GOOD NEWS
The Life and Teachings of Jesus

Chapter 1 – Two Birth Announcements and John's Birth

<u>An Introduction</u> Luke 1:1-4
(Glossary Articles: Biblical Names; Maturity / Perfection; Luke's Gospel; Theophilus)

¹A lot of people have written about what happened during Jesus' life. The message we Christians are bringing is based on the testimony of eyewitnesses from the earliest days – eyewitnesses who also became ministers of this message.

²So since I've carefully researched this information and now have extensive knowledge of the details from the beginning, it seemed like it would be good for me to write an orderly version of these things to provide you[1] with assurance that the message you've accepted is really true.

<u>The Announcement of John's Birth – June, 4 BC</u> Luke 1:5-25
(Glossary articles: Agent / Angel; Biblical Chronology; Biblical Names; Birth of Jesus – The Date; Elijah; Herod; Herod's Temple; High Priest; Judea; Priests; Repentance; Sin / Rebellion)

³During the time that Herod the Great was king of Judea, there was a Jewish priest[2] whose wife was named Elizabeth. She was a descendant of the first Jewish high priest[3], and both of them were living as faithful servants of God by observing all God's commandments and rules. But this couple had no children – Elizabeth had been unable to get pregnant – and they were both getting old[4].

⁴While he was serving in the temple complex along with the rest of his division of the priests, as was customary for the Jewish priests, he was chosen by a drawing to have the honor of burning incense in the temple of the Lord.

⁵As usual, a large crowd of people stood outside in the courtyards praying while he offered the incense. But while he was at the Altar of Incense, an agent from God suddenly appeared with him inside the temple, standing on the right side of the Altar of Incense.

⁶When this priest saw God's agent, at first he was terrified, but the agent reassured him: "Don't be afraid! God's heard your prayer. Your wife, Elizabeth, will have your son, and you're to call him John.

⁷"Your son will bring great joy to you, and many others will rejoice because of his birth. This son will be a great prophet in the Lord's sight, but he's not to drink any wine or alcoholic beverage as long as he lives.

⁸"He'll be filled with God's Holy Spirit from the moment he's born. He'll cause many of his Israelite countrymen to turn their lives around to focus on the Lord their God[5].

⁹"This child will live before the Lord with the same spirit and power seen in the prophet Elijah, turning the hearts of the fathers to their children. He'll cause those who are living in rebellion[6] against God to see the wisdom of those who serve God, and he'll prepare all the people for the Lord to come among them."

¹⁰The priest replied with skepticism, "How'm I supposed to believe what you're telling me? After all, I'm an old man, and my wife is no spring chicken."

¹¹The agent of God responded: "I am Gabriel! I have the authority to stand in the very presence of almighty God himself! I was sent to bring you this good news, but now, since you seem to have trouble believing my message, you'll be mute, unable to say a word, until the day when all of these things are fully accomplished. And everything I've said will happen in its proper time!"

¹²Meanwhile all the people were waiting for the priest, wondering why he was taking so long in the temple. When he finally did come out, he couldn't speak a word. He made gestures with his hands until they realized that he'd seen a vision while he was in the temple.

¹³As soon as his time to serve in the temple was completed he went to his own home, and it wasn't long until Elizabeth was pregnant.

¹⁴For the first five months of her pregnancy Elizabeth kept herself hidden from others saying excitedly, "This is how the Lord's brought me to life; taking away the shame I used to feel when I was around others[7]."

---

[1] 1:2-Literally, "you, most excellent Theophilus." See Theophilus in the Glossary.
[2] 1:3-See Zechariah in the Glossary.
[3] 1:3-Aaron.
[4] 1:3-This could've been any age after normal child-bearing age for Elizabeth.
[5] 1:8-See Belief / Faith and Repentance in the Glossary.
[6] 1:9-Literally, "the disobedient," but disobedience is rebellion and either of those is sin. Since those with faith will naturally be faithful, disobedience is also evidence of a lack of faith (see Hebrews 3:18-19 to see the link between faith and obedience).
[7] 1:14-When Elizabeth responded to her pregnancy, her words were literally, "This is how the Lord has made me," but the implication has to do with finally coming into being or into the reality always intended. In Elizabeth's culture, childbirth was considered the crowning event in a woman's life. Since she'd been childless up until this time, her joy in becoming pregnant was understandably overwhelming.

The Announcement of Jesus' Birth to Mary – December, 4 BC Luke 1:26-38
(Glossary articles: Agent / Angel; Biblical Chronology; Birth of Jesus – The Date; Galilee; Jewish Marriage Customs; Joseph; Mary; Son of God; Sons and Fathers in Biblical Thinking)

[15] About the time Elizabeth was six months pregnant, God sent his agent Gabriel again, this time to a young virgin named Mary who was living in a town in Galilee[1].

[16] She was in a contract to marry a man named Joseph who was a descendant of King David. And having come into her home, Gabriel said, "Rejoice, blest woman. The Lord himself is with you."

[17] This greeting left Mary confused, trying to understand the significance of the agent's words.

[18] Sensing Mary's confusion the agent said, "Don't be afraid, Mary – God's extremely pleased with you. Because of this, you'll become pregnant and give birth to a son, and you'll name your son 'Jesus.'

[19] "He'll be truly great, and he'll be called the son of the Most High, and the Lord God will give him the throne of his ancestor, King David. He'll rule Israel forever, and his kingdom will never end!"

[20] "How can that happen?!" Mary asked. "I'm a virgin – I've never had sex with anyone!"

[21] "God's Holy Spirit will come over you," answered the agent, "and the dynamic strength of the Most High will surround you[2] so that from the moment he's born, the baby will be holy, and he'll be called the Son of God.

[22] "If you've got any doubt about what I'm telling you, your relative, Elizabeth, has become pregnant even in her old age; though in the past people said she'd never have children. In fact, she's now in the sixth month of her pregnancy, because absolutely nothing's out of range when God commands it[3]."

[23] "Wow! OK! I'm the Lord's slave," said Mary, "so let it all happen, just like you said."

[24] Having received her reply, Gabriel left.

Mary Visits Elizabeth – December, 4 BC Luke 1:39-45
(Glossary article: Judea)

[25] Shortly after Gabriel's visit, Mary left in a rush to see Elizabeth. Elizabeth lived in a town in the hill country of Judea. As soon as Mary stepped into Elizabeth's house to greet her, Elizabeth's child jumped in her womb.

[26] After greeting Mary, Elizabeth was filled with God's Holy Spirit and practically shouted for joy, "Boy, have you been blessed – more than all other women. And how much more blessed is the child you're carrying! How did I rate this, that the one who'll be the mother of my Lord should come to visit me?

[27] "I'm telling you: as soon as I heard your voice greeting me, the baby leaped inside me for pure joy. And the joy you're feeling now comes from your faith that the Lord would do exactly what he told you he'd do."

Mary's Poem Luke 1:46-56
(Glossary articles: Abraham; In the Name of...; Poetry in the Bible)

[28] During this time Mary wrote this poem:

> [29] From the depths of my soul I praise the Lord[4]!
> How my spirit's rejoiced in God my savior
> Because he's cared so deeply for his lowly slave girl!
> And from now on, women of all generations will call me blessed
> Because the Mighty One did such great things for me!
> His very nature is holy!
> [30] He also shows mercy to all those who reverence him[5],
> From generation to generation
> His arm has done great things!
> He's scattered those who are arrogant in the attitude of their hearts;
> He's cast down rulers from their thrones;
> He's exalted the humble;
> And he filled the hungry with the finest food,
> While he sent the wealthy away empty-handed.

---

[1] 1:15-Nazareth.

[2] 1:21-There's never been a pregnancy as protected as this one.

[3] 1:22-Most translations record the words of Gabriel to Mary as saying that nothing is impossible for God. This wording can create a paradox when other passages say, for instance, that it's impossible for God to lie. This is straining at gnats trying to find fault with the biblical record. First, such efforts to find any tiny fault with the Bible's message is entirely inappropriate in for a book that has to deal—in human language—with things that are far, far beyond human experience. Second, in this case the wording is better understood as Gabriel telling Mary that God can do whatever he wants to do—the point being that God would never want to do evil.

[4] 1:29-Mary's whole poem has strong echoes of Psalm 103—"Bless the Lord, O my soul!" Mary turned this around and did what the psalm encourages us to do.

[5] 1:30-The poem shifts here from a focus on what God is doing in Mary's life to a focus on what God had done for Israel.

He's come to the rescue of his child, Israel,
To bring to mind his compassionate nature,
Just as he gave his word to our fathers,
To Abraham and his descendants forever!

³¹So Mary stayed with Elizabeth about three months and then returned to her own home.

The Birth of John – March, 3 BC Luke 1:57-66
(Glossary articles: Biblical Chronology; Birth of Jesus – The Date; Immediately / Quickly)

³²When the time came for Elizabeth's baby to be born, of course she had a son. When her neighbors and relatives heard that the Lord had shown such mercy on her, they threw a party.

³³Then when the baby was eight days old and it was time for him to be named and circumcised, they all came to the house. These friends assumed that the child would be named after his father, but Elizabeth said, "No! He'll be called John."

³⁴The neighbors and relatives all said, "There's nobody by that name in your whole family!"

³⁵So they gestured to his father[1] asking him what he'd name his son. He motioned for a writing tablet and wrote, "His name is John."

³⁶The neighbors and relatives were all amazed, but as soon as he'd written this, the old priest started talking again, praising God.

³⁷Everybody in the house was struck with awe, and the news of this became a hot topic of conversation all through the Judean hill country.

³⁸Everybody who heard about what had happened tried to figure out the meaning, saying, "What will become of this kid?" And they soon saw that God had his hand on John.

Chapter 2 – Two More Birth Announcements and Jesus' Birth

The Announcement to Joseph – March, 3 BC Matthew 1:18-25
(Glossary articles: Agent / Angel; Biblical Chronology; Birth of Jesus – The Date; Isaiah; Jewish Marriage Customs; Joseph; Mary; Prophecies and Fulfillments; Sin / Rebellion)

¹As mentioned earlier, Jesus' mother, Mary, was in a contract to marry Joseph. But before they actually had sexual relations, it was obvious that she was pregnant. (Of course her pregnancy was from God's Holy Spirit.)

²Joseph, her contracted husband, didn't know the origin of her child[2]. He was a good man and didn't want to make a public example of her infidelity, so he decided to break his contract with her quietly.

³But while Joseph was thinking over his options, an agent of the Lord appeared to him in a dream to say, "Joseph, son of David, don't be concerned about taking Mary as your wife. The child she's carrying comes from God's Holy Spirit. She's going to have a son, and you're going to name him Jesus[3], because he'll save his people from their sins[4]."

⁴All of this happened to give full meaning to what the Lord had said through the prophet Isaiah: "Behold, a virgin will conceive and bear a son, and they'll call his name Immanuel[5]." (The name Immanuel means "God with us.")

⁵When Joseph woke in the morning, he did as the agent of the Lord had commanded him. He and Mary went through with the wedding ceremony, but he didn't have sex with her until after Jesus was born.

Jesus' Birth in Bethlehem – September 11, 3 BC Luke 2:1-7
(Glossary articles: Augustus Caesar; Bethlehem; Biblical Chronology; Birth and Childhood of Jesus-Events; Birth of Jesus – The Date; Joseph)

⁶Shortly before the birth of Mary's son, the Roman emperor[6] ordered a registration for his whole empire. So each person went to his own home town to be registered.

⁷Since Joseph was a descendant of King David, he and his pregnant wife, Mary, had to travel to Bethlehem[7] to be registered, because that had been King David's hometown.

---

[1] 1:35-The fact that the people gestured to John's father may indicate that he'd been struck deaf as well as mute. However, there are other possibilities. It's possible he was already getting deaf in his old age; it's possible that the people so associated being mute with being deaf that they used gestures when they could've just talked to him, and it's possible that Elizabeth's choice of the name "John" created so much commotion that they had to use gestures.

[2] 2:2-Joseph probably knew nothing about Mary's pregnancy until she came back to Nazareth after her visit with Elizabeth. Mary had been away for about three months, so her pregnancy would've been visible when she came home. Since Joseph hadn't yet heard from God about Mary's pregnancy, his natural assumption was that she'd been unfaithful to him. Such unfaithfulness would've been considered adultery, and according to the Law of Moses, such adultery was a capital offense—punishable by stoning.

[3] 2:3-Jesus is the Greek version of the Hebrew name Joshua, meaning Jehovah is Salvation.

[4] 2:3-Remember, sin is always treason—rebellion against God.

[5] 2:4-Isaiah 7:14.

[6] 2:6-Augustus Caesar.

[7] 2:7-Literally, "leave Nazareth in Galilee."

⁸That's how it came about that they were in Bethlehem when she gave birth to her first son. She wrapped him in cloth strips and laid him in an animal's feeding trough because there wasn't room for having a baby in the family's guest quarters.

<u>The Announcement to the Shepherds – September 11, 3 BC</u> Luke 2:8-20
(Glossary articles: Agent / Angel; Bethlehem; Biblical Chronology; Birth and Childhood of Jesus-Events; Birth of Jesus – The Date)

⁹That night in the fields not far from Bethlehem there were some shepherds taking care of their flock. Suddenly an agent of the Lord stood before them and the radiant glory of God himself[1] shone around them – and they were terrified.

¹⁰Then the agent said, "Don't be afraid. Look, I'm bringing good and joyful news for everybody, news that a savior – Christ, the Lord – has been born for you today in David's hometown. This is what to look for: you'll find a baby wrapped in strips of cloth and lying in an animal's feeding trough."

¹¹And suddenly a vast contingent of the army of heaven appeared with this agent praising God and saying, "Glory to God in the highest; and on earth, peace to men who are favored by God."

¹²So when these agents of God returned to heaven, the shepherds talked excitedly among themselves saying, "Let's go to Bethlehem and see for ourselves what the Lord's revealed to us." So they hurried off to Bethlehem and there they found Mary and Joseph; and in an animal's feeding trough they saw the baby.

¹³After seeing for themselves, they left the stable and told people all through the area what the agents of the Lord had told them about this child. Everybody who heard it was amazed by what the shepherds told them. But Mary kept quiet, carefully thinking over all these things.

¹⁴So the shepherds returned to their flock, glorifying and praising God for all that they'd heard and seen – just as the Lord's agent had told them it would be.

<u>Jesus' Family Tree</u> Matthew 1:1-17; Luke 3:23-38
(Glossary articles: Abraham; Biblical Names; Christ / Messiah; Jericho; Genealogy of Jesus)

¹⁵Jesus was about 30 years old when he began his public ministry. Here's the background that establishes Jesus' birthright to claim the title of Christ[2]:

- Jesus was born as a Hebrew, a descendant of Abraham, as God had promised Abraham.
- He was born into the Israelite tribe of Judah, from which the prophets all agree that God's Christ would come.
- He was of the family of King David, to whom God promised that one of his descendants would reign forever.

¹⁶In every way his ancestry qualified him to be the Jewish Christ, but that ancestry also included women who weren't Jewish but who were famous in the history of Israel: a woman of Jericho[3] who protected the Israelite spies; a woman named Ruth[4] who followed her mother-in-law to Israel and accepted the God of Israel; and a woman[5] who married King David and became the mother of King Solomon.

Chapter 3 – Jesus' Childhood
<u>Going Through the Jewish Rituals – September, 3 BC</u> Luke 2:21-39
(Glossary articles: Agent / Angel; Biblical Chronology; Biblical Names; Birth and Childhood of Jesus-Events; Birth of Jesus – The Date; Christ / Messiah; Gentiles / Nations; Herod's Temple; Jerusalem; Law of Moses)

¹Eight days after Jesus was born [September 19, 3 BC] it was time for him to be named and circumcised[6]. His parents named him Jesus, just as the agent of the Lord had instructed them even before this baby was conceived.

²When it was time for Mary's purification ceremony [October 14, 3 BC] (as specified in the Law of Moses), they brought the baby to Jerusalem to present him before the Lord, because the Law of Moses says that every male who's a woman's firstborn shall be dedicated to the Lord.

³As a sign of this dedication they offered a sacrifice as required by the Law of the Lord – "two turtledoves or two young pigeons[7]."

⁴Now there was a man in Jerusalem named Simeon who lived a righteous life and who worshipped God faithfully. He was looking forward to the coming of God's Christ[8] as the hope of the people of Israel. God's Holy Spirit had revealed to him that he wouldn't die before he'd seen God's Christ.

⁵He'd come into the temple that day, compelled by the Holy Spirit, and when Mary and Joseph brought the young child Jesus to fulfill the customs required by the Law of Moses, he took the child up in his arms and blessed God, saying, "Lord,

---

[1] 2:9-A radiant glory is often associated with the presence of the Lord's agents.
[2] 2:15-This part of the account is drastically abbreviated. For all the details, see Genealogy of Jesus in the Glossary.
[3] 2:16-Rahab.
[4] 2:16-From the country of Moab.
[5] 2:16-Bathsheba.
[6] 3:1-Leviticus 12:3 requires circumcision on the eighth day of life.
[7] 3:3-Leviticus 12:1-8. This was the sacrifice to be offered if the family were too poor for the standard sacrifice of a lamb and a bird.
[8] 3:4-Literally, "the consolation of Israel."

I'm your servant, and now you can let me die in peace. You've done what you promised. I've seen the salvation that you've prepared for all humanity – the Christ who'll be a light to bring understanding to the nations[1] and who'll be the splendor of your people, Israel."

⁶Joseph and Mary were amazed at what he said about their child. Then Simeon blessed them and said to his mother, Mary, "You know, this child's destined to be the cause of the rise and of the fall of many in Israel. He'll be a sign from God – though there'll be those who'll stand against him – that the thoughts of many hearts may be revealed. And yes, a sword will also pierce through your own soul."

⁷At this time there was also a prophetess named Anna[2]. She was very old, having lived with her husband for seven years and then as a widow until she was eighty-four years old. She never left the temple, serving God with fasting and prayers night and day. She came up just as Simeon was talking and she gave thanks to the Lord and spoke of the child to all in Jerusalem who were looking expectantly for the promised Christ who'd rescue Israel[3].

⁸Then when they'd finished the rituals required by God's law, they went home[4].

Scholars Come to Bethlehem – April/May, 2 BC Matthew 2:1-18
(Glossary articles: Agent / Angel; Bethlehem; Biblical Chronology; Birth and Childhood of Jesus-Events; Chief Priests; Christ; Herod; Jerusalem; Joseph; Scribes)

⁹A few months after Jesus was born in Bethlehem (during the rule of Herod the Great), scholars from the east came to Jerusalem saying, "Where's the one who's been born to be king of the Jews? We saw his star when it first rose[5], and we've come to worship him."

¹⁰When King Herod heard about this, he was extremely disturbed, as was everybody else in Jerusalem[6]. He called a meeting of the chief priests and the scribes, asking them to tell him where the Christ was to be born. "In Bethlehem in the province of Judea," they told him, "because this is what the prophet wrote:

¹¹And as for you, Bethlehem in Judah's land,
You're not the least among the rulers of Judah,
For a ruler will come from you who'll shepherd my people, Israel[7]."

¹²Once Herod had this answer, he called for a secret meeting with the scholars, asking them exactly when the star first appeared. When he'd learned all he could, he sent them on to Bethlehem, saying, "Go search carefully for the child. When you've found him, come back to me and tell me where he is so that I too may go and worship him."

¹³After hearing what the king had learned about Bethlehem, they left the city, and the star that they'd seen when they were in the east went ahead of them. When they saw the star again, they were overjoyed, and it stood over the place where the toddler was.

¹⁴When they arrived in the house [May 8, 2 BC], they saw the child with Mary his mother. On seeing the child, they fell on their faces to worship him, presenting gifts of gold, frankincense, and myrrh. But God warned these scholars in a dream not to return to King Herod, so when they left Bethlehem they headed for home by a different route that would avoid Jerusalem.

¹⁵After these scholars had gone, an agent of the Lord warned Joseph in a dream: "Get up now and take this child and his mother! Flee to Egypt, because Herod will be looking for the child in order to destroy him."

¹⁶So Joseph got up and took his family by night heading for Egypt and remained there until he heard that Herod was dead. This happened to give fuller meaning to what the Lord said through his prophet: "I called my son out of Egypt[8]."

¹⁷When Herod realized that he'd been tricked by these scholars he was furious. He sent soldiers to kill all the male children in Bethlehem and in all the area around Bethlehem from two years old down (based on the time he'd learned from the scholars).

¹⁸This gave fuller meaning to what Jeremiah the prophet had said: "A sound was heard in the land[1] – weeping and anguished mourning – Rachel, weeping for her children and refusing to be comforted because they were dead[2]."

---

[1] 3:5-This prophecy about bringing "understanding to the nations" would've left a serious impression on Mary. In Jewish culture of that time, the Christ was expected to rescue Israel from foreign oppressors, but few if any would've understood that his role would be to bring understanding to the nations other than Israel. There'd have been more who believed that the Christ would bring death to these nations.
[2] 3:7-From the tribe of Ashur.
[3] 3:7-Literally, "the redemption of Israel" rather than "the promised Christ who'd rescue Israel," but "the promised Christ who'd rescue Israel" is clearly implied.
[4] 3:8-In Luke's Gospel, the account says that the family went home to Nazareth in Galilee. Luke simply skipped over the return to Bethlehem, the visit of the eastern scholars, the move to Egypt to avoid Herod's plots, and the return from Egypt that ended up in Nazareth.
[5] 3:9-The wording here seems to imply a star that rose in the sky in the normal pattern of stars rather than something that suddenly appeared overhead. See Birth of Jesus – The Date in the Glossary for more information on this star.
[6] 3:10-Herod the Great was infamous for his willingness to kill anybody who got in his way—even favored members of his own family. So when Herod got upset, at least the leaders in Jerusalem would've been in a turmoil.
[7] 3:11-Micah 5:2.
[8] 3:16-Hosea 11:1. See Prophecies and Fulfillments in the Glossary to understand better what Matthew was doing when he wrote this. This wasn't actually a prophecy that the Christ would spend time in Egypt.

Joseph and Mary Return to Galilee – Spring, 1 BC Matthew 2:19-23
(Glossary articles: Agent / Angel; Biblical Chronology; Biblical Names; Birth and Childhood of Jesus-Events; Galilee; Herod; Joseph; Judea; Nazareth)

[19]After Herod died, an agent of the Lord appeared to Joseph in a dream while he was still in Egypt saying, "Get up and take the child and his mother back to the land of Israel, because those who wanted to kill the child are dead." So Joseph got up and took his family to Israel, but when he heard that Herod's son[3] was ruling in Judea in place of his father he was afraid to go there.

[20]After a warning from God in another dream, he bypassed Judea and traveled to Galilee where he settled back in Nazareth. This gave fuller meaning to what the prophets had said: "He'll be called a Nazarene[4]."

Jesus Takes on Manhood – About April 5-15, 11 AD Luke 2:40-52
(Glossary articles: Biblical Chronology; Birth and Childhood of Jesus-Events; Galilee; Herod's Temple; Jerusalem; Jewish Feasts; Joseph; Mary)

[21]So the child grew into a strong young man, filled with wisdom and clearly gifted by God.

[22]When Jesus was twelve years old, the family went up to Jerusalem for the Passover feast, just as they did every year.

[23]When the feast was over, Joseph and Mary started back to Galilee[5], but Jesus stayed behind in Jerusalem.

[24]His mother and Joseph[6] didn't realize that Jesus wasn't with them. They thought he was with others in their group. But after a day's travel, they began looking for Jesus among their relatives and friends. When they didn't find him, they hurried back to Jerusalem to look for him.

[25]After three days[7] they found Jesus in the temple[8], sitting with a group of teachers, listening to them and asking questions – and all who heard him were astonished at his understanding and the answers he gave to their questions.

[26]When Mary and Joseph saw Jesus, they were amazed, and Mary said, "Son, why did you do this to us? Your father and I have been worried sick, searching high and low for you."

[27]Jesus asked them, "Why were you searching so hard? Didn't you understand that it's time for me to start working in my Father's business?" But Mary and Joseph didn't understand what he was talking about.

[28]Then Jesus returned to Galilee[9] with his parents as an obedient son, but his mother kept going over these things in her heart. So Jesus grew up, and as his body grew he also grew in wisdom and in the way both God and people looked on him with favor.

Chapter 4 – Jesus Is God with Us
Jesus Is God with Us John 1:1-14
(Glossary articles: Belief / Faith; Common Gender; Jesus as the Logic)

[1]At the very beginning of all things there existed a Logic that controls every aspect of this creation. This Logic is an aspect of who God is – an essential part of who God is. Everything in this universe was made through this Logic – nothing in this universe ever came into existence without this Logic. This Logic is the very source of life – the life that enlightens all humans. The light of this Logic shines in the darkness of this world, but the darkness just doesn't get it.

[2]So God sent a man named John to tell everybody about that Light so that people could focus their lives on the Light. John wasn't the Light – he was just sent to tell people that the Light was coming. That Light is the true light that lights up every person, and now the Light himself was coming into the world[10].

[3]But although everybody in the world was made through him, the world in general didn't recognize him when he came. He came as the one who'd made everything and everyone, and even his own people didn't accept him.

---

[1] 3:18-Literally, "heard in Ramah."

[2] 3:18-Jeremiah 31:15. Other than the weeping for dead children, there's no obvious connection between what Jeremiah wrote and what happened in Bethlehem. See Prophecies and Fulfillments in the Glossary to understand what Matthew was doing when he wrote this.

[3] 3:19-Archelaus, who was also known as Herod Archelaus.

[4] 3:20-Today we have no clear idea what prophecy Matthew had in mind.

[5] 3:23-Literally, "Nazareth."

[6] 3:24-The wording Luke used here was meant to emphasize that Mary was Jesus' biological mother, but Joseph wasn't his biological father.

[7] 3:25-We don't know if the three days included a day of travel from Jerusalem and a day or possibly more of travel back looking for Jesus among the crowds leaving Jerusalem, or whether this was three days of searching in Jerusalem.

[8] 3:25-It's not important, but using the chronology assumed in this translation, the date of Jesus' resurrection (Nisan 24) was also most likely the date that Jesus' parents found him in the temple.

[9] 3:28-Literally, "Nazareth."

[10] 4:2-This sentence has three possible meanings, each of which could be what John intended: 1) that this Light enlightens people when the people come into the world—he gives us life; 2) that the Light that enlightens all people (gives them life) was coming into the world; or 3) that the Light came into the world to give light to every man.

⁴But when some did accept him for who he is, he gave them the right to be the very children of God – even to those who'd focus their lives on God. These have been reborn – not by a physical birth, nor as the result of human passion or planning, but by a spiritual birth brought about by God himself.

⁵So the Logic of God took on flesh and came to live among us. We actually saw in him the very majesty of God, overflowing with grace[1] and truth.

Chapter 5 – The Ministry of John the Immerser
John's Ministry Begins – April, 29 AD Matthew 3:1-2, 4-6; Mark 1:4-6; Luke 3:1-3; John 1:15-18
(Glossary articles: Baptize / Immerse; Caesar; Christ; Jesus and the Law; John the Immerser; Judea; Preaching / Proclaiming; Sin / Rebellion; Son of God; Sons and Fathers in Biblical Thinking)

¹In the spring of 29 AD[2] the word of God came to John the Immerser (the son of Elizabeth and her husband[3]) while he was living in uncultivated areas near Judea. Then John traveled into all the areas along the Jordan River, announcing immersion[4] as a sign of a life turned around[5] in order to gain forgiveness for sin against God[6].

²"Turn your life around," he proclaimed, "because the ruler of heaven is about to establish his authority on earth."

³John himself was dressed in camel's hair and wore a leather belt around his waist. His diet consisted of locusts and wild honey. Everybody from Jerusalem, Judea, and all the area around the Jordan River went out to hear him, and they were immersed by him in the Jordan, confessing their sins.

⁴John made it very plain that he wasn't the Christ, saying, "The one who's coming after me is greater than I am. He existed before I did. And we've all received benefits from his overwhelming bounty – one gift after another."

⁵(Now the Law was given through Moses, but grace and truth came through Jesus Christ. Nobody's ever seen God. The only son born of God who comes from the very heart of the Father is the one who's revealed the reality of God to us.)

John's Message Matthew 3:7-10; Luke 3:7-14
(Glossary articles: Abraham; Baptize / Immerse; John the Immerser; Pharisees; Sadducees; Tax Collectors; Third Person Commands)

⁶When John saw many of the Pharisees and Sadducees in the crowds coming to be immersed he said, "You sons of snakes! Who warned you to try to escape the wrath of God? If you really want to escape, start living in a way that shows you've actually turned your lives around[7].

⁷"And don't even think you can find safety by claiming you're descendants of Abraham. I'm telling you that God's able to raise up children of Abraham from the stones you see around you. Even now there's an ax sitting next to the root of each tree. Every tree that doesn't bear good fruit will be cut down and thrown into the fire."

⁸So the people asked him, "What should we do?"

⁹John answered, "If you've got two tunics, give one to the person who doesn't have one; and if you've got food, share with someone who doesn't have any[8]."

¹⁰Then tax collectors also came to be immersed and asked him, "Teacher, what should we do?"

¹¹John told them, "Collect only as much tax as you're supposed to collect."

¹²Jewish policemen[9] also asked him, "And what shall we do?"

¹³John told them, "Don't use your authority to intimidate or extort money from anyone, don't accuse anyone falsely, and be content with your wages."

John's Ministry Challenged Matthew 3:3, 11-12; Mark 1:2-3, 7-8; Luke 3:4-6; 15-18; John 1:19-28
(Glossary articles: Baptize / Immerse; Christ; Elijah; John the Immerser; Judeans / Jewish Authorities; Levites; Pharisees; Preaching / Proclaiming; Priests; The Prophet; Tax Collectors)

¹⁴People were thinking that surely the Christ would come soon, and they were wondering whether John might be the Christ.

---

[1] 4:5-Grace is well defined as the gift that makes a person's eyes light up.
[2] 5:1-Literally, "In the 15th year of Tiberius Caesar's reign, with Pontius Pilate as governor of Judea, Herod [Antipas] as ruler of Galilee, Herod's brother, Philip, as ruler of Iturea and Trachonitis, and Lysanias as ruler of Abilene," but that translates to a time between the fall of 28 AD and the fall of 29 AD—most likely the spring of 29 AD.
[3] 5:1-See Zechariah in the Glossary.
[4] 5:1-The word for immersion here can also imply cleansing as a result of the immersion. See Baptize / Immerse in the Glossary.
[5] 5:1-The concept of a life turned around is generally translated "repentance," but that word has come to have meanings in our culture that don't express the real idea here. See Repentance in the Glossary.
[6] 5:1-Remember, sin is always treason—rebellion against God.
[7] 5:6-Note that a prerequisite to the immersion John taught was this willingness to change how you live.
[8] 5:9-These are third person commands in the Bible, but they've been converted to second person commands for English readers. The meaning is the same, but it doesn't come through as strongly in many other translations.
[9] 5:12-These were actually Jewish soldiers, but the job of the Jewish soldiers was more that of policemen than that of soldiers. The Romans provided the real soldiers (who also served as policemen in some circumstances).

¹⁵Then the Jewish authorities sent priests and Levites from among the Pharisees to ask him, "Who are you?"

¹⁶John never denied the truth. He openly admitted it, testifying, "I'm not the Christ."

¹⁷Then they asked him, "What then? Are you Elijah[1]?"

¹⁸John said, "I am not."

¹⁹"So are you the Prophet?" they asked.

²⁰Again he answered, "No!"

²¹So they asked, "Who are you? We need to give some answer to the ones who sent us. So what would you say about yourself?"

²²John replied, "It's like what the prophets said:

²³See, I'm sending my own messenger ahead of you
He'll prepare the road for you[2].
²⁴The voice of one crying in the wilderness,
'Prepare the way of the Lord;
'Make his paths straight.
²⁵'Every valley shall be filled,
'And every mountain and hill cut down;
'The crooked places shall be made straight,
'And the rough roads shall be made smooth;
'And all people shall see the salvation of God[3].'"

²⁶Then the Pharisees asked him, "If you're not the Christ or Elijah or the Prophet, why are you immersing people?"

²⁷John replied, "I'm immersing people in water, but there's someone standing among you now that you don't know – someone who's greater than I am. He's going to immerse[4] you in God's Holy Spirit and in fire! He's the one who's coming after me. I'm not even worthy to bow down and untie the straps of his sandals[5].

²⁸"He's carrying the tool in his hand to separate the wheat from the worthless husks, and before he's done, he'll thoroughly clean the entire grain-processing area. He'll gather his wheat into the barn, but he'll burn up the husks with fire so hot it can't be put out." John used many such warnings as he proclaimed this news.

²⁹All this happened in a town[6] on the east side of the Jordan River where John was immersing people.

Jesus' Immersion Matthew 3:13-17; Mark 1:9-11; Luke 3:21-22; John 1:29-34
(Glossary articles: Baptize / Immerse; Heaven / Sky; Immediately / Quickly; Lamb of God)

³⁰While everybody was being immersed, Jesus came from the district of Galilee[7] to be immersed by John in the Jordan River. John tried to talk him out of this, saying, "I really need to be immersed[8] by you. Why are you coming to me?"

³¹But Jesus answered him, "Just accept it. If I'm going to do everything God wants me to do, this has to be included."

³²So John agreed, and when Jesus had been immersed he came out of the water quickly and began to pray. Suddenly the sky opened up and John saw God's Holy Spirit descending on Jesus like a dove and resting on him. Then a voice from the sky said, "This is my dearly loved son in whom I find great joy!"

³³The day after Jesus was immersed[9], John saw Jesus approaching him, and he said to those around him, "Look there. That's God's sacrificial lamb taking away the guilt of the whole world.

³⁴"This is the man I was talking about when I said, 'After my time, someone greater than me – someone who existed before me – is coming.'

³⁵"I didn't realize that Jesus was actually God's Christ[1], but the reason I've been immersing[2] you in the water was to prepare you for when he'd be revealed to Israel."

---

[1] 5:17-See Good News 25:12.

[2] 5:23-Malachi 3:1.

[3] 5:25-Isaiah 40:3-5.

[4] 5:27-Note the significance of translating this concept as "immerse" here. As Christians, we're immersed in the very Spirit of God, and we live immersed in that presence.

[5] 5:27-It was the job of the lowest of slaves to untie guests' footwear and wash their feet. See Servants / Slaves in the Glossary.

[6] 5:29-See Bethabara in the Glossary.

[7] 5:30-Literally, "from Nazareth in the district of Galilee."

[8] 5:30-The word "immersed" used here implies a cleansing as a result of the immersion. John understood that Jesus didn't need cleansing while he did. But Jesus was coming to institute a practice that would be a Christian's first expression of his or her faith in God, and he needed to set the example as he began his ministry. Like Jesus, when a Christian is immersed, he or she's to begin a life of ministry. See Baptize / Immerse in the Glossary.

[9] 5:33-John's Gospel says "the day after," but doesn't specify after what. At first glance the passage reads as if this were the day after the Jewish leaders questioned John, but that doesn't work since when those leaders questioned John he apparently didn't know who the Christ was, but on this "day after" he pointed Jesus out as the lamb of God and testified that he'd seen God's Holy Spirit descending onto him. Given those facts, this translation assumes that "the day after" refers to the day after Jesus was baptized.

³⁶Beyond this John also testified, "I saw God's Holy Spirit descending from the sky like a dove and resting on this man.

³⁷"As I said, I didn't realize that he was God's Christ, but when God sent me to immerse people in water, he told me, 'When you see my Holy Spirit descending and resting on a person, you'll know that this is the one who'll immerse[3] people into my Holy Spirit.'

³⁸"I saw this happen to Jesus, so I can bear witness that he's God's own Son[4]."

Chapter 6 – A Preview of Things to Come
Jesus Attracts a Following John 1:35-51
(Glossary articles: Agent / Angel; Andrew; Biblical Names; Christ / Messiah; Disciples; John the Immerser; Lamb of God; Moses; Nathanael; Nazareth; Peter; Son of Man and Son of God; Sons and Fathers in Biblical Thinking)

¹The day after John the Immerser proclaimed who Jesus was to his disciples, he was standing with two of them when he saw Jesus walking by, and he said again, "Look there. That's God's sacrificial lamb."

²When the two disciples heard this, they decided to follow Jesus. Jesus looked around and saw them following him, so he asked, "What are you looking for?"

³They answered, "Teacher, where are you staying?"

⁴"Come and see," said Jesus. It was about 4:00 in the afternoon when they joined him, and they spent the rest of the day with him.

⁵One of the men who heard what John said and joined Jesus that afternoon was Andrew, Simon Peter's brother. The first thing he did was find his brother, Simon, to tell him, "We've found the Messiah." ("Messiah" means the same thing as "Christ.") So Andrew brought Simon to meet Jesus, and when Jesus looked at him, he said, "Your name is Simon, son of John, but from now on you'll be called Peter."

⁶The following day Jesus decided to go back to Galilee[5], and when he got there, he found Philip and said to him, "Follow me." Philip was from Andrew and Peter's hometown[6].

⁷Soon Philip went to look for Nathan[7] and told him, "We've found the Christ[8] that Moses and the prophets wrote about! It's a man named Jesus from the town of Nazareth."

⁸Nathan responded, "Can anything good come from Nazareth?"

⁹"Come see for yourself!" Philip replied.

¹⁰As soon as Jesus saw Nathan coming toward him, he said, "Look who's coming! Here's an Israelite who'd never try to deceive anybody[9]!"

¹¹"How do you know anything about me?" Nathan asked.

¹²Jesus answered, "Before Philip found you, when you were under the fig tree, I was watching."

¹³Stunned, Nathan answered, "Teacher, you're the very son of God! You're the king of Israel!"

¹⁴Jesus said, "You believe me just because I said that I saw you under the fig tree? I'm telling you the absolute truth: you'll see greater things than that! Before we're through you'll see the sky break open and the agents of God descending on me as a human[10]."

The Marriage Feast in Cana John 2:1-12
(Glossary articles: Baptize / Immerse; Belief / Faith; Capernaum; Disciples; Jewish Marriage Customs)

¹⁵On the third day after Jesus was immersed, there was a wedding in the town of Cana in Galilee, and Jesus' mother was present.

¹⁶Jesus and his disciples[11] were also invited to the wedding. When the wedding wine ran out, Jesus' mother told him, "They're out of wine[1]!"

---

[1] 5:35-Neither the word "Messiah" nor the word "Christ" is actually used in this verse or verse 36, but the implication is very clear. John literally said, "I didn't know him" in both cases.

[2] 5:35-Remember that the word for "immersing" here also implies cleansing as a result of the immersion.

[3] 5:37-This is a good example of why the word "immerse" is used in this translation to clarify such things as the fact that Christians are actually immersed in the very Spirit of God and live constantly in his presence.

[4] 5:38-This has been translated as if John the Immerser testified to having seen the Holy Spirit descend on Jesus, and that seems like the right translation, but it could also be John the Disciple who wrote these words who was testifying that he was present and that he also saw this happen. Either option works.

[5] 6:6-Back from the Jordan where Jesus was immersed.

[6] 6:6-See Bethsaida in the Glossary.

[7] 6:7-Literally, Nathanael, but Nathan is used throughout this translation.

[8] 6:7-Literally, "the one" rather than "the Christ," but the implication is very clear.

[9] 6:10-I can imagine Jesus looking at Nathanael with a twinkle in his eye as he pointed out this honest man to those around him.

[10] 6:14-Literally, "on the son of man…" Jesus frequently used these words to focus on his humanity. He was a real human like any of us, but unlike us, God, who is spirit, lived in him with no limitations.

[11] 6:16-We think of Jesus and his 12 disciples, but he hadn't called the twelve yet. We don't know who these disciples were or how many there were.

[17]Jesus said to her, "Yes, ma'm, but what business is that of ours? It's not time yet for me to demonstrate my power[2]."

[18]But Mary told the servants, "You do whatever he tells you."

[19]Now there were six stone water jars nearby that were used for the ceremonial washings practiced by Jews. Each of these jars would hold about twenty-five gallons of water. Jesus told the servants, "Fill those jars with water." Then when they'd done this he said, "OK, now dip some out and take it to the master of the feast."

[20]So the servants did as he said. When the master of the feast tasted the water (which had now turned to wine) – not knowing the source of this wine – he called the bridegroom over and chided him: "A host always serves the best-tasting wine first. Once people have had a lot to drink, then he brings out the cheaper wine. But you've kept the best until now!"

[21]This was the first time Jesus had used his miraculous power publicly to reveal his glory, and his disciples put their trust in him.

[22]After this wedding Jesus went to Capernaum for a few days with his mother, his brothers, and his disciples.

Chapter 7 – The Wilderness Temptation

The Wilderness Temptation Matthew 4:1-11; Mark 1:12-13; Luke 4:1-13
(Glossary articles: Angel / Agent; Herod's Temple; Immediately / Quickly; Jerusalem; Jesus and Temptation; Sacred Writings; Satan; Son of God; Sons and Fathers in Biblical Thinking)

[1]About this time, Jesus, feeling the power of God's Holy Spirit within him, was led quickly into a wilderness area to be tempted by the devil. He spent forty days alone in the wilderness with only wild beasts around him[3], going without food day and night, and by the end of that time, he was close to starvation. Just then the tempter[4] came by and said, "If you're the Son of God, why don't you command these stones to be loaves of bread?"

[2]But Jesus responded, "In the sacred writings[5] we read, 'Man shall not live just by eating bread, but by every word that comes out of God's mouth[6].'"

[3]Later the devil took Jesus to Jerusalem where they climbed to the top edge of the temple. The devil said to him, "If you're really the Son of God, why not jump off this tower? After all, the sacred writings say[7], 'God will command his own agents to protect you so that you won't even stub your toe[8].'"

[4]"The sacred writings also say[9], 'You shall not try to test the Lord your God[10].'" Jesus answered.

[5]Next the devil took Jesus to a high mountaintop where he gave him a vision[11] of all the inhabited kingdoms of the world and all their glory. "All these kingdoms have been given to me and serve me," he said. "I can give authority over them to anybody I please, and I'll give them all to you if you'll simply bow down and worship me."

[6]At this point Jesus strongly rebuked him saying, "Get out of here! You're God's own Adversary! The sacred writings say[12] very clearly, 'You shall worship the Lord your God, and he's the only one you're to serve[13].'"

[7]After that the devil left him alone for a while and agents from God came to comfort and care for Jesus.

Chapter 8 – Getting Started

Back to Jesus' Hometown Matthew 13:53-58; Mark 6:1-6a; Luke 4:16-30; John 4:44
(Glossary articles: Belief / Faith; Biblical Names; Capernaum; Elijah; Isaiah; Joseph; Mary; Preach / Proclaim; Prophecies and Fulfillments; Sabbath; Sacred Writings)

[1]Then Jesus returned with his disciples[14] to his hometown in Galilee[15], filled with the power of God's Holy Spirit, and people were talking about him throughout the whole area.

---

[1] 6:16-Wedding feasts were community parties. To run out of wine in the middle of such a party would be a social disaster.

[2] 6:17-Jesus didn't want to go public with his miracles in this way. We don't know what Mary had seen him do in the past, but she was convinced that he could help if he chose to do so.

[3] 7:1-Of course there'd be wild beasts in such wilderness areas, but the fact that Mark mentioned them with Jesus may imply that in Jesus' presence in this lonely area, the wild beasts were as tame as they'd been in the original garden paradise where Adam and Eve lived.

[4] 7:1-See Jesus and Temptation in the Glossary for a better picture of what may have actually happened during these temptations.

[5] 7:2-Literally, "it is written."

[6] 7:2-Deuteronomy 8:3.

[7] 7:3-Literally, "it is written."

[8] 7:3-Psalm 91:11-12.

[9] 7:4-Literally, "it is written" (Matthew) or "it has been said" (Luke).

[10] 7:4-Deuteronomy 6:16.

[11] 7:5-The Bible doesn't literally say that this was a vision, but this is strongly implied where Luke says that the devil showed Jesus all the kingdoms of the world "in a moment of time."

[12] 7:6-Literally, "it is written."

[13] 7:6-Deuteronomy 6:13.

[14] 8:1-We don't know who these disciples were or how many there were at this point in Jesus' ministry.

[15] 8:1-Nazareth.

²As he usually did on Sabbath days, he went to the worship center and stood up to read from the sacred writings[1]. The attendant handed him a scroll containing the writings of Isaiah. Jesus opened the scroll to the passage he wanted and began to read:

³The Spirit of the Lord is on me
Because he's anointed me
To bring good news to the poor,
To bring healing to the brokenhearted,
To announce liberty for those in captivation,
To restore sight to the blind,
To free all those who are oppressed,
And to announce that God's time has come[2]!

⁴Having read this, he closed the scroll, gave it back to the attendant, and sat down, and everyone in the worship center was watching him with anticipation[3].

⁵Then Jesus began to speak: "Today this prophecy is being fulfilled as you hear it."

⁶As he continued to speak, the people were astonished at what he was saying and began to whisper among themselves: "Isn't this the carpenter, the son of Joseph and his wife, Mary? Don't we know his four brothers[4] and don't his sisters live right here with us?

⁷"Where did he get this message of grace[5], and who gave him the wisdom to do such powerful signs?" The people were also offended by the things he was saying[6].

⁸Jesus told them, "Of course you'll quote me the old proverb, '"Physician, heal yourself." We've heard what you did in Capernaum. Let's see you do those things here in your own home town.'

⁹"I'll tell you what's true: a prophet is honored everywhere but in his own hometown, among his own relatives, and even in his own home.

¹⁰"There were a lot of widows in Israel that Elijah could've helped when there was no rain from the sky for three and a half years, and extreme famine was everywhere in Israel. He could've helped them if they'd been willing to take him in, but God sent him to a widow who wasn't even a Jew[7].

¹¹"And there were many people with leprosy in Israel who could've used help from Elisha, but the only one cleansed of leprosy was a man who wasn't a Jew[8]."

¹²When the people in the worship center heard this, they were filled with indignant anger[9]. They took Jesus by force to the top of a cliff, meaning to throw him down to his death. But Jesus passed right through them and went on his way.

¹³So Jesus wasn't able to do much in his hometown except to lay his hands on a few sick people and heal them[10]. And he was amazed that these people refused to trust him.

---

[1] 8:2-"From the sacred writings" isn't stated but is clearly implied.

[2] 8:3-Isaiah 61:1-2. This is a watershed in Jesus' ministry. He went home to Nazareth to proclaim more clearly than ever that he's the son of Almighty God. The anointing he has isn't an anointing of oil, but an anointing of God's Holy Spirit. And that anointing dedicated Jesus to a ministry to the poor, the brokenhearted, those in captivity, the blind, and the oppressed—to bring hope to all of these. When we receive God's Holy Spirit, those are the things that become our job.

[3] 8:4-The hometown people had to give this now-famous rabbi the honor of reading from the sacred writings and delivering a message in the worship center, but they were skeptical.

[4] 8:6-James, Joses, Simon, and Judas. Though three of these brothers shared the names of some of Jesus' disciples, these brothers weren't those disciples. The reference to Joseph and Mary makes it clear that these were their children, not the children of Joseph by a previous marriage.

[5] 8:7-This is often translated as "gracious words" and could indicate a gift with words, but given his message, it seemed more appropriate to translate as "message of grace," which is equally possible from the Greek.

[6] 8:7-From what follows, it seems Jesus must have been talking about people who weren't Jewish coming to the Lord. For anyone stuck in tradition (and we all have that tendency), what Jesus was saying seemed all wrong. We put God in a box of our design, but when we come face to face with the reality of God, he never fits in our boxes.

[7] 8:10-Literally, "a woman of Zarephath in the region of Sidon."

[8] 8:11-Literally, "Naaman, the Syrian."

[9] 8:12-Jesus said that traditional Judaism wasn't what God wanted from them—and they refused to hear this message from a hometown boy. They completely rejected the spiritual healing he so wanted to give them.

[10] 8:13-From what the Bible says, it seems that the problem in Nazareth wasn't that Jesus was unable to heal, but that those who needed healing wouldn't come to him to get it.

Move to Capernaum Matthew 4:13-17, 23-25; 7:28-29; 9:35-36; 12:15-21; Mark 1:15, 21-22, 39; 6:6b, 34b; Luke 4:14-15, 31-32, 44; 8:1-3
(Glossary articles: Belief / Faith; Capernaum; Evil Spirits; Gentiles / Nations; Herod; Immediately / Quickly; Mary Magdalene; Preach / Proclaim; Prophecies and Fulfillments; Nazareth; Repentance)

[14] So Jesus left his hometown[1] and set up a base of operations in Capernaum on the north shore of the Sea of Galilee in an area given to two of the tribes of Israel[2]. This gave fuller meaning to the prophet's words:

[15] The land shared by two tribes[3],
Toward the sea, on the west side of the Jordan River,
Galilee of the nations:
The people dwelling in darkness saw a great light,
And for those who lived in the very land of death's own shadow,
The light has dawned[4].

[16] The power of God's Spirit was on him, and right away Jesus began to teach in the worship center in Capernaum and in all the worship centers around that region[5].

[17] He traveled in a regular circuit, proclaiming, "The time's up; God's kingdom is right here right now. Change the focus of your life – put your trust in the good news I'm bringing you[6]!" Everyone who heard him was captivated by his message, because he taught with authority, not like the scribes[7].

[18] Jesus went through all the cities and villages of the area with his disciples, teaching in the worship centers, announcing the good news of God's kingdom, and healing every kind of sickness – pains, evil spirits, epilepsy, paralysis, and infirmity. Whatever the illness, Jesus healed the people who came to him.

[19] Soon word of his ministry spread even into territories that weren't Jewish[8].

[20] Huge crowds from the provinces of Galilee, the Ten Cities[9], and Judea (including many from Jerusalem) came to listen to him and followed him around as he taught.

[21] But when Jesus saw the huge crowds around him, his heart ached for them because they were so confused with no one to help them – like sheep with no shepherd.

[22] There were also some women that Jesus had healed of evil spirits and various illnesses who traveled with the group. One of these was named Mary Magdalene – Jesus had cast seven evil spirits out of her.

[23] Many other women[10] were also with Jesus and his disciples, and these women were instrumental in providing financial support for the group.

Jesus Calls Four Fishermen Matthew 4:18-22; Mark 1:16-20; Luke 5:1-11
(Glossary articles: Andrew; Immediately / Quickly; James; John; Peter; Scribes)

[24] One day as Jesus was walking along the shore of the Sea of Galilee[11], the crowds were pressing in on him to try to hear what he was teaching them about God.

[25] Jesus spotted a couple of empty boats on the shore where the owners had left them to clean and repair their fishing nets.

[26] Jesus stepped into the one owned by Simon and asked him to move the boat a little way from the shore. Then Jesus sat down in the boat and began teaching the crowds again.

[27] When he finished teaching, he told Simon to go out farther into the deep part of the water and let down his nets to catch some fish. "Master," Simon argued, "we've worked all night without catching a thing. Nevertheless, if you say so, I'll put the nets down again[1]."

---

[1] 8:14-Nazareth.

[2] 8:14-Zebulon and Naphtali.

[3] 8:15-Literally, "The Land of Zebulon and the Land of Naphtali."

[4] 8:15-Isaiah 9:1-2.

[5] 8:16-Information about various trips around Galilee is combined in this section.

[6] 8:17-Here is the essence of God's message from the very beginning, repeatedly reinforced in Jesus' ministry. Change the focus of your life from a focus on yourself and the things of this world to a focus on God and the reward he offers; then put your trust in God and the message he provides as the guiding principle for all the rest of your life. The first is repentance—a change in the focus of your life. The second is faith, maintaining the long-term focus on God.

[7] 8:17-This was a common reaction to Jesus' teaching. The scribes would typically talk about what this or that teacher or prophet had said to establish the authority of what they were saying, much like what some scholars do today. Jesus needed no such references. He could say what he knew first hand to be true.

[8] 8:19-Syria.

[9] 8:20-The Bible also names Perea.

[10] 8:23-Two women are mentioned by name: Joanna who was the wife of Herod's steward and Susanna. Some of these women were obviously wealthy.

[11] 8:24-Literally, "the Lake of Gennesaret," but this is another name for the Sea of Galilee, also called the Sea (or Lake) of Tiberius.

[28] When Simon's crew had done this and tried to bring the net in, it was so full of fish that it started breaking. Simon signaled for his partners[2], (James and John[3], who owned the other boat) to come help. Before they were through pulling in the net, both boats were so full of fish that they were about to sink!

[29] When they came to land and Simon Peter saw all the fish, he turned and dropped to his knees in front of Jesus, saying, "Oh Lord, get away from me! I'm just a sinful man!" (Indeed, everyone on both crews was astonished at the huge catch of fish they'd taken in.)

[30] Then Jesus told Simon and his brother Andrew, "Don't be afraid. Just follow me. I'm going to teach you to fish for men." So they quickly left everything and followed him.

[31] Next Jesus walked over to where James and John were now in the boat with their father[4] mending their nets and he called them to follow him. They also left their father and the hired servants with all the fishing equipment and followed Jesus.

A Sabbath in a Worship Center with Jesus Matthew 8:14-17; Mark 1:23-34; Luke 4:33-41
(Glossary articles: Andrew; Capernaum; Evil Spirits; Galilee; Immediately / Quickly; Isaiah; Nazareth; Prophecies and Fulfillments; Sabbath; Son of God; Sons and Fathers in Biblical Thinking)

[32] In the worship center in Capernaum there was a man with an evil spirit. During the Sabbath service this man shouted, "Why don't you let us alone, Jesus of Nazareth[5]? I know you're the holy one sent from God, but what business is it of yours what we do? Are you here to destroy us?"

[33] "Hush!" Jesus rebuked him, "Now, come out of him!"

[34] The evil spirit threw the man to the ground in a fit, and then with a loud yell, he came out of the man, leaving him unharmed.

[35] The people in the worship center were all amazed and murmured among themselves, "What's going on? What kind of new message is this? He doesn't just teach as if he has authority; he even commands evil spirits and they obey him!"

[36] (And with healings like this, Jesus' fame spread quickly from one end of Galilee to the other.)

[37] That afternoon Jesus went to Simon and Andrew's house along with James and John. There they found Simon's mother-in-law lying in bed, sick with a fever.

[38] The family asked Jesus what he could do for her, so he came and took her by the hand and ordered the fever to leave her. Then he helped her up. As soon as he did this, the fever was gone and she got up and cared for them.

[39] When the sun had set[6], people brought all those who were sick and those with evil spirits to Jesus for healing.

[40] Everybody in town tried to gather around the door to see what was happening. Jesus simply laid his hands on the sick and healed them. When Jesus gave the order, evil spirits came out yelling and saying, "You're the Christ, the son of God!" But Jesus immediately made them shut up because they knew he was the Christ[7].

[41] All of this happened to give full meaning to what Isaiah the prophet wrote saying, "He took our illnesses on himself and carried away our sicknesses[8]."

Jesus' Ministry Plan Mark 1:35-39; Luke 4:42-44
(Glossary article: Jesus and Temptation)

[42] Very early in the morning, long before daybreak, Jesus got up and went out to pray where no one would be around[9].

[43] When Simon and the others got up, they went looking for him, and when they found him, they told him, "Everybody's out looking for you! They don't want you to leave."

---

[1] 8:27-Peter and his team had worked all night with nothing to show for it, and now this rabbi who apparently knew nothing about fishing was asking him to have his crew put down the nets in full daylight. Simon thought this would be a total waste of effort, and he may also have been thinking that the nets would need additional work after doing this. Little did he know!

[2] 8:28-Visualize Simon whistling and yelling to get the attention of his partners who'd probably been standing on the shore laughing at Simon and what this rabbi was making him do.

[3] 8:28-Literally, "James, the son of Zebedee, and John, his brother."

[4] 8:31-Zebedee.

[5] 8:32-By calling him "Jesus of Nazareth," the evil spirit in this man was trying to create contention by implying that this man from Nazareth had no business interfering with life in Capernaum.

[6] 8:39-This day was a Sabbath and the Sabbath rules called for no work. Bringing someone to get healed would be considered work. But as soon as the sun set, it was a new day and there were no restrictions on work.

[7] 8:40-Jesus didn't want or need the testimony of demons. In addition, Jesus' plan didn't include identifying himself clearly as the Christ until he was ready, because such a claim would've brought the wrong result. The Jews were expecting a worldly Christ, and too many would've wanted to force him into their idea of what the Christ should be, while others would've wanted to destroy him because too many had made such claims and brought down the wrath of the Romans on their nation. Jesus didn't publicly make a clear claim to be the Christ until he was on trial.

[8] 8:41-Isaiah 53:4

[9] 8:42-Such private prayer time appears to have been an important part of Jesus' life. In order to be our savior, Jesus had to experience life as we experience it. He had to be really tempted, and he had to communicate with God in prayer. From the information in the Bible, it seems likely that in most cases God's responses were generally no more audible to him than his responses to our prayers are to us.

⁴⁴Jesus replied, "It's time for us to move on to other towns so that I can bring the good news of the kingdom of God to them as well – after all, that's why I was sent into this world."

Calling Matthew Matthew 9:9-13; Mark 2:13-17; Luke 5:27-32
(Glossary articles: Disciples; Matthew; Pharisees; Repentance; Scribes; Sin / Rebellion; Tax Collectors and "Sinners")

⁴⁵Not long afterward Jesus was out by the sea again teaching the crowd that kept coming to him. As he walked along near the sea, he saw a man named Matthew (also called Levi[1]) sitting in a booth collecting taxes.

⁴⁶Jesus said to him, "Follow me," so he got up, left everything behind, and went with Jesus.

⁴⁷Matthew arranged a great feast at his house in honor of the Lord, and there were many tax collectors as well as others who were looked on as sinners (but who were following Jesus) gathered for the feast along with Jesus and his disciples.

⁴⁸When the scribes and Pharisees saw this, they asked his disciples, "Why do you and your teacher eat and drink with tax collectors and other sinners?"

⁴⁹Jesus heard this and told them, "Folks who are well don't need a doctor – it's folks who are sick who need the doctor.

⁵⁰"You need to go learn what God meant when he said, 'I desire mercy and not sacrifice[2].'

⁵¹"I didn't come to tell righteous people that they need to change the focus of their lives – I came to call sinners back to God."

Issues for Possible Followers Matthew 8:18-22; Luke 9:57-62
(Glossary articles: Heaven / Sky; Scribes; Son of Man)

⁵²When Jesus saw huge crowds gathering around him, he told his disciples to prepare to cross over to the other side of the Sea of Galilee[3].

⁵³Then as he was walking on the road toward the boat, a scribe came up and told him, "Teacher, I'll follow you wherever you go."

⁵⁴"Foxes have dens," Jesus replied, "birds in the sky have nests, but I as a human[4] don't own a place to lay my head[5]."

⁵⁵Another time one of his disciples told him, "Lord, I'll follow you, but first let me go home to be with my dad until he dies[6]."

⁵⁶"Follow me," Jesus told him, "and let those who are spiritually dead take care of burying the physically dead[7]. Your job is to go and announce the kingdom of God!"

⁵⁷Still another time a disciple said, "Lord, I'm ready to follow you, but first let me go and tell my family goodbye."

⁵⁸"No one," Jesus said, "who puts his hand to the plow and then looks back is fit for the kingdom of God[8]!"

Chapter 9 – Teaching about Growing Up Spiritually – Part 1
The Blessings Matthew 5:1-12; Luke 6:17-23
(Glossary article: Evil Spirits)

¹Jesus was on a large, level area[9] with his disciples, and a huge crowd of people surrounded him. Some had come from as far north as the seacoast of Lebanon[10] and as far south as Judea and Jerusalem.

²They'd come to listen to him teach, to be healed of their diseases, and to have evil spirits cast out. And as Jesus was healing them, the whole crowd was trying to touch him.

³Power flowed from him as he healed all who came to him. Then looking over the huge crowds, he began teaching them:

---

[1] 8:45-Literally, "Levi, the son of Alphaeus."
[2] 8:50-Hosea 6:6.
[3] 8:52-Matthew has this happening as Jesus was preparing to cross the Sea of Galilee. Luke has it happening in Samaria on the way to Jerusalem. Matthew only mentioned the first two encounters, while Luke mentioned all three. The way these encounters are recorded, it's likely they happened at three different times and were recorded together because of the similar subject matter. If that's true, it's likely one of them occurred on the way to a boat, another occurred in Samaria, and we have no idea where the third happened. That's something we don't really need to know.
[4] 8:54-Literally, "the son of man doesn't own a place to lay his head."
[5] 8:54-Literally Jesus said that he didn't own a place to sleep, though others often provided him with a place to sleep.
[6] 8:55-Literally, "Let me bury my father first." But if the man's father were already dead, he wouldn't have been in a crowd listening to Jesus. He was saying that he wanted to stay with his father until his father died.
[7] 8:56-Literally, "Let the dead bury the dead."
[8] 8:58-To plow a straight furrow you had to focus your eyes on an object at the far end of the field and never take your eyes off of that object. As Christians, we're to focus our lives on God and never take our eyes off of him.
[9] 9:1-Matthew records Jesus going up onto a hill to say these things to the crowds, while Luke records Jesus saying these things as he stood on a level area. However, Luke says that Jesus came down to this level area. Some have suggested that Jesus had to go up on a hill get to down to this level area. Others point out that Jesus certainly taught these same things repeatedly during his ministry, and the differences between what Luke wrote and what Matthew wrote would be consistent with two different occasions. In any case, the material Jesus covered is so similar in these two accounts that it's been blended here for convenience.
[10] 9:1-Literally, "Tyre and Sidon."

⁴"There's great joy for those who recognize their own spiritual poverty, because that's what it takes just to get into the kingdom of heaven.

⁵"There's great joy for those who are mourning now, because the time's coming when they'll find comfort and even laughter.

⁶"There's great joy for those who allow God to be in control, because it's these people that God will eventually put in charge of the whole world!

⁷"There's great joy for those who desire to do right as much as a man who's starving desires food or a man dying of thirst desires water, because such people will find their desires satisfied indeed.

⁸"There's great joy for those who show mercy to others, because in the end, it's those people who will receive God's mercy.

⁹"There's great joy for those whose intentions are pure and true, because those are the people who'll actually have a clear understanding of God.

¹⁰"There's great joy for those who seek to bring peace where there's strife, because they'll be called the very children of God.

¹¹"There's great joy even for those who are abused and mistreated for always doing what's right, because such people truly own the kingdom of heaven.

¹²"Yes, there's great joy indeed for you when people hate you, curse you, exclude you, and falsely accuse you of doing wrong because you serve me.

¹³"Rejoice and celebrate, jump up and down for joy, because when that happens you know that your reward in heaven will be truly wonderful. After all, that's exactly how people treated the prophets who served me before you.

The Curses Luke 6:24-26
(Glossary article: Cursing, Swearing, and Profanity)

¹⁴"But there's great sorrow in store for you who are wealthy, because you've already got all the reward you're going to get.

¹⁵"There's great sorrow in store for you whose bellies are full now, for the time's coming when you'll be very hungry.

¹⁶"There's great sorrow in store for you who party and laugh now, for your time of mourning and weeping is coming.

¹⁷"There's great sorrow in store for you when everybody talks about how wonderful you are, because that's exactly how your ancestors treated the false prophets in their time.

Salt and Light Matthew 5:13-16; Mark 4:21-25; 9:50; Luke 8:16-18; 11:33; 14:34-35
(Glossary article: Third Person Commands)

¹⁸"You're the salt of the earth[1]. Salt's good, but if it loses its flavor, what good is it? When that happens it's not good for the soil or even for the manure pile. All you can do is throw it out someplace where people walk on it[2].

¹⁹"Have that saltiness in yourselves that adds zest to life, and still be at peace with each other.

²⁰"You're the light of the world.

²¹"There's no way to hide a city if it's built on a hilltop.

²²"And when you turn on a table lamp, you don't cover it with a bucket or hide it under a bed, but you place it where it can provide light for everyone in the room[3].

²³"Let your light shine in such a way that people will see the good things you do and give the praise to your Father in heaven[4].

²⁴"I assure you: there's nothing hidden now that won't be brought out into the open. Yes indeed, all secrets will be brought into the light of day.

²⁵"So take what I'm telling you very seriously.

²⁶"Anybody who begins to understand the things I'm telling you will be given even greater understanding. But anyone who doesn't put out the effort to get it – even the understanding that person seems to have will be taken away.

²⁷"If you've got ears at all, pay attention[5] to these things!

---

[1] 9:18-Salt added a zesty flavor to food, it was used to preserve meats, and it was also used as money. Jesus had all of these in mind.
[2] 9:18-In New Testament times, salt was never pure, and moisture in the air would dissolve the salt, leaving impurities with enough salt to make what was left useless for flavoring food, to preserve meats, or to be used as money. If thrown into the field, these impurities contained enough salt to harm crops. Thus the residue would be thrown onto a pathway.
[3] 9:22-Literally, "the house," but in his day most houses consisted of just one room.
[4] 9:23-As Christians, when we do something good, we're to give the credit to God who's enabled us and taught us.
[5] 9:27-This is a third person command in the Bible, but it's been converted to a second person command for English readers. The meaning is the same, but it doesn't come through as strongly in many other translations.

The Law Fulfilled Matthew 5:17-48; 18:8-9; Mark 9:43-49; Luke 6:27-30, 32-36, 38a; 12:57-59; 16:16-18
(Glossary articles: Caring Love; Common Gender; Cursing, Swearing, and Profanity; Hell; Jesus and Divorce; Jesus and the Law; John the Immerser; Law of Moses; Maturity / Perfection; Pharisees; Satan; Scribes; Sin / Rebellion; Tax Collectors and "Sinners")

^{28}"Don't even think that I've come to tear down the Law of Moses and the things taught by the prophets.

^{29}"My purpose isn't to tear down what those men wrote, but to give full meaning to their messages.

^{30}"I assure you that this is the absolute truth: even the smallest stroke of a pen in the Law of Moses still applies until everything in that Law is given its full meaning[1].

^{31}"Therefore, if someone violates even one of the least significant commandments in the Law of Moses and influences others to do the same, that person shall be considered the lowest in rank in the kingdom of heaven.

^{32}"But if someone lives by those teachings and influences others to do the same, that person will be considered great in the kingdom of heaven[2].

^{33}"I'm telling you: unless your goodness is better than the 'goodness' of the scribes and the Pharisees, you won't even get into the kingdom of heaven.

^{34}"You've heard the saying, 'You shall not commit murder[3].' And you know that anyone who does commit murder will be found guilty in a court of law.

^{35}"But I'm telling you that anyone who's just angry with someone for no good reason will be found guilty in God's judgment. Even if you call someone an idiot, you may be brought before God's Supreme Court.

^{36}"And you could be condemned to the fires of hell just for calling someone a fool[4].

^{37}"But why can't you even judge your own selves properly?

^{38}"So if you want to bring an offering to God and you remember that a brother has some grudge[5] he's holding against you, put down your gift and go find your brother. First make peace with him, and then come present your gift to God.

^{39}"And if an adversary is taking you to court[6], find a way to settle your differences before you get to court. Otherwise your adversary may bring you before the judge and the judge may turn you over to the officers who'll throw you into the prison.

^{40}"If you let that happen, you'll be stuck there until you can pay the whole penalty down to the last penny.

^{41}"You've heard it said, 'You shall not have sex with anyone other than your own spouse[7].'

^{42}"But I'm telling you that anyone who even looks on another person with lust is already guilty of the intent[8].

^{43}"In fact, if you think it's your right eye that's causing you to sin against God[9], you should tear it out and throw it away.

^{44}"After all, it would sure be better for you to enter eternal life with just one eye rather than go into the garbage dump of hell with both eyes.

^{45}"Or if you think it's your right hand or foot that's causing you to sin against God, just cut it off and throw it away.

^{46}"Again, it would be better for you to enter eternal life lame or maimed than have all your limbs intact and be thrown into the garbage dump of hell – where 'the fire never goes out[10].'

^{47}"You've also heard it said, 'Anyone who divorces his wife[11] must give her a certificate of divorce[12].'

---

[1] 9:30-It's important to note that Jesus said that absolutely nothing in the Law of Moses would go away until everything in it was given its full meaning, but that he'd come to do exactly that. In other words, if we accept the fulfillment of the law that Jesus brought—a life focused on living for God—that law doesn't apply, but if we don't accept what Jesus brought, then everything in that law still applies.

[2] 9:32-Given what Jesus said later in this section about divorce, swearing, and an eye for an eye and what he later taught about eating "unclean" foods and observing the Sabbath (all of which are part of the Law of Moses), it's obvious that the teachings he talked about in these two verses must apply only prior to accepting the fulfillment Jesus brought. However, the fulfillment Jesus taught does fulfill the real intent of the Law of Moses—thus providing a true fulfillment.

[3] 9:34-Exodus 20:13; Deuteronomy 5:17.

[4] 9:36-Jesus prefaced this section to be about unjustified anger, and he's talking about these words as expressions of unjustified anger. The issue isn't the words, but the unforgiving, worldly attitude behind what a person says. (See Good News 27:15 and Proverbs 4:23.)

[5] 9:38-This isn't about who's angry, but about finding a way to make peace as a child of God.

[6] 9:39-Jesus' point is still that his followers are to be peacemakers. (See 1Corinthians 6.)

[7] 9:41-Exodus 20:14; Deuteronomy 5:18

[8] 9:42-Jesus worded this instruction as for men who might lust for women because in his culture the fact that women do lust wasn't accepted, but the principle applies equally to men or women.

[9] 9:43-Remember, sin is always treason—rebellion against God.

[10] 9:46-Isaiah 66:24. Mark 9:44 and 9:46 aren't included here because the ancient manuscript evidence indicates that these verses accidentally came into Mark's Gospel long after Mark wrote it.

[11] 9:47-In biblical times, a woman generally couldn't divorce her husband. Today these principles apply regardless of who instigates a divorce.

[12] 9:47-See Deuteronomy 24:1. This demonstrates that Jesus intended to fulfill the law (verse 30 above) in such a way that he'd replace it with a higher standard of the heart.

⁴⁸"But I'm telling you that anyone who divorces a spouse for any reason except sexual unfaithfulness[1] and then marries another is guilty of sexual unfaithfulness and causes that spouse to commit sexual unfaithfulness, and anyone who marries a divorced person is guilty of sexual unfaithfulness[2].

⁴⁹"And you've heard it said, 'You shall not swear falsely, but you shall fulfill what you swear to the Lord[3].'

⁵⁰"But I'm telling you that you shouldn't swear at all. You shouldn't swear by heaven, because that's 'God's throne[4].'

⁵¹"You shouldn't swear by the earth, because that's 'God's footstool[5].'

⁵²"You shouldn't swear by the city of Jerusalem, because that's the city of the great king[6].

⁵³"You shouldn't even swear by your own head, because you can't cause a single one of your hairs to be either black or white.

⁵⁴"When you say 'Yes,' let that be the end of the matter. And when you say 'No,' let that be the end of the matter. Anything else comes from Satan himself.

⁵⁵"You've heard the saying, 'An eye for an eye and a tooth for a tooth[7].'

⁵⁶"But I'm telling you that you shouldn't even try to resist someone who wants to do evil to you.

⁵⁷"So if someone slaps you on your right cheek[8], you should simply turn your head and offer that person the opportunity to strike your left cheek, too.

⁵⁸"If someone sues you to take away your shirt, offer that person your jacket, too[9].

⁵⁹"When someone forces you to go a mile, go two miles[10].

⁶⁰"If someone asks you for help, give the help. If someone wants to borrow from you, don't turn away as if you didn't hear. And if someone takes away your things, don't even ask to have those things returned.

⁶¹"Give generously and you'll find you receive even more – good measure, pressed down, shaken together, and running over. The way you measure what you give, whether generous or stingy, is exactly the way God will measure how he gives to you.

⁶²"Again, you've heard the saying, 'You shall care about your neighbor' (and hate your enemy[11]).

⁶³"But I'm telling you that you're to truly care for your enemies, do good to those who hate you.

⁶⁴"Pray for the needs of those who abuse and persecute you. Lend to them without expecting to get paid back.

⁶⁵"When you do this, you'll have a great reward in heaven and you'll show that you're truly children of your Father in heaven, because he causes his sun to shine on both the good and the evil, and he sends rain on those who are unjust as well as on those who are just.

⁶⁶"Think about it. If you only care about those who care about you, why should you be rewarded for that? People who are evil and even the most crooked tax collectors do that!

⁶⁷"If you're only kind to your friends and family, how are you different from anyone else? Even pagans do that.

⁶⁸"If you only lend money to those who can pay you back in full, what good is that? Even sinners[12] do that.

⁶⁹"Grow up! Show the kind of maturity that you see in your Father in heaven[13].

⁷⁰"The Law of Moses and the words of the prophets," Jesus continued, "were the rule until John the Immerser came[14].

⁷¹"Starting with John, we've been announcing the kingdom of God, and everyone who really listens to the message is eager to get in.

---

[1] 9:48-Did Jesus mean that sexual unfaithfulness justifies divorce or that you can't make someone sexually unfaithful if that person already is? Either way, Jesus opposed divorce.

[2] 9:48-See Good News 23:26-35.

[3] 9:49-Numbers 30:2.

[4] 9:50-Isaiah 66:1.

[5] 9:51-Isaiah 66:1.

[6] 9:52-Psalm 48:2. The great king may refer to God himself or to the Christ. From our perspective, both are the same.

[7] 9:55-Exodus 21:24; Leviticus 24:20; and Deuteronomy 19:21. This again demonstrates that Jesus intended to fulfill the law (verse 30 above) in such a way that he'd do away with its authority.

[8] 9:57-If a right-handed person slaps you on the right cheek, it has to be a back-handed slap—an insult as well as an injury. Hitting back escalates the conflict. Jesus wants you to stop the battle—to be a true peacemaker.

[9] 9:58-In Jesus' time most people owned just one set of clothing, so this was a big thing!

[10] 9:59-A Roman soldier could compel a non-Roman to carry his burden for a mile. Jesus was saying that if a despised Roman soldier forced you to carry his burden for a mile, you should offer to just keep carrying it for another mile. In other words, you overcome the bad by finding a way to go beyond the bad and do something good.

[11] 9:62-Leviticus 19:18. "Hate your enemy" isn't in Moses' law, but is a common human response to enemies.

[12] 9:68-Remember, sin is always treason—rebellion against God.

[13] 9:69-This is often translated as if Jesus commanded his followers to "be perfect even as your Father in heaven is perfect." That's obviously impossible for humans, and Jesus never commanded us to do something we couldn't do. See Maturity / Perfection in the Glossary.

[14] 9:70-When John announced the coming kingdom, that marked the beginning of a transition away from the Law of Moses.

Chapter 10 – Teaching about Growing Up Spiritually – Part 2

The Practice of Charity Matthew 6:1-4

¹"Be sure you don't go around doing good things just so people will see what a good person you are.

²"If you're getting your praise from people, you needn't expect any reward from your Father in heaven.

³"So whether you're in a worship center or out in the street, don't hire some trumpeter to call attention to what you're doing when you're helping someone in need. That's what the fakes do. They want to get their recognition from other people.

⁴"I'm telling you the absolute truth when I say that they already have all the reward they'll ever get.

⁵"So when you're doing something good for someone in need, don't even let your left hand know what your right hand's doing.

⁶"Keep the things you do for those in need absolutely secret. Then your Father who knows all secrets will be the one to reward you quite openly.

The Practice of Prayer Matthew 6:5-15; Mark 11:25-26; Luke 6:37b; 11:1-4
(Glossary articles: Agent / Angel; Forgiveness; John the Immerser; Satan; Sin / Rebellion)

⁷"In the same way, don't pray like the fakes do. They love to get everybody's attention by standing up in the worship center or even out on the street and showing off how holy they are.

⁸"I'm telling you the absolute truth when I tell you that they already have all the reward they'll ever get.

⁹"But when you want to talk to your Father in prayer, go into your own room and shut the door. Then when you're alone, talk to your Father who's already in this private place, and your Father who knows all secrets will be the one to reward you quite openly.

¹⁰"And when you're talking to your Father in prayer, don't use a lot of useless repetitive words like pagans do.

¹¹"They think that God will pay attention to them because of all the words. Don't be like them! Remember, your Father knows what you need even before you ask for anything."

¹²Then one of the disciples said, "Lord, teach us to pray like John taught his disciples."

¹³Jesus responded, "Your prayers should be something like this:

¹⁴"Our Father in heaven; may your name always be honored as sacred. May all men come to honor you as the ruler of their lives. May all people do what you would want done just as your agents in heaven do.

¹⁵"For this day, give us the bread we need for food.

¹⁶"And forgive us for the times we've hurt you, just as we forgive those who hurt us.

¹⁷"And don't lead us into situations where we'd be tempted to turn against you, but rather keep us safe from Satan[1], our adversary.

¹⁸"Remember, whenever you pray, if you've got some grudge against anyone, start by forgiving that person so that your Father in heaven will also be able to forgive you.

¹⁹"For if you forgive people when they hurt you, your Father in heaven will also forgive you when you hurt him; but if you don't forgive people who hurt you, your Father isn't going to forgive the times when you've hurt him.

Going without Food Matthew 6:16-18

²⁰"Also, when you go without food as a way to grow spiritually, don't be like the fakes who make a show of how miserable they are.

²¹"They put on a long face so that everyone will know how much they're suffering. I'm telling you the absolute truth: they already have all the reward they'll ever get.

²²"So when you do go without food, make sure you care for your appearance so that no one but your Father (who sees all secrets) will even suspect that you're hungry. Your Father who knows all secrets will be the one to reward you quite openly.

Treasure in Heaven Matthew 6:19-34; Luke 11:34-36; 12:22-34; 16:13-15
(Glossary articles: Belief / Faith; Pharisees)

²³"Don't store up wealth in this world where anything can go wrong: moths can eat fabrics, corrosion can destroy metals, thieves can steal anything else – nothing's really secure.

²⁴"Instead, store up your wealth in heaven. There moths won't eat your wealth, corrosion won't destroy your wealth, and thieves can't get to your wealth.

²⁵"Provide for yourself with wallets that bulge and never wear out, full of treasure in heaven that will never run out. I assure you that your heart's going to be focused on what you think of as your treasure[2].

²⁶"Where you focus your eyes is what controls your whole body.

---

[1] 10:17-Literally, "the evil one."
[2] 10:25-This is a very important point. Jesus knew that you win a person's heart by winning their wealth—not the other way around. If you haven't given your wallet to the Lord, you'll find it impossible to truly give your heart. But if you've given your wallet to the Lord, you'll find it impossible to hold back your heart.

²⁷"If your eyes are focused on what's good, your whole being will be lit up with the light of goodness like a bright shining lamp.

²⁸"But if your eyes are focused on what's bad, your whole being will be in the utter darkness of evil. If what's coming into your eyes is actually the darkness of evil, how terrible that darkness can be!

²⁹"So be sure that what you think is 'light' isn't really darkness. But if your entire being's filled with light, with no dark corners left unlit, then your whole being will be bright just like a lamp can light up an entire room.

³⁰"No one can serve two masters. Either you'll hate the first one and love the second one or the other way around. In the same way, you just can't serve God and at the same time serve the things of this world."

³¹Now some of the Pharisees (who care a lot about money) heard what Jesus was saying and made fun of him.

³²But Jesus told them, "You like to justify what you do in front of the people around you, but God knows what's really in your hearts.

³³"And I assure you: what people think is very important is actually an abomination in God's sight.

³⁴"So don't worry about this life at all. Don't worry about what you're going to eat or what you're going to drink. Don't worry about what you're going to wear.

³⁵"Isn't life more important than food? Isn't your body more important than the clothes you put on it?

³⁶"Look at the birds in the sky. They don't plant any seeds or reap any crops to put in barns, but your Father in heaven still feeds them. Don't you understand that you're more important to him than those birds?

³⁷"When it gets right down to it, which one of you can extend your life[1] just by worrying about it?

³⁸"If you can't do something that small, why should you worry about what you're going to wear?

³⁹"Think about the lilies growing out in a field. They don't go out and work at a job or make clothes to wear, but I'm telling you that even King Solomon, when he was decked out in his finest royal robes, didn't look as good as one of those flowers.

⁴⁰"If God's that generous to flowers that grow up one day and may be tossed in the fire the next day, won't he do much more for you in spite of the weakness of your faith?

⁴¹"So don't go around saying, 'What are we going to eat?' or 'What are we going to drink?' or 'What are we going to wear?' Don't worry about such things!

⁴²"Those are the things all the pagans worry about, but your heavenly Father knows you need those things.

⁴³"Instead, make the kingdom of God and the righteous ways he teaches your first priority, and you'll find that you'll get all the worldly things you really need.

⁴⁴"Oh my little flock, don't worry, about tomorrow – tomorrow will worry about its own problems. Each day brings enough problems without borrowing problems from tomorrow.

⁴⁵"Remember, in the end it's your Father's pleasure to give you the whole kingdom. So in this life, sell what you've got and give to the poor.

Chapter 11 – Teaching about Growing Up Spiritually – Part 3
Proper Judgment Matthew 7:1-6; Luke 6:37a, 38b, 41-42

¹"Don't pick at others for what they do so that you won't wind up being picked at for what you do. Don't condemn others for what they do so that you won't wind up being condemned for what you do.

²"Remember, the standard you use in judging others will be the same standard that's used against you.

³"Why do you look for a speck of dust in your brother's eye when you've got a log sticking out of your own eye? How can you go around saying, 'Brother, let me get that speck of dust out of your eye,' when you've got that log in your eye.

⁴"You two-faced fake! First take the log out of your own eye so you can see clearly enough to help your brother with the speck of dust in his eye.

⁵"But don't give sacred things to dogs – don't throw your pearls out for pigs to trample on them just before they come at you to tear you to pieces[2]."

Asking, Seeking, Knocking Matthew 7:7-11; Luke 11:5-13
(Glossary article: Law of Moses)

⁶Then Jesus continued, "Let's say one of you pounds on a friend's door in the middle of the night, calling him by name and saying, 'Lend me some food! A friend of mine just showed up unexpectedly, and I haven't got a thing to feed him.'

---

[1] 10:37-Literally, "Which of you can add one cubit to his (height or age)?" The word Jesus used here for height or age gives two possible meanings: 1) which of you can make yourself one foot taller by worrying? or 2) which of you can extend your life by worrying? This translation assumes the second of these options because it seems more likely to be the focus of worry for more people.

[2] 11:5-There's an obvious and important point here. While we aren't to condemn others or pick at them for what they do, we're to show enough judgment to distinguish between the dogs and pigs on one hand and those who'll recognize the value of spiritual treasures on the other hand. There's an important difference between condemning others and picking at them versus wasting spiritual treasures on those who'll only turn against us.

⁷"You know what the man's friend will answer: 'Go away and don't bother me! The door's locked and the whole family's in bed. I'm not about to get up just to get food for somebody I don't even know!'

⁸"But you also know that even though the guy won't get up because the person at the door is his friend, he'll get up and give him as much food as he wants if he keeps on knocking!

⁹"So I'm telling you: if you need something, just keep asking for it and you'll get it.

¹⁰"If you want to find something, just keep looking for it and you'll find it.

¹¹"If you want in, just keep on knocking and the door will be opened[1].

¹²"Anyone who keeps on asking will get what's needed. Anyone who keeps on looking will find what's needed. Anyone who keeps on knocking will find that the door will be opened.

¹³"If your son were to ask you for some bread, which of you would give your son a stone? Or if he asked for a fish, would you give him a snake? If he asks for an egg, will you give him a scorpion?

¹⁴"If you who live in this environment of evil still know how to give good gifts to your children, how much more will your Father in heaven give his Holy Spirit[2] to those who keep on asking him?

The Golden Rule Matthew 7:12; Luke 6:31
(Glossary article: Law of Moses)

¹⁵"In every way, treat people the way you wish they'd treat you. That's the point of everything God ever told you in the Law of Moses and the writings of the prophets."

A Narrow Gate and a Wide Gate Matthew 7:13-14; Luke 13:23-30
(Glossary article: Abraham)

¹⁶Then someone asked, "Lord, are there only a few who'll actually be saved?"

¹⁷"Use the narrow door," Jesus responded, "to get into God's reward.

¹⁸"The wide door and the broad roadway lead to eternal destruction, and most folks are following that way.

¹⁹"But the way that leads to eternal life is by the narrow door and the difficult road. Only a few actually find that way.

²⁰"So try hard to enter through that narrow door, because I'm telling you the absolute truth: there are a lot of folks who'll want to get in and won't be able to.

²¹"Once the master of the house has closed and locked the door, you'll find yourself standing outside knocking and yelling, 'Lord! Lord! Open the door for us!'

²²"But he'll answer back, 'I don't know you or even where you've come from.'

²³"Then you'll cry out, 'We ate and drank with you and you taught in the streets where we lived.'

²⁴"But he'll say, 'I'm telling all of you, I don't know you or even where you've come from. But I do know that you've spent your lives doing evil.'

²⁵"Then you'll be weeping and grinding your teeth in anguish when you see Abraham, Isaac, Jacob, and all the prophets in the kingdom of God and you yourselves locked out.

²⁶"Yes, people will come from the east and the west, from the north and the south, to sit down in the kingdom of God.

²⁷"And there are indeed many who are now counted as last who'll be first in that kingdom, and many who are now counted as first will be last.

Discerning False Leaders Matthew 7:15-23; 12:33-37; Luke 6:43-46
(Glossary articles: Evil Spirits; Profanity; In the Name of...; Miracles; Prophecies)

²⁸"Beware of those who claim to bring a message from God when it's really something they've made up. They're like hungry wolves on the inside but dressed up to look like gentle sheep.

²⁹"You can recognize them by what their lives produce, just as you identify a tree by the fruit it produces.

³⁰"Do you get grapes from thorn bushes? Do you get figs from thistles? Good trees bear good fruit and bad trees bear bad fruit. A good tree is incapable of bearing bad fruit, and a bad tree is incapable of bearing good fruit.

³¹"A good person will always produce good actions straight out of the good treasures in that person's heart, and an evil person will always produce evil actions straight out of the evil treasures in that person's heart.

³²"You sons of snakes! You're so evil, how could you ever say anything good?

³³"After all, it's what's in a person's heart that comes out of his mouth.

³⁴"I tell you, in the judgment you'll have to give account for every single word of profanity you've ever spoken.

³⁵"The very things you've said will reveal whether you've been justified or whether you'll be condemned.

---

[1] 11:11-This passage is often translated with the English verbs, "ask," "seek," and "knock," without the emphasis on continuing action (keep asking, keep seeking, keep knocking). However, the verbs Jesus used clearly indicated continuing in these actions until you get the desired result.

[2] 11:14-If God granted all our worldly requests, he'd reinforce our worldliness. By giving himself—his Holy Spirit, God gives us the greatest gift we could ever have and teaches us to rely on him instead of worldly goods.

³⁶"And remember, when a tree doesn't bear good fruit, it's cut down and burned up. In the same way, you can recognize those with false claims of messages from God by looking at what their lives produce.

³⁷"So why do you call me 'Lord, Lord,' if then you don't do the things I tell you to do?

³⁸"Just because people call me 'Lord, Lord,' doesn't mean they'll get into the kingdom of heaven. You've got to do what my Father in heaven wants you to do.

³⁹"On the Day of Judgment, many people will come to me saying, 'Lord, Lord! Didn't we proclaim powerful messages[1] in your authority and cast out evil spirits in your authority and do marvelous miracles in your authority?'

⁴⁰"That's when I'll look at them and say, 'Get away from me, you who live with no regard for what God requires. I've never known you at all.'

True Wisdom Matthew 7:24-27; Luke 6:47-49
(Glossary article: Immediately / Quickly)

⁴¹"So here's how it is. Anybody who listens to these things I'm telling you and then puts them into practice, I'd compare that person to a wise man who built himself a house and started by digging deep to lay the foundation on bedrock.

⁴²"When it poured down rain and flood waters beat against it and the storm winds blasted it, that house stood firm because its foundation was on rock.

⁴³"On the other hand, anybody who hears the things I'm telling you and does nothing about them, I'd compare that person to a foolish man who built his house on sand with no foundation.

⁴⁴"When it poured down rain and the flood waters beat against it and the storm winds blasted it, that house collapsed rapidly into a huge pile of rubble."

Chapter 12 – The Great Physician
A Leper Healed Matthew 8:1-4; Mark 1:40-45; Luke 5:12-16
(Glossary articles: Capernaum; Immediately / Quickly; Law of Moses)

¹On Jesus' way back to Capernaum after teaching these things, huge crowds followed him. Then a man eaten up with leprosy came to him and fell to his knees to worship him, saying, "Lord, if you're willing, you can heal me."

²Jesus, filled with compassion for this man, reached out his hand, placed it on the leper[2], and said, "I certainly am willing. Be healed!" As soon as he said it, the leprosy was gone[3].

³Then Jesus told him, "Be sure you don't tell anyone how this happened. Just go to the priest[4] and offer the sacrifice required in the Law of Moses as a witness to them that you're now well."

⁴(In spite of what Jesus said, this man spread the word of how Jesus had healed him wherever he went. Before long Jesus couldn't even go into the city for the crowds, so he had to spend most of his time in open areas away from towns. And the crowds just kept coming from all over to listen to his message and to be healed. During these times Jesus often went aside into remote areas to pray.)

A Roman Commander's Servant Healed Matthew 8:5-13; Luke 7:1-10
(Glossary articles: Abraham; Belief / Faith; Capernaum; Jewish Elders; Romans and Jews)

⁵After healing the man with leprosy, Jesus continued on his way into the city of Capernaum.

⁶There was a Roman military commander[5] in that city who had a servant who was very dear to him, but the servant was at the point of death, unable to move and in terrible pain.

⁷When the commander heard about Jesus' power to heal, he sent some of the Jewish elders[6] to Jesus to plead with Jesus to come and heal his servant.

⁸When the elders came to Jesus, they earnestly presented the commander's request to have his servant healed. They told Jesus that this Roman deserved such consideration because he really loved the Jews and had even built one of their worship centers out of his own funds.

---

[1] 11:39-The word used here is for prophecy, but see the Glossary article on Prophecies and Fulfillments.
[2] 12:2-Touching a person with leprosy was strictly forbidden. It must have shocked the crowd to see Jesus reach out and touch this man.
[3] 12:2-This is a case where the word generally translated "immediately" is used and it's obvious from the context that the effect was immediate.
[4] 12:3-If you had leprosy, you couldn't return to society until the priest examined you. Then you had to present a sacrifice and go through a specific ritual.
[5] 12:6-Literally, "centurion," a commander over about 100 Roman soldiers.
[6] 12:7-As a Roman authority, this commander probably doubted a Jewish rabbi would help him, so he sent Jewish elders. Then rather than expose Jesus to criticism for entering the home of a non-Jew, this commander sent another message. This caused Jesus to tell these Jews something they could hardly believe—that foreigners from all over would eventually be able to sit with the patriarchs of the Jews in the kingdom of heaven.

⁹So Jesus went with them, but as they approached the house, the commander[1] sent a message with some of his friends, saying, "Don't bother coming into my house, Lord. I'm not worthy to have you under my roof – that's why I didn't come to you myself. I know that all you need to do is say the word and my servant will be fine.

¹⁰"After all, I'm a man accustomed to real authority. If I tell one of my soldiers, 'Go,' he goes. And if I tell another one, 'Come,' he comes. And if I tell my servant, 'Do this,' that's exactly what he does."

¹¹When Jesus heard the message, he was quite surprised[2]. He turned to the crowd of people following him and said, "I'm telling you: I haven't found anybody with that much faith – not in all Israel!

¹²"And I assure you all: there'll be many who'll come from the east and the west to sit down beside Abraham, Isaac, and Jacob in the kingdom of heaven.

¹³"But there'll be those who were the children of the kingdom who'll be thrown out into the outer darkness where they'll weep and grind their teeth in anguish because of their loss."

¹⁴Then he told the messengers, "Go back to this commander and tell him, 'It will be done in accordance with your faith.'"

¹⁵And when the elders and the commander's friends returned to the commander's house, they found the servant fully recovered.

A Widow's Son Raised Luke 7:11-17
(Glossary article: Judea)

¹⁶The next day Jesus went to a city[3], accompanied by many of his disciples and a huge crowd of others.

¹⁷As they approached the city gates, they met a funeral procession carrying a man's body. This man had been the only son of a woman who'd been widowed[4], and many of the city's people were with the procession.

¹⁸When Jesus saw this woman, he felt great sympathy for her and told her, "Don't cry." Then he went over to the coffin and touched it, causing the men carrying it to stop. "Young man," he said, "I'm telling you: get up!"

¹⁹At that the dead man sat up and began talking. Then Jesus led him back to his mother.

²⁰The whole crowd was struck with awe and praised God, saying, "God's raised up a great prophet among us," and "God's surely come among his people."

²¹People were soon talking about this even in Judea and throughout all the surrounding areas.

A Daughter Healed Matthew 15:21-28; Mark 7:24-30
(Glossary articles: Belief / Faith; Evil Spirits; Gentiles; Third Person Commands)

²²Once Jesus traveled to a non-Jewish area north of Galilee[5]. He went into a house and tried to keep his presence a secret, but the word soon got out. (There was just no way to keep Jesus hidden!)

²³While he was there, a woman from that area who wasn't a Jew[6] came to him. "Have mercy on me, Lord, son of David!" she cried out, "An evil spirit's severely tormenting my little girl!"

²⁴She kept calling out to him, but Jesus wouldn't say anything. Then the disciples urged Jesus, "This woman just keeps yelling at us. Send her away!"

²⁵At that point Jesus turned to the woman. "I wasn't sent to anybody," he said, "except the lost sheep who are Israelites."

²⁶The woman then came up and fell on her knees before him. "Lord, help me!" she pleaded.

²⁷But Jesus replied, "Let the children eat their fill first. It's not right to take the children's bread and throw it to the dogs[7]!"

²⁸"Yes, Lord," she replied, "But even the dogs eat the crumbs that fall from their master's table."

²⁹At this Jesus responded, "Woman, you truly have a strong faith in me! Because you said this, what you desire shall be done[8]. The evil spirit's left your daughter."

---

[1] 12:9-Literally, "centurion."

[2] 12:11-Jesus' surprise is consistent with his humanity. In the Bible, it's clear that Jesus had access to whatever knowledge he needed, but that in most cases he functioned without drawing on his access to divine knowledge for his own benefit—he functioned just as we would.

[3] 12:16-The city was Nain in south-central Galilee.

[4] 12:17-In New Testament times, a widow would generally rely on her children to care for her. It was extremely hard for a woman to make it on her own. So the loss of this son would've been devastating. In most cases, such a widow would've been reduced to begging.

[5] 12:22-Around Tyre and Sidon (southern Lebanon today).

[6] 12:23-Matthew's account tells us that this woman was a Canaanite (a native of the land of Canaan, which took in several ethnic groups). Mark is more specific, telling us that she was of Syrian and Phoenician heritage. Mark's comment that she was Greek doesn't mean much. Jews tended to think of non-Jews as all being "Greek," since at that time most of the Roman Empire spoke Greek.

[7] 12:27-This seems very heartless and even cruel, but there were two important things going on here. First, Jesus was testing this woman to see how she'd respond. Was she coming to him as just another healer, hoping for a cure for her daughter, or did she really believe that Jesus was special and different? If she believed that Jesus was special and different, this response wouldn't stop her; but if she thought of him as just another healer, this response would cause her to leave. Second, Jesus truly did need to focus his ministry on the Jews. The non-Jews were to be the work of his disciples.

[8] 12:29-This passage is very difficult to translate into English. This is a third person command in the Bible, and there's no convenient way to translate it into English. What Jesus did was command that the healing would already have taken place.

³⁰(And that very hour when she got home, she found her little girl in bed, and the evil spirit was gone.)

A Blind Man Healed Mark 8:22-26
(Glossary articles: Biblical Names; Capernaum)
³¹Later they came to a town near Capernaum[1] where some people brought a blind man to Jesus. They begged him to touch the man.

³²Jesus took the blind man by the hand and led him out of the town. Next he spit on the man's eyes and put his hands on the blind man. After doing this he asked the blind man, "Do you see anything?"

³³"I see men," he said, "but they look like trees walking[2]."

³⁴Jesus put his hands on the man's eyes again and made him look up. As soon as he did this, his eyesight was completely restored.

³⁵Then Jesus sent him away and told him, "Don't go into the town or tell anyone in the town."

Healing a Man on a Sabbath at a Pharisee's Home Luke 14:1-6
(Glossary articles: Immediately / Quickly; Lawyers; Pharisees; Sabbath)
³⁶One of the chief Pharisees invited Jesus to have a meal with him on the Sabbath.

³⁷All the Pharisees and Lawyers present were watching him closely to see what he'd do, because there was a man present who suffered from severe swelling.

³⁸"According to God's law," Jesus asked, "is it acceptable to heal a man on the Sabbath?" None of those present offered any response, so Jesus took the man aside, healed him, and then let him leave.

³⁹Then Jesus turned to those present and asked, "If you own a donkey or an ox that falls into an open pit on the Sabbath, which one of you wouldn't quickly pull him out even though it's a Sabbath?"

⁴⁰Once again, none of them could find anything to say.

Chapter 13 – Warnings about Selfish Pride and Worldly Focus

Warnings about Seeking Titles and Honors Matthew 23:1-12; Mark 12:38-39; Luke 14:7-14; 20:45-47
(Glossary articles: Law of Moses; Pharisees; Scribes)

¹At a wedding feast that Jesus attended, people were rushing to get the places of honor for the feast. When Jesus saw this he said, "When you're invited to a wedding feast, don't try to take the places of honor.

²"If you do, when someone the host respects more than you comes in, he'll come and tell you, 'Get up and give this man that place.'

³"Then you'll be embarrassed and slink off to take the most obscure place you can find.

⁴"But when you're invited to a feast, go find an obscure place. Then if the host thinks you should be honored, he'll come to you and say, 'My friend, come take your place at the front!'

⁵"When that happens you'll have the respect of all those at the feast with you. I tell you, people who try to show off will get humiliated, but those who humble themselves will be the ones who are praised."

⁶Then Jesus told the Pharisee who'd invited him to the feast, "When you give a banquet, don't just ask your friends and family and your wealthy neighbors.

⁷"If you do that, you know they'll return the favor and you'll have received your reward.

⁸"Instead, when you give a banquet, invite the poor, the disfigured, the lame, and the blind. They can't repay you, so you'll receive your reward from God when the righteous are raised from the dead."

⁹Later Jesus told his disciples and the crowds that followed him[3], "The scribes and Pharisees are the authorities on the Law of Moses, so do whatever they tell you to do, but don't imitate how they live.

¹⁰"They tell others how to live, but that's not how they live. They burden people down with rules that are hard to obey, but then they won't lift a finger to help.

¹¹"Beware of the Pharisees and scribes who like going around in lordly robes. The good things they do are done to show off in front of people.

¹²"They wear jewelry and clothing that's supposed to identify them as righteous people. They love being honored at the head table for religious feasts and getting the seats of honor in your worship services. They love having people greet them as 'Reverend[4] ' when they walk through the supermarket.

---

[1] 12:31-See Bethsaida in the Glossary.

[2] 12:33-Why did Jesus take this man out of town? Why did he spit on the man's eyes? Why did the miracle require two steps? The Bible doesn't tell us. These are questions for which the answers aren't important, but if this had been a made-up account, it's very unlikely it would've included those things.

[3] 13:9-Notice the distinction between disciples (those trying to learn to live as Jesus taught) and the crowds that followed Jesus around.

[4] 13:12-Literally 'rabbi.' 'Reverend' carries the meaning better for American Christians. Christians aren't to use titles that imply they're somehow better than others. The Spirit of Christ speaks most powerfully through those who seek honor from God rather than men.

¹³"You who want to follow me, don't let anybody call you 'Reverend' because for my followers there's only one guide – the Christ – and all of you are brothers.

¹⁴"And don't call anyone on earth your father[1] because for my followers there's only one Father, and he's in heaven.

¹⁵"And don't let people call you 'Doctor[2]' because for my followers there's only one master teacher – the Christ! Instead, the greatest among you must be your servant.

¹⁶"If you go around taking on the titles of greatness, God will humble you. But if you seek to humbly serve those in need, God will exalt you."

The Kingdom and a Banquet Matthew 22:1-14; Luke 14:15-24
(Glossary articles: Dining Customs; Jewish Marriage Customs; Slaves)

¹⁷When he heard this, one of the people reclining around the feast with Jesus said, "There'll be great joy for anyone who gets to feast in the kingdom of God!"

¹⁸Then Jesus told this story: "The kingdom of heaven," he said, "is like a king who made preparations for the marriage of his son. When everything was ready, he sent his slaves to tell the people he'd invited, 'Everything's ready. Come to the feast.' But they weren't willing to come.

¹⁹"At this the king sent other slaves with this message: 'Look! I've got the feast all prepared. I've had my oxen and my fat cattle slaughtered and everything's ready. Come to the wedding!' But those who were invited just made a joke of the invitation.

²⁰"One of them said, 'Please have me excused. I bought some land and I need to go inspect it.'

²¹"Another one said, 'I've bought a new truck and I need to take a test drive. Please have me excused.'

²²"A third one said, 'I can't come; I just got married.'

²³"Others went on about their business: one to his farm, another to his store. Still others grabbed the slaves and beat them, even killing some of them.

²⁴"When a slave reported to the king about all that had happened, the king was furious. He sent his soldiers to kill those who'd abused his slaves and to destroy their whole city.

²⁵"Then he told his slaves, 'The wedding feast's ready, but those I invited weren't worthy to share in my feast. So go all through the city and invite everyone you find. I don't care if they're poor, maimed, lame, or blind!'

²⁶"Then one of the slaves told the king, 'Master, we've done just as you commanded, and there's still room for more.'

²⁷"At this the king said, 'Go out on the highways beyond the city and even search the hedges along the roadsides. Force anyone you find to come to the feast. I want the house to be filled. And I'm telling you: none of those who were invited will get even a taste of this feast!'

²⁸"The king's slaves did as instructed and brought in everybody they could find, good or bad, until the wedding facilities were packed with guests.

²⁹"But when the king came to greet the guests he saw a man who wasn't wearing the wedding outfit[3].

³⁰"'Friend,' the king asked, 'how did you get in without a wedding garment?' But the man had no answer.

³¹"Then the king told his servants, 'Tie his hands and feet and throw him out into the darkness where there'll be weeping and grinding of teeth in anguish.'

³²"Understand the point:" Jesus said, "The kingdom calls many to come, but only a few actually get in."

Jesus Curses Religious Leaders with a Worldly Focus Matthew 23:13-36; Mark 12:40; Luke 11:37-54
(Glossary articles: Belief / Faith; Caring Love; Dining Customs; Hell; Lawyers; Pharisees; Scribes)

³³One day as Jesus was teaching, a Pharisee invited him to dinner. Jesus accepted the invitation, but when he lay on the cushions for the meal, the Pharisee expressed surprise that he hadn't washed his hands before the meal.

³⁴"There's great anguish coming to you, scribes and Pharisees!" Jesus told those who were present, "You're a bunch of fakes!

³⁵"You look good on the outside, like cleaning the outside of a cup or dish, but inside you're full of greed and wicked selfishness!

³⁶"Foolish blind Pharisees! Didn't the one who created the outside create the inside too?

³⁷"First clean what's inside as you would clean a cup or dish so that the outside may also be clean.

---

[1] 13:14-Jesus wasn't talking about how we address our biological fathers. The subject he was addressing here is people taking on titles of honor as if they were somehow better than others. Jesus intentionally chose fishermen, tax collectors, and those whom the world would consider uneducated to accomplish his mission so that the glory would obviously be God's. Christian leaders are right to seek training, but they should never use any title that might imply that a trained leader is somehow better than a faithful servant of God. They both have God's Holy Spirit, and that's all that matters.

[2] 13:15-This is about religious scholars who like to be called "Doctor" as an indication of status. The word "doctor" means "teacher," and the best teacher is the one who's trained but relies on God more than on the training and seeks honor from God rather than men.

[3] 13:29-In New Testament times, kings would provide festive wedding garments for their guests. Since there was no cost to the guest, there was no excuse for this man to be at the feast without the garment.

³⁸"Give what you have to those in need and then everything will be clean for you.

³⁹"There's great anguish coming to you, scribes and Pharisees! You're a bunch of fakes!

⁴⁰"You slam the doors of the kingdom of heaven in the faces those who want in. You yourselves aren't getting in, and you're barring the way for others.

⁴¹"There's great anguish coming to you, scribes and Pharisees! You're a bunch of fakes!

⁴²"You repossess widows' homes and then you pretend to make long prayers in public. That's why your condemnation will be so great!

⁴³"There's great anguish coming to you, scribes and Pharisees! You're a bunch of fakes!

⁴⁴"You search land and sea to win one convert, and then you turn your converts into twice the children of hell you are!

⁴⁵"There's great anguish coming to you, blind guides! You say, 'An oath isn't binding if you swear by the temple, but if you swear by the gold of the temple the oath is binding.'

⁴⁶"Blind fools! Which is truly greater, the gold or the temple that sanctifies the gold?

⁴⁷"And you say, 'An oath isn't binding if you swear by the altar in the temple, but if you swear by the gift on the altar your oath is binding.'

⁴⁸"Blind fools! Which is truly greater, the gift on the altar or the altar that sanctifies the gift?

⁴⁹"Understand! If you swear by the altar, you're swearing by it and by whatever's on the altar.

⁵⁰"And if you swear by the temple, you're swearing by it and by the God who inhabits the temple.

⁵¹"If you swear by heaven, you're swearing by the throne of God and by God himself who sits on that throne.

⁵²"There's great anguish coming to you, scribes and Pharisees! You're a bunch of fakes!

⁵³"You carefully give a tenth of even the herbs you grow in your garden – mint, anise, and cumin, but you fail to give anything from the more important matters such as justice, mercy, faith in God and the caring love God's commanded.

⁵⁴"These are the things you should've done first – without neglecting your material giving.

⁵⁵"Blind guides! You strain out the gnat and swallow the whole camel!

⁵⁶"There's great anguish coming to you, scribes and Pharisees! What you crave is having the best seats in the worship centers and being recognized in the shopping mall!

⁵⁷"There's great anguish coming to you, scribes and Pharisees! You're a bunch of fakes!

⁵⁸"You're like burial chambers that have been whitewashed! On the outside you look good, but inside you're as unclean as a chamber full of dead bones.

⁵⁹"You're like graves where men have been buried and now a garden grows on the burial site where men walk on the unseen bones below.

⁶⁰"Just like those burial chambers, on the outside you look like you're so righteous, but inside you're filled with falseness and lawlessness[1]."

⁶¹On hearing this, one of the experts in the Law reclining around the feast said, "Teacher, when you say those things you're insulting us too!"

⁶²"There's great anguish coming to you who are supposed to be experts in the Law, too!," Jesus replied. "You tell others how to live, but that's not how you live, laying terrible burdens on them that you wouldn't touch with so much as a finger.

⁶³"There's great anguish coming to you, scribes, Pharisees, and experts in the Law! You're a bunch of fakes!

⁶⁴"You build the tombs of the prophets and provide ornate monuments to the righteous men of the past, and you say, 'If we'd lived in the times of our ancestors when these holy men were living, we wouldn't have joined our ancestors in killing the prophets.'

⁶⁵"But in saying that you testify that you're indeed the children of those who murdered the prophets. Now complete what your ancestors started!

⁶⁶"Serpents! Children of poisonous snakes! How can you hope to escape being condemned to hell?

⁶⁷"That's why God in his wisdom has said, 'I'm going to send you messengers, prophets, wise men, and scribes. You'll murder and crucify some of them. Others you'll beat with whips or run out of town while you chase them from city to city.

⁶⁸"Thus you'll bring upon yourselves the guilt for all the blood of prophets that's been shed from the blood of that righteous man, Abel, to the blood of the man[2] you murdered between the temple and the altar.

⁶⁹"I'm telling you the absolute truth: all of these curses will come down on this generation.

⁷⁰"Yes, there's great anguish coming to you, experts in the Law! You've taken away the very key to understanding. You didn't enter the kingdom yourselves, and when anyone somehow gets close, you've done your best to keep that person out!"

⁷¹As Jesus was saying these things, the scribes and Pharisees started getting hostile, trying to pin Jesus down with questions about all sorts of things. They were trying to entrap him in something he might say, looking for anything they could use to bring an accusation against him.

---

[1] 13:60-There's no theme Jesus pounded on more consistently than the theme that God cares about what's in a person's heart, not what's on the outside. Fine clothing and "Christian" jewelry are no substitute for a heart surrendered to God.

[2] 13:68-Zechariah the son of Berechiah. See Zechariah in the Glossary.

Chapter 14 – The Twelve Disciples

Appointing Twelve Disciples Matthew 10:1-4; Mark 3:13-19; Luke 6:12-16
(Glossary articles: Andrew; Biblical Names; Evil Spirits; Disciples; James; John; Judas; Matthew; Nathanael; Peter)

^{1}As he gathered more and more disciples, Jesus went by himself to a mountain to pray and spent the whole night in prayer to God.

^{2}When day broke he called his disciples and chose twelve whom he appointed as messengers[1] to go out with the message, giving them power to heal all kinds of illness and disease and to deal with evil spirits.

^{3}These are the names of the twelve he chose:
- Simon who was also called Peter
- Andrew (Simon Peter's brother)
- James
- John (James' brother, Jesus called them "Sons of Thunder[2]")
- Philip
- Nathan[3]
- Thomas
- Matthew the tax collector (also known as Levi)
- James the Younger[4]
- Judas son of James (not the one who betrayed Jesus[5])
- Simon known as the Zealot
- Judas (the one who betrayed Jesus[6])

Sending Out the Twelve Disciples Matthew 10:5-16; 11:1; Mark 6:7-13; Luke 9:1-6
(Glossary articles: Evil Spirits; Messengers; Gentiles; Preaching / Proclaiming; Repentance; Samaritans)

^{4}Then Jesus called these twelve messengers[7] together, having given them the power to deal with any evil spirits and to cure any diseases, and he sent them out to proclaim the coming kingdom of God and to heal the sick. He sent them out in pairs and gave them these instructions:

^{5}"Don't go into non-Jewish or Samaritan areas. Instead, stick with just the lost sheep who are Israelites. As you go, announce the news with these words: 'The kingdom of heaven is about to come.'

^{6}"Heal the sick, even those with leprosy, raise the dead, cast out evil spirits. You've received this power as a free gift, so give it out freely.

^{7}"Take nothing with you except one staff. Don't take any money or provisions for your trip – not even bread to eat. Don't take an extra jacket or extra sandals or an extra staff, because you're doing God's work and you deserve the support of those to whom you go.

^{8}"Whenever you enter a city or town, ask around for a worthy person and stay with that person as long as you're in that town.

^{9}"Whenever you go into a house, greet the people of the house warmly. If these people are worthy, let your peace come on them.

^{10}"If anyone refuses to let you in or listen to your message, shake off even the dust from your feet when you leave that house or that city as a witness against them and let your peace return to you.

^{11}"I assure you: cities that God destroyed for their wickedness[8] will have it better on judgment day than that city!

^{12}"See, I'm sending you out like a little flock of sheep into a howling pack of wolves. You'll need to be as clever as serpents and as innocent as doves."

^{13}So these disciples went through the towns proclaiming the good news, warning people to turn their lives around, and healing people wherever they went, anointing the sick with oil[9].

---

[1] 14:2-The word here is normally translated "apostles" rather than "messengers." "Apostle" is a word with a Greek root meaning "one sent out on a mission." Over the years, this word has come to be viewed as a religious word, but in New Testament times the word Jesus used was a common secular term for someone sent out to accomplish some task.

[2] 14:3-James and John were also called Zebedee's sons.

[3] 14:3-Literally, Nathanael. He was also known as Bartholomew (meaning Tolmai's Son).

[4] 14:3-Also known as James Alphaeus' son.

[5] 14:3-Literally, "not Iscariot." This Judas was also known as Thaddaeus.

[6] 14:3-Literally, "Judas Iscariot."

[7] 14:4-These are the twelve who became Jesus' closest followers and are generally known as "the twelve disciples," but the word here is the one generally translated "apostles." "Messengers" is a better term today to express this idea.

[8] 14:11-Sodom and Gomorrah.

[9] 14:13-We don't know if the disciples anointed the sick with oil when they were with Jesus, or if Jesus routinely anointed the sick with oil, or if this anointing was something Jesus told them to do only on their journey.

¹⁴And when Jesus finished these instructions to his disciples he also left to teach and proclaim God's message in the cities to which he'd sent them.

¹⁵When the disciples[1] Jesus had sent out returned, they told him all about what they'd done and what they'd taught.

Chapter 15 – A Trip to Jerusalem

First Cleansing of the Temple John 2:13-25
(Glossary articles: Belief / Faith; Crucifixion Timing Issues; Herod's Temple; Jerusalem; Jewish Feasts; Miracles; Sacred Writings)

¹One time when it was about time for the Jewish Passover, Jesus went up to Jerusalem, and when he came to the temple, he found merchants in the temple complex selling oxen, sheep, and doves for sacrifices as well as people exchanging foreign currencies for the coins accepted in the temple services.

²Making a whip out of some rope, Jesus began to drive out all the merchants along with their animals, and he knocked over the tables of money, scattering the coins on the ground.

³Jesus told the merchants, "Get that stuff out of here! Don't you dare turn my Father's house into a merchandise market!"

⁴When Jesus' disciples saw this, they recalled the psalm that says, "Zeal for your house consumes me[2]!"

⁵Then the Jewish temple authorities asked Jesus, "Who gave you the right to do this? Can you show us some kind of miracle to prove that you have this right?"

⁶Jesus answered, "Destroy this temple, and in just three days I'll raise it up."

⁷The Jews replied, "That's crazy. It's taken forty-six years to build this temple, and you're going to raise it up in just three days?"

⁸(They had no idea Jesus was speaking of his body as the temple he'd raise up. But when he rose from the dead, his disciples recalled what he'd told them, and it gave them confidence both in the passage in the Psalms[3] and in what Jesus had taught them.)

⁹While Jesus was in Jerusalem for the Passover, many who were there saw the miracles he was doing and trusted his message.

¹⁰But Jesus wouldn't entrust himself to any of them since he knew all about humanity and didn't need anyone to tell him how he should deal with people.

Meeting with a Supreme Court Judge John 3:1-21
(Glossary articles: Belief / Faith; Caring Love; Common Gender; Moses; Nicodemus; Pharisees; Supreme Court; Son of Man; Wind, Breath, Spirit)

¹¹One night a member of the Jewish Supreme Court[4] named Nicodemus (a member of the Pharisees) came to see Jesus and said, "Teacher, we know that you've come from God – nobody could do the things you're doing except by the power of God himself."

¹²Jesus responded, "I'm telling you the absolute truth: unless you're born anew[5], you can't even see God's kingdom."

¹³Nicodemus replied, "What are you talking about? How can anybody be born when he's already old? Are you saying that somehow I need to get back into my mother's womb to be born again?"

¹⁴Jesus answered, "Again, I assure you that this is absolute truth: unless you've been born of water[6] and spirit, you cannot possibly get into God's kingdom.

¹⁵"Anyone born as flesh is only flesh, but when you're born of the Spirit, your essence becomes spirit. So you shouldn't be surprised that I said you must be born again.

¹⁶"The wind[7] blows wherever it wants and you can hear the sound it makes, but you can never know where it came from or where it's going.

¹⁷"Those who are born of the Spirit are like that – the rest of the world can tell they're there but they don't understand where they're coming from."

¹⁸Nicodemus responded, "I don't understand what you're trying to say."

¹⁹Jesus answered, "You call yourself the man who teaches all of Israel, and you don't understand this?

---

[1] 14:15-Literally, "the messengers," or "the ones sent out."
[2] 15:4-Psalm 69:9.
[3] 15:8-Literally, "the writing."
[4] 15:11-Often translated as "Council" or "Sanhedrin."
[5] 15:12-The word Jesus used for "anew" also implies "from above"—a new start on life with a whole different focus, discarding the past and growing as a new being.
[6] 15:14-From the context we cannot tell if Jesus was referring to the "water" associated with human birth or the water of immersion when a person becomes a Christian. The answer isn't important since there are plenty of other passages that deal with Christian immersion.
[7] 15:16-"Wind," "breath," and "spirit" are all different translations of the same word in the Bible. Only the context can tell the translator which word to use.

²⁰"I'll tell you[1] the absolute truth: we tell you what we know and we bear witness to what we've seen and you still don't put your faith in us.

²¹"If I've told you things that apply to this earth and you can't accept them, how can you expect to understand when I talk to you about heavenly things?"

²²(Nobody here on earth has ever been in heaven except Jesus. He came down from heaven as a human[2], and he's in heaven now.)

²³"Furthermore," Jesus continued, "just as Moses erected a pole with a serpent on it in the wilderness to save the Israelites, even so I as a human[3] must be lifted up so that whoever entrusts his life to me absolutely shall not perish but shall instead have life forevermore."

²⁴You see, this shows how very much God cared for the world in that he gave[4] his unique son so that anyone entrusting his or her life to Jesus would escape destruction and have life forevermore.

²⁵God didn't send his son into this world to condemn the world, but to bring salvation to the world through him.

²⁶If you entrust your life to Jesus, by that decision you're no longer condemned. But if you don't entrust your life to Jesus, you're already condemned just because you haven't surrendered your life to God's unique son.

²⁷And this is why you're condemned – because the very source of light has come into the world, but you prefer the darkness over the light because what you're doing is wrong and you know it.

²⁸After all, when you're doing wrong, you don't want to come into the light where the evil of your deeds will be exposed.

²⁹But if you're living right, you welcome the light so that it's obvious to everybody that you're living to please God.

Chapter 16 – Back in Galilee
A Storm Calmed Matthew 8:23-27; Mark 4:35-41; Luke 8:22-25
(Glossary article: Belief / Faith)

¹One evening after teaching along the shore[5] of the Sea of Galilee all day, Jesus got into a boat with his disciples and said, "Let's take the boat to the other side."

²Some other smaller boats were crossing with them, but suddenly a severe storm came up with waves washing across the boat.

³Meanwhile, Jesus was in the back of the boat sound asleep on a cushion while the boat was taking on water rapidly.

⁴In their panic, his disciples were yelling, "Teacher! Master! Save us! Can't you see that we're all about to die?"

⁵"Why are you so scared?" Jesus responded. "What's happened to the faith you have in me, even as small as it is?"

⁶Then he got up, rebuked the wind, and told the sea, "Peace, be still." Immediately the wind died down and the waters were calm.

⁷The disciples were in awe, saying, "Who is this guy? He tells the wind and the sea what to do, and they do what he says!"

A Herd of Evil Spirits Chased Out Matthew 8:28-34; 9:1a; Mark 5:1-20; Luke 8:26-39
(Glossary articles: Biblical Names; Evil Spirits; Disciples; Gentiles; Immediately / Quickly; Son of God)

⁸Once the sea was calm they sailed into a non-Jewish territory[6]. As soon as they reached the shore, two naked men possessed by evil spirits came out of the nearby tombs where they were living.

⁹When one of the men approached him, Jesus said, "Come out of that man, you evil spirit!"

¹⁰(This man was so fierce that no one would go near him. He'd been captured and tied up with chains under guard before, but he always broke the chains and escaped into uninhabited areas. He was like a wild animal, and he couldn't be tamed[7]. This man roamed the mountains and the graveyards, cutting himself with stones.)

¹¹When Jesus ordered the evil spirit to come out, the man ran to him, fell to his knees before him, and cried out, "What are you doing here, Jesus. I know you're the Son of God Most High! I impose an oath on you before God, don't send me to hell ahead of the time[8]!"

---

[1] 15:20-"You" is plural in this paragraph, referring to the religious leaders of Israel.
[2] 15:22-Literally, "the son of man…"
[3] 15:23-Literally, "the son of man…"
[4] 15:24-The tense of the verb indicates that this isn't what Jesus said, but what John wrote about something that had already happened.
[5] 16:1-There are places along the shore of the Sea of Galilee where the shape of the land creates an amphitheater where a large crowd could hear a speaker.
[6] 16:8-Literally, "the land of the Gergesenes" (Matthew) or "the land of the Gadarenes" (Mark and Luke). These two groups lived in the same general area.
[7] 16:10-The details here may have come out as the man talked with Jesus and his disciples, or he may have told others years later after he became a Christian.
[8] 16:11-The Bible doesn't make it clear exactly what "time" the evil spirits were talking about. The words of the demon are very difficult to translate. In their language, it was possible to express a concept where you placed another person under oath. In this case, the demon tries to impose an oath on Jesus, but Jesus ignores his trick. The concept here is similar to that involved in Third Person Commands.

[12]Then Jesus asked the evil spirit, "What's your name?"

[13]The evil spirit replied, "My name's 'Brigade[1]' because there are so many of us."

[14]Then the evil spirits urged Jesus not to send them out of the country, but to send them into a herd of about two thousand pigs nearby at the base of the mountains[2].

[15]Jesus gave the evil spirits permission to go into the pigs, and the whole herd began to stampede, running headlong over a cliff and drowning in the sea.

[16]The herdsmen who took care of the pigs ran to the city telling everyone along the way about what had happened including what had happened to the man who'd been possessed by the evil spirits.

[17]Then a crowd from the city went out to see for themselves what had happened. When they came to the place, they saw Jesus talking with the man who was now sitting with Jesus, fully clothed and in his right mind.

[18]Then the crowd from the city begged Jesus to leave their area, afraid of what might happen if he stayed[3].

[19]When Jesus got into the boat to return to Galilee, the man who'd been healed begged to go with him, but Jesus refused his request saying, "Go home to your friends and tell them about the wonderful things the Lord's done for you, and how he's had compassion on you[4]."

[20]So the man left that area and began spreading the news. He travelled throughout the area known as Ten Cities telling everyone about his experience. And Jesus and his disciples returned to Galilee.

A Woman Healed and a Child Raised Matthew 9:1b, 18-26; Mark 5:21-43; Luke 8:40-56
(Glossary articles: Belief / Faith; Capernaum; Disciples; Immediately / Quickly; James; Peter)

[21]As soon as Jesus stepped out on the shore near Capernaum, a huge crowd greeted him. (They'd all been eagerly waiting for him to get back.)

[22]Then a man[5], an officer in the local worship center, fell to his knees in front of Jesus and begged him, "Please come lay your hand on my little daughter! She's dying, and you can bring her back!"

[23](This was his only daughter – a 12-year-old.)

[24]Jesus got up to follow the man, accompanied by his disciples and surrounded by such a huge crowd that it was hard to move.

[25]In the crowd there was a woman who'd suffered from constant bleeding for twelve years and who'd spent everything she had on doctors who couldn't help her. Indeed, she'd suffered through the treatments of several doctors and the problem just got worse.

[26]Hearing about all the things Jesus had done, she came up behind him thinking, "If only I can touch the edge of his clothes, I'll be healed."

[27]And as soon as she touched the edge of his robe, she could tell that the source of the bleeding had dried up and that she truly had been healed.

[28]Jesus knew right away that healing power had gone from him. He turned around to face the crowd and asked, "Who touched my clothes?"

[29]Those in the crowd all denied having touched him. "Master," said Peter, speaking for himself and the other disciples, "The crowds are pressing in on you from all sides. What do you mean, 'Who touched me?'"

[30]"Somebody touched me," Jesus insisted. "I felt the healing power going out."

[31]Jesus began looking around in the crowd, and the woman realized that she couldn't hide from him. She came and fell to her knees in front of him, trembling with fear, and confessed to him right in front of everyone what she'd done and how she'd been healed as soon as she touched the edge of his robe.

[32]"Daughter," Jesus responded, "cheer up! Your faith in me has brought you this healing. Go in peace."

[33]While he was still talking to this woman, a messenger came from the worship center officer's home to tell him, "Your daughter's just died. There's no reason to bother the teacher anymore."

[34]When Jesus heard these words he told the man, "Don't be afraid. Just trust in me and she'll be fine."

[35]At that point Jesus told everybody to stay behind except Peter and the brothers James and John. When they reached the house, they found chaos. People were wailing at the top of their lungs, flute players were playing dirges, and everyone was in mourning.

[36]"Why are you all weeping?" Jesus asked. "Let me through! This little girl isn't dead; she's just sleeping!"

---

[1] 16:13-Literally, "legion," which was a military group of a few thousand. The closest American equivalent would be a brigade.

[2] 16:14-When these demons failed to impose an oath on Jesus that Jesus had no intention of accepting, they came up with another plan and urged it on Jesus. They were subject to Jesus, and they knew it, but they refused to behave as if they were subject to him.

[3] 16:18-Jesus, a Jewish rabbi, had come into their territory and caused the death of about 2,000 pigs. It was well-known that Jews despised pigs and anybody who ate pigs. The folks from town appreciated that a man with evil spirits, one of their own, had been healed; but they didn't want an international incident over it.

[4] 16:19-If Jesus let this non-Jew go with him, it could cause a lot of trouble for both of them. Jesus had made his point—the God of Israel has compassion on non-Jews as well as Jews. This was staggering news.

[5] 16:22-Jairus.

³⁷At this the mourners started ridiculing him, knowing that she was indeed dead. But Jesus had everyone leave the house except his three disciples and the parents.

³⁸Then Jesus took the girl by the hand and said, "Little girl, get up!"

³⁹The girl started breathing again, got up quickly, and began walking around like the 12-year-old she was. Then Jesus told them to bring her some food.

⁴⁰The worship center officer and his wife were astonished, but Jesus strictly ordered them not to tell anybody what had gone on in that room. However, the news of her recovery was soon the talk of the whole area.

A Paralyzed Man Forgiven and Healed Matthew 9:2-8; Mark 2:1-12; Luke 5:17-26
(Glossary articles: Belief / Faith; Immediately / Quickly; Lawyers; Pharisees; Scribes; Sin / Rebellion; Son of Man)

⁴¹Whenever word got out that Jesus was back in town, huge crowds would gather at the house to hear him teach.

⁴²One day people just kept coming until very quickly there was no more room for anyone to get in the house or even close to the door as Jesus explained his message to them.

⁴³On that day there were Pharisees and scribes and lawyers sitting in the house. They'd come from Jerusalem, Judea, and all over Galilee. And the power of God was simply flowing through Jesus to heal people.

⁴⁴While Jesus was teaching, four men came carrying a bed with a paralyzed man lying on it. They tried to bring the paralyzed man to Jesus, but when they couldn't get into the house, they carried the man and his bed up onto the roof of the house and took off enough tiles to use rope and let the man and his bed down in front of Jesus.

⁴⁵When Jesus saw how much faith they had in him, he said to the paralyzed man, "Son, cheer up. Your sins[1] are now forgiven."

⁴⁶The scribes and Pharisees seated near Jesus were thinking to themselves, "Who does this guy think he is? His own words are sinful! No one but God can forgive sin!"

⁴⁷Jesus was immediately aware of what they were thinking, so he said, "Why are you entertaining such evil thoughts about what I've just done?

⁴⁸"After all, which is easier – to say, 'Your sins are forgiven' or to say 'Get up, pick up your bed, and walk?'

⁴⁹"But just so you'll know that I as a human[2] have power on earth to forgive sin – " Then he said to the paralyzed man, "Get up, pick up your bed, and go home."

⁵⁰As soon as Jesus said these words, the man who'd been paralyzed got up in front of the whole crowd, picked up the bed he'd been lying on, and left the house praising God.

⁵¹Everyone was amazed and filled with awe. They said, "We've certainly seen some strange things today!" and "We've never seen anything like that!" And they praised God for giving such power to a human.

Asking about Fasting Matthew 9:14-17; Mark 2:18-22; Luke 5:33-39
(Glossary articles: Immediately / Quickly; John the Immerser; Pharisees)

⁵²Then one day while the Pharisees and the disciples of John the Immerser were fasting some of John's disciples asked Jesus, "Why do we and the Pharisees fast frequently while your disciples never fast?"

⁵³"Can the bridegroom's friends fast," Jesus asked, "and go around looking mournful while the bridegroom's with them?

⁵⁴"No, as long as the bridegroom's with them, they can't go around fasting! The time's coming when the bridegroom will be taken away. When that time comes, then they'll fast."

⁵⁵Then Jesus gave them these illustrations: "Nobody's dumb enough to put a patch of new, unshrunk wool on an older woolen garment. If you do that, the patch shrinks the first time it's washed and pulls at the old garment, making the tear worse than ever.

⁵⁶"In the same way, people know better than to put new wine into wineskins that have become brittle with age. If they do that, when the wine ferments it expands breaking the wineskin and spilling the wine. New wine has to be put into new skins so that both will go through the fermentation process safely.

⁵⁷"But once folks have had the old wine, they won't soon want to change. They think the old's better."

Blindness and an Evil Spirit Matthew 9:27-33; 12:22-23; Luke 11:14
(Glossary articles: Belief / Faith; Evil Spirits)

⁵⁸When Jesus left that group, two blind men followed him calling out, "Son of David[3], have mercy on us!"

⁵⁹When Jesus reached the house where he was staying, the blind men came in to him. Jesus asked them, "Do you have faith in me, that I can really do this?"

⁶⁰"Yes, Lord," they replied.

⁶¹Then as Jesus touched their eyes, he said, "May it be done exactly according to your faith in me."

---

[1] 16:45-Remember, sin is always treason—rebellion against God.
[2] 16:49-Literally, "the son of man has power on earth…"
[3] 16:58-"Son of David" was another name for the Christ.

⁶²At this their sight returned. Then Jesus warned them sternly, "See to it that you don't tell anybody about this!" But when they left the house, they spread the news about him all through that area.

⁶³Later when he was in a crowd, a man was brought to Jesus with an evil spirit that caused him to be both blind and mute. Jesus cast out the evil spirit and healed the man so that he could see and talk.

⁶⁴The crowd was simply amazed, and people were asking, "Could this really be the son of David[1]?"

Healing a Woman on the Sabbath Luke 13:10-17
(Glossary articles: Immediately / Quickly; Sabbath; Satan)

⁶⁵Jesus was teaching in various worship centers on Sabbath days, and on one occasion there was a woman present who was so bent over that she could no longer stand straight up[2].

⁶⁶When Jesus saw her, he called her to himself and told her, "Lady, you're now released from your ailment." As he said this, he laid his hands on her, and she was immediately healed and began praising God.

⁶⁷But the leader of the worship center was offended because Jesus had done work on the Sabbath by healing this woman.

⁶⁸"There are six days in the week for working," he said, "so come and be healed on those days – not on the Sabbath!"

⁶⁹"You fake!" Jesus replied. "Don't you release your ox or your donkey from of the stall and lead it to water on the Sabbath? Think! For eighteen years Satan's kept this woman in bondage. Isn't it appropriate for her to be released from those bonds on a Sabbath?"

⁷⁰When Jesus said this, the leaders who'd been angered by the healing were put to shame, and the congregation all expressed their joy at the wonderful things Jesus was doing.

Chapter 17 – Some Additional Teaching

A House Divided Matthew 9:34; 12:24-29; Mark 3:22-27; Luke 11:15, 17-22
(Glossary articles: Evil Spirits; Pharisees; Satan; Scribes)

¹But some of the scribes and Pharisees from Jerusalem said, "He's actually in league with the very prince of evil spirits[3]. That's how he's able to cast out these evil spirits."

²Jesus knew what they were saying so he called them over to himself and said, "Every kingdom torn apart by civil war winds up being destroyed, and even a city or a family torn apart by internal divisions will bring about its own destruction.

³"So if Satan's casting out his own evil spirits, he's divided against himself. In that case, how can his kingdom hold up?

⁴"And do you really want to say that I'm casting out evil spirits by the prince of evil spirits? Then by whose power do your own children cast out evil spirits? Let them be your judges!

⁵"But if I'm casting out evil spirits by the spirit of God, it's obvious that the kingdom of God has really arrived.

⁶"Think about it! How can someone plunder a powerful man's house without first tying up the owner? Once he's done that, he can plunder the strong man's house to his heart's content.

Unforgivable Sin Matthew 12:31-32; Mark 3:28-30; Luke 12:10
(Glossary articles: Evil Spirits; Hell; Sin / Rebellion; Son of Man; Unforgivable Sin)

⁷"But because you've said these things, I have a warning for you.

⁸"I can assure you that people can be forgiven of every sin against God[4] and every false doctrine except lying about the Holy Spirit as if he were evil. That falsehood won't be forgiven.

⁹"Again, anybody who says something against me as a human[5] can be forgiven, but anyone who calls the Holy Spirit[6] evil, that person won't be forgiven either in this world or in the age to come. The person who does that will be condemned to spend eternity in hell."

¹⁰(Jesus said this because they'd said, "He has an evil spirit.")

---

[1] 16:64-"Son of David" was another name for the Christ.

[2] 16:65-The wording here generally implies timidity, but in this case it was probably a curvature of the spine (kyphosis) that forced the woman into a posture often associated with timidity.

[3] 17:1-Literally, "Beelzebub." This name appears in 2Kings 1 as the god of the pagan city of Ekron. The word may mean "Lord of the Flies, and there may be a connection with people thinking of flies as disease-causing evil spirits, but that's not clear. In this passage, the word is clearly used as another name for Satan.

[4] 17:8-Sin is always treason—rebellion against God.

[5] 17:9-Literally, "the son of man…"

[6] 17:9-Jesus made a clear distinction here between who he is as a human and who God's Holy Spirit is living in and manifest in him. These people crossed a very dangerous line by saying that his miracles were the work of evil spiritual powers.

Asking for Proof Matthew 12:38-42; 16:1-4; Mark 8:11-12; Luke 11:16, 29-32; 12:54-56
(Glossary articles: Biblical Names; Crucifixion Timing Issues; Immediately / Quickly; Jesus' Resurrection; Miracles, Pharisees, Repentance; Scribes; Son of Man)

[11]Then while Jesus was teaching a large crowd, a committee of scribes and Pharisees confronted him. "Do a miracle, teacher," they demanded. "We want to see some miraculous sign[1] from heaven as proof of your claims."

[12]Jesus gave a deep sigh. "Why does this generation insist on proof?

[13]"A wicked generation given to adultery looks for proof by some obvious sign, but the only sign they'll be given is the sign of the prophet Jonah. Just as Jonah was in the great fish for three days and three nights, so I as a human[2] will be in the ground for three days and three nights. As Jonah was a sign to the people of a great pagan city[3], so too, I as a human will be a sign for the people of this generation.

[14]"Then in the judgment day, the people to whom Jonah announced God's judgment[4] will stand up and testify against this generation because they turned their lives around when all they had was Jonah's announcement, and someone much greater than Jonah is here now[5].

[15]"In the same way, the queen of the South will stand up and testify against this generation because she came from far away to witness Solomon's wisdom, and someone much greater than Solomon is here with you now[6]."

[16]Then Jesus turned to the crowd and said, "When there's a red sunset you say, 'The sky's red, so fair weather's coming today.'

[17]"When there's a red sunrise, you say, 'The sky's red and threatening, so foul weather's coming today.'

[18]"When you see clouds gathering in the west, right away you say, 'We'll get a shower today,' and that's what happens.

[19]"And when the south wind blows, you say, 'It'll be a hot day today,' and that's what happens.

[20]"You fakes! You know how to read these signs in the sky and in the winds on earth, so why can't you understand the signs of the times[7]?" Then he walked away from their committee.

The Bad Fig Tree Luke 13:6-9
[21]Later Jesus told this story to help people understand:
[22]"A man who owned a vineyard had some fig trees planted in the vineyard. When he came to harvest the figs, one tree had produced none at all.

[23]"The owner told the fellow he'd hired to take care of the vineyard, 'Look here. I've been looking for figs on this tree for three years now, and every year I get nothing. Cut it down. Why let it keep drawing nutrients from the soil?'

[24]"But the vineyard keeper answered, 'Sir, let's give it one more year. I'll dig around it to keep moisture near the roots and I'll fertilize it. Then if it bears figs, great. And if it doesn't, then we'll cut it down[8].'"

Is He Insane? Matthew 12:46-50; Mark 3:20-21, 31-35; Luke 8:19-21
[25]One day the crowds sitting around trying to hear Jesus were so large and tightly packed that people in the crowds couldn't even eat.

[26]Then while Jesus was talking to the crowds, his mother and brothers showed up at the edge of the crowd. They'd heard about this huge crowd and they'd said among themselves, "He's out of his mind!"

[27]But because of the crowds they couldn't get near him, so they sent a message. The message reached Jesus when someone pointed them out, saying, "Look, your mother and your brothers are out there at the edge of the crowd, and they want to talk to you."

[28]"Who is my mother and who are my brothers?" Jesus asked.

[29]Then he stretched out his hand toward his disciples sitting around him and said, "Here are my mother and my brothers!

[30]"Indeed, anyone who'll listen to God's message and do what my Father in heaven wants is my brother, my sister, and my mother."

---

[1] 17:11-Jesus didn't hide his miracles, but he didn't show off his miracles either. The miracles were for those in need, not for the curious. This committee was from the leaders (probably from Jerusalem), so these men wouldn't have seen Jesus' daily miracles, and Jesus wasn't about to give them a command performance. God never works that way.

[2] 17:13-Literally, "the son of man…" (God cannot be buried. Jesus as a human was.)

[3] 17:13-Literally, people of Nineveh.

[4] 17:14-Literally, "people of Nineveh."

[5] 17:14-Jonah did no miracles, yet the city repented in response to his announcement of God's word. If the people of Nineveh could recognize the truth of Jonah's words, these religious leaders should be able to recognize the truth of Jesus' words even without miracles.

[6] 17:15-When the queen of Sheba heard of Solomon's wisdom, she came to test him. When she left Solomon's court, she said that the reports hadn't told half the story. Solomon did no miracles. The queen was won over just by his words. If a pagan queen could be so convinced just by the words of Solomon, a human with no divine powers, then those who listened to Jesus should not need miracles. This applies today. People should be able to recognize God in Jesus' words without any need for miracles.

[7] 17:20-Jesus' message was, "With all your understanding of weather signs, you need to pay attention to the much more important signs of God at work here."

[8] 17:24-The warning in this story is that God won't wait forever for people to respond to him.

Unrepentant Cities Cursed Matthew 11:20-24; Luke 10:13-15
(Glossary articles: Biblical Names; Capernaum; Miracles; Sin / Rebellion)

³¹Then Jesus started to condemn the cities in which he'd done most of his miracles, saying, "Oh, how terrible it will be for you cities of Galilee[1] that haven't responded to my ministry!

³²"Indeed, if the miracles done in your cities had been done in ancient pagan cities that were destroyed for their evil ways[2], they would've turned their lives around long ago, sincerely mourning their sins against God[3].

³³"I assure you: the people of those cities will be better off in the judgment than your people.

³⁴"And oh, my hometown of Capernaum. You think you're so high and mighty, but you'll be brought down to your graves!

³⁵"Indeed, if the wonderful miracles that have been done in your streets had been done in a pagan city that God destroyed for its evil ways[4], that city would still be here today.

³⁶"I promise you: in the judgment it'll be better for the people of that city than for your people."

Revealed to Babes Matthew 11:25-30; Luke 10:21-24

³⁷At that point Jesus' spiritual joy overflowed into prayer, saying, "Thank you, Father, Lord of heaven and earth, that you hid these things from those who are proud of how wise and clever they are and you revealed them to such innocent children, because this is how your good will[5] comes to reality in this world."

³⁸Jesus continued to his disciples: "My Father's handed over everything to me. Nobody really understands me as his son except the Father, and nobody really understands the Father except me and anyone to whom I decide to reveal him."

³⁹Up to this point Jesus had been speaking openly with others around him, but now he took his disciples aside and told them, "There's great joy for you in being able to see the things you now see!

⁴⁰"I promise you: there were a lot of prophets and kings who really wanted to see what you now see and to hear what you now hear, but they didn't get to see or hear these things."

⁴¹Then Jesus continued to the crowd, "Come to me, all of you who work so hard and who are carrying such heavy loads, and I'll give you rest. Put on the harness to work for me and find out what it's like to serve me.

⁴²"You'll find that I'm gentle and humble, and you'll find the rest that really matters – rest for your souls! For the harness I'll put on you is easy to wear and the burden I'll give you to carry is light[6]."

A Sabbath Healing in Galilee Matthew 12:9-14; Mark 3:1-12; Luke 6:6-11
(Glossary articles: Biblical Names; Evil Spirits; Gentiles / Nations; Herod; Isaiah; Law of Moses; Pharisees; Sabbath; Son of God)

⁴³On a Sabbath Jesus went into the worship center to teach as was his custom.

⁴⁴In the worship center there was a man whose right hand was shriveled up.

⁴⁵Then the leaders of the worship center watched Jesus closely and asked him, "Does the Law of Moses allow a person to be healed on Sabbath days?"

⁴⁶(They were looking for a way to accuse Jesus of breaking the religious laws[7].)

⁴⁷"Which of you men," Jesus responded, "who owns one sheep and finds that it's fallen into a pit on a Sabbath day won't do whatever work's needed to get that sheep out of the pit?

⁴⁸"Isn't a human more valuable than a sheep? So if you'll do that for a sheep, it must be lawful to do good on Sabbath days."

⁴⁹Then Jesus told the man with the shriveled hand, "Step forward."

⁵⁰Turning toward those who'd questioned him, he said: "I'm going to ask you one thing. Now you tell me – on Sabbath days, do you think it's lawful to do good things or to do evil things, to save life or to kill?"

⁵¹When no one would answer him, he looked around at them in anger, saddened by their refusal to deal with the truth.

⁵²So he told the man with the shriveled hand, "Reach out your hand." When the man did this, it was healed and as healthy as the other hand.

⁵³After this the Pharisees who'd raised this question left the worship center quickly and, working with those who politically supported the rule of Herod's family, they tried to figure out some plot that would work to destroy Jesus.

⁵⁴Meanwhile, Jesus and his disciples left the worship center and went down to the seashore.

---

[1] 17:31-Chorazin and Bethsaida. (See Bethsaida in the Glossary.)

[2] 17:32-Tyre and Sidon.

[3] 17:32-Remember, sin is always treason—rebellion against God.

[4] 17:35-Sodom.

[5] 17:37-The word Jesus used here for "good will" is the same as the word the agents of God used in announcing Jesus' birth to the shepherds. The blessings God promised are brought to reality through his followers.

[6] 17:42-Jesus promises a burden we can carry. It's the burden of stress, sorrow, and care that he promises to lift.

[7] 17:46-These worship center leaders had obviously arranged for this man to be there so they could accuse Jesus if he healed the man.

⁵⁵Having heard of the wonderful things Jesus was doing, a huge crowd gathered around him including people from Jerusalem, Lebanon[1], and various areas on the east side of the Jordan River, and Jesus healed the sick among them.

⁵⁶Jesus told his disciples to have a small boat ready just in case the crowd pushed in too much and threatened to crush him. He was healing many in the crowd and even more were trying to push in just to touch him.

⁵⁷Whenever those with evil spirits saw him, they'd fall to their knees in front of him crying out, "You're the Son of God!" Yet he warned them not to advertise who he was, and this gave fuller meaning to what the prophet Isaiah had said:

⁵⁸Behold, my chosen servant
The one I love and in whom I am extremely pleased
I'll put my own spirit in him
And he'll declare justice to the nations[2] even beyond Israel
⁵⁹He won't quarrel, nor will he cry out
No one will hear this one shouting in the streets
Even if the stem of the plant is damaged, he won't break it off
Even if the flame's gone and only smoke remains, he won't quench it
Until he brings victory for justice
And he'll be the hope of all the nations[3].

Lord of the Sabbath Matthew 12:1-8, 30; Mark 2:23-28; Luke 6:1-5; 11:23, 27-28
(Glossary articles: Law of Moses; Pharisees; Sabbath; Sacred Writings; Son of Man)

⁶⁰On a Sabbath day when Jesus and his disciples were walking through grain fields, his disciples were hungry and ate some of the grain, rubbing the kernels in their hands to separate the husks.

⁶¹When some of the Pharisees saw this they said, "Look at what your disciples are doing. You know that's not lawful to do on Sabbath days[4]!"

⁶²"Haven't you read in the sacred writings[5]," Jesus replied, "what David and those who were with him did when they were in need and hungry – how they went into the house of God and ate the sacred bread even though the Law of Moses strictly prohibited anyone from eating that bread except the priests[6]?

⁶³"Or haven't you read in the Law of Moses how it's OK for the priests who serve in the temple to break the Sabbath restrictions by their work?

⁶⁴"Yet I'm telling you that even beyond those things, you need to realize that there's one here among you now who's greater than the temple itself.

⁶⁵"Remember how the sacred writings[7] say, 'I desire mercy and not sacrifice[8]?' If you'd understood the meaning of that passage, you wouldn't have condemned those who are really guilty of nothing at all.

⁶⁶"The Sabbath," he told them, "was made for people, and not people for the Sabbath. Therefore the fact is that I as a human[9] am lord over even the Sabbath.

⁶⁷"And know this: the person who's not with me is against me, and the person who doesn't help me gather the harvest is by that fact scattering it abroad."

⁶⁸Just then a woman from the crowd called out, "What a joy it must have been for the woman whose womb carried you and whose breasts fed you as a babe!"

⁶⁹But Jesus replied, "OK, but there's much more joy for those who hear God's message and live according to that message!"

Unless You Turn your Life Around Luke 13:1-5
(Glossary articles: Biblical Names; Pilate; Repentance; Sin / Rebellion)

⁷⁰Later, as Jesus was teaching, some in the group told him about some Galileans whom Pilate had executed as they were offering their sacrifices at the temple.

---

[1] 17:55-Literally, "Tyre and Sidon"
[2] 17:58-The word translated "nations" here also means "non-Jews," and both words carry implications that apply in this context. The message that the Christ was to bring would be for the entire world, and even for the pagans who knew nothing about God.
[3] 17:59-Isaiah 42:1-5.
[4] 17:61-The Law of Moses allowed people passing through a grain field to eat some of the grain. But since this involved crushing the grain to separate the chaff, the Pharisees counted that as "work" (technically it was "harvesting" the grain). All "work" was forbidden on the Sabbath.
[5] 17:62-'In the sacred writings" is clearly implied but not specifically stated.
[6] 17:62-1Samuel 21:1-6.
[7] 17:65-"The sacred writings" is clearly implied by the quotation but not specifically stated.
[8] 17:65-Hosea 6:6.
[9] 17:66-Literally, "the son of man is…"

⁷¹"Do you suppose," Jesus replied, "that these Galileans were worse sinners against God[1] than other Galileans just because they died that way?

⁷²"No, I assure you: they were not. Unless you turn your life around, you'll all die like they died.

⁷³"Or those eighteen men who were killed when Messenger Tower fell on them – do you think they were worse sinners against God than others living in Jerusalem?

⁷⁴"Again I assure you: they were not. Unless you turn your life around, you'll all die like they did."

An Evil Spirit Returns Matthew 12:43-45; Luke 11:24-26
(Glossary article: Evil Spirits)

⁷⁵Another time Jesus told the crowds, "When an evil spirit leaves a man he wanders through dry places looking for rest and finding none.

⁷⁶"Then he says, 'I know what I'll do. I'll just go back to the house I came from.'

⁷⁷"So when he returns he finds that house empty, swept clean, and with everything in order. In fact, it looks so nice that he goes out and finds seven other evil spirits more evil than himself to share the house.

⁷⁸"Thus that person's condition is worse afterward than it was before. And that's the way it'll be with this wicked generation."

Paying the Temple Tax Matthew 17:24-27
(Glossary articles: Capernaum; Peter)

⁷⁹When Jesus and his disciples returned to Capernaum, those responsible for collecting the temple tax came to Peter asking, "Doesn't your teacher pay this tax?"

⁸⁰Peter responded with a simple, "Yes."

⁸¹But when Peter came back to the house, Jesus asked him, "What do you think, Simon? Do the kings of this world collect taxes from their children or from strangers?"

⁸²Peter responded, "From strangers."

⁸³Jesus replied, "Then the children are free from such taxation.

⁸⁴"However, just so we don't offend anybody, go cast a hook into the sea and take the first fish that comes up. Open its mouth and you'll find a coin[2].

⁸⁵"Take that and give it to them to pay the tax for both of us."

Chapter 18 – Stories about Seeds that Jesus Used

The Seeds and the Soils Matthew 13:1-9; Mark 4:1-9; Luke 8:4-8
(Glossary articles: Immediately / Quickly; Third Person Commands)

¹Jesus used many stories to help illustrate his teachings. One time Jesus left the house where he was staying and sat down in a boat near the seashore to teach. Huge crowds from all over that area stood on the shore and listened. Then he told them this story:

²"Listen to this! A farmer went out to scatter seed in his field[3]. As he scattered the seed, some fell on the road where it was trampled down and the birds in the sky came to eat it.

³"Other seed fell on rocky areas where there was very little soil. In the rocky areas the seed sprouted quickly[1] because there was no soil into which the roots could grow, and in the sun's heat the plants just withered and died.

⁴"Still other seed fell where there were a lot of weeds, so when the seed sprouted, the weeds quickly choked the grain plants and they died. None of these seeds produced any crop.

⁵"But some of the seed fell on the good soil. Those seeds sprouted and grew up to produce good grain. Some produced thirty grains from one seed, some produced sixty grains, and some produced even a hundred.

⁶"If you've got ears to hear, pay attention to this[4]!"

The Purpose of Illustration Stories Matthew 13:10-17; Mark 4:10-12; Luke 8:10
(Glossary articles: Belief / Faith; Isaiah; Prophecies and Fulfillments)

⁷Later when he was away from the crowds, several of Jesus' disciples came to him and asked, "Why do you use these stories so much when you're teaching?"

---

[1] 17:71-Remember, sin is always treason—rebellion against God.

[2] 17:84-Was this literally a coin in the fish's mouth or was "open its mouth and you'll find a coin" an idiom for selling the fish to get the coin? The important point was that as God's only son, the temple tax was one tax Jesus didn't owe, and he wouldn't pay it out of his funds as a matter of principle.

[3] 18:2-In biblical times a farmer would carry a sack of seed and throw the seed out into the field with a sweeping motion of the hand and arm.

[4] 18:6-This is a third person command in the Bible, but it's been converted to a second person command for English readers. The meaning is the same, but it doesn't come through as strongly in many other translations.

[8]"Because you've been given the right to know the secrets of the kingdom of heaven," Jesus replied, "but those who haven't given their lives to follow me don't have that right[1]. They only hear nice stories.

[9]"When you put forth the effort to gain some understanding, you'll be given more, and soon you'll have great understanding. But if you don't even try to get it, what little you do get will be taken from you.

[10]"Those who don't get it give full meaning to what Isaiah wrote:

[11]When you listen you'll hear,
But you won't understand,
And when you look you'll see,
But you just won't get it.
For the hearts of these people have become dull;
Their ears have become hard of hearing;
And they've closed their eyes
Lest their eyes should see
And their ears should hear
And they should turn and focus their lives on me.
If that were to happen,
I would surely heal them[2].

[12]"That's why I use these stories when I teach the crowds, so that what's right there for them to see, they'll still fail to see, and what's right there for them to hear and understand, they'll still fail to understand[3].

[13]"But there's great news for your eyes because they see the importance of these things and for your ears because they truly listen to these things. I promise you: many prophets and many very righteous people have wanted to see what you now see and to hear what you now hear, and they never had that opportunity."

The Seeds and the Soils Explained Matthew 13:18-23; Mark 4:13-20; Luke 8:9, 11-15
(Glossary articles: Belief / Faith; Immediately / Quickly; Satan)

[14]Then the disciples asked Jesus, "So what does that story mean[4]?"

[15]"Didn't you understand this story?" asked Jesus. "How are you ever going to understand all the other stories I'm going to tell? OK, here's what the story of the farmer and his seeds means:

[16]"The seed is the message of the kingdom of God, and the farmer is the one who carries that message out into the world.

[17]"The seed that fell on the road represents the people who hear the message with hardened hearts and just don't get it. Satan comes quickly to see that the message doesn't linger in their minds, lest they should entrust their lives to God and be saved.

[18]"The seed that fell onto rocky areas represents those who quickly receive the message with great joy, but who don't dig deep to establish roots. These people put their faith in God only for a time, and when some difficulty or opposition comes along because of their faith, they just as quickly turn away from God[5].

[19]"The seed that fell in the weeds is like those who really get the message, but the cares of this world and the riches and pleasures of worldly life choke out their spiritual lives so that their fruit never gets ripe[6].

[20]"But the seed that fell on fertile soil represents those who, when they hear and comprehend the message, accept it with a good and fertile heart and produce a bountiful crop. Some will bring in thirty more, some sixty more and some a hundred more."

---

[1] 18:8-There were crowds who showed up for a while and then went home, and then there were disciples who seriously wanted to learn.

[2] 18:11-Isaiah 6:9-10

[3] 18:12-God always presents his message in a form that we could understand if we wanted to do so, but in a form that we can ignore if we choose to do so. He doesn't force us to hear and understand his message, but he does warn us about the danger of not listening.

[4] 18:14-We're so familiar with this story and its meaning that we may think, "How could the disciples ask this question?" But to them, Jesus had just told a story about a farmer who had varying success in planting his crop. If we'd heard that story for the first time, we, too, might be asking, "So what?" Jesus was teaching them to look for the meaning in his stories, and in the process he was reinforcing the story and its meaning.

Notice that there are four groups mentioned. One group rejects the message without any thought. It's just not of interest to them. The next group accepts initially, but this group allows others to push them out. The third group also accepts initially, but this group is drawn away by their own worldly desires. The fourth group refuses to be pushed out and refuses to be distracted by worldly desires, and that fourth group is the real harvest. They have shown what it takes to be part of God's eternity.

[5] 18:18-These are the people who aren't discipled. When Christians don't intentionally train new converts, they contribute to this problem and they are guilty of terrible treason against God, because the command in Jesus' great commission is to make disciples (Good News 52:33-35). Too many times Christians focus on making initial converts rather than disciples.

[6] 18:19-These are the people who do become disciples, seriously trying to follow the Lord, but who then become distracted by the things of this world and turn away from God. This group is generally made up of those who don't have a strong Christian support group, and again, God holds Christians responsible for their failure to provide support to each other.

The Seed and the Weeds Matthew 13:24-30
(Glossary article: Slaves)

²¹Later Jesus told another story. "The kingdom of heaven," he said, "is like a farmer who planted good wheat seed in his field, but while everybody was sleeping his enemy came and in the same field this enemy planted weeds[1] that would initially look a lot like wheat and then left.

²²"When the grain sprouted and began to grow and produce wheat, the weeds became obvious.

²³"The farmer's slaves came to the farmer and asked, 'Lord, didn't you plant good clean seed in your field? Why are these weeds coming up?'

²⁴"'Some enemy must have done this,' he told them.

²⁵"Then the slaves asked him, 'Do you want us to go pull up the weeds?'

²⁶"But the farmer replied, 'No, if you do that you'll pull up a bunch of the wheat along with the weeds. We'll let them both grow in the field until harvest time. At the harvest I'll tell the reapers, "First gather up the weeds and tie them into bundles to burn. Then gather the wheat and put that in my barn[2].""'

The Seed and the Weeds Explained Matthew 13:36-43
(Glossary articles: Agent / Angel; Belief / Faith; Son of Man; Third Person Commands)

²⁷After telling this story Jesus sent the crowds away and went back to the house where he was staying. When he got there, his disciples approached him and asked him to explain the story about the good seed and the weeds.

²⁸"The farmer who plants good seeds," he answered, "is me as a human[3]. The field is the world.

²⁹"The good seeds are the children of the kingdom who've put their faith in me. The weeds are the children of Satan. The enemy who planted the weeds is Satan.

³⁰"The harvest is the end of time for this world, and of course those who gather the crop are the agents of God.

³¹"Just as in the story the weeds were gathered and burned in a bonfire, so it will be for the children of Satan when the time of this world is ended.

³²"I as a human[4] will send out my heavenly agents and they'll gather up everything offensive out of my kingdom and all who simply disregard law and order.

³³"All of these will be cast into a fiery furnace where there'll be wailing and grinding of teeth in anguish.

³⁴"At that time God's righteous people will shine like the sun in their Father's kingdom.

³⁵"If you've got ears at all, pay attention to these things[5]!"

The Kingdom and the Mustard Seed Matthew 13:31-32; Mark 4:30-32; Luke 13:18-19

³⁶Then Jesus used another story: "What shall I use to describe the kingdom of heaven?" he said. "What story would help you visualize it?

³⁷"The kingdom of heaven is like a tiny mustard seed that a farmer planted in his field. Though this is the smallest seed that a farmer plants, once planted it grows larger than any of the other herbs that farmers plant. In fact, it grows large enough that it has branches like a tree where birds can build nests in its shade[6]."

7-The Kingdom and the Seeds that Grow Mark 4:26-29
(Glossary article: Immediately / Quickly)

³⁸Then Jesus told this story: "The kingdom of God can be compared to a farmer who scatters seed in his field.

³⁹"That night he goes to bed and the next day he gets up to find that the seed has sprouted and is growing, though he has no idea how this has happened.

⁴⁰"Then in the soil the crop just grows from a seedling to the harvest all by itself: first a blade like grass, then the head on that blade where the grain will appear, and finally the full grain appears.

⁴¹"Then when the grain has ripened, the farmer quickly starts cutting the grain because it's time for the harvest[7]."

---

[1] 18:21-The word used here is for a weed that looks a lot like wheat in the early stages of growth. The Romans had a law against planting this weed in an enemy's wheat field.

[2] 18:26-This is a very important lesson from Jesus. In effect, he was telling his followers that there'd be people in their Christian teams who'd act like Christians and who'd look like Christians on the outside, but who wouldn't be Christians. And he was telling his followers that it's God's decision to let these fake Christians mingle with the real ones until judgment day—but when that time comes, the fakes will burn.

[3] 18:28-Literally, "the son of man…" Jesus came as a human to plant the seed.

[4] 18:32-Literally, "the son of man…"

[5] 18:35-This is a third person command in the Bible, but it's been converted to a second person command for English readers. The meaning is the same, but it doesn't come through as strongly in many other translations.

[6] 18:37-Starting from a king with a few followers, within 300 years Jesus' kingdom took over the Roman Empire without a single battle fought.

[7] 18:41-When good seed is set in fertile ground, the crop just grows. In the same way, when God's good news is proclaimed to people who'll listen, the kingdom grows even though we have no clue how it grows.

Chapter 19 – Other Stories Illustrating the Kingdom
The Kingdom and Yeast Matthew 13:33; Luke 13:20-21

[1]In another story Jesus said, "The kingdom of heaven might be compared to a bit of yeast that a woman mixed into her dough causing the whole lump of dough to expand.

2-The Kingdom and Treasures Matthew 13:44-46

[2]"In another way the kingdom of heaven could be compared to a treasure hidden in a field that a man stumbled on and then hid again. Overjoyed with his good luck, he then sold everything he owned in order to buy that field.

[3]"Or the kingdom of heaven might be compared to a pearl merchant who finds a pearl so beautiful that he knows it would be impossible to estimate the pearl's worth. Having found it, he sells everything he owns to buy that one pearl.

The Kingdom and a Fishing Net Matthew 13:47-50
(Glossary article: Agent / Angel)

[4]"And from yet another perspective, the kingdom of heaven could be compared to a large fishing net cast into the sea. When it's drawn in, the net's full of all kinds of fish.

[5]"Then the fishermen sit down and separate the fish into good fish they can sell and everything else, and they throw away everything but the good fish.

[6]"So at the end of time the agents of God will come and separate the evil people from the good people, and the evil people will be thrown into the fiery furnace. Then there'll be sobbing and grinding of teeth in anguish."

Chapter 20 – Stories about Wealth that Jesus Used
The Rich Fool Luke 12:13-21

[1]Once someone in the crowd called out, "Teacher, tell my brother to divide the inheritance with me[1]."

[2]"Man," Jesus responded, "who made me a judge or negotiator in charge of settling your affairs?" Then Jesus told the crowd, "Beware of envying what others have and wanting it for yourselves, because real life doesn't have anything to do with your earthly possessions."

[3]Then he told them this story to illustrate his point:

[4]"There was a wealthy man whose fields produced unusually bountiful harvests one year. The man thought, 'What am I going to do with all this bounty?

[5]"'I know! I'll build more storage facilities[2] where I can store all my crops and other goods. Then I'll say to myself, "Self, you've got plenty of wealth stored up to last for many years. Now it's time to relax – eat, drink, and party on!"'

[6]"But God said to that man, 'You fool! This very night they require your soul[3]! Then who's going to enjoy all those things you've stored up?'

[7]"That's exactly how it is with anyone who stores up earthly treasures selfishly while not providing the spiritual riches that would please God."

The Lost Sheep Matthew 18:11-13; Luke 15:1-7
(Glossary articles: Common Gender; Dining Customs; Pharisees; Scribes; Sin / Rebellion; Son of Man; Tax Collectors)

[8]Another time there were a lot of tax collectors and other people who were generally looked on as sinners gathered around listening to Jesus.

[9]On noticing this, the Pharisees and scribes started griping, saying, "This guy claims to be righteous, but he's allowing a bunch of sinners among his followers – and he even eats with them[4]!"

[10]Jesus realized what they were saying and responded with this story: "If one of you had a hundred sheep and one of those sheep got lost, wouldn't you leave the ninety-nine in the open range and go into the mountains searching for the lost sheep until you found it?

[11]"And when you've found it, wouldn't you gladly lift that sheep up on your shoulders to carry it back to the rest of the flock?

[12]"Then when you got home, wouldn't you call your friends and neighbors together and tell them, 'I'm throwing a party today, and you're invited, because I found my sheep that was lost?'

[13]"In the same way, I assure you that there's more joy in heaven over one sinner[1] who turns his or her life around than over ninety-nine righteous people who don't need to turn their lives around.

---

[1] 20:1-This man wasn't that concerned about losing his father; he just wanted to get his father's wealth—wealth he hadn't earned.
[2] 20:5-Literally, "I'll tear down my storage facilities and build bigger ones." Grain storage in that climate was dug into the ground. To increase the size, the owner would "tear down" the sides.
[3] 20:6-The implication here is that at a certain point Satan and his followers have enough control of a man's soul that they can demand it.
[4] 20:9-Eating with a person was like saying, "I accept this person as my friend." For a man who claimed to be the Christ, eating with sinners was shocking!

¹⁴"It's my job as a human[2] to rescue those who are lost.

Lost Money Luke 15:8-10
(Glossary articles: Common Gender; Sin / Rebellion)
¹⁵"Or as another example, if a woman has ten hundred dollar bills and loses one, wouldn't she turn on all the lights and sweep the house, searching carefully until she found the missing hundred dollar bill?

¹⁶"And when she did find it, wouldn't she be so glad that she'd want to go out and party with her friends? In the same way, I assure you that there's joy in heaven over one sinner[3] who turns his or her life around."

A Juvenile Delinquent Luke 15:11-32
(Glossary articles: Sin / Rebellion; Slaves)
¹⁷Then Jesus said, "There was a wealthy man who had two sons, and the younger of the sons told his dad, 'Give me my portion of the inheritance right now[4].' So his dad divided all that he had between his sons.

¹⁸"Shortly after that, the younger son gathered up everything he now owned and left home, traveling to a distant country[5].

¹⁹"When he got there, he began to party as if the wealth he had from the inheritance would never run out – but it did.

²⁰"Worse yet, about the time he ran out of money, the country where he was living went through a serious economic downturn[6], and he was left with nothing.

²¹"He finally managed to get a job with a farmer in that country, working out in the fields feeding the pigs[7]. He was so hungry that he'd gladly have relieved his hunger by eating the pig slop.

²²"And though he'd been generous when he was partying, now no one would show an ounce of generosity to him.

²³"Finally he got his head on straight. 'How many paid laborers does my dad have,' he thought, 'and all of them are well fed? They have more than enough, and here I am starving to death.

²⁴"'I've got to get up and go back to my dad. I'll tell him, "Dad, I know that I've sinned[8] against you and against God, and I know that I no longer have any right to be called your son. All I ask is that you hire me just like any of your paid laborers."'

²⁵"So the young man got up and managed to get back to his dad, but his dad saw him long before he reached the house and his heart went out to his son.

²⁶"Then his dad ran to this son, hugged him tightly, and kissed him on his cheeks.

²⁷"The son told his dad, 'Dad, I know I've sinned against you and against God, and I know that I no longer have any right to be called your son[9].'

²⁸"But his dad called to his slaves and said 'Bring out the best clothes in the house and get him properly dressed! Put a ring on his hand and good shoes[10] on his feet!

²⁹"'Butcher the calf we've been fattening up for a feast! Let's eat and have a party, because my son was dead and now he's alive, he was lost and now he's found[11]!'

³⁰"Meanwhile, the older brother[12] happened to come in from working in the fields and as he got close to the house he heard dancing music.

³¹"He called a boy over and asked what was going on. The boy replied, 'Your brother's come back, and because he's made it back safely, your dad's killed the calf he was fattening up for a party.'

---

[1] 20:13-Remember, sin is always treason—rebellion against God.

[2] 20:14-Literally, "it's the job of the son of man…"

[3] 20:16-Remember, sin is always treason—rebellion against God.

[4] 20:17-According to Deuteronomy 21:17, the inheritance would be divided between a man's sons with twice as much going to the oldest son as to any younger sons. The younger son knew that he'd never inherit the farm and that either he'd be like a servant to his older brother or he'd have to leave the farm.

[5] 20:18-This young Jewish man traveled to some country far from Israel—a country with very different customs.

[6] 20:20-Literally, a famine—a period when the farmers were unable to produce adequate crops. The price of food would skyrocket, devastating the whole national economy.

[7] 20:21-To a Jew there are few things more disgusting than a pig. But this young Jew was reduced to feeding pigs—pigs who fared better than he did.

[8] 20:24-In this case, sin isn't only rebellion against God, but it's also rebellion against the young man's father. In most cases, sin is a double rebellion like this.

[9] 20:27-The son didn't get to finish his planned speech. Before he could finish, his father broke in and effectively said, "Nonsense! Let's throw a party. You're my son!"

[10] 20:28-The father took away all the stigmas of poverty and gave his son the marks of at least some level of wealth.

[11] 20:29-Up to this point the message has been about the grace of God. God's not just willing to forgive us, he's eager enough to run to us, embrace us, and throw a party for us. He welcomes us back as his children.

[12] 20:30-At this point the story changes to a warning for those who resent God's grace for a rebel who's willing to turn his or her life around. The reality is that such people are generally envying the life of rebellion this convert was able to live before turning to God. Somehow, such people haven't realized how great God's reward is and how fake the rewards of rebellion are.

³²"This made the older brother furious, and he refused to even enter the house. His dad came out and begged his son to join the party¹.

³³"But the son replied, 'Look, I've served you faithfully for a lot of years now, and I've never gone against you even once – but you never even gave me a goat² to celebrate with my friends.

³⁴"Now as soon as your son³ shows up you kill the fattened calf and throw a party, even though he's wasted the wealth you earned – sleeping with harlots⁴!'

³⁵"'Son,' his dad replied, 'you're always here with me and everything I have rightfully belongs to you⁵.

³⁶"But it was the right thing to do⁶ to have a party and rejoice because your brother was as good as dead to us, and now he's alive. He was lost, and now he's found.'"

The Unfaithful Steward Luke 16:1-12
(Glossary article: Belief / Faith)

³⁷Another time Jesus gave this illustration to his disciples: "There was a wealthy businessman who had a manager for his business.

³⁸"Someone reported to him that his manager was wasting his resources, so the wealthy man called the manager to his office.

³⁹"'What's going on?' he demanded. 'I've found out you haven't been faithful in managing my resources. You're fired, and I want a full accounting of everything before you go.'

⁴⁰"The manager was shocked. 'I've been fired!' he thought. 'What am I going to do? I can't dig ditches for a living and I'd be too ashamed to beg for a living.'

⁴¹"Then he came up with a plan to be certain that other wealthy people would take care of him. He set up meetings with those who owed anything to his master. When the first one came in he asked him, 'How much do you owe?'

⁴²"'4,000 liters of oil,' the man replied.

⁴³"The manager said, 'Take out your invoice and write 2,000 liters and I'll sign it.'

⁴⁴"Then he asked the next man, 'How much do you owe?'

⁴⁵"'3,500 liters of wheat,' this man replied.

⁴⁶"The manager told him, 'Take out your invoice and write 2,800 liters and I'll sign it.'

⁴⁷"Then the wealthy man had to congratulate the dishonest manager's shrewd actions. You see the children of this evil world can be shrewder in their time than the children of light⁷?

⁴⁸"This is the lesson: If you want people to gladly welcome you into your eternal home in heaven, use the earthly wealth you have (which is in no way an indication of your righteousness) to help others and gain their friendship.

⁴⁹"Then when all your earthly things are gone, those same people will rejoice as they welcome you into your eternal home⁸.

⁵⁰"If you're faithful in how you use the little things of this world, God can trust you to be faithful in the truly large things of his eternity⁹.

⁵¹"But if you abuse the trust God's placed in you with the little things of this world, he'll know that you would be unfaithful in handling the truly great things of his eternity¹⁰.

⁵²"So if you've not been faithful in handling the worldly goods that have nothing to do with how righteous you are, who in the world would entrust the real riches of heaven to you?

⁵³"And if you aren't faithful as a steward of someone else's goods, who'd trust you with something of your own?

---

[1] 20:32-Jesus came freely offering God's grace to all who'd surrender their lives in faith to God. But the religious leaders resented this offer of God's grace. Jesus was doing everything he could to try to get them to join the party, but they wouldn't have anything to do with it.

[2] 20:33-The father has killed a fat calf while the son hasn't even had a tough old goat.

[3] 20:34-The elder son can't bring himself to call the returnee his brother. There are those who feel this way about people who've lived all their lives in selfish rebellion against God only to find God's grace later in life.

[4] 20:34-Here's a hint of the envy this elder son felt. He might as well say, "When was I supposed to get some harlots?"

[5] 20:35-Not having a fattened calf was this son's choice. The entire farm belonged to him.

[6] 20:36-It's right to rejoice that a fellow human has found the riches of God's grace. What God's to offer far exceeds all the pleasures of rebellion, and he's got more than enough for everybody.

[7] 20:47-Every story breaks down if we try to get more out of it than Jesus intended. In this story, a man is congratulated for being dishonest and unfaithful, but the point of the story is that this man thought ahead and made preparations for his future. If we want to be welcomed into heaven, we need to use the things of this sinful world in a way that will prepare us for that end.

[8] 20:49-The wealth of this world has nothing to do with how righteous a person is, so why not use it to build friendships that will last for eternity? If we want to go there, we need to practice what will be welcome there.

[9] 20:50-This passage is one of several that tell us there are great responsibilities for those who get to heaven, so God must choose only those who give their lives to him now so that he can trust them there.

[10] 20:51-If God can't trust you with the little things of this world, obviously you can't be trusted with the much more valuable things of heaven.

A Rich Man and a Man Named Lazarus Luke 16:19-31
(Glossary articles: Abraham; Agent / Angel; Hell; Lazarus; Moses)

^{54}"There was a wealthy man," Jesus continued, "who dressed in the finest designer clothing and lived in luxury.

^{55}"There was another man, a beggar named Lazarus, whose body was covered with sores.

^{56}"The beggar was laid just outside the wealthy man's complex, begging for scraps that might fall from the wealthy man's table, and the dogs in that neighborhood licked the beggar's sores.

^{57}"Eventually the beggar died and was carried by God's agents to find comfort in Abraham's embrace[1]. The wealthy man also died and was buried.

^{58}"Then the wealthy man, tormented in the world of the dead, spotted Abraham in the far distance embracing Lazarus, so he called out, 'Father Abraham, have mercy on me! Send Lazarus[2] to dip the tip of his finger in water and place it on my tongue to cool it. I'm in anguish in these flames!'

^{59}"'Son[3],' Abraham responded, 'don't you remember that in your life on earth, you received many good things while Lazarus lay right outside your gate and received only bad things?

^{60}"'Now the tables have turned – he's being comforted and you're being tormented.

^{61}"'Besides, even if I wanted to send him, there's a great divide between us so that anyone who did want to go to you from here couldn't go, nor could those in the torments you're experiencing come to us.'

^{62}"'Then I'm begging you, father,' the wealthy man cried, 'send Lazarus to my family home! I've got five brothers! Send Lazarus to warn them! I don't want them to wind up in this place[4]!'

^{63}"'They've already got the writings of Moses and the prophets. My only message to your brothers is, "Listen to them!"'

^{64}"'No, father Abraham!' the wealthy man cried out. 'I know them! They won't listen to those old writings! But if someone went back to them from the dead, then they'd turn their lives around.'

^{65}"'If they won't pay attention to what Moses and the prophets have written,' replied Abraham, 'then they wouldn't pay attention even if someone rose from the dead[5].'"

Chapter 21 – More Stories that Jesus Used

Unprofitable Slaves Luke 17:7-10
(Glossary article: Slaves)

^{1}Then Jesus said, "Suppose one of you has a slave out plowing in the field or tending the sheep. When your slave comes in from the field, which of you would say, 'Here, sit down at the table and eat a good meal'?

^{2}"In fact, wouldn't you tell your slave, 'Fix my meal, make yourself presentable, and then serve the meal. And see to it that I have enough to eat and drink. Then after I've had my meal and I'm completely satisfied, you can have your meal.'

^{3}"And after your slave's done all that, what do you think? Would you thank your slave for doing what he was told to do? I certainly don't think so!

^{4}"So in the same way, when you've done everything God commands you to do, you should say to yourselves, 'As God's slaves, we've still not earned any credit for our master. We've only done the things that were our job to do[6].'

Equal Pay for Unequal Work Matthew 20:1-16
(Glossary article: Money in the Bible)

^{5}"Here's another way that you can think of the kingdom of heaven," said Jesus. "It's like a landowner with a vineyard.

^{6}"When it was time for the harvest, he began looking for men he could hire.

^{7}"Early in the morning at first light[7] he found some men[8] and agreed to pay them a normal day's wage[9] for working in his vineyard, and then he put them to work.

^{8}"About 9:00 in the morning he went out again and found some men just standing around in the town market, so he told them, 'Go work in my vineyard, and at the end of the day I'll give you fair wages.'

^{9}"So these men went into his vineyard to work the harvest.

---

[1] 20:57-The picture here is a person who's been suffering finding an embrace of love. When we get to heaven, we'll need a time of adjustment—we'll need the embrace of those who love us to help us recover.

[2] 20:58-This man who'd been so wealthy still thought of Lazarus as if he were a servant to be sent into the flames for his comfort. Even in this torment, he hadn't learned to deal with God's reality.

[3] 20:59-Abraham addressed this man as one of his physical children, but being Abraham's child physically didn't determine the judgment.

[4] 20:62-The wealthy man showed some concern, but only for his own family. He still wanted to treat Lazarus as a servant.

[5] 20:65-This statement was proved true by Jesus' resurrection from the dead!

[6] 21:4-We, like slaves, can't do anything that would ever earn us credit with God. If we were to do everything good we could possibly do, that would be what we owe God as our creator. Our righteousness can't pay for even one act of rebellion.

[7] 21:7-The typical work day during harvest lasted from sunup to sundown.

[8] 21:7-Free men would wait in the town market for someone to hire them. The owner of a large vineyard might well run to the market more than once looking for laborers, especially if he saw that the harvest was too great for the number of laborers he'd hired.

[9] 21:7-Literally, a denarius, but that was a typical wage for a day laborer.

¹⁰"All day the man kept going back and finding more men, once at noon and again about 3:00 in the afternoon. Each time he just promised fair wages.

¹¹"Then about 5:00 in the evening he went back to the market and found other men just standing around. 'Why have you been standing around all day doing nothing?' he asked.

¹²"'Because nobody's offered to hire us,' they replied.

¹³"'Well, go to my vineyard and get busy,' the owner said, 'I'll pay you what's fair.'

¹⁴"At the end of the day the owner told his manager, 'Call the men in and pay them, starting with the men I hired last and working back to the men I hired first.'

¹⁵"When the men hired at 5:00 came to be paid, they each received a full day's pay. Then working down to the ones hired early that morning, the manager gave each one a full day's pay.

¹⁶"Those who were hired first started complaining and criticizing the landowner. 'These last guys only worked about an hour,' they told the landowner, 'and you've made them equal to us after we've carried the main load and suffered the full heat of the day.'

¹⁷"But the landowner answered one of them who complained, 'Friend, I haven't cheated you. Didn't you agree to work for a day's wage?

¹⁸"'Take the pay you've earned and go on home. I just wanted to give the last man I hired the same amount that I gave you.

¹⁹"'Is there some law that says what I can or can't do with my own money? Or are you looking for evil when I'm doing good[1]?'

²⁰"It'll be the same way in the kingdom of heaven – those who were last on earth will be first there and the first here on earth will be last there.

A Story of Two Sons Matthew 21:28-32
(Glossary articles: Belief / Faith; Tax Collectors)

²¹"But what do you think about this?" Jesus continued. "A man had two sons. He went to the older son and told him, 'Son, go out and work in my vineyard today.'

²²"'I'm not going to work in your vineyard,' the son replied. But later he regretted what he'd said and went out into the vineyard to work.

²³"Meanwhile the man approached his younger son and said the same thing to him. 'I'm on my way,' the younger son responded, but then he didn't go.

²⁴"Now, which of these two kids did what his dad wanted him to do?"

²⁵Those in the crowd around Jesus replied, "The older one."

²⁶"I tell you the absolute truth," Jesus said: "there are tax collectors and whores[2] who'll enter the kingdom of God ahead of you!

²⁷"Indeed, John came to you urging you to live righteously, but you didn't put your faith in his message.

²⁸"Tax collectors and whores put their faith in his message, but even when you saw that, you still refused to put your faith in his message."

Using Stories To Teach Matthew 13:34-35, 51-52; Mark 4:33-34
(Glossary articles: Prophecies and Fulfillments; Scribes)

²⁹When Jesus was talking to the crowds, his message was constantly in the form of these stories to illustrate his points – he never used any other teaching method.

³⁰Then when they were alone, Jesus would explain everything to his disciples.

³¹This brought full meaning to the words of the prophet who wrote, "I'll speak in stories; I'll tell things that have been secrets since the very beginning of creation[3]."

³²After such teaching Jesus would ask his disciples, "Do you understand what I've been saying?"

³³"Yes, Lord," the disciples would generally respond.

³⁴Then Jesus would add something like this: "Every scribe trained in the things of the kingdom of heaven is like a homeowner who uses things of value in his house, both old and new[4]."

---

[1] 21:19-We should rejoice that God is generous to us and not envy what someone else gets.
[2] 21:26-Jesus constantly confronted those who relied on the forms of religion rather than giving their hearts to God. And here he made the point that even the worst sinner whose heart is set on trying to live for God will be accepted by God.
[3] 21:31-Psalm 78:2
[4] 21:34-While the good news of the kingdom is a wonderful new thing, there are still valuable lessons to be learned from the Jewish sacred writings.

Chapter 22 – About Forgiveness and Christian Love

Forgiveness-How Much and How Many Times? Matthew 18:21-35; Luke 17:3-4
(Glossary articles: Caring Love; Forgiveness; Money in the Bible; Slaves)

^{1}At this point Peter approached Jesus and asked, "Lord, how often do I have to forgive my brother[1] when he hurts me? Seven times[2]?"

^{2}"Seven times?" Jesus responded. "Certainly not! I'm telling you: seventy times seven times[3]!

^{3}"Be very careful about this! If a brother hurts you, it's OK to confront him, but if he apologizes, you must forgive him. And if he hurts you seven times a day[4] and then apologizes[5], you must still forgive him!"

^{4}Then Jesus told this story to illustrate the reason for such forgiveness: "The kingdom of heaven can be compared to a king who wanted to settle accounts with his slaves.

^{5}"As soon as he started settling accounts, one of his slaves was brought into court owing over $5 billion[6].

^{6}"Since he couldn't repay what he owed, the king ordered that he, his family, and everything he owned be sold to new owners in order to recover as much of the debt as possible.

^{7}"Upon hearing this judgment, the slave fell to his knees before the king. 'Have patience with me, master,' he said, 'and I'll pay back every cent[7].'

^{8}"When he heard his slave's plea, the king felt sorry for him, released him from custody, and forgave the entire debt.

^{9}"As soon as he was released, he found a fellow-slave who owed him about $10,000[8]. He grabbed his fellow-slave by the throat, saying, 'Pay me what you owe right now!'

^{10}"The fellow-slave fell to his knees before him. 'Be patient,' he begged, 'and I'll pay back every cent.'

^{11}"But the slave who'd just been forgiven his huge debt refused to forgive his fellow-slave. Instead, he had this slave sentenced to imprisonment[9] until the entire debt might be paid.

^{12}"When the other slaves heard what had happened, they were angry. They went to the king and told him everything that had happened.

^{13}"Then the king was furious and had the servant whom he'd forgiven arrested again. 'You evil slave!' he said. 'I forgave you all that money just because you begged me to have mercy. Shouldn't you have had some pity for your fellow-slave just as I had pity on you?'

^{14}"So the king reinstated his debt and sent him to prison to be tortured until he paid the entire debt.

^{15}"And that's exactly what my heavenly Father will do to every one of you if you don't truly, from your heart, forgive your fellow disciples when they offend you.

Handling Offenses Matthew 18:15-20
(Glossary articles: Common Gender; In the Name of...; Team / Church)

^{16}"So if someone hurts you," Jesus continued, "go to that person and discuss the problem between just the two of you[10]. If you can resolve the issue by doing that, you've restored your relationship.

^{17}"But if that doesn't resolve the issue, take one or two others with you to witness your exchange so that if you need to go further, they can testify to what was actually said. If the issue still can't be resolved, share it with the Christian team.

^{18}"If a fellow Christian refuses to listen to the team's judgment, then that person should be treated as if he or she weren't even a Christian at all and not part of your team[11].

^{19}"I'm telling you the absolute truth," Jesus said: "whatever you bind here on earth will be bound in heaven, and whatever you release here on earth will be released in heaven.

---

[1] 22:1-Peter was probably talking about his biological brother, Andrew. When we're thrown together day after day, it's hard to avoid offending each other—and that applies especially to family members.

[2] 22:1-Seven was seen as a significant number with God. Peter thought, "Seven should certainly be enough."

[3] 22:2-The squaring of a number (seven times seven) would be almost like infinity, but to say seventy times seven times meant much more than 490 times. Jesus was telling his disciples, "If you want to be my disciple, your willingness to forgive should know no end."

[4] 22:3-Jesus returned to Peter's use of "seven." It's hard to imagine a person hurting you seven times in one day. Jesus was using a combination of exaggeration (something he used frequently) and giving Peter's word back to him.

[5] 22:3-In this case Jesus was talking about a restored relationship when someone asks for forgiveness. There are different standards if a person doesn't ask forgiveness, but we must always let God handle retribution.

[6] 22:5-Literally, "ten thousand talents."

[7] 22:7-This promise was ridiculous, and the king knew it. The debt was too large to even imagine that this man could repay it.

[8] 22:9-Literally, "a hundred denarii."

[9] 22:11-There were no bankruptcy laws and a person would be thrown into prison or sold as a slave for not paying a debt. Of course prison made it impossible for that person to ever pay the debt, so it was like a life sentence.

[10] 22:16-Jesus indicated that it's not the job of the offender to resolve the issue, it's the job of the one who's been offended to go seek to resolve the matter. Often the offender doesn't realize that he or she's offended anyone. It's about being a peacemaker, and it applies to Christian brothers and sisters.

[11] 22:18-We let things go without seeking resolution. This is wrong both for the Christian team and for the offender. The officers of a congregation need to use their authority carefully but firmly.

[20] "And in the same way, if two of you here on earth agree about anything you ask, my Father in heaven will grant the request because wherever two or three of you get together in my authority, I'll be right there with you[1]."

A Samaritan Who Cared Luke 10:25-37
(Glossary articles: Caring Love; Jericho; Jerusalem; Jews and Samaritans; Law of Moses; Lawyers; Levites; Money in the Bible; Priests)

[21] Then an expert in Jewish laws stood up in the crowd to test Jesus. "Teacher," he asked, "what should I do to gain eternal life?"

[22] "What does it say in the Law of Moses?" Jesus asked. "How do you understand what it says?"

[23] "'You shall care for Jehovah your God with all your heart, with all your soul, with all your strength, and with all your mind[2],'" the lawyer responded, "and 'you shall care for your neighbor as you care for yourself[3].'"

[24] "Well," said Jesus, "you've got the right answers. Do that and you'll have eternal life."

[25] Wanting to show off how correct he was, the lawyer asked Jesus, "And just who is my neighbor?"

[26] "There was a Jewish man[4]," Jesus responded, "who was traveling on the road down from Jerusalem to Jericho[5]. On this trip, he was attacked by thieves who stripped off his clothing, beat him, and then ran off leaving him for dead.

[27] "As it happened, the next man to come down that road was a Jewish priest[6], but when he saw the man who'd been robbed, he moved over to the far side of the road and just kept going.

[28] "Not long after that a Levite[7] came by and looked at the man, but then he did exactly what the priest had done.

[29] "Then a Samaritan who was traveling that way came to the place where the man lay bleeding. When he saw the man, his heart went out to this Jew[8].

[30] "He went to the man's side and started caring for him, bandaging his wounds and pouring on oil and wine to prevent infection.

[31] "Then he set the man on his own animal and brought him to a traveler's inn where he continued to care for him.

[32] "The next day, before he left the inn, the Samaritan gave $200[9] to the man in charge of the inn and told him, 'Take care of that fellow. If you have to spend more than this, I'll cover the bill next time I come through here.'

[33] "So now," Jesus asked, "Which of these three men was a neighbor to the one who was attacked by thieves?"

[34] "The one who cared for him[10]," answered the lawyer.

[35] "Go and demonstrate that kind of caring love[11]," Jesus concluded.

Chapter 23 – A Trip to Judea

Jesus' Feet Anointed Matthew 19:1a; Mark 10:1a; Luke 7:36-50
(Glossary articles: Anointing Jesus; Belief / Faith; Biblical Chronology; Caring Love; Dining Customs; Forgiveness; Jewish Feasts; Judea; Money in the Bible; Pharisees; Sin / Rebellion)

[1] After Jesus finished this teaching, he left Galilee and went to Judea[12].

[2] There was a Pharisee named Simon[13] living in the town of Bethany, a town near Jerusalem. He invited Jesus to dinner, so Jesus went to Simon's house and reclined to eat.

[3] Now there happened to be a woman in that city who had a really bad reputation.

[4] When she heard that Jesus was eating at Simon's house, she brought a small box[1] filled with perfumed oil and, standing behind Jesus at his feet, she broke open the box and began to wash his feet with her tears and to wipe them with her hair. She kissed his feet and anointed them with the perfumed oil.

---

[1] 22:20-The promises here are for those who've focused their lives on God and who'll therefore seek the things that are consistent with who God is and what he wants.
[2] 22:23-Deuteronomy 6:5.
[3] 22:23-Leviticus 19:18.
[4] 22:26-The Bible only says a man, but the fact that he was Jewish is clearly implied and necessary for the story.
[5] 22:26-This was a steep and winding mountain road.
[6] 22:27-The Bible doesn't specifically say "Jewish," but the fact that he was Jewish is clearly implied and necessary for the story.
[7] 22:28-Members of the Levite tribe were responsible for various duties at the temple. Among the Israelites, all Levites were considered especially dedicated to God's service.
[8] 22:29-This story is Jesus' definition of Christian love, and it starts with forgiveness when a Samaritan, whose people had been abused, maligned, and mistreated by Jews for centuries, decided to turn retribution over to God and care for this suffering Jew.
[9] 22:32-Literally, "two denarii." See Money in the Bible in the Glossary.
[10] 22:34-This lawyer couldn't even bring himself to say "Samaritan."
[11] 22:35-The word here is for the caring love that is Christian love.
[12] 23:1-Various gospel accounts dealing with trips Jesus made to Jerusalem, Bethany, and elsewhere in Judea are combined in this section.
[13] 23:2-In Good News 37:50-58 we have the account of a former leper healed by Jesus whose name was also Simon. He lived in Bethany and he also invited Jesus to his home for a meal. Jesus had no criticism for that Simon. Is this the same Simon? In the time between these meals, Simon may have developed leprosy and have gone to Jesus to be healed both physically and spiritually, or this may be an entirely different Simon. After all, we know that Simon was a very common name.

⁵When Simon saw this, he thought, "If this guy were really a prophet, he'd know who this woman is and what a sinner she is, and he wouldn't even let her touch him."

⁶Jesus turned to his host and said, "Simon, I want to tell you something."

⁷Simon replied, "Teacher, you may say whatever you wish."

⁸So Jesus said, "There was a man who loaned money to two others. He loaned $50,000 to one man and $5,000[2] to the other.

⁹"Then when neither one was able to repay the loan, he graciously forgave them both. Now, tell me: which one of these men will hold their creditor in higher esteem?"

¹⁰Simon responded, "I guess the guy who was forgiven the larger amount."

¹¹"You're right," Jesus said.

¹²Then turning to the woman he continued: "Simon, do you see this woman?

¹³"When I came into your house, you didn't even give me water to wash the filth of the street off of my feet as any good host should, but she's washed my feet with her tears and wiped them with her hair.

¹⁴"You didn't greet me with a kiss as any courteous host should, but this woman has kissed my feet over and over ever since I got here.

¹⁵"You didn't anoint my head with oil as any kind host should, but this woman has anointed my feet with her perfumed oil.

¹⁶"Therefore I tell you, her sins against God[3] (and indeed there are a lot of them) are forgiven because of her great care[4] for me.

¹⁷"But the one who thinks he only has a few sins to be forgiven – hardly worth mentioning – isn't likely to show such caring love."

¹⁸Then Jesus spoke to the woman saying, "Your sins against God are forgiven."

¹⁹When they heard this, the people at the table with him started muttering among themselves saying, "Who does this guy think he is to claim that he can forgive sins against God?"

²⁰But Jesus said to the woman, "Your faith in me has saved you. Go in peace."

Martha's Complaint Luke 10:38-42

²¹While Jesus and his disciples were in Bethany, a woman named Martha welcomed him into her home.

²²She had a sister named Mary who was there and who sat on the floor near Jesus to hear him teaching. Meanwhile, Martha was stressed out and irritated, trying to care for all her guests without her sister's help.

²³Finally Martha came to Jesus and said, "Sir, don't you even care that my sister's left me to take care of everything? Tell her to give me a little help here[5]!"

²⁴Jesus replied, "Martha, Martha! You're fretting about all these things, and they're just things. Only one thing's really necessary, and Mary's chosen that good thing. Nobody's going to take that away from her."

Teaching About Divorce Matthew 19:1b-12; Mark 10:1b-12; John 3:22
(Glossary articles: Common Gender; Baptize / Immerse; Jesus and Divorce; Judea; Law of Moses; Moses; Pharisees; Sacred Writings)

²⁵Jesus and his disciples then came to the area of Judea on the east side of the Jordan River where they were immersing[6] converts. As usual, huge crowds gathered around him in that area to hear him teach, and he healed those who came.

²⁶Then some Pharisees came to test him. "According to the Law of Moses," they asked, "is it OK for a man to divorce his wife for whatever reason he chooses?"

²⁷"Haven't you read in the sacred writings[7]," asked Jesus, "where it says that at the beginning God 'created them as male and female[8] ' and said, 'This is why a man leaves his dad and mom and is joined to his wife, and the two of them become one flesh[1] '?

---

[1] 23:4-The box was made of alabaster and such boxes for preservation of perfumes generally had a wax seal. Various translations use terms like "flask," "vial," "cruse," or "jar," but the term used in the Bible doesn't specify the form, and archeological finds favor a box. The Bible literally says that she "broke" the "*alabastron*," but the meaning is probably that she broke the wax seal.

[2] 23:8-Literally, "500 denarii" and "50 denarii." See Money in the Bible in the Glossary.

[3] 23:16-Remember, sin is always treason—rebellion against God.

[4] 23:16-The word here is for the caring love that is Christian love.

[5] 23:23-God certainly knows how important it can seem to have everything right for our guests. And thirteen extra men to prepare for would've been a lot of work for Martha. It's right to show respect and kindness to guests by trying to have good food and a clean place to eat and sleep, but those things aren't of eternal significance. As Christians, we need to get our priorities straight. Jesus emphasized over and over—the things of this world will be destroyed along with those who focus their lives on those things. Christians need to focus constantly on God's work as the top priority.

[6] 23:25-The word used here for "immersing" also implies cleansing as a result of the immersion.

[7] 23:27- "In the sacred writings" is clearly implied but not stated.

[8] 23:27-Genesis 5:2.

²⁸"So from that time on, they're no longer two in God's eyes. They've become one. Therefore, no human has the right to separate what God considers to be joined as one."

²⁹"So," they asked, "then why did Moses include a commandment in the law that a man should give a certificate of divorce when he divorces his wife?"

³⁰"Moses," Jesus replied, "allowed you to divorce your wives because your hearts are so hard, but from the beginning that was never God's intent.

³¹"I'm telling you now that in God's eyes, unless someone's spouse has been sexually unfaithful, anyone who divorces a spouse to marry someone else is guilty of being sexually unfaithful, and anyone who marries a divorced spouse is guilty of being sexually unfaithful[2]."

³²Then Jesus' disciples came to him when they'd gone back into the house where they were staying and said, "If that's the case for a husband and wife, it would be better never to get married."

³³"This isn't something that everybody can handle," Jesus replied. "The ability to hold with this teaching is a gift God gives

³⁴"Remember, there are some men who were born incapable of having sex, and there are some men whose sexual organs have been removed to keep them from being able to have sex, and there are some who choose not to have sex so as not to bring dishonor on the kingdom of heaven[3].

³⁵"If you're able to accept this teaching, accept it!"

John the Immerser's Final Testimony to Jesus Matthew 4:12; Mark 1:14; Luke 3:19-20; John 3:23-4:3
(Glossary articles: Baptize / Immerse; Belief / Faith; Christ; Galilee; Herod; John the Immerser; Pharisees; Son of God)

³⁶At the same time that Jesus and his disciples were immersing converts, John (who hadn't been taken to prison yet) was immersing converts not too far from where Jesus was, because there was plenty of water available there, and people were coming to him for immersion.

³⁷Meanwhile, John's disciples got into a discussion about purification with some of the Jewish authorities, and the topic of Jesus' activities came up.

³⁸Then they came to John and told him, "Teacher, the man who was with you on the other side of the Jordan River – you know, the one you pointed out as God's Christ[4] – he's immersing people and everybody's going to him!"

³⁹John replied, "Everything we humans ever get comes from God in heaven. You heard me. You know that I always said, 'I'm not the Christ' and 'I'm just the one who's been sent to prepare the way for him.'

⁴⁰"It's the groom who gets the bride. The groom's best man stands by to hear the groom's words, and he feels great joy in just listening to the groom's voice.

⁴¹"That's my joy – to hear the groom's voice and know that he's indeed here. But he must increase in popularity, and it's time for me to step back.

⁴²"Don't you understand? He's the one who comes from above, and therefore he's Lord over everything.

⁴³"I'm just a man of this earth, and the best I can do is speak from my earthly experience. But he comes straight from heaven and is in charge of everything!

⁴⁴"He acts as an eyewitness to tell us what he's actually seen in heaven and heard from God – though nobody wants to listen. Yet anybody who does accept what he's telling us takes a stand to say that God is true to his word.

⁴⁵"Indeed, he's the one whom God himself has sent, and therefore he speaks the very words of God, for God has placed no limit on the presence of his Spirit with this one[5]."

⁴⁶(Yes, the Father loves this son and he's turned everything over to him. Anyone who entrusts his life to the son has everlasting life; but the one who doesn't entrust his life to the son won't experience real life at all – by his rejection of God's own son, he brings the wrath of God on himself.)

⁴⁷During this time, John (who immersed Jesus) was publicly criticizing Herod, the ruler of four areas that included Galilee, because among his other evils he'd married his brother's wife[6]. Then Herod added to his list of evils by throwing John into prison.

---

[1] 23:27-Genesis 2:24.
[2] 23:31-See Good News 9:47-48 above.
[3] 23:34-This third group are those who've been divorced or separated from their spouses and who abstain from sex to avoid bringing discredit to God's kingdom.
[4] 23:38-Literally, "he to whom you testified," but the implication of Christ is very clear.
[5] 23:45-There's no way we will ever fully understand how God came in Jesus, but here we have an important clue. Jesus clearly emphasized his humanity over and over, but he also emphasized his divinity. How could both be true? What this passage tells us is that at least part of the solution has to do with how God's Holy Spirit lives in us—but with his presence limited by our sinfulness and rebellion. If we seek to follow the Holy Spirit's leading, we find that he works in our lives more and more in ways that become very obvious to us and even to others. But our experience is still limited by our sinfulness—Jesus' experience of God's presence within was unlimited by sin.
[6] 23:47-This was Herod Antipas, son of Herod the Great, his brother was Philip and his brother's wife was Herodias.

⁴⁸When Jesus realized that the Pharisees knew that he was making and immersing more disciples than John (though it was actually his disciples who were immersing converts rather than Jesus himself) and heard¹ that John had been imprisoned, he left Judea to return to Galilee.

Chapter 24 – Returning to Galilee
A Samaritan Woman Matthew 9:37-38; Luke 10:2; John 4:4-43
(Glossary articles: Belief / Faith; Christ; Jews and Samaritans)

¹Traveling back to Galilee, Jesus had to go through Samaria².

²Along the journey he came into the area of a city³ in Samaria near a section of land that Jacob gave to his son Joseph where a well (known as Jacob's Well) was located.

³It was about noon, and Jesus was tired from the journey, so he sat down beside the well while his disciples went into the town to get some food.

⁴While he was sitting there, a Samaritan woman came to the well to get water, and Jesus said, "Give me a drink."

⁵The woman responded, "Why would you, a Jew, ask me, a Samaritan woman, for a drink⁴?" (Jews generally wanted nothing to do with Samaritans.)

⁶Jesus replied, "If you only knew the wonderful gift of God and who it is who's saying, 'Give me a drink,' you'd have asked me, and I would've given you living water."

⁷So the woman asked him, "Just where do you think you're going to get that 'living water'? You don't even have anything to lower into the well and draw water out.

⁸"Do you think you're greater than Jacob, our ancestor⁵ who gave us this well and drank from it himself along with all of his sons and their livestock?"

⁹Jesus told her, "Anyone who drinks this water will just get thirsty again, but anyone who drinks the water that I can give will never be thirsty again.

¹⁰"Indeed, the water that I give will become like a spring that just shoots out the water that gives life forevermore."

¹¹So the woman told Jesus, "Well sir⁶, then give me this water so that I won't get thirsty again and I won't have to come to this well to get water⁷."

¹²Jesus replied, "Go get your husband and come back."

¹³The woman answered, "I don't have a husband."

¹⁴Then Jesus said, "Good answer! How right you are to say, 'I don't have a husband.' In fact, you've had five husbands, and the man you're living with now isn't your husband, so you were certainly telling the truth."

¹⁵"OK, lord," she replied, "it's obvious that you're a prophet. So tell me who's right. Our ancestors have always worshipped on this mountain here⁸, but you Jews say that Jerusalem's the proper place to worship⁹."

¹⁶"Woman," Jesus said, "trust me, the time's coming very soon when people won't worship the Father either on this mountain or in Jerusalem.

¹⁷"You don't even know what you worship, while we do know what we worship, because salvation comes through the Jews.

¹⁸"But the time's coming soon – in fact it's already here – when true worshippers will simply worship the Father in spirit and in truth wherever they are because that's what God really wants.

¹⁹"God is spirit¹. Anybody who wants to worship him must worship him in spirit and in truth."

---

¹ 23:48-Just before he left Judea Jesus learned two things: 1) John, who'd been proclaiming his message in Galilean areas, had been arrested; and 2) opposition to Jesus was growing in Judea. John's disciples in Galilee could benefit from Jesus' leadership, while serious confrontation in Judea would've been too early at this point.

² 24:1-There are two possibilities for saying that Jesus "had to go through Samaria": 1) the Jordan was flooded, closing off other roads to Galilee (but this was the wrong season for floods); or 2) the phrase could be translated "Jesus insisted on going through Samaria."

³ 24:2-Sychar.

⁴ From this woman's perspective, there were three strange things here: 1) a man normally wouldn't speak to a woman he didn't know, and that would apply that much more for a Jewish rabbi speaking to a Samaritan woman of low reputation; 2) a Jew normally wouldn't speak to a Samaritan, and that went triple for a Jewish rabbi speaking to a foreign woman; and 3) a Jew (and especially a Jewish rabbi) wouldn't ask for water from a Samaritan woman—and especially a woman with such a bad reputation. Asking for water would imply a bond of friendship.

⁵ 24:8-This woman was baiting Jesus to see if this claim of Jacob as the ancestor of the Samaritans would shut him up or make him angry.

⁶ 24:11-The woman's reply was sarcastic. First, the woman has no reason to think of Jesus as any more than some Jewish rabbi. Second, this woman had been hardened by life. Jesus looked past any sarcasm to see the person this woman could be.

⁷ 24:11-This woman didn't like the daily chore of having to come for water. She avoided the gossip of the other village women by coming in the heat of the day.

⁸ 24:15-The Samaritan temple was on Mount Gerazim. The Samaritans had their own version of the sacred writings and insisted that they were the true people of God.

⁹ 24:15-As soon as this woman realized that Jesus was more than just another Jewish rabbi, she wanted to turn the conversation away from her past by getting it onto a religious controversy.

²⁰"Well, I know that the Christ's is coming." the woman said, "When he comes, he'll tell us everything."

²¹Jesus replied, "As surely as I'm speaking to you now, I AM the Christ[2]."

²²About this time Jesus' disciples showed up and they were astonished that he was talking with a woman, but no one asked Jesus "What in the world did you want from her?" or "Why in the world are you talking with that woman?"

²³Meanwhile the woman hurried back into the city, leaving her pot of water behind[3].

²⁴When she got to the city she told the men, "Come, you've got to meet this man who told me all about everything I've ever done! Do you think this could be the Christ?"

²⁵When they'd listened to the woman's report, they left the city to see for themselves.

²⁶While this was going on, the disciples were urging Jesus, "Teacher, eat something."

²⁷But Jesus simply answered, "I have food about which you still don't know anything."

²⁸So the disciples were talking among themselves, saying, "Has someone brought him food?"

²⁹Jesus told them, "My nourishment comes from doing the will of the one who sent me – to finish the work he's given me[4].

³⁰"Wouldn't you normally say that there are still four months before harvest time? Well I'm telling you: open your eyes and just look at the fields – they're already white with ripe grain ready for the harvest.

³¹"And the one who gets busy to reap this harvest will receive his wages now and at the same time gather fruit for life everlasting so that both the one who plants the seed and the one who reaps the harvest may rejoice together.

³²"In this case the proverb is true, 'One sows and another reaps.'

³³"I sent you out to reap a crop when you'd done nothing to get the crop ready – others did that work, and you've joined in their work by reaping the harvest.

³⁴"There's an abundant crop to be harvested, and there just aren't enough workers on the job, so pray to the Lord of the harvest and ask him to send more workers into his harvest fields."

³⁵Meanwhile, based on the woman's report of how Jesus had told her all about her life, many of the men of that town already believed that he was the Christ[5]. So when these men arrived where he was, they urged him to stay with them.

³⁶Jesus agreed and stayed there two days – long enough for many more to hear what he was saying and to put their trust in him and his message.

³⁷Then the people of that town told the woman, "Now we accept that he's the Christ not only because of what you told us, but also because we've heard him for ourselves. Indeed, now we're quite sure that he's truly the savior of the world."

³⁸After those two days in that town, Jesus continued his journey.

A Nobleman's Son Healed John 4:45-54
(Glossary articles: Belief / Faith; Capernaum; Galilee; John's Gospel; Miracles)

³⁹Jesus continued on his way into Galilee where he was welcomed eagerly since so many had seen what he'd done in Jerusalem during the Passover celebration.

⁴⁰While traveling through Galilee, Jesus came to the town of Cana where he'd changed the water to wine. There he met a nobleman from Capernaum whose son was sick.

⁴¹The nobleman had heard that Jesus had come back to Galilee from Judea, so he went to Jesus imploring him to come heal his son who was at the point of dying.

⁴²Jesus said, "Unless you see signs and wonders, you just won't put your faith in me."

⁴³"Lord," the nobleman pleaded, "come with me before my child dies."

⁴⁴"Go back home," Jesus told him. "Your child's alive."

⁴⁵The nobleman had faith in what Jesus told him, so he started home. As he was on his way down to Capernaum, some of his servants met him and told him, "Your son's alive!"

⁴⁶Then he asked them when his son had recovered. They told him, "Yesterday afternoon, about 1:00, the fever just left him."

⁴⁷The boy's dad knew that this was exactly the time when Jesus had said, "Your son's alive." So he and everyone in his household came to have faith in Jesus.

⁴⁸(This was actually the second miracle Jesus did after he returned from Judea into Galilee[1].)

---

[1] 24:19-This is one of those very important statements in the Bible, and it should always have been obvious. The prohibition in the Ten Commandments against images to represent God should've been a good clue. God walked among us in the physical person of Jesus, but it was the spirit, not the body, that made him God with us. It's that same exact Holy Spirit (for God is holy) who comes to us (in a very limited way) and lives in us. There's no image of God that would be appropriate—he can inhabit any form, but he's not bound by any physical form.

[2] 24:21-Rather than "I AM the Christ," Jesus literally said "I AM," using a very emphatic form of "I AM." However, "the Christ" is clearly implied.

[3] 24:23-This is what the good news of Jesus does. She'd forgotten the very reason she'd come to the well. She had good news to share!

[4] 24:29-When people get really busy doing God's work, they can go long periods without getting hungry for food.

[5] 24:35-Literally, "believed in him," but as "the Christ" is clearly implied.

Chapter 25 – John the Immerser's Ministry Ends

John in Imprisoned Luke 7:18-23
(Glossary articles: Biblical Names; Evil Spirits; Herod; John the Immerser; Miracles)

^{1}Meanwhile, in Herod's prison, John the Immerser heard from his disciples about all the miracles Jesus was doing, so he sent two of his disciples to ask Jesus, "Are you the real Christ[2], or should we be looking for someone else[3]?"

^{2}While these disciples were there, Jesus cured many who had various diseases and physical ailments, and he threw evil spirits out of those who were possessed – he even cured several who were blind.

^{3}Then Jesus replied to John's disciples, "Go back to John and tell him what you've seen and heard here.

^{4}"Those who were blind now see, those who were lame now walk, those who had leprosy are now clean, those who were deaf now hear, even those who were dead now live, and above all the poor have the good news brought to them.

^{5}"There's great joy for anyone who's not offended by the way I do things."

Jesus Testifies about John Matthew 11:7-15; Luke 7:24-30
(Glossary articles: Baptize / Immerse; Elijah; John the Immerser; Law of Moses; Lawyers; Pharisees; Prophecies and Fulfillments; Tax Collectors)

^{6}As John's disciples were leaving, Jesus started talking to the crowds about John, saying, "What did you go to the wilderness to see? Were you looking for a reed shaking in the wind?

^{7}"Tell me what you went out there to see. Were you looking for a man wearing soft designer clothing? That would certainly be dumb! People who wear such clothing live in kings' palaces, not in the wilderness.

^{8}"So what was it that you went out to see? Were you looking for a prophet? Yes indeed, and more than a prophet.

^{9}"John's the one described in the sacred writings where we read[4], 'Behold, I'm sending my own messenger ahead of you. He'll prepare the way for your coming.'

^{10}"I assure you: among all those of human birth to this point there's never been one greater than this John the Immerser. Yet the one who's least in the kingdom of heaven is greater than John[5].

^{11}"From the time that John the Immerser came until now the kingdom of heaven has been under attack, and it's violent men who are attacking it.

^{12}"Before John came, it was the prophets and the Law of Moses that foretold this coming; and if you will accept what I'm telling you: John's the 'Elijah' the prophets said would come[6].

^{13}"If you've got ears to hear, pay attention to this."

^{14}So when the people heard what Jesus had to say about John, even the tax collectors glorified God, having been immersed by him.

^{15}But the Pharisees and the experts in Moses' Law had already rejected God's plan for them, having not been immersed by John.

Contrasting John and Jesus Matthew 11:16-19; Luke 7:31-35
(Glossary articles: Evil Spirits; John the Immerser; Sin / Rebellion; Son of Man; Tax Collectors)

^{16}Jesus continued, "What comparison can I make to help you understand what this generation is like?

^{17}"You're like a group of children sitting in the city park calling to other children, 'We played flutes for you, but you wouldn't come dance, so we played like funeral mourners, but you wouldn't weep or act out your sorrow.'

^{18}"When John came, he didn't go to feasts or drink wine with his companions, so people said, 'He's got an evil spirit.'

^{19}"Then I came as a human[7], eating at feasts and drinking with my companions, and you all say, 'Look at that! He's a glutton and a wino – a friend of tax collectors and sinners against God!'

^{20}"But you can always find some way to justify your own 'wisdom.'"

---

[1] 24:48-This was the second miracle Jesus did after returning to Galilee from Jerusalem. We don't know what the first miracle was.

[2] 25:1-Literally, "the coming one," but "Christ" is clearly implied.

[3] 25:1-Like most Jews, John expected the Christ to be a conquering king, not a homeless itinerant rabbi. John probably hoped that Jesus would take over and release him from prison, but that wasn't God's plan.

[4] 25:9-Literally, "This is the one of whom it is written," but clearly implying "written in the sacred writings."

[5] 25:10-How tragically we miss our calling. God offers us the opportunity to be greater than John in his kingdom, and we stay locked in our worldly pursuits.

[6] 25:12-See Malachi 4:5-6. There are obvious parallels between the ministries of Elijah and Elisha on one hand and the ministries of John and Jesus on the other. People needed to see that even though his ministry style differed from John's, they were both part of the same plan just as Elijah and Elisha were part of that plan long ago.

[7] 25:19-Literally, "the son of man came…"

The Death of John the Immerser Matthew 14:1-12; Mark 6:14-29; Luke 9:7-9
(Glossary articles: Biblical Names; Elijah; Herod; Immediately / Quickly; John the Immerser; The Prophet)

²¹Now Herod was ruler over four provinces including Galilee. Herod had taken his brother's wife[1] as his own, and John had openly condemned him saying, "It's against Moses' Law for you to have her as your wife[2]."

²²Because of this, Herod had imprisoned John, and he really wanted to kill John, but he was afraid of how his people might respond[3]. Most people believed that John was a prophet of God.

²³The woman Herod had married[4] was furious with John and wanted to kill him, but she couldn't because Herod was still in awe of John, knowing him to be a good and holy man[5].

²⁴Before his marriage, Herod had listened to John gladly and protected him, doing many good things in response to John's message[6].

²⁵Then Herod gave a great feast for his birthday, inviting his nobles, the top army brass, and the leading citizens of Galilee.

²⁶At the feast, his wife's daughter danced for Herod and all his guests, and Herod was so pleased that he promised with an oath to give her whatever she wanted up to half of his kingdom.

²⁷She went to her mother to ask what she should tell Herod, and her mother saw her chance. She told her daughter, "Ask for the head of John the Immerser on a platter."

²⁸The girl rushed back to the feast and said, "I want you to give me the head of John the Immerser on a platter right now."

²⁹Herod was trapped. He'd sworn in front of all his nobles and guests that he'd give this girl whatever she wanted. He certainly didn't want to fulfill this request, but because of his oath in front of so many leading people there was nothing else he could do.

³⁰So the king sent one of his guards quickly with orders to bring John's head, and the guard beheaded John in the prison and brought the head on a platter. Then the girl took the head and gave it to her mother.

³¹When John's disciples heard about this, they came and got his body for burial. Then they went to tell Jesus what Herod had done.

³²Later, when Herod heard about the things Jesus was doing (by this time Jesus had become well-known), he told his advisers, "I know I had John beheaded, so who's this man I'm hearing so much about? This has to be John the Immerser risen from the dead – that's why he has such powers."

³³Many people were saying the same thing while others said, "This is Elijah who's supposed to come before the Christ" and still others were saying, "This is the prophet who's to come as companion to the Christ, or at least he's like one of the prophets."

³⁴But Herod insisted, "I beheaded John, and now he's come back from the grave[7]!"

Chapter 26 – The Bread of Life-Part 1
Feeding Five Thousand Matthew 14:13-23; Mark 6:31-34a, 34c-46; Luke 9:10-17; John 6:1-15
(Glossary articles: Andrew; Biblical Names; Capernaum; Immediately / Quickly; Money in the Bible; The Prophet; Sacred Writings)

¹Not long after Jesus heard about John's death, he told his disciples. "Come away where we can be by ourselves and rest."

²(There were so many people coming to hear him and be healed by him that he and his disciples hardly had time to eat.)

³So they took a boat to a remote area[8]. But when people found out where he was going, they ran ahead on foot from the cities of that area because they'd seen how he could heal the sick.

⁴When Jesus got out of the boat, he was met by a large crowd.

⁵So Jesus went up on a hill[9] with his disciples and began healing their sick and teaching the crowd many things about the kingdom of God.

---

[1] 25:21-This was Herod Antipas, son of Herod the Great. The brother was named Philip and the woman was named Herodias.
[2] 25:21-Herod claimed the right to be ruler in Jewish territories by claiming Jewish heritage, but that claim also bound him to at least appear to observe the laws God had given to Moses.
[3] 25:22-Herod was ruler over Galilee at the pleasure of the Romans, but if there was anything the Romans wouldn't tolerate it was public unrest. If Herod did something that caused his people to riot, he could be sure the Romans would find a replacement for him.
[4] 25:23-Herodias.
[5] 25:23-Herod was in awe of John, not because of John's goodness and holiness, but because of the power and influence John had over the people due to his goodness and holiness. Herod wanted John dead, but he didn't want to be blamed for John's death.
[6] 25:24-Herod's response to John's message wasn't a sign of conversion, but rather a means to gain political advantage through John's popularity.
[7] 25:34-The world of the New Testament was permeated with a lot of superstition, and Herod was already feeling guilty about having John killed.
[8] 26:3-Near Bethsaida. This wasn't that far from Capernaum, probably a spot between the two cities. See Bethsaida in the Glossary.
[9] 26:5-Going up on the hill would allow Jesus to be heard by the crowd. Jesus used his disciples to maintain order and keep the crowds from becoming a danger.

⁶That evening Jesus' disciples came to him and said, "This is a remote area and it's already getting late. Send these crowds away so they can get to the nearby villages and buy food and lodging for themselves, because they haven't got anything to eat here."

⁷Looking over the crowds, Jesus tested Philip by asking him, "Where do you think we could buy enough bread to feed all of these people?"

⁸"It would take more than sixteen thousand dollars[1] to give each one even a little bread!" Philip exclaimed.

⁹"Well they don't need to go away," Jesus told the disciples. "You give them something to eat."

¹⁰"Are you saying," they asked, "that we should go out and buy sixteen thousand dollars' worth of food?"

¹¹"How many bread cakes do you have?" Jesus asked. "Go find out."

¹²Andrew, Simon Peter's brother, told him, "There's a youngster here who has five barley cakes and two small fish, but what's that for such a huge crowd?"

¹³Then Jesus had his disciples order the crowd to sit down on the grass in groups of fifty or a hundred. (This was close to time for Passover[2].)

¹⁴Jesus took the five cakes of bread and the two fish in his hands, and looking up to the sky, he prayed for God's blessing on this food. Then he broke these items into small pieces and gave the pieces to his disciples.

¹⁵The disciples distributed this food to the crowd, and by the time they were through, everyone had plenty to eat. Then Jesus told the disciples, "Collect all the leftovers so that we don't waste anything."

¹⁶The disciples gathered up twelve baskets full of leftover fish and barley cake. (There were about five thousand men in that crowd plus women and children.)

¹⁷Upon seeing this miracle, some of the men in the crowd said among themselves, "This man must be the prophet who was predicted in the sacred writings[3]."

¹⁸Jesus realized that these men wanted to force him to set himself up as king. So Jesus told his disciples to get into the boat quickly and head toward Capernaum while he dismissed the crowds.

¹⁹Then when Jesus was alone, he went up on the hillside to pray. As it grew dark, he was alone, praying.

Walking on Water Matthew 14:24-36; Mark 6:47-56; John 6:16-21
(Glossary articles: Belief / Faith; Capernaum; Immediately / Quickly; Peter)

²⁰Now during the night, as the disciples had rowed about three or four miles toward Capernaum, a strong wind came up blowing against them, and the boat was being tossed around by the waves.

²¹Jesus was still on the land by himself, but about three o'clock in the morning, he saw them straining against the wind and he came toward them walking on the water.

²²The disciples saw Jesus walking on the water as if he were going to pass by them, and they were terrified. "It's a ghost[4]!" one of them cried out and they were screaming out in terror, because all of them saw him[5].

²³Then Jesus quickly called to them, "Cheer up, guys! It's just me[6] – no need to be afraid."

²⁴"Lord," called Peter, "If it's really you, tell me to come to you walking on the water."

²⁵"Come on," Jesus replied.

²⁶Peter climbed out of the boat and began walking on the water toward Jesus. But when he started paying attention to the fierce wind, he was suddenly terrified and began to sink. "Lord," he cried out, "save me!"

²⁷At that Jesus quickly reached out and took Peter by the hand. "Oh you!" Jesus said. "Your faith is so weak! Why did you doubt me?"

²⁸When Peter and Jesus reached the boat and got in, the wind stopped.

²⁹Then the disciples worshipped Jesus, saying, "It's really true! You're God's own son!" (The disciples were still struggling with skepticism and hadn't truly understood the significance of Jesus feeding all those people.)

³⁰They continued to row and soon anchored not far west of Capernaum[7].

³¹Some of the men in that area recognized Jesus right away, and they sent messengers all through that area to let people know to bring their sick to him. People soon came, often carrying them to him on their beds.

³²People brought their sick to Jesus wherever he was. It didn't matter whether he was in a village, a city, or out in remote locations. Wherever Jesus was they brought the sick into the marketplaces and begged him to let them even touch the hem of his garment. And all who did this were cured of whatever ailments they had.

---

[1] 26:8-Literally, "two hundred denarii."

[2] 26:13-Passover was in the spring and the grass would've been green.

[3] 26:17-Literally, "who is to come into the world," which clearly implies "predicted in the sacred writings."

[4] 26:22-It was night and stormy, which would make it hard to recognize Jesus and easy to think of ghosts.

[5] 26:22-Mark brings out the point that this wasn't just something one of them saw, they all saw this man walking on the water in the night and they were all terrified.

[6] 26:23-Literally, Jesus said, "I AM," very emphatically.

[7] 26:30-From the different gospel accounts it seems they were headed for Capernaum on the north shore of the Sea of Galilee, but with no instruments and at night they landed somewhere west of town.

Jesus – The Bread of Life John 6:22-58
(Glossary articles: Belief / Faith; Capernaum; Moses; Sacred Writings; Son of Man)

³³The morning after Jesus had walked on the water, some of the people were still in the area where Jesus had given thanks for the bread and fed them, but they were puzzled. They knew that the disciples had left in a boat without Jesus, and they knew that this had been the only boat available, but Jesus was nowhere to be found.

³⁴When some other boats happened to come close enough, they got in and rode to Capernaum looking for Jesus. When they finally found Jesus, they asked him, "Teacher, how did you get here?"

³⁵"I'm telling you the absolute truth," Jesus replied: "you're not looking for me because you saw the miraculous signs and understand that you need to be my disciples, but because I gave you all the free food you wanted!

³⁶"You need to quit being so concerned about the food that perishes and focus on the food that lasts and brings you to real life – the life that lasts forever!

³⁷"I as a human[1] can give you this food, and you should understand this because you saw the signs that prove that God the Father is working through me."

³⁸"What should we be doing," they asked, "in order to be doing the things God wants?"

³⁹"This is the only work that God asks:" Jesus answered, "for you to put your full faith in me[2], the one whom God's sent to you."

⁴⁰At this they replied, "OK then, what miraculous sign are you going to do to prove that we really should put our full faith in you? What evidence do you have?

⁴¹"Our ancestors ate manna in the desert where there was no food, as it says in the sacred writings[3], 'He gave them bread that fell from the sky[4].'"

⁴²"I absolutely assure you," Jesus responded: "It wasn't Moses who gave you bread from the sky. No indeed! It's God my Father who gives you the true bread from above.

⁴³"I'm the real bread of God – I, who came down from heaven, yes, I, who will give my life for the world!"

⁴⁴"Lord," they answered, "just give us that bread from now on[5]."

⁴⁵"I AM[6] the bread that brings real life" Jesus replied. "Those who come to me will never be hungry again, and those who put their faith in me will never be thirsty again[7].

⁴⁶"But here's the problem: you've seen me and the evidence of who I am, and still you won't put your faith in me.

⁴⁷"Everyone that the Father gives me will turn to me, and I certainly won't turn away anyone who turns to me.

⁴⁸"I didn't come down from heaven to do my own will, but to do the will of the one who sent me.

⁴⁹"And this is what my Father, the one who sent me, wants: of all those whom he's given me, he desires that none be lost, but when the end comes, he wants me to raise them back to life.

⁵⁰"My father wants all who see me as his son and who put their full faith in me to have real life – life everlasting. And I'll raise all of them up when the end comes."

⁵¹The Jewish religious leaders who were present grumbled about his words, "I AM[8] the bread that brings real life" that "came down from the sky."

⁵²"Isn't this Jesus, the son of Joseph?" they grumbled. "Don't we know exactly who his dad and mom are? How can he say, 'I came down from heaven'?"

⁵³"Don't start grumbling," Jesus said. "Nobody can come to me unless my Father, who sent me here, draws that person to me. And if a person comes to me, I'll raise that person up at the end.

⁵⁴"You recall what the prophet wrote, 'And God will teach all of them[9].' So everybody who's listened to and learned from the Father naturally comes to me.

⁵⁵"And it's not that anybody's really seen the Father (except me, since I came from God – I've certainly seen the Father). And I'm telling you the absolute truth: those who've truly put their faith in me have everlasting life.

⁵⁶"I AM[10] the very bread of life. Your ancestors ate the manna in the wilderness, but they're dead. What I'm bringing is the bread that comes down from heaven itself – bread of such a nature that, if you eat it, you'll never die.

---

[1] 26:37-Literally, "the son of man..."
[2] 26:39-Those with this kind of faith are faithful. Their lives are focused on living according to Jesus' teachings. And those teachings can all be summed up in Christian love first for God and then for others.
[3] 26:41-Literally, "as it is written," but "in the sacred writings" is clearly implied.
[4] 26:41-Psalm 78:24 (which refers to events recorded in Exodus 16:4-36).
[5] 26:44-This reply was probably meant to be sarcastic.
[6] 26:45-This was a very emphatic "I AM."
[7] 26:45-Obviously Jesus wasn't talking about physical hunger or thirst. Recall that in Good News 9:7 Jesus said that those who hunger and thirst for righteousness will certainly be filled.
[8] 26:51-The "I AM" here is very emphatic.
[9] 26:54-Isaiah 54:13.
[10] 26:56-The "I AM" here is very emphatic.

⁵⁷"I AM[1] the living bread that came down from heaven. Whoever eats this bread will live forever! And the bread that I'm going to give you is my own flesh – my flesh that I'm going to give for those in this world to find life."

⁵⁸At this the Jewish religious leaders began to dispute: "How can this man," they argued, "give us his flesh to eat?"

⁵⁹"I'm telling you the absolute truth," Jesus responded: "Unless you eat my human flesh[2] and drink my blood, you aren't even alive at all. But anybody who eats my flesh and drinks my blood already has everlasting life, and I'll raise that person up in the end. My flesh is the real food, and my blood is the real drink.

⁶⁰"The person who eats my flesh and drinks my blood lives in me[3] – and I live in that person. Just as the Father who lives forever sent me, and I'm alive because of the Father, so he who feeds on me will live forever because of me.

⁶¹"This is the real bread that came down from heaven – not like the manna your ancestors ate that couldn't give everlasting life. They're dead. But the one who eats this bread that I bring will live forever."

Losing Some Followers John 6:59-71
(Glossary articles: Belief / Faith; Capernaum; Christ; Judas; Son of Man and Son of God)

⁶²Jesus was in the worship center in Capernaum when he said these things. When they heard what he said there, many of his disciples complained: "That's a tough one! What in the world is that supposed to mean?"

⁶³Understanding that they were whispering such things, Jesus asked, "Does this shock you? How, then, are you going to feel when you see me as a human[4] ascending back to where I was before?

⁶⁴"It's the spirit that gives life. In the end, what value can the flesh be? You have to understand the words that I've spoken spiritually – that's when you'll find that they are the source of life.

⁶⁵"I know that there are some of you who haven't really put your trust in me." (Jesus said this because he knew from the first who didn't really trust in him and even who would betray him.) "That's why I told you that no one can join with me unless my Father gives his permission."

⁶⁶At that point many of his disciples turned back, no longer traveling with him. Then Jesus took the twelve he'd chosen aside and asked, "Are you thinking about leaving too?"

⁶⁷"Lord," said Simon Peter, "to whom do you think we'd go? You're the only one who has the message of eternal life. And besides that, we've truly come to trust in you, knowing that you're the Christ, the son of the one true living God."

⁶⁸Jesus answered, "Yes, I know I chose you twelve with good reason; yet one of you is evil to the core."

⁶⁹(He was talking about Judas, the son of Simon, because he knew that Judas was going to betray him, even though he and the others had just pledged to stay with him.)

Chapter 27 – The Bread of Life-Part 2

What Goes In or What Comes Out Matthew 15:1-20; Mark 7:1-23; Luke 6:39
(Glossary articles: Isaiah; Jerusalem; Jewish Elders; Pharisees; Scribes)

¹Then some scribes and Pharisees[5] came from Jerusalem. As they watched Jesus, they found fault with his disciples when they noticed that some of them were eating bread without washing their hands.

²(The Pharisees and all the Jewish religious leaders always wash their hands in a special way passed down from the ancient elders as tradition. Any time they come from the market, they always wash before they eat. They also have similar traditions about washing cups, pitchers, copper pans, and even the cushions that they lie on when they eat.)

³"Why don't your disciples keep the traditions of the elders?" these men asked. "They don't wash their hands when they eat."

⁴"You'd rather keep your traditions about washing pitchers and cups and such than keep the commandments of God," Jesus said. "Tell me, why do you allow a tradition that keeps you from honoring the commandment of God?

⁵"God gave you the commandment to 'Honor your father and your mother[6],' and he also said, 'You shall execute anyone who curses father or mother[7]!'

⁶"But you say, 'If someone tells father or mother, "I've promised to give God anything I might have provided for you," then that person can no longer do anything for father or mother.'

⁷"So by your tradition you allow people to get around God's commandments and make his commandments meaningless – and there are lots of things like that where your traditions override God's commandments.

---

[1] 26:57-The "I AM" here is very emphatic.

[2] 26:59-Literally, "the flesh of the son of man..."

[3] 26:60-This is often taken as a prediction of the Lord's Supper (also called the Eucharist), but there's more here than a ritual. God isn't impressed by human rituals. The rituals are meant for us, not for God. The point here is that we take on Jesus' very life, we become his body carrying out the ministries he demonstrated. And as Paul later wrote, in doing so we become flesh and blood relatives of each other—we're one family, one blood.

[4] 26:63-Literally, "the son of man…"

[5] 27:1-These men from Jerusalem would be in more of a leadership role than the local scribes and Pharisees in Galilee.

[6] 27:5-Exodus 20:12 or Deuteronomy 5:16.

[7] 27:5-Exodus 21:17 or Leviticus 20:9.

⁸"Fakes!" Jesus exclaimed. "Isaiah was right when he described you, saying, 'This nation pretends to honor me in what they say, but their hearts aren't focused on me at all! Their so-called worship is worthless because the rules they teach are just things made up by men[1].'"

⁹Then Jesus called the crowd over and said to them, "Listen to me and understand what I'm telling you! What goes into a person's mouth isn't what defiles that person. Instead, it's what comes out of that person's mouth. If you've got ears at all, pay attention to this!"

¹⁰Jesus' disciples came to him later, after they were in the house away from the crowds, and asked, "Did you know that you offended the Pharisees by what you said?"

¹¹But Jesus replied, "Every plant that my heavenly Father hasn't planted will be pulled up by the roots.

¹²"Let those folks alone – they're blind guides to blind followers. And of course, if a blind person leads blind people, they'll all wind up in a ditch."

¹³Then Peter said, "Explain this illustration to us."

¹⁴"Don't you get it yet?" Jesus asked. "Isn't it obvious that whatever goes into a person's mouth can't defile him because it doesn't go into his heart? Instead it goes through the stomach and comes out when the person goes to the bathroom.

¹⁵"But what comes out of a person's mouth is an expression of what's in that person's heart, and in those words you see how defiled a person really is.

¹⁶"Think of it – everything evil comes from a person's heart – things like evil thoughts, murder, adultery, sexual offenses of various sorts, theft, envy, lying about others, lust, pornography, and speaking against God. Those are the things that defile a person, but eating with dirty hands doesn't have anything to do with defiling a person in God's eyes."

¹⁷(By saying this, Jesus made it clear that food of any sort cannot make a person unclean before God.)

Four Thousand Fed Matthew 15:29-39; Mark 7:31-37, 8:1-10
(Glossary articles: Biblical Names; Immediately / Quickly)

¹⁸Jesus then left that area and traveled around the western edge of the Sea of Galilee through the area of the Ten Cities.

¹⁹Along the way, Jesus set up camp on top of a high hill. Huge crowds came to him bringing people who had all kinds of health problems – the lame, the blind, the mute, the maimed, and those afflicted with many other illnesses.

²⁰Friends would lay these people down at Jesus' feet, and he healed them all. The crowds were amazed to hear the mute speaking and to see the maimed made whole, the lame walking, and the blind seeing. They all praised the God of Israel for these healings.

²¹For example, one man was brought to him who was deaf and couldn't speak clearly. Those with him begged Jesus to place his hand on this man.

²²In this case Jesus took the man over away from the crowds, put his fingers in the man's ears, spit on his fingers and then touched the man's tongue. Then Jesus looked up into the sky, sighed deeply, and looking back at the man he said, "Open!" Instantly the man could hear and speak plainly.

²³Then Jesus ordered the man and those with him to keep this a secret, but the more he commanded people not to tell about being healed, the more widely they spread the news. Astonished, they went around saying, "Everything he's done has been done well! He even causes the deaf to hear and the mute to talk!"

²⁴As the crowds continued to stay with Jesus day after day, he called over his disciples. "I'm concerned about this crowd," he said. "They've been with us for three days now, and they don't have a thing left to eat.

²⁵"I don't want to just send them away lest they faint from hunger before they're able to get food. After all, some of them are from distant places."

²⁶"Where could we get enough bread in this remote area to feed such a huge crowd?" the disciples asked.

²⁷"How many bread cakes do you have?" asked Jesus.

²⁸"Seven," they replied, "and a few small fish."

²⁹So Jesus ordered the crowd to sit on the ground. He took the seven bread cakes along with the fish and gave thanks to God for this food. Then he broke the bread and fish into pieces and gave the pieces to the disciples who passed this food out to the crowd.

³⁰The whole crowd ate until they were all full, and the disciples took up seven large baskets of leftovers. (There were four thousand men in that crowd besides the women and children.)

³¹After the crowd had eaten and the leftovers had been collected, Jesus sent them all away. Then Jesus and his disciples quickly got into a boat and took it to an area on the west coast of the Sea of Galilee[2].

---

[1] 27:8-Isaiah 29:13.
[2] 27:31-Near Magdala and Dalmanutha.

A Warning about Bad Yeast Matthew 16:5-12; Mark 8:13-21; Luke 12:1
(Glossary articles: Belief / Faith; Herod; Pharisees; Sadducees)

³²When they landed, the disciples realized they'd forgotten to bring any of the bread – there was only about one loaf among them in the boat. About that time Jesus told them, "Beware of the Pharisees' leaven and the leaven of Herod."

³³"He said that because we forgot the bread," they whispered among themselves.

³⁴But Jesus, aware of their whisperings, said, "You've got eyes, so why can't you see? You've got ears, so why can't you hear? Don't you get it? Your faith in me is still so small!

³⁵"Why are you all upset because you didn't bring any bread?

³⁶"Don't you remember the five bread cakes that fed five thousand? How many baskets of food did you take up after they were fed?"

³⁷"Twelve," they responded.

³⁸"And don't you remember the seven bread cakes we used to feed four thousand?" Jesus continued. "How many large baskets of bread did you take up after they were fed?"

³⁹"Seven," they replied.

⁴⁰"So how can you fail to understand," Jesus concluded, "that I wasn't talking about bread? No, you need to beware of the leaven of the Pharisees and the Sadducees!"

⁴¹Finally they got it. They understood that he wasn't talking about the leaven in bread but about the teaching of the Pharisees and the Sadducees.

Chapter 28 – A Feast in Jerusalem

A Sabbath Healing in Jerusalem John 5:1-16
(Glossary articles: Immediately / Quickly; Jerusalem; Jewish Feasts; Judeans & Jewish Authorities; Law of Moses; Pool of Healing; Sabbath)

¹Jesus then went up to Jerusalem for one of the Jewish feasts[1].

²In Jerusalem there was a pool[2] by the city gate known as the Sheep Gate. This pool was surrounded by five porches, and many sick people (blind, lame, paralyzed, etc.) lay on these porches.

³(They lay there because from time to time the water was stirred, and people believed that the first person in the pool when this happened would be cured.)

⁴There was one man at the pool who'd been ill for thirty-eight years. Jesus saw him lying there and knew that he'd been ill for so long. "Do you want to be healed?" Jesus asked.

⁵"Sir," the man replied, "I don't have anyone to help me into the pool when the water's stirred up. While I'm trying to get there, somebody else gets there first."

⁶"Then get up," said Jesus, "pick up your bed and walk!"

⁷At Jesus' word the man was immediately well. He took up his bed and walked away as instructed.

⁸Now that day was a Sabbath. Some Jewish religious leaders met him and told him, "It's a Sabbath, and it's against the Law of Moses for you to carry your bed."

⁹"The man who cured me," he replied, "told me, 'Take up your bed and walk.'"

¹⁰"Who told you 'Pick up your bed and walk'?" they demanded.

¹¹But the man who'd been healed didn't know who'd healed him, because Jesus had slipped away in the crowd around the pool.

¹²Later Jesus found him in the temple. "OK, now you're well. See to it that you stop sinning[3], or something worse may happen to you."

¹³Once the man knew who'd healed him, he ran to the Jewish authorities and told them that it was Jesus.

¹⁴It was for challenges like this – intentionally healing on a Sabbath – that the Jewish religious leaders persecuted Jesus and wanted to kill him.

Jesus as God's Son John 5:17-47
(Glossary articles: John the Immerser; Moses; Sabbath; Sacred Writings; Son of Man and Son of God; Sons and Fathers in Biblical Thinking)

¹⁵Then they heard Jesus say, "My Father's been busy up until now, and I've been busy too."

¹⁶This further infuriated the Jewish authorities making them want to kill him more than ever.

¹⁷It wasn't just that he healed people on the Sabbath. No, now he was claiming that God was actually his father, and in their minds, that would make him equal with God.

¹⁸"I tell you the absolute truth," Jesus told them: "I as the son[1] can't do anything on my own.

---

[1] 28:1-The Bible doesn't tell us for certain, but the feast most commonly known as "the feast of the Jews" was Passover, and that's the wording used in this passage.
[2] 28:2-The Pool of Bethesda or House of Mercy Pool.
[3] 28:12-Remember, sin is always treason—rebellion against God.

¹⁹"As the son, I can only do what I've seen my Father do – and in the same way he does things.

²⁰"The Father loves me as his son[2] and shows me everything that he himself is doing. And he'll show me even greater things so that you'll all be amazed.

²¹"Indeed, just as the Father raises the dead and gives them life[3], even so I as the son give life to anyone I choose.

²²"In fact, the Father won't be the judge for anyone – he's given all authority for judgment to me as his son[4] so that everybody will come to honor me[5] just as they honor God.

²³"Anyone who doesn't honor me as the son[6] doesn't honor my Father who sent me.

²⁴"I'm telling you the absolute truth: those who seriously listen to what I teach and put their faith in the Father who sent me already have life everlasting. These won't have to face judgment. They've already passed from death into eternal life.

²⁵"Again I'm telling you the absolute truth: the time's coming – in fact it's already here – when the dead will hear my voice, the voice of God's own son, and those who listen to me will live forever[7].

²⁶"Just as life itself is an inherent part of who my Father is, so he's granted me as his son to have life inherently in myself. He's given me authority to mete out justice because I've lived here as a human and experienced what it is to be human[8].

²⁷"Does this surprise you? I tell you, the time's coming when everyone in the graves will hear my voice and come out.

²⁸"Those who've done what's good will rise to life everlasting. Those who've done what's wrong will rise to find themselves condemned eternally.

²⁹"Now, by myself I can't do anything[9]. I judge people based on what I hear, and my judgment is right because I'm not looking out for my own interests, but for what my Father (the one who sent me) wants.

³⁰"If I were just bragging about myself with nothing to support my bragging, you really shouldn't believe me. But that's not the case at all. God himself testifies to my truth, and I certainly know that what he says is true.

³¹"Furthermore, you yourselves sent messengers to John the Immerser, and he also testified to the truth of my claims.

³²"But I don't need testimony from any human. I'm saying these things so that you'll pay attention and find salvation.

³³"John was like a lamp burning brightly, and you were happy to find joy in his light for a while.

³⁴"But I have a witness who's greater than John –

³⁵"The miraculous works I'm doing – works I do by the power God gave me – these very works stand as witness that the Father truly has sent me. Besides that, the Father himself has testified that my message is true.

³⁶"But you've never heard his voice or seen his reality. You don't have his message living in your hearts because you haven't put your faith in me, the one he's sent to you.

³⁷"You look diligently through the sacred writings[10], thinking that you'll find eternal life in those writings. Yet it's those very writings that tell about me, but you're not willing to turn to me and receive the life I offer.

³⁸"I don't depend on humans to give me honor.

³⁹"And I know all about you. You don't have the caring love of God in your hearts.

⁴⁰"How can you put your faith in me when you're so busy trying to gain honor from each other[11]? You're not looking for the honor that comes only from God.

⁴¹"I've come in my Father's authority, and you won't accept me. But if somebody else comes in his own authority, you'll accept him!

⁴²"Don't even think that I'm the one who'll accuse you to the Father. No, the one who'll accuse you is Moses, the very one in whom you've supposedly placed your trust.

⁴³"If you really did trust in Moses, you'd have trusted in me. After all, he wrote about me[12]. But if you won't put your faith in what he wrote, how can you put your faith in what I've been saying?"

---

[1] 28:18-Literally, "the son can't do…" Throughout this passage Jesus literally referred to himself as "the son" and "the son of man," translated here as "I," "I as a human," "I as the son," etc. These phrases emphasize that Jesus was speaking of his human incarnation, not of the spiritual God who was present in him without limit.

[2] 28:20-Literally, "the Father loves the son," but "me as the son" is clearly implied.

[3] 28:21-Literally, "the son gives life," but "I as the son" is clearly implied.

[4] 28:22-Literally, "judgment to the son," but "me as his son" is clearly implied.

[5] 28:22-Literally, "the son," but "me" is clearly implied.

[6] 28:23-Literally, "honor the son," but "me as the son" is clearly implied.

[7] 28:25-Jesus repeatedly made the point that as Christians, we don't die. Our bodies are left behind, but the reality of our selves—the soul and spirit—take on a new body that lasts forever.

[8] 28:26-Literally, "because he's the son of man."

[9] 28:29-Here again Jesus separates his human self—the self that can do nothing, from the spiritual presence of God within him with unlimited power.

[10] 28:37-Literally, "the writings."

[11] 28:40-This is such an important point for Christians to see. When we seek honor from other humans, we're on dangerous ground! We need to focus on seeking honor from God and him only.

[12] 28:43-Deuteronomy 18:18.

Chapter 29 – Beginning Preparations for the End
"You Are the Christ" Matthew 16:13-20; Mark 8:27-30; Luke 9:18-21
(Glossary articles: Biblical Names; Christ; Elijah; Hell; John the Immerser; Peter; Son of Man and Son of God; Team / Church)

¹At one point Jesus and his disciples traveled to an area close to a Roman center of government not far northeast of Galilee[1].

²As they were leaving the area, he took some time by himself to pray. Then, as they continued their journey, he asked his disciples, "What are people speculating about who I am (humanly speaking[2])?"

³"Some are saying that you're John the Immerser come back from the dead," they began, "and others say you're Elijah or Jeremiah or one of the other ancient prophets who's come back to life."

⁴"OK," Jesus responded, "But who do you say I am?"

⁵"You're the Christ of God," answered Simon Peter, "the very son of the living God!"

⁶"There's indeed great joy in store for you, Simon, son of John," Jesus continued. "It wasn't some flesh and blood human who revealed that to you. No indeed, it was my Father in heaven!

⁷"And I tell you, you're Peter, and it's on the bedrock of that statement that I'll build my team[3]. And I promise you: the very gates of hell won't be able to hold up against that team!

⁸"I'm going to give you the keys to the kingdom of heaven! Whatever you make binding here on earth will be what's binding in heaven, and whatever you allow on earth will be allowed in heaven."

⁹Then he commanded his disciples not to tell anyone that he, Jesus, was the Christ.

The Crucifixion and Resurrection Predicted Matthew 16:21-23; 17:22-23; Mark 8:31-33; 9:30-32; Luke 9:22, 43b-45
(Glossary articles: Jerusalem; Jewish Elders; Peter; Chief Priests; Satan; Scribes; Son of Man)

¹⁰Now the crowds were all amazed by the power and majesty of God that they saw in Jesus.

¹¹But while all the people were marveling, Jesus began to warn his disciples about what was coming – that he was going to Jerusalem where the elders, chief priests, and scribes would cause him extreme suffering and finally have him put to death, but that he'd be raised from the dead on the third day.

¹²"Let this message sink deeply into your ears!," he said, "I as a human[4] will soon be betrayed, and I'll have to endure a lot of suffering, be rejected by the elders and the chief priests and scribes, and be killed – but I'll be raised up on the third day."

¹³When Peter heard this, he took Jesus aside and rebuked him. "That'll never happen to you, Lord! Never in a million years!"

¹⁴But turning toward the disciples so that all could hear, Jesus responded, "Get away from me, Satan[5]! You make me sick! All you can think about is the things of this world – not the things that matter to God."

¹⁵Then they left that area and started walking south through Galilee.

¹⁶This time Jesus didn't want anybody to know about his movements because of what he was trying to teach his disciples.

¹⁷"I as a human[6] am about to be betrayed," he said, "and the men into whose hands I'm going to be betrayed will kill me. But after they've killed me, I'll rise from the dead on the third day."

¹⁸But though Jesus was plainly telling them what was coming, they didn't get it, and they were afraid to ask questions.

Chapter 30 – The Greatest and the Least
The Danger of Wealth Matthew 19:16-30; Mark 10:17-31; Luke 18:18-30
(Glossary articles: Caring Love; Maturity / Perfection; Peter; Son of Man)

¹One time as Jesus was walking up the road to Jerusalem, a young ruler came running to him. He dropped to his knees in front of Jesus and asked, "Good teacher, what good deed must I do to gain everlasting life?"

²"Why do you call me 'good'?" asked Jesus. "The only one who can truly be called 'good' is God[7] But if you really want to enter the realm of everlasting life, just keep the commandments."

³"Which ones?" the man asked.

⁴"Don't murder," Jesus answered, "don't offend sexually against your wife or anyone else's, don't steal, don't testify to a falsehood, don't cheat, honor your father and mother, and care about your neighbor just as much as you care about yourself."

---

[1] 29:1-Caesarea Philippi, a non-Jewish area where Jesus could avoid crowds.
[2] 29:2-Literally, "who I, the son of man, am."
[3] 29:7-The name "Peter" means "a stone." The word Jesus used for the rock on which he'd build his team was the feminine form for bedrock, while Peter's name was the masculine form for a stone—not the bedrock.
[4] 29:12-Literally, "the son of man..."
[5] 29:14-The word "Satan" means "adversary." The real Satan was working through Peter.
[6] 29:17-Literally, "the son of man is..."
[7] 30:2-Jesus wanted this young man to realize that he'd just addressed Jesus as God. Jesus then answered his question—as God.

⁵"But teacher, I've done all of those ever since I was a child," the young man responded. "How much more do I need to do?"

⁶Jesus looked closely at the man and cared deeply for him.

⁷"One thing's still missing," Jesus told him. "If you really want to be a spiritual grown-up, here's what you need to do. Go sell all the earthly treasures you have and give to the poor. If you do that, you'll have real wealth in heaven[1].

⁸"Then when you've done that, come, accept that you'll die in my service, and follow me."

⁹When the young man heard this message, he left Jesus with a downcast expression, because he had a lot of earthly treasures.

¹⁰Then Jesus told his disciples, "I'm telling you the absolute truth: it's hard indeed for a rich person to get into the kingdom of heaven.

¹¹"In fact, I'll tell you what – it's easier for a camel to go through the eye of a needle than for a rich man to get into the kingdom of God."

¹²When the disciples heard that, they were amazed. "Then who in the world can be saved?" they asked[2].

¹³Jesus looked at them closely and replied, "Actually, it's impossible as a human, but God can save anyone he wants to save. Things that are impossible for humans are possible for God."

¹⁴"Look," said Peter, "we've left everything we owned to follow you. What reward can we expect?"

¹⁵"I absolutely assure you," replied Jesus: "When God's rule is restored and I as a human[3] sit on my glorious throne, the twelve of you who've followed me so faithfully will sit on twelve thrones exercising authority over the twelve tribes of Israel.

¹⁶"More than that, anybody who's left houses or brothers or sisters or dad or mom or wife or kids or lands for my sake and the sake of the good news I've taught shall indeed get back a hundred times as much in this present life – houses, brothers, sisters, mothers, children and lands (along with personal abuse) – and in the age to come they'll get everlasting life[4].

¹⁷"But many who think they're at the head of the line for everlasting life will find themselves at the back of the line. And those who are thought to be at the back of the line will be at the front."

James and John Request Kingdom Leadership Matthew 20:20-28; Mark 10:35-45
(Glossary articles: Baptize / Immerse; Gentiles / Nations; James; John; Slaves; Son of Man)

¹⁸Then the mother of James and John[5], came to Jesus with her sons, kneeling down in front of Jesus and saying, "Teacher, will you promise to do what we ask?"

¹⁹"What do you want me to do?" asked Jesus.

²⁰"In your kingdom," she replied, "grant that my sons may sit next to you in your glory, one at your right hand and one at your left hand."

²¹"You have no idea what you're asking for," Jesus replied. "Can you really drink the cup that I'm about to drink? Can you stand to be immersed[6] in the same depths into which I'm about to be immersed?"

²²"We are able!" the men replied.

²³ "Yes," Jesus answered, "you certainly will drink from this cup, and the time will come when you'll be immersed into the same depths into which I'm about to be immersed.

²⁴"However, even I don't have the right to decide who sits on my right hand and my left hand. That's for my Father to decide."

²⁵When the other ten disciples heard what James and John had done, they were angry with the brothers.

²⁶But Jesus called them all together and said, "You know how the rulers of the nations boss people around, and how those in authority flaunt their power over others. But that's not how things are to work among you!

²⁷"Among my followers, if you want to be thought of as great, be a servant to the others, and if you want to be at the top, be a slave to all the others!

²⁸"You need to imitate the way that I as a human[1] didn't come to have people wait on me, but rather to serve people and, in the end, to give my own life to ransom many people from the power of evil."

---

[1] 30:7-This young man was so used to his focus on worldly wealth that he didn't even see how that focus kept him from caring for others as he cared for himself. Jesus had a drastic prescription for his spiritual illness. It's possible to have wealth and still serve God (think of Abraham or David), but to do so a person must be ready to get rid of all worldly wealth and possessions in God's service at any time. The focus of a Christian's life cannot be worldly possessions.

[2] 30:12-In New Testament culture, it was assumed that the wealthy were blessed by God, so they should be the ones being saved.

[3] 30:15-Literally, "the son of man sits..."

[4] 30:16-Notice that Jesus didn't criticize his disciples for wanting a reward for their service. Instead, he promised his disciples a great reward, just not in this world. God does provide motivation (the carrot) for his servants, but he wants us to have our focus beyond this world. (Read Hebrews 11.)

[5] 30:18-Literally, "the mother of Zebedee's sons."

[6] 30:21-Translating this as "immersed" gives a better understanding of what Jesus was saying to his disciples. He was about to be plunged into the very depths of suffering greater than any of them could imagine.

Who's the Greatest? Matthew 18:1-7, 10, 14; Mark 9:33-40, 42; Luke 9:46-50; 17:1-2; John 7:1
(Glossary articles: Agent / Angel; Belief / Faith; Capernaum; Evil Spirits; Miracles)

²⁹After this, Jesus returned to Galilee, avoiding Judea, because the Jewish authorities wanted to kill him. Jesus came back to Capernaum, and when he was in the house he asked his disciples, "What were you arguing about along the way?"

³⁰However, not one of them would speak up. (They'd actually been disputing among themselves about who'd be the greatest.)

³¹So Jesus sat down, called the twelve disciples to him and said, "I'm telling you the absolute truth: unless you turn your life around and start over like a little child, you'll never get into the kingdom of heaven. So, who's greatest in the kingdom of heaven?"

³²Then he took a little child, set him on his lap, hugged him, and told his disciples, "Anybody who's willing to be as humble as this little child is the greatest in the kingdom of heaven.

³³"But anybody who wants to be first in my kingdom will wind up being last of all and servant to everybody else.

³⁴"And anybody who accepts a little child like this one because that's what I would want, that person accepts not just me, but the Father who sent me.

³⁵"Don't worry, the least among you will be great.

³⁶"But don't you dare despise one of these little ones, because I'm telling you: in heaven the agents God has assigned to them have direct access to my Father.

³⁷"It's not God's will that even one of these little ones should perish. So anybody who causes one of these little children who have faith in me to turn against me – I'll tell you what, it would be better for that person to be drowned deep in the sea with a millstone for a necktie.

³⁸"Terrible things are coming to this world because of how this world continually offends God! These offenses must come, but there'll be great anguish for the person who brings about such offenses!"

³⁹Then John said, "Teacher, we saw somebody casting out evil spirits in your name, and we told him to stop because he isn't one who travels with us."

⁴⁰"Don't stop someone from doing our work in my name," Jesus responded. "If the man was doing miracles in my name, he's not likely to turn around and say anything bad about me. Anybody who's not against us is on our side."

Blessing the Children Matthew 19:13-15; Mark 10:13-16; Luke 18:15-17

⁴¹Then some in the crowd started bringing little children and infants for Jesus to put his hands on them and pray for them. When Jesus' disciples saw what was going on, they began telling the parents to go away and not bother Jesus with these children.

⁴²But when Jesus realized that this was happening, he was irritated and called his disciples over and told them, "Let the little children come to me. Don't turn them away, because the kingdom of heaven is for those who are like these children.

⁴³"Indeed, I assure you that anybody who doesn't accept the kingdom of heaven like a little child absolutely won't get in!"

⁴⁴Then Jesus started taking the little children up in his arms. For each one he'd place a hand on the child and offer a prayer that the child's life might be blessed.

Chapter 31 – A Changing Ministry

Sending Out Seventy Disciples Luke 10:1, 3-12; 16-20
(Glossary articles: Evil Spirits; Disciples; Heaven / Sky; In the Name of...; Satan)

¹Another time Jesus chose seventy of his disciples and sent these out two-by-two with instructions to go into all the cities and towns that he was getting ready to visit.

²He told them, "As you go, be aware that I'm sending you out like lambs into a pack of wolves. Don't take money, don't pack a bag, and don't take extra sandals.

³"Don't take time with anybody you meet along the road, but find a house where the people welcome you and start by saying, 'May peace be on this home.'

⁴"If a child of peace lives there, your blessing of peace will be on that home, but if not, your blessing of peace will simply return to you.

⁵"And don't move from house to house. Just stay in the first house that welcomes you, eating and drinking only the things they offer you, because your work's worthy of that payment. Just eat whatever things people offer you in any city that welcomes you.

⁶"Heal the sick in that place and tell them, 'The kingdom of God is very near.'

⁷"And if any city won't welcome you, then go out into the street and tell them, 'We wipe off even the dust of this city that clings to our feet as a witness against you. But know this: the kingdom of God's come this close to you, and you missed it!'

---

¹ 30:28-Literally, "the son of man..."

⁸"I'm telling you: it will be better on judgment day for a pagan city that God destroyed for its wickedness[1] than for that city!

⁹"Understand this: the person who listens to you is listening to me, and anybody who rejects me has really rejected the one who sent me."

¹⁰When the seventy returned from their assignments, they were bubbling over with joy. "Lord," they said, "Even the evil spirits did whatever we told them to do in your authority[2]!"

¹¹"I saw Satan fall like lightning from the sky!" Jesus responded. "See, I've given you authority[3] to walk over snakes and scorpions and over all the power of your enemy[4] and absolutely nothing[5] will harm you!

¹²"However, the rejoicing you do shouldn't be focused on your authority over Satan's powers, but rather over the fact that you're now citizens of heaven."

Jesus' Glory Matthew 17:1-13; Mark 9:2-13; Luke 9:28-36
(Glossary articles: Elijah; James; Jerusalem; John; John the Immerser; Moses; Peter; Sacred Writings; Scribes; Son of Man)

¹³One day about a week after Jesus had questioned his disciples about who he was, he took Peter, James, and John up on a mountain by themselves, and as he was praying, his appearance was changed right before them.

¹⁴His face was as radiant as the sun and his clothing became as bright as light itself, whiter than any earthly cleaning could do.

¹⁵Then Moses and Elijah appeared with them, talking with Jesus about his coming death in Jerusalem.

¹⁶The disciples (Peter, James, and John) had all been sleeping and were still drowsy, but when they were fully awake, they saw his glory and the men with whom Jesus was talking.

¹⁷As Moses and Elijah were about to part from Jesus, Peter said, "Lord, it's so good for us to be here. Just say the word and we'll build three shrines here, one for you, one for Moses, and one for Elijah[6]."

¹⁸(Peter said this because he was so awestricken that he didn't know what to say.)

¹⁹Peter hardly got the words out of his mouth before a brilliant cloud overshadowed them, and a voice from the cloud said, "This is my dearly loved son in whom I'm extremely pleased. Pay attention to him!"

²⁰When the disciples heard this voice, they were overcome by awe and fell down with their faces to the ground in worship, but Jesus simply walked over and touched them, saying, "You can get up now; there's no need to be afraid." And when they looked up, the only one there with them was Jesus.

²¹As they were coming down the mountain, Jesus gave them strict orders: "Don't tell anybody about that vision until I as a human[7] rise from the dead." So these disciples kept this to themselves, but they questioned among themselves what Jesus meant about rising from the dead.

²²Continuing on their way, the disciples asked him, "Why do the scribes say that Elijah must come before the Christ[8]?"

²³Jesus answered, "Actually, Elijah does come first to put everything back in order. But I can tell you now that Elijah has already come, and those religious leaders didn't recognize him. Indeed, they did whatever they wanted to him.

²⁴"But why do you think the sacred writings[9] say that I as a human[2] must suffer terribly and be treated with contempt? Indeed, in much the same way that they treated John, it won't be long until they do the same kind of things to me as a human[10]."

²⁵Then the disciples understood that Jesus was talking about John the Immerser being the fulfillment of that prophecy[11]. And the disciples kept silent about these events as Jesus had instructed them.

---

[1] 31:8-Literally, "Sodom"
[2] 31:10-Literally, "in your name."
[3] 31:11-The word Jesus used means authority, not dynamic power. If Jesus had been giving his disciples power to stomp on snakes and scorpions, he would've used the word for dynamic power, not authority.
[4] 31:11-The word for enemy is singular—Satan.
[5] 31:11-Jesus actually used a triple negative to emphasize his point. Even if Satan were to kill us, he'd be doing us a favor. Even pain and suffering can work out for good for Christians.
[6] 31:17-Moses had built a tabernacle—a building to worship God—at Mount Sinai. Peter was ready to build three tabernacles. It was a great leap for him to put Jesus in the same category as Moses and Elijah, but God wanted these disciples to know that Jesus is far, far above those prophets.
[7] 31:21-Literally, "the son of man rises…"
[8] 31:22-Literally, "must come first," but "before the Christ" is clearly implied. See Malachi 4:5.
[9] 31:24-Literally, "And how is it written…" with "in the sacred writings" clearly implied.
[10] 31:24-Literally, "the son of man…" in both places.
[11] 31:25-John the Immerser said that he wasn't Elijah, and in a very literal sense he was not. Jesus was saying that although John wasn't literally Elijah, he was the one figuratively pointed out by the prophecy that Elijah would come as forerunner to the Christ. Elijah was a desert dweller like John, announcing an in-your-face message like John, dressed much like John had dressed. The prophet who followed Elijah was Elisha, and while he still strongly proclaimed God's word for Israel, he was more of a town person than a desert dweller. The parallels between the ministries of Elijah and Elisha as compared to John and Jesus easily show how John, without actually being Elijah come back from the dead, yet fulfilled the intent of the prophecy in Micah.

An Epileptic Healed Matthew 17:14-21; Mark 9:14-29; Luke 9:37-43a; 17:5-6
(Glossary articles: Belief / Faith; Evil Spirits; Immediately / Quickly; Scribes)

²⁶The next day Jesus, Peter, James, and John came down the mountain to join the other disciples. When they got close, Jesus saw that a large crowd had gathered around some scribes who were arguing with his disciples.

²⁷The crowd, overjoyed to see him, began running toward Jesus. When they arrived he asked the scribes, "What were you talking about with my disciples?"

²⁸At this, a man rushed forward from the crowd and dropped to his knees in front of Jesus. "Lord," he pleaded, "Have mercy on my son, he's my only child. He's just crazy!

²⁹"He has an evil spirit that causes him to suddenly scream and then go into convulsions. The evil spirit throws him to the ground and he gets rigid, foaming at the mouth and grinding his teeth so that he can't even talk.

³⁰"When the evil spirit finally leaves him alone, he's bruised and exhausted. I begged your disciples to cure him, but they couldn't."

³¹"How long must I bear with this wicked generation of people who don't trust God?" Jesus cried out. Then he said, "Bring the child to me."

³²They brought the child to Jesus, and as he was walking to Jesus, the evil spirit sent him into a convulsion so that he fell to the ground foaming at the mouth. "How long has he been like this?" Jesus asked.

³³"Ever since he was a toddler," his dad replied. "Many times it's caused him to fall into a fire or into the water as if trying to kill him. If you can do anything, please take pity on us and help us!"

³⁴"'If you can?'" Jesus demanded. "To a person who really has faith in God, all things are possible."

³⁵Right away the child's dad cried out, "I do have faith in God! Help me with whatever's lacking in my faith!"

³⁶When Jesus saw that more people were running to get into the crowd and see what would happen, he rebuked the evil spirit. "Deaf-mute spirit! Get out of this child and never enter him again!"

³⁷At this the spirit cried out, threw the boy into a powerful convulsion, and then obeyed and came out of the child. Then the child lay so still that many in the crowd were whispering, "He's dead!"

³⁸But Jesus took the child by the hand, lifted him up, and gave him to his dad. From that time on the boy was cured[1]. And the whole crowd was amazed by this demonstration of God's power.

³⁹Later, when they were in the house, the disciples got Jesus aside and asked, "Why couldn't we deal with that evil spirit?"

⁴⁰"Your faith in God is just not strong enough," Jesus replied. "I'm telling you the absolute truth: if your faith's like a mustard seed, you'll be able to tell a tree[2] to be pulled up by the roots and cast into the sea or to tell a mountain to move, and it will do as you say. You'll be able to do anything.

⁴¹"But some like this one require that you spend serious time in prayer."

Chapter 32 – To Jerusalem for the Feast of Tents

The Feast of Tents John 7:2-29, 33-43
(Glossary articles: Belief / Faith; Christ / Messiah; Evil Spirits; Herod's Temple; Jerusalem; Jewish Feasts; Judea; Judeans / Jewish Authorities; Law of Moses; Moses; The Prophet; Sabbath; Sacred Writings)

¹Then as time for the Jewish Feast of Tents was approaching, his brothers told him, "You need to get out of here and go to Judea so that your disciples there can see the things you're doing.

²"After all, anyone who really wants to make a name for himself won't hide what he's doing. So if you can really do all this stuff, go show off to the whole world[3]."

³(Even his brothers didn't have faith in what he was doing.)

⁴"It's not time for me to go there yet," Jesus said. "You don't have anything to hold you back because those whose focus is on this world certainly can't find any reason to hate you.

⁵"But they do hate me because I tell them bluntly that the things they're doing are evil. You go on up to the feast. It's just not time for me to go yet."

⁶So his brothers left for the feast while Jesus stayed in Galilee. But after they'd left, he went to the feast too—though he arrived without any fanfare, as if keeping his arrival a secret. The Judeans were looking for him, asking each other, "Where is he?"

⁷There was a lot of muttering about him. Some folks said, "He's a good man." Others said, "No, quite the opposite! He's a deceiver." But no one was openly talking about him for fear of the Jewish authorities.

⁸Then about the middle of the feast, Jesus went into the temple and began teaching the crowds. Hearing him, the Jewish authorities were astonished and asked each other, "Where in the world did this uneducated hick get such knowledge?"

---

[1] 31:38-This indicates that the family was known to early Christians.
[2] 31:40-Literally, "a sycamine tree" that looks a lot like a mulberry tree but has fruit more like a fig tree.
[3] 32:2-Galilee was a backwater politically and religiously. Jerusalem was the political and religious center of Judaism throughout the known world. Jesus' brothers thought the religious leaders in Judea would quickly bring him down.

⁹Jesus knew what they were saying and responded, "What I teach isn't just my thoughts as a human. My teachings come from the one who sent me. If anybody wants to do his will, that person will know whether this teaching is from God or from me speaking as just another human.

¹⁰"Anybody who teaches his own thoughts is looking for people to honor him. But the man who wants to honor the one who sent him is sure to speak the truth, and there's nothing evil in him.

¹¹"Wasn't it Moses who gave you the law? Yet not one of you really keeps the law. So why do you want to kill me?"

¹²Some of the people who heard him responded, "You've got an evil spirit! Who's trying to kill you?"

¹³"Here I've done one thing," Jesus said, "and you're all astonished because I did it on a Sabbath[1].

¹⁴"Moses gave you the law of circumcision (though it really came from your ancestors before Moses), and because of this law you circumcise a male infant on the Sabbath[2].

¹⁵"Now, if a male child gets circumcised on a Sabbath to keep the Law of Moses, why are you angry with me because I healed a man on a Sabbath?

¹⁶"Don't set your standards based on appearance. Set your standards based on what's right!"

¹⁷Some of the people who lived in Jerusalem asked, "Isn't this the man they're trying to kill? Look! He's speaking out as if he didn't have a care in the world. Is it possible that the authorities actually know that he's the Christ?

¹⁸"But we know where this man's from. When the Christ comes, no one will know where he's from[3]."

¹⁹"You know me and you know where I'm from—or so you think," Jesus exclaimed, "but I haven't come for my own purposes. The one who sent me is truth itself, but you don't know him. I know him because I came from him and he sent me.

²⁰"I'll be with you a little longer, and then I'll return to the one who sent me. You'll look for me, but you won't find me. You can't go where I'll be."

²¹Then the Judeans whispered among themselves, "Where do you think he's planning to go that we wouldn't be able to find him? Do you think he's planning to go to the distant groups of Jews dispersed throughout the Roman Empire and teach those who speak Greek?

²²"And what's this about, 'You'll look for me but you won't be able to find me' and, 'You can't go where I'll be'?"

²³Then on the last day, the great day of the feast, Jesus stood and called out, "If you're thirsty, come to me and drink! The one who has faith in me, as the sacred writings[4] say, 'Rivers of living water will flow from that person's heart[5].'"

²⁴(Jesus was, of course, speaking of the Holy Spirit who'd come to those who put their faith in him. Remember, the Holy Spirit hadn't been given to his followers yet, because he himself hadn't gone back to glory.)

²⁵"Truly, this must be the Prophet," said many in the crowd when they heard Jesus' teachings.

²⁶Others said, "This is actually the Christ!"

²⁷But some asked, "Since when does the Christ come from Galilee? Don't the sacred writings[6] say that he'll be from King David's family and that he'll be born in Bethlehem just like King David was?"

²⁸So among the people at the feast there was disagreement about who he was.

An Arrest Attempt John 7:30-32; 44-53; 8:1
(Glossary articles: Belief / Faith; Christ / Messiah; Judeans / Jewish Authorities; Law of Moses; Nicodemus; Pharisees; Chief Priests; Sacred Writings)

²⁹Hearing what Jesus was saying, the Jewish authorities wanted to arrest him, but no one touched him because it wasn't his time yet.

³⁰Many of the ordinary people put their faith in him. "When the Christ comes," they asked, "how could he possibly do more than this fellow's done?"

³¹The Pharisees heard things like this in the crowd's murmurings. Then they and the chief priests sent temple policemen[7] to arrest him.

³²After a time the temple policemen came back to the chief priests and the Pharisees without Jesus.

³³"Why didn't you arrest him?" they asked.

³⁴"Nobody ever talked like this man!" they replied.

³⁵"Has he tricked you, too?" the Pharisees asked. "Have any of the Pharisees or other authorities put their faith in him? This crowd, they're all cursed. They don't know the Law of Moses at all."

³⁶"Does our law condemn a man before the evidence has been heard in court and we know what he's doing?" asked Nicodemus. (He was one of them, but some time earlier he'd come to Jesus by night expressing his faith in Jesus.)

---

[1] 32:13-The last time Jesus had been in Jerusalem, he'd healed a man on the Sabbath. See Good News 28:1-16 above.
[2] 32:14-A male infant was circumcised on the eighth day of life (Leviticus 12:3), regardless what day of the week that was. These people were taking Sabbath requirements too far in some areas while in other areas they routinely ignored these same requirements.
[3] 32:18-This was a tradition that had no basis in the sacred writings of Moses and the prophets.
[4] 32:23-Literally, "the writing."
[5] 32:23-This passage is from some sacred writing now lost.
[6] 32:27-Literally, "Doesn't the writing…"
[7] 32:31-Literally, "soldiers"—but the role of the temple soldiers was more that of policemen than soldiers.

³⁷"Are you one of those hick Galileans?" they sneered. "Search the sacred writings[1] as much as you like. No prophet's supposed to come from Galilee!"

³⁸After this exchange they all went home, but Jesus went out to the Mount of Olives.

A Woman Caught in Adultery John 8:2-11
(Glossary articles: Herod's temple; John's Gospel; Law of Moses; Pharisees; Scribes; Sin / Rebellion)

³⁹Early the next morning Jesus went back into the temple, and everybody came over to where he was. As was his custom, Jesus sat down and began teaching.

⁴⁰Then the scribes and Pharisees brought in a woman and made her stand in front of everybody[2].

⁴¹"Teacher," they sneered, "This woman was caught in the very act of adultery. As we're sure you know, the Law of Moses commands that such a woman should be stoned. So what do you think we should do[3]?"

⁴²(Of course they were testing him, trying to find something they could claim he'd done wrong[4].)

⁴³But Jesus just stooped down, and with his finger he started writing in the dirt, acting as though he didn't even hear them as they kept after him trying to get him to answer.

⁴⁴Finally he stood up and told them, "Go ahead and stone her[5], but make sure the one who throws the first stone isn't guilty of any sin against God[6]." Then he stooped down and started writing on the ground again[7].

⁴⁵Those who'd brought the woman were stunned. Each of them knew in his own conscience that he was certainly not innocent. So beginning with the older ones, every one of them walked away, leaving the woman standing in front of the crowd.

⁴⁶Jesus stood up again and saw that only the woman was left. "Woman," he said, "where are the people who brought this accusation against you? Has no one stayed here to condemn you?"

⁴⁷"No one, Lord," she replied.

⁴⁸"Then I'm not going to condemn you either[8]," Jesus told her. "Go your way and stop sinning against God."

Chapter 33 – Teaching in the Temple – Part 1

The Light of the World John 8:12-29
(Glossary articles: Belief / Faith; Herod's Temple; Judeans / Jewish Authorities; Law of Moses; Pharisees; Sin / Rebellion; Son of Man)

¹Jesus then returned to teaching. "I AM[9] the light of the world," he said, "Those who follow me will find themselves walking in the light of life, not in darkness at all."

²At this the Pharisees said, "You're bragging about yourself. If you don't have any proof in the form of others who'll testify to what you're saying, your testimony isn't worth your breath."

³"Even if I were bragging about myself," Jesus responded, "my testimony would still be true because I know where I've come from and I know where I'm going.

⁴"You don't have a clue where I came from or where I'm going. You can only judge by human standards.

⁵"I'm not trying to judge anybody. Still, if I were to judge, my judgment would be right on. After all, I'm not alone—the Father who sent me is with me.

⁶"So let's see what testimony I have. In the Law of Moses it says that the testimony of two witnesses should be considered true. OK, I AM[10] the first one who bears witness to myself, and the Father who sent me also bears witness to what I say."

⁷"So where's your 'father'?" they demanded.

⁸"You don't know me or my Father," Jesus replied. "If you'd known me, you'd also have known my Father."

⁹(Jesus said these things while he was in the treasury area of the temple teaching, and no one arrested him because it wasn't time yet.)

¹⁰Then Jesus continued: "I'm going away, and you'll look for me, but you'll die in your sins. You can't come where I'm going."

---

[1] 32:37-Literally, "Search as much as you like," but "in the sacred writings" is clearly implied.

[2] 32:40-This account is missing in some of the most ancient manuscripts. However, it certainly fits with both Jesus and his adversaries.

[3] 32:41-We can't help but wonder, if this woman was caught in the very act of adultery, where was the adulterer?

[4] 32:42-Obviously Jesus had a reputation for mercy and forgiveness that made his adversaries think he wouldn't condemn this woman.

[5] 32:44-Jesus commanded them to stone the woman. That was what the Law said to do if there were two or more witnesses.

[6] 32:44-Remember, sin is always treason—rebellion against God.

[7] 32:44-Some have speculated that Jesus was writing various sins that he knew these accusers had committed, and as they looked at what he was writing, they were convicted by their own consciences. That's certainly possible.

[8] 32:48-When all the witnesses against this woman were gone, Jesus again followed the Law by not condemning her.

[9] 33:1-The "I AM" here is very emphatic.

[10] 33:6-The "I AM" here is very emphatic and would remind these religious leaders of God bearing witness to himself when Moses asked who God is (Exodus 3:14).

¹¹At this the Judeans began asking each other, "Is he going to kill himself? Is that what he means by saying, 'You can't come where I'm going'?"

¹²"You're from below." Jesus told them. "I'm from above. You're of this physical world. I'm not a part of this physical world.

¹³"That's why I told you that you'll die in your sins. And if you don't have faith that I AM[1] who I claim to be, you definitely will die in your sins."

¹⁴"OK," they replied, "so who are you?"

¹⁵"Haven't you been paying attention?" Jesus asked. "I've been telling you ever since the beginning, and I've got lots more to tell you (and to judge about what you're doing).

¹⁶"But the bottom line is that the one who sent me is true, and the things I say in this world I heard from him."

¹⁷(These Judeans still didn't understand that he was talking about God as his Father.)

¹⁸Then Jesus told them, "When you lift me up as a human[2], then you'll realize that I AM[3] exactly who I've always claimed to be, and that nothing I do comes strictly from my human nature.

¹⁹"Rather, I talk about these things just as my Father's taught me to do. He's the one who sent me, and he's with me now.

²⁰"The Father's never left me alone because I always do what I know will please him[4]."

Children of Abraham or Satan? John 8:30-59
(Glossary articles: Abraham; Belief / Faith; Caring Love; Evil Spirits; Herod's Temple; Judeans / Jewish Authorities; Satan; Slaves; Sin / Rebellion)

²¹As Jesus was teaching these things in the temple, many in the crowd put their faith in him.

²²Then Jesus told the Judeans who did put their faith in him, "If you continue to live by the things I teach, you're truly my disciples, and you'll know the truth when you see it, and the truth will always set you free."

²³At this some of the Judeans said, "We're descendants of Abraham, and we've never been slaves to anybody! How can you tell us that we will be set free?"

²⁴"I'm telling you the absolute truth," Jesus said: "anybody who commits even one act of sin against God[5] becomes a slave to sin.

²⁵"Although you think of yourselves as slaves in God's house, a slave isn't a permanent part of the family, but a son is a permanent part of the family. So if the son sets you free, then you really are free.

²⁶"I know you're descendants of Abraham, but you want to kill me because the things I've said to you don't fit in your idea of things. I'm talking about what I've seen with my Father. Similarly, you're doing what you've seen with your father."

²⁷"Abraham's our father!" they exclaimed.

²⁸"If you were really Abraham's children," Jesus responded, "you'd do the things Abraham would do. But instead you're looking for a way to kill me—a human who's only told you the truth that I heard from God.

²⁹"Abraham never did anything like that! Yes, you really are doing the thing that your father does."

³⁰"We're no bastards!" they exclaimed. "We've got one father—and that's God himself!"

³¹"If God were really your father," Jesus said, "you'd love me since I'm an integral part of God, and I came out from God. And I didn't come out on my own—he sent me.

³²"Why do you think you can't understand what I'm telling you? It's because you can't comprehend what I'm saying. You're actually of your father, just as I said, and your father's the devil himself.

³³"The things you want to do are the things your father wants to do. He was a murderer from the very beginning.

³⁴"He doesn't hold to the truth, because there's no truth in him. When he tells a lie, he's speaking from his very nature. He's a liar and the father of all lies.

³⁵"And because I come telling you the truth, you won't believe a thing I say.

³⁶"Which one of you can show that I've ever committed any sin against God? And if you can't, then I must be telling the truth, so why won't you believe me?

³⁷"Anybody who belongs to God listens to what God has to say. That's why you don't listen to me, because you don't belong to God."

³⁸"Well," some of the Jewish authorities responded, "aren't we justified in calling you a Samaritan and saying that you've got an evil spirit[6]?"

---

[1] 33:13-The "I AM" here is very emphatic.
[2] 33:18-Literally, "when the son of man is lifted up…"
[3] 33:18-The "I AM" here is very emphatic.
[4] 33:20-Jesus avoided a clear statement of who he really is at this point. It wasn't time yet for the final confrontation, but neither would he deny who he really is.
[5] 33:24-Remember, sin is always treason—rebellion against God.
[6] 33:38-When these leaders called Jesus a Samaritan, they resorted to name-calling. If you resort to name-calling, you make it clear that you yourself think you're wrong and you have no better defense of your position.

³⁹"I don't have an evil spirit," Jesus responded. "I honor my Father, and because I honor my Father, you try to smear me. I'm not looking to glorify myself. God's the one who'll glorify me, and he's the one who'll judge you!

⁴⁰"I'm telling you the absolute truth: if anybody lives by my teachings, that person will never experience death."

⁴¹"Now we know for a fact that you've got an evil spirit!" the Jewish authorities exclaimed. "Abraham's dead, and so are the prophets; yet you're saying, 'If anybody lives by my teachings, that person will never experience death.'

⁴²"Are you greater than Abraham? Because he's certainly dead. And what about the prophets. What are you trying to make yourself out to be?"

⁴³"If I try to get honor for myself," Jesus replied, "that honor isn't worth anything. It's my Father who honors me. And my Father's the one you call your God, but you've never known him.

⁴⁴"I know him, and if I were to say, 'I don't know him,' I'd be a liar like you. But I do know him, and I live by the things he says.

⁴⁵"Abraham, whom you claim as your father, rejoiced to see the day when I came to the world. He saw that day, and he was glad to see it."

⁴⁶At this the Jewish authorities scoffed, "You're not even fifty years old, and are you claiming that you've seen Abraham?"

⁴⁷"I'm telling you the absolute truth," Jesus replied: "before Abraham even existed, I AM¹!"

⁴⁸At this the religious authorities picked up stones to throw at him, but Jesus slipped out of sight and left the temple, walking right through the middle of the crowd.

Chapter 34 – Teaching in the Temple – Part 2
<u>Healing a Man Born Blind</u> John 9:1-41
(Glossary articles: Belief / Faith; Herod's Temple; Judeans / Jewish Authorities; Miracles; Moses; Pharisees; Sabbath; Sin / Rebellion; Son of God; Sons and Fathers in Biblical Thinking)

¹As Jesus walked away, he and his disciples spotted a man who'd been blind from birth². "Teacher," his disciples asked, "why was this fellow born blind? Was it his own sin against God³ or his parents'⁴ sins?"

²"This affliction wasn't the result of this fellow's sin or of his parents' sins," Jesus responded. "It happened so that God's power could be demonstrated in this man's life.

³"I need to do the work God sent me to do as long as the light of day lasts. There's a dark night coming when no one will be able to work, but as long as I'm in this world, I AM⁵ the very light of the world."

⁴Having said this, he spit on the ground and used the damp earth to spread over the blind man's eyes. Then he told the man, "Go wash in Messenger Pool⁶.'"

⁵The blind man obeyed, and when he came back, he could see clearly. Others in the neighborhood realized that he was no longer blind, and they questioned among themselves, "Isn't this the guy who used to sit and beg as a blind man?"

⁶Some said, "Yes, it's definitely him."

⁷Others said, "It sure looks like him."

⁸Then the man himself said, "Absolutely, that was me⁷!"

⁹People in the neighborhood gathered around him asking, "How were you healed of your blindness?"

¹⁰"A man called Jesus made some mud and coated my eyes with it," He answered. "Then he told me, 'Go wash in Messenger Pool.' So I went and washed in the pool, and as soon as I did, I could see."

¹¹"Where is this guy?" they were all asking.

¹²"I don't know," replied the man who'd been healed.

¹³So they brought the man who'd been blind to the Pharisees⁸. (It was a Sabbath when Jesus healed the man.) They had the man repeat the story about how he'd gained his sight.

¹⁴"Jesus put clay on my eyes," he replied, "and when I washed my eyes, I could see."

¹⁵"It's obvious that this man isn't doing God's will," some of the Pharisees scoffed. "He doesn't obey the Sabbath restrictions."

---

¹ 33:47-The "I AM" here is very emphatic.
² 34:1-The Bible doesn't tell us how they knew this man was born blind.
³ 34:1-Remember, sin is always treason—rebellion against God.
⁴ 34:1-Jesus had probably been telling his disciples that God doesn't punish a person for his or her ancestors' sins (see Ezekiel 18). So if it wasn't ancestors' sins and the man was born blind before he could sin, what was the cause of this affliction? The disciples didn't consider the possibility that just the environment of sin in this world brings all kinds of afflictions (see Genesis 3).
⁵ 34:3-The "I AM" here is very emphatic.
⁶ 34:4-This pool is generally referred to in other translations as "the Pool of Siloam," but in this passage John takes care to translate "Siloam." So why the mud? Why wash in this specific pool? Why did John translate "Siloam?" We don't know the answers.
⁷ 34:8-Literally, "I AM, and the "I AM" here is very emphatic.
⁸ 34:13-This formerly blind man was brought to the Pharisees because they asked people to do this, looking for evidence against Jesus.

¹⁶However, others of the Pharisees asked, "How can a sinner who isn't obeying God perform such miracles?" This led to a disagreement among the Pharisees about Jesus.

¹⁷Then some of them asked the blind man, "What's your opinion about this guy who healed your blindness?"

¹⁸"He's a prophet!" replied the man who'd been healed.

¹⁹At this the Jewish authorities questioned whether he'd actually been blind. They called for his parents and asked them, "Is this man your son? And do you claim that he was born blind? If so, how can he see now?"

²⁰"We know that this is our son," they responded, "and we know that he was born blind. But we don't have a clue how he can see now, and we don't know who healed his blindness. He's an adult, let him speak for himself."

²¹(The man's parents said this because they were afraid of the Jewish authorities who'd already made it clear that anyone who held that Jesus was the Christ would be barred from the worship center[1]. That's why his parents said, "He's an adult, let him speak for himself.")

²²So the authorities called for the man who'd been blind and told him, "Give the glory to God. We know that this Jesus is a sinner."

²³"Whether or not he's a sinner," the man replied, "I don't know. What I do know is that I was blind, and now I can see."

²⁴"But what did he do to you?" the authorities asked. "How did he cure your blindness?"

²⁵"I already told you," the man responded, "but you weren't listening. Why would you want to hear it again? Do you want to become his disciples?"

²⁶At this the authorities began insulting him. "You're his disciple!" they scoffed, "We're Moses' disciples! We know that God spoke to Moses! As for this guy, we don't know what he's up to."

²⁷"That's pretty surprising," the man replied, "that you don't know what he's up to; yet he opened my eyes!

²⁸"We all know that God doesn't listen to those who sin against him. He listens to those who worship him and do his will.

²⁹"Yet ever since the world began, nobody has ever heard of anyone born blind whose eyes were then opened. If this guy weren't sent by God, he couldn't do anything!"

³⁰"You've been covered in sin from the day you were born!" they responded. And they barred him from the worship centers.

³¹Jesus heard that he'd been barred from the worship centers, so he went to him and asked, "Are you ready to put your faith in the son of God?"

³²"I'm ready to put my faith in him, lord," the man replied. "Who is he?"

³³"Well you've seen him," Jesus said, "because he's talking with you right now."

³⁴"Lord," the man responded, "I put my faith in you!" And he fell to his knees before Jesus.

³⁵"I came into this world," Jesus said, "to bring judgment—so that those who are spiritually blind may see and so that those who claim to have spiritual sight may be blinded."

³⁶Some of the Pharisees were in the crowd around Jesus and heard him say this. "Are you saying that we're blind too?" they asked.

³⁷"No," Jesus replied. "If you were blind, you wouldn't be guilty of sin, but because you claim, 'We see,' you're indeed guilty.

The Good Shepherd John 10:1-21
(Glossary articles: Caring Love; Evil Spirits; Judeans / Jewish Authorities)

³⁸"I'm telling you the absolute truth," Jesus continued: "anybody who enters a sheepfold without using the gate is sure to be a thief—a person intent on stealing sheep.

³⁹"The person who enters by the gate is the shepherd, and the guard at the gate opens the gate for the shepherd. The shepherd calls his sheep by name, and they listen to his voice.

⁴⁰"The shepherd leads his sheep out, walking in front of them, and the sheep follow him because they know his voice.

⁴¹"The sheep won't follow a stranger—indeed, they'll run from him because they don't recognize his voice."

⁴²Jesus used this illustration, but the people didn't understand what he was getting at, so he continued:

⁴³"I'm telling you the absolute truth," he said: "I AM[2] the gate for the sheep.

⁴⁴"All those who previously claimed to be the gate to God were thieves, intent on stealing sheep, but the sheep wouldn't listen to them.

⁴⁵"I AM[3] the gate. Anyone who comes in through me will be rescued. That person will freely enter and leave the sheepfold, finding safe pastures.

⁴⁶"The thief comes to steal, to kill, and to destroy the flock. But I've come to bring life—a life more abundant than the sheep have ever known before.

⁴⁷"I AM[1] the good shepherd. A truly good shepherd will give his life for the sheep.

---

[1] 34:21-To be barred from worship center meant being pushed out of family and community affairs. It would be hard even to buy food in the market. This was far from trivial.

[2] 34:43-The "I AM" here is very emphatic.

[3] 34:45-The "I AM" here is very emphatic.

⁴⁸"Someone who doesn't own any of the sheep but who's just a hired hand watching the sheep for pay will run away when he sees a wolf pack coming. Then the wolves can take a sheep and scatter the whole flock.

⁴⁹"The hired hand runs away because he's a hired hand and doesn't really care what happens to the sheep.

⁵⁰"I AM[2] the good shepherd. I know my sheep, and my sheep know me. Just as the Father knows me, I know the Father, and I give my life for the sheep.

⁵¹"I have other sheep, too, who aren't part of this flock. I need to bring them into the flock. They'll hear my voice and join the flock so that there'll be just one flock all under one shepherd.

⁵²"That's why my Father cares so much for me, because I'll surrender my life so that I can take it up again.

⁵³"No one can take my life from me. But I volunteer to surrender my life. I have the ability to give up my life and I have the ability to take it back again. This is what my Father told me to do."

⁵⁴All of this led to controversy among the Judeans. A lot of them said, "He's a madman and possessed by an evil spirit. Why even listen to him?"

⁵⁵"This isn't how someone with an evil spirit talks," others replied. "Can an evil spirit heal blind eyes?"

"My Father and I Are One" John 10:22-39
(Glossary articles: Belief / Faith; Christ; Herod's Temple; Judeans / Jewish Authorities; Law of Moses; Son of God; Sons and Fathers in Biblical Thinking)

⁵⁶During the Dedication Festival (a winter festival) Jesus was in the temple in the area known as Solomon's porch, and there was a crowd of Judeans around him.

⁵⁷"How long," they asked, "are you going to keep us in suspense? If you're the Christ, just tell us in plain words."

⁵⁸"I already told you," Jesus responded, "and you don't have faith in what I told you.

⁵⁹"The miraculous works that I'm doing in my Father's name are a solid testimony to who I am, but you don't put your faith in me because you're not part of my flock.

⁶⁰"As I told you, my sheep listen to what I have to say. I know them, and they follow me. I'm giving them life everlasting. They'll never die, and nobody can take them out of the protection of my Father.

⁶¹"The Father and I are one!"

⁶²At this some of the Judeans began to pick up stones, planning to stone him to death. Jesus asked them, "Of all the many good things I've demonstrated by my Father's power, which of them causes you to want to stone me?"

⁶³"We're not going to stone you because of something good you've done," they replied, "but because you've lied about God. You—just a human—claim to be God!"

⁶⁴"Well," said Jesus, "doesn't the Law of Moses quote God as saying, 'I said, "You're gods[3]"'?

⁶⁵"So if God called those to whom his message had come gods (and you can't get around that passage), how can you say 'You're lying about God,' just because I've said, 'I'm the son of God?'

⁶⁶"You'd be right not to trust me if I weren't doing things that are obviously from my Father.

⁶⁷"But if I'm doing those things, even though you don't trust me, put your faith in the things you see me doing. In that way, maybe you'll understand and have faith that the Father is in me and that I am in him."

⁶⁸Then the Jewish authorities tried to arrest Jesus, but he slipped away.

Chapter 35 – Encamped along the Jordan[4]
Warnings of Future Trouble[5] Matthew 10:17-39; 16:24-28; Mark 8:34-38; 9:1; 13:9-13; Luke 6:40; 9:23-27; 12:2-9, 11-12, 49-53; 14:25-33; 17:33; 21:12-19; John 10:40-42; 12:25
(Glossary articles: Baptize / Immerse; Biblical Names; Gentiles / Nations; Hell; Miracles: Preaching / Proclaiming; Satan)

¹Jesus went to an area just across the Jordan River where John had been immersing converts during his ministry. He set up camp there, and many of the people from that area came out to him.

²"John performed no miracles," they said, "but everything he said about this man turned out to be true." So many of these people put their faith in him while he was there.

³Then he turned to them and said, "Don't be too trusting of others. Some people will arrest you and take you to court, and they'll whip you right in their places of worship!

⁴"Everybody's going to hate you and you'll be dragged in front of the authorities and governors and even kings. You'll be thrown into prison just because you're my disciples.

---

[1] 34:47-The "I AM" here is very emphatic.
[2] 34:50-The "I AM" here is very emphatic.
[3] 34:64-Psalm 86:6.
[4] The title of this chapter assumes that the first two sections occurred during the time that Jesus was encamped by the Jordan, but the Bible doesn't actually say where Jesus was when these things happened. Where this happened isn't important. The third section did happen during that encampment.
[5] This section is a blend of several passages sharing common themes. These are things Jesus taught over and over at different times during the latter part of his ministry, so blending them here is as reasonable as any other point this late in the ministry.

⁵"When you appear before these rulers, you'll be able to testify to them and to all the nations. The good news I've brought you must be proclaimed to every nation before the end comes.

⁶"And when you're arrested and turned over to the authorities, take that as an opportunity to give your testimony to them. The decision should already be firm in your mind not to worry about or even try to plan ahead for what you should say.

⁷"When it's time for you to speak up, you'll be given exactly the right words to say because your Father's Holy Spirit will be speaking through you. Just say what he gives you to say.

⁸"I'll give you wisdom so that none of your adversaries will be able to contradict you or deny the truth of what you say.

⁹"I've come to set the world afire, and I wish that fire were already burning! I've got an immersion[1] to go through, until I get that done I'm severely limited in what I can do!

¹⁰"Did you think I came to bring peace on earth? Not even close[2]!

¹¹"My coming here will bring division and even the sword more than it will bring peace! From now on if there are five people living in a house, there'll be two on one side and three on the other.

¹²"A man will turn his own brother over to the authorities to be killed, and a father will turn in his own children. Children will turn against their own parents and have them executed.

¹³"A mother will turn against her daughter, and a daughter will turn against her mother, and the same between a daughter-in-law and her mother-in-law.

¹⁴"Your enemies will often be those in your own home! You'll be betrayed by parents, brothers, relatives, and friends.

¹⁵"People from all over will turn against you just because you're my disciples. But whoever remains faithful to the end will be saved[3].

¹⁶"When they treat you cruelly in one city, run to the next one. I'm telling you the absolute truth: you won't get through all the cities in Israel before I come.

¹⁷"I'm the master of God's house, but if people have called me Satan[4], you shouldn't be surprised by anything they call my followers. But don't let them scare you. The time's coming when all secrets and all hidden things will be brought out into the light[5].

¹⁸"So the things that I tell you during the dark of night, you're to talk about openly in the light of day, and what you hear me whisper in your ear, you're to proclaim from the housetops.

¹⁹"They'll kill some of you, but don't be afraid of people who can kill your body but who cannot kill your soul[6].

²⁰"Instead, fear the one who can destroy both the body and the soul in the garbage dump of hell. Yes indeed, you need to be in awe of him!

²¹"You can buy two sparrows for one copper coin, can't you? Yet not one of those sparrows falls to the ground unless your Father allows it.

²²"And I tell you, God even knows exactly how many hairs there are on your head, and in the end not one of them will be lost. By being steadfast in your commitment to me, you'll gain your souls for all eternity.

²³"So I'm telling you: don't be afraid. You're worth a lot more than an entire flock of sparrows.

The Cost of Discipleship[7] Matthew 10:24-25, 32-33, 37-39; 16:24-28; Mark 8:34-38; 9:1; Luke 6:40; 9:23-27; 12:8-9; 14:25-33; 17:33; John 12:25
(Glossary articles: Agent / Angel; Caring Love; Slaves; Son of Man)

²⁴"And if you care about[8] your dad or your mom more than you care about me, you're not worthy to be my disciple.

²⁵"Yes, even if you care about[9] your own children more than you care about me, you're not worthy to be my disciple.

²⁶"Indeed, if you want to follow me, and yet you aren't willing to turn against your dad, your mom, your wife, your kids, your brothers, your sisters, yes, and even your own life too, you can't be my disciple.

²⁷"Disciples aren't greater than their teachers, nor are slaves greater than their masters.

²⁸"It's the goal of a teacher to train the mature disciples to be like their teacher, and it's the goal of a master to teach his slaves to do things as the master would do them.

---

[1] 35:9-Translating this word as "immersion" brings out the depths of suffering into which Jesus was about to be plunged.
[2] 35:10-Jesus calls on his disciples to be peacemakers and people of peace, but in this passage he was prophesying what would happen, not because of what Christians would do, but because of how the world would respond to Christians.
[3] 35:15-Those with saving faith are faithful. Those who aren't faithful don't have saving faith. It's that simple.
[4] 35:17-Literally, "Beelzebub" rather than "Satan," but the meaning is obvious.
[5] 35:17-Jesus has a very important lesson here. Living with secrets is unhealthy physically and spiritually, and in the end it's a wasted effort.
[6] 35:19-The soul is who you are at your inner most being. God will give you a new, better, and eternal body, but it's your soul that matters.
[7] This section is a blend of several passages sharing common themes. These are things Jesus taught over and over at different times during the latter part of his ministry, so blending them here is as reasonable as any other point this late in the ministry.
[8] 35:24-This refers to the caring love that is Christian love.
[9] 35:25-This refers to the caring love that is Christian love.

²⁹"If anyone speaks up for me in front of others, I'll speak up for that person in front of my Father in heaven and his holy agents.

³⁰"But if anyone speaks against me in front of others, I'll speak against that person in front of my Father in heaven and his holy agents.

³¹"Indeed," Jesus told his disciples and those standing around him, "if you want to follow my ways, you've got to take the focus of your life off of yourself!

³²"You've got to face every day ready to be executed as a criminal just because you're my disciple—living as I've taught you. Otherwise you're not worth anything to me, and you cannot be my disciple[1].

³³"If one of you decided to build a tower, wouldn't you first sit down to calculate the cost and see if you can afford to build it? Otherwise, you might get the foundation done and run out of money.

³⁴"Then every time people looked at the unfinished foundation, they'd start laughing at you, saying, 'This guy started out to build his great tower, but he couldn't get the job done.'

³⁵"Or if one king were about to go to war against another king, wouldn't he first sit down and see if he had some strategy for using his ten thousand soldiers to defeat a king with twenty thousand soldiers? And if he couldn't come up with that strategy, he'd send messengers to negotiate for peace.

³⁶"In the same way, if you're not willing to give up all your worldly possessions for me, you cannot be my disciple!

³⁷"And anyone who tries to cling to this life will surely lose it, but anyone who loses this worldly life for following me and spreading the good news of the kingdom will find true life indeed!

³⁸"What good is it if you get so rich that you own the whole world and then lose your eternal soul? Really, what earthly treasure do you think you could exchange for your soul?

³⁹"If you're ashamed of me and the things I've taught in this unfaithful and rebellious world, then I as a human[2] will be ashamed of you when I return in the glory of my Father with all the holy agents of God.

⁴⁰"Yes, I as a human[3] will surely come in the glory of my Father with his heavenly agents to reward everybody according to each one's deeds in this world.

⁴¹"I'm telling you the absolute truth: there are some of you here who won't experience the bitter taste of death before you see me as a human[4] coming into my royal authority[5].

Being on God's Side Matthew 10:40-42; Mark 9:41; John 13:20

⁴²"Anyone who accepts you is accepting me, and anyone who accepts me is accepting the one who sent me.

⁴³"Anyone who accepts a prophet as a prophet will certainly receive a prophet's reward, and anyone who accepts a righteous man as a righteous man will certainly receive a righteous man's reward.

⁴⁴"And anyone who, acting as my disciple, gives a cup of cold water, even though just to a little child, I'm telling you the absolute truth: that person's certain to receive the appropriate reward."

Lazarus Dies John 11:1-16
(Glossary articles: Belief / Faith; Caring Love; Lazarus; Judeans / Jewish Authorities; Son of God)

⁴⁵Now a man named Lazarus became very ill. He was the brother of Mary and Martha, and the three of them lived in Bethany. The sisters sent word to Jesus saying, "Lord, our brother, for whom you care so deeply, is very ill."

⁴⁶When Jesus received this message, he told his disciples, "This illness isn't fatal. Rather, Lazarus' illness is to bring glory to God so that I as the Son of God may also be glorified through this illness." (Jesus did deeply care for Lazarus and his sisters.)

⁴⁷After hearing that Lazarus was sick, Jesus stayed put for two more days. Then he said to his disciples, "Now, let's go back to Judea."

⁴⁸"Teacher," the disciples responded, "the Jewish authorities there were just trying to stone you to death. Why on earth do you want to go back?"

⁴⁹"There are just twelve hours in a day, right?" Jesus replied, "And when you travel in the daylight, you don't stumble because you can see the road clearly in the daylight.

⁵⁰"But if you try to travel at night, you'll stumble for sure, because you don't have the light shining on you."

⁵¹After saying this, Jesus continued, "Our friend Lazarus is sleeping, but I'm headed there to wake him up."

---

[1] 35:32-This whole section is extremely important. Christianity is serious business. Remember, this section is made up of things Jesus said repeatedly during his ministry. You cannot be his disciple, and you cannot be saved, if you don't make him first in your life—above all worldly possessions, above all family members and loved ones, and even above your own life in this world. The word "Christian" means "slave of Christ," and that's what Christ demands. When a person is immersed as a Christian, that person needs to understand that this is the decision he or she is making.

[2] 35:39-Literally, "the son of man..."

[3] 35:40-Literally, "the son of man..."

[4] 35:41-Literally, "the son of man..."

[5] 35:41-This is a reference to Jesus coming in his kingly authority at his resurrection, not a reference to the second coming.

⁵²"Lord," the disciples responded, "If he's sleeping, he'll get well on his own." (Of course, Jesus was talking about Lazarus having died, but the disciples thought he meant that Lazarus was just getting some rest that would help him heal.)

⁵³Then Jesus told the disciples frankly, "Lazarus is dead, and for your sakes, I'm glad I wasn't there when he died so that this will strengthen your faith. But now let's go to him."

⁵⁴Thomas (who's also known as 'the Twin') told the other disciples, "Let's go too, so that we can die with him."

Chapter 36 – A Trip to Bethany

<u>Lazarus Raised from the Dead</u> John 11:17-44
(Glossary articles: Belief / Faith; Christ / Messiah; Caring Love; Lazarus; Judeans / Jewish Authorities; Son of God; Sons and Fathers in Biblical Thinking)

¹The town of Bethany where Mary, Martha, and Lazarus lived was about two miles from Jerusalem. When Jesus got close to Bethany, he heard that Lazarus had been buried four days earlier.

²As soon as Martha heard that Jesus was in town, she went out to meet him. (Mary was still sitting in the house.)

³When Martha came to Jesus, she said, "Lord, if you'd only been here, my brother wouldn't have died. And even now, I know that God will grant you anything you ask."

⁴"Your brother will rise again," Jesus responded.

⁵"I know he's going to rise again," Martha replied, "in the resurrection at the end of time."

⁶"I AM[1] the resurrection and the very essence of life," Jesus told her. "If you put your faith in me, even though you may die, you'll still be alive.

⁷"In fact, anyone who's alive and who has faith in me will absolutely never die. Do you trust me in this matter?"

⁸"Yes, Lord," Martha said. "I have faith in you because you're the Christ, the son of God. You're the one the prophets told us would come into our world."

⁹After saying this, Martha went back to the house and quietly told Mary, "The teacher's here, and he's asking for you."

¹⁰Jesus was still outside town where Martha had met him. As soon as Mary heard that Jesus was asking about her, she got up and went to him.

¹¹Several Judeans had come to Bethany to comfort Mary and Martha in the loss of their brother, and when they saw Mary get up suddenly and leave the house, they followed her. They said to themselves, "She's going to the tomb to mourn there."

¹²When Mary got to Jesus she fell to her knees in front of him and said, "Lord, if you'd been here my brother wouldn't have died."

¹³When Jesus saw her crying, and the Judeans who'd come with her also crying, he was so troubled that his breathing became labored.

¹⁴"Where have you laid his body?" he asked as he started to weep.

¹⁵"See how much he cared for him!" some of the Judeans said.

¹⁶Others asked, "If this man was able to heal a man born blind, couldn't he also have kept this man from dying?"

¹⁷Then Jesus, still deeply troubled, came to the tomb—a cave with a large stone in front of the entrance. Jesus told the people with him, "Remove the stone from the entrance!"

¹⁸"Lord," exclaimed Martha, "He's been in there four days! He'll stink!"

¹⁹"Didn't I tell you," Jesus replied, "that if you put your faith in me, you'll see the very glory of God?"

²⁰At this some men removed the stone from the entrance to the cave where Lazarus' body was lying.

²¹Then Jesus looked up toward heaven and prayed, "Father, I'm so grateful that you've listened to me.

²²"I know you always listen to me, but I'm saying this for the benefit of the people standing here, so that they may come to have faith in me as the one you've sent into this world."

²³When he'd finished praying, he called out at the top of his voice, "Lazarus, come out of there!"

²⁴As soon as he said it, Lazarus came shuffling out of the tomb, bound hand and foot with the strips of cloth used to prepare him for burial and with a cloth covering his face.

²⁵Then Jesus told the people standing near him, "Get him out of those grave clothes."

<u>A Resolution to Kill Jesus</u> John 11:45-54
(Glossary articles: Belief / Faith; Biblical Names; Disciples; High Priest; Judeans / Jewish Authorities; Miracles; Pharisees; Chief Priests; Romans and Jews; Supreme Court)

²⁶When they saw what Jesus had done, many of the Judeans who'd been with Mary and Martha put their faith in him. But some of the Judeans went straight to the Pharisees and told them what Jesus had done.

²⁷Then the chief priests and the Pharisees called together the Jewish Supreme Court[2]. "What are we going to do?" they said. "This man's working all kinds of miracles!

---

[1] 36:6-The "I AM" here is very emphatic.
[2] 36:27-This court was the supreme authority for religious matters among the Jews and was also the local political authority. It is often translated as the Council or Sanhedrin, but Supreme Court does a better job of communicating who these men were. See Supreme Court in the Glossary.

^{28}"If we let things go on like this, soon everybody will put their faith in him instead of us. Then the Romans will come with their soldiers to remove us from office and take away our status as a nation!"

^{29}"You don't get it!" said one of the group[1] who was high priest that year. "You're just not thinking! After all, it's better for one man to die for the nation than for the whole nation to perish."

^{30}(Now when the high priest said this, he didn't have a clue that, as the high priest, he was being led to predict that Jesus would die for the nation—and it wasn't just for that nation that Jesus would die. No, his death would gather together as one people all the children of God scattered around the whole world.)

^{31}From that day on the Jewish authorities began to seriously plot Jesus' death.

^{32}Because he was aware of their plots, Jesus wouldn't move openly among the Judeans. Instead he left there and went to a city[2] on the edge of a wilderness area, and he remained there with his disciples.

Chapter 37 – The Final Trip from Galilee to Jerusalem

A Lament for Jerusalem Matthew 23:37-39; Luke 13:31-35
(Glossary articles: Caring Love; Evil Spirits; Herod; In the Name of...; Jerusalem; Pharisees)

^{1}One day some Pharisees came to Jesus when he was back in Galilee and said, "Get out of here! Herod[3] wants to kill you!"

^{2}"Go tell that old fox," Jesus replied, "'Look here, I'm going to chase evil spirits out of people and cure people today and tomorrow, and the third day my job will be done.'

^{3}"Nevertheless, I will need to travel today and tomorrow and the day after that because it just can't be that a prophet would get killed outside of Jerusalem.

^{4}"O Jerusalem, Jerusalem! You're the one who kills the prophets and stones the messengers that God sends!

^{5}"You don't know how many times I've wanted to gather all your children together as a mother hen gathers her chicks under her wings, but you wouldn't tolerate my caring love.

^{6}"Now just look at what's coming. Your home will be a scene of destruction.

^{7}"I'm telling you the truth: you'll not see me after this until the time when you're ready to say, 'Great joy to the one who comes in the power and glory of God[4]!'"

Ten Lepers Healed Luke 9:51a; 17:11-19
(Glossary articles: Belief / Faith; Jerusalem; Jews and Samaritans)

^{8}When Jesus knew that it was time for him to be killed, he set out for Jerusalem, determined to fulfill God's plan. On his way to Jerusalem near the border between Galilee and Samaria, Jesus entered a village where he met ten men with leprosy. They actually stood some distance away from Jesus and called out, "Jesus, Master, have mercy on us!"

^{9}When Jesus noticed them he simply said, "Go show yourselves to the priests!"

^{10}As soon as they started toward the priests their disease was healed. One of them, when he noticed that the disease was healed, hurried back shouting praises to God.

^{11}Then he fell on his face in front of Jesus, thanking him over and over. (This man was a Samaritan.)

^{12}"Didn't I heal ten men?" asked Jesus. "Where are the other nine? Didn't any of them except this foreigner come back to praise God?"

^{13}Then Jesus told the man in front of him, "Get up and be on your way. Your faith in me has brought you this healing."

Fire from the Sky Luke 9:51b-56
(Glossary articles: Elijah; James; Jews and Samaritans; John; Son of Man)

^{14}As he continued toward Jerusalem, Jesus sent messengers ahead to arrange lodgings for the group.

^{15}The messengers came to a Samaritan village along the way, expecting to arrange lodgings there for Jesus. But the Samaritans wouldn't provide lodgings because he was headed for Jerusalem.

^{16}When James and John heard this, they asked, "Lord, should we command fire from the sky to come down and destroy them like Elijah did[5]?"

^{17}"You don't understand what spiritual power has hold of you," Jesus answered.

^{18}"I didn't come as a human[6] to destroy the lives of other humans, but to save them." So they went on to another village.

---

[1] 36:29-Caiaphas, the high priest appointed by the Romans.
[2] 36:32-The city was called Ephraim.
[3] 37:1-This was Herod Antipas, son of Herod the Great.
[4] 37:7-Literally, "in his name."
[5] 37:16-Elijah prayed for fire from the sky to consume a sacrifice and to consume some soldiers sent to take him, but he never prayed for destruction of a town.
[6] 37:18-Literally, "the son of man didn't come…"

Final Warnings of Jesus' Death Matthew 20:17-19; Mark 10:32-34; Luke 13:22; 18:31-34
(Glossary articles: Chief Priests; Jerusalem; Scribes; Son of Man)

¹⁹On this final trip to Jerusalem, Jesus walked ahead of the group, and those who followed felt a growing sense of dread.

²⁰Then Jesus took his twelve disciples aside along the road and told them, "Pay attention now. We're on our way up to Jerusalem, and when we get there, everything the prophets predicted about me as a human[1] will actually happen.

²¹"There I'll be[2] betrayed to the chief priests and scribes, and they'll condemn me to death.

²²"They'll deliver me to the Romans who'll make fun of me, insult me, whip me, spit on me, and finally crucify me. But the third day I'll rise up from the dead."

²³But the disciples just couldn't grasp any of this. They'd become so certain of his power that their minds just wouldn't accept the meaning.

The Kingdom of God Is in Your Heart Luke 17:20-21
(Glossary article: Pharisees)

²⁴Along the way some Pharisees asked Jesus when the kingdom of God would come on earth.

²⁵"The kingdom of God," Jesus replied, "isn't something you'll be able to see. You won't be able to point it out saying, 'Look, here it is!' or 'Look, there it is!'

²⁶"The fact is, God's kingdom comes in your heart[3]."

A Widow and an Unjust Judge Luke 18:1-8
(Glossary articles: Belief / Faith; Son of Man)

²⁷Then Jesus told a story to teach that people should be constant in their prayers without getting discouraged.

²⁸"There was a city judge who didn't have any respect for God or men," Jesus said. "There was also a widow in the same town, and she just kept coming to this judge saying, 'Give me justice in my dispute with my adversary!'

²⁹"For a while the judge wouldn't listen to her, but eventually he said to himself, 'I don't have any respect for God or men, but this widow just keeps on irritating me.

³⁰"'I'll give her the justice she wants because I'm getting tired of her constant appeals.'

³¹"So pay attention," Jesus continued, "to what this wicked judge said.

³²"If he'll give relief to a widow just because she keeps pestering him, won't God make things right for his own chosen ones who call to him day and night, and demonstrate his patience with them? I assure you: he certainly will give them justice quickly.

³³"However, I wonder. When I come again as a human[4], will I find the faith anywhere in the world?"

Blind Men Healed Matthew 20:29-34; Mark 10:46-52; Luke 18:35-43
(Glossary articles: Belief / Faith; Immediately / Quickly; Jericho)

³⁴Just outside Jericho a huge crowd surrounded Jesus.

³⁵Two blind men happened to be sitting on the roadside begging. One of the blind men was known as Timothy's son[5].

³⁶When these men heard the crowd passing, they asked what was going on, and some in the crowd told them that Jesus[6] was passing by. Hearing that, they called out, "Jesus! Lord! Son of David! Have mercy on us!"

³⁷Several toward the front of the crowd tried to hush the men, but they just called out more and more, "Son of David! Have mercy on us!"

³⁸When Jesus got near, he stood still and gave orders to have the blind men brought to him. So some of the crowd close to them said, "Cheer up! Come on now! Jesus is calling for you."

³⁹At this they got up, dropping their cloaks, and made their way to Jesus. "What do you want me to do for you?" Jesus asked the men.

⁴⁰"Lord," they answered, "we want to be able to see!"

⁴¹Then Jesus touched their eyes and said, "You can go now. Your faith in me has brought you this healing."

⁴²Immediately the men were able to see, and they joined the crowd following Jesus, singing their praises to God. And the people in the crowd joined them in praising God.

---

[1] 37:20-Literally, "the son of man…"
[2] 37:21-Literally, "the son of man will be..."
[3] 37:26-God's kingdom comes to an individual when that individual accepts God as king in his or her heart.
[4] 37:33-Literally, "when the son of man comes again, will he…"
[5] 37:35-This name is often translated "Bartimaeus," but that name means "Son of Timothy."
[6] 37:36-Literally, "Jesus of Nazareth."

A Tax Collector Finds Jesus Luke 19:1-10, 28
(Glossary articles: Abraham; Jericho; Son of Man; Tax Collectors and "Sinners")

⁴³As Jesus passed through the city of Jericho, there was a wealthy man[1] (a chief of tax collectors) who wanted to see who he was.

⁴⁴However, this tax collector was short, and the crowd around Jesus prevented him from getting close enough to even catch a glimpse of Jesus. So he ran ahead of the crowd and climbed into a sycamore tree in order to get a good view as Jesus passed by.

⁴⁵When Jesus reached that tree, he looked up and said, "Quickly now, come on down out of that tree. Didn't you know? I'm going to stay at your house today." So the tax collector scrambled down out of the tree and joyfully welcomed Jesus.

⁴⁶But the crowd around Jesus started complaining, saying, "He's gone to stay with that sinner!"

⁴⁷Then the tax collector stood up and told Jesus, "Look here, Lord. I now promise to give half of my wealth to the poor. And if I've taken anything from anybody by fraud, I promise to restore four times what I took."

⁴⁸So Jesus said, "This day salvation has come to this man's home. After all, he, too, is a child of Abraham. Remember, I came as a human[2] for this very purpose, to find and bring salvation to those who are lost."

⁴⁹Then Jesus continued his journey toward Jerusalem.

Jesus' Head Anointed – Friday, Nisan 8 Matthew 26:6-13; Mark 14:3-9; John 12:1-8
(Glossary articles: Anointing Jesus; Belief / Faith; Biblical Chronology; Dining Customs; The Gospels; Lazarus; Jewish Feasts; Judas; Money in the Bible; Preaching / Proclaiming)

⁵⁰Six days before Passover, Jesus arrived in Bethany where Lazarus (the one Jesus had raised from the dead) lived. A man named Simon[3] (a man Jesus had cured of leprosy) welcomed Jesus into his home and prepared a special meal for him. Lazarus was at the meal and his sister, Martha, was serving the meal.

⁵¹During the meal Lazarus' other sister, Mary, arrived with an alabaster flask containing almost a pound of very expensive perfumed oil[4]. She came up to Jesus where he was reclining on the floor, broke the flask open, and poured the oil on his head and on his feet, wiping his feet with her own hair. The house was filled with the fragrance from the oil.

⁵²But seeing this, some of his disciples started murmuring about the expense.

⁵³Judas (Simon's son and the one who was going to betray Jesus) rebuked her, saying, "Why did you waste that? We could've sold that oil for more than a year's wages[5] and given the funds to the poor!"

⁵⁴(Judas said this, not because he cared about the poor, but because he was the one who kept the group's funds, and he was a thief, sometimes taking money for himself.)

⁵⁵But Jesus responded, "Let her alone! What right do you think you have to criticize her? She's done a good thing for me. After all, you'll always have people who need financial help, and there'll be plenty of opportunities to do good for them, but I won't always be here.

⁵⁶"She's done what she could, anointing my body for burial even before I die. And I promise you: wherever the good news I've brought is proclaimed—anywhere in the world—what this woman just did will be recounted as a memorial to her."

A Plot against Lazarus John 12:9-11
(Glossary articles: Judeans / Jewish Authorities; Lazarus; Chief Priests)

⁵⁷When they heard that Jesus was in Bethany, large crowds of Judeans came, not just to see Jesus, but also to see Lazarus, because they'd heard how Jesus raised him from the dead.

⁵⁸Because of that, the chief priests, who were already trying to think up ways to kill Jesus, began plotting to kill Lazarus. Too many of their own followers were turning away from them and putting their trust in Jesus after meeting Lazarus.

Wealth Entrusted to Three Men Matthew 25:14-30; Luke 19:11-27
(Glossary articles: Immediately / Quickly; Money in the Bible; Servants / Slaves)

⁵⁹People were thinking that the kingdom of God was going to take over very soon because they were getting close to Jerusalem, so Jesus told this story to illustrate the kingdom[6]:

⁶⁰"A wealthy nobleman was getting ready to travel to a distant land where he'd be put in charge of a kingdom[7].

---

[1] 37:43-The tax collector's name was Zacchaeus.
[2] 37:48-Literally, "the son of man came…"
[3] 37:50-In Good News 23:2-20, we have the account of a Pharisee named Simon living in Bethany who invited Jesus to his home for a meal. Jesus severely criticized that Simon. Is this the same Simon? In the time between these meals, Simon may have developed leprosy and have gone to Jesus to be healed both physically and spiritually, or this may be an entirely different Simon. After all, we know that Simon was a very common name. See Anointing Jesus in the Glossary.
[4] 37:51-The flask contained oil of spikenard.
[5] 37:53-Literally, "three hundred denarii."
[6] 37:59-This section combines two similar stories told by Jesus at different times.
[7] 37:60-This account is consistent with practices in the Roman Empire where kings traveled to Rome to receive their authority.

⁶¹"Before he left he called for three of his slaves and entrusted one with two and a half million dollars, one with one million dollars, and one with half a million dollars[1]—each according to his abilities. He told them, 'See what you can do with this while I'm gone.' Then he left quickly.

⁶²"But the citizens he'd be ruling hated him and sent representatives to say, 'We won't put up with this man as our king[2]!'

⁶³"Then when the man returned as king, he ordered his slaves to report on the profit they'd made by their use of the money he'd entrusted to them.

⁶⁴"The first of the slaves reported, 'Master, with the two and a half million you entrusted to me, I've made another two and a half million.'

⁶⁵"'Well done,' the king responded. 'You've earned the right to share in my joy. You were faithful in the little I gave you, so now I'm putting you in charge of ten cities[3].'

⁶⁶"The second of the slaves reported, 'Master, with the million dollars you entrusted to me, I've made another million.'

⁶⁷"'Well done,' the king responded. 'You've earned the right to share in my joy. You were faithful in the little I gave you, so now I'm putting you in charge of five cities.'

⁶⁸"Then the third slave came in and told the king, 'I kept your money hidden in the ground, wrapped in a cloth, because I was afraid of you. I knew that you're a harsh man. You collect money that was deposited by others, and you harvest fields that were planted by others. So here's your money back.'

⁶⁹"'You wicked, lazy slave! I'll condemn you out of your own mouth!' the king roared. 'You knew that I'm a harsh man, did you? You knew that I collect money that I never deposited and that I harvest fields that were planted by others?

⁷⁰"'Then why didn't you at least deposit the money with the bankers so I'd get my money back with interest?'

⁷¹"Then he told his bodyguard, 'Take the money from him, and give it to the man who has five million.'

⁷²"'But Lord,' they exclaimed, 'he's already got five million!'

⁷³"'Those who have will be given vastly more, but those who have nothing—even what little they do have will be taken away[4].

⁷⁴"'So take this worthless slave and throw him out into the outer darkness where there'll be weeping and grinding of teeth in distress.

⁷⁵"'But bring those enemies who didn't want me to be their king here and kill them where I can watch[5]!'"

Chapter 38 – Jesus Enters Jerusalem
The Final Passover Approaches John 11:55-57
(Glossary articles: Herod's Temple; Jerusalem; Jewish Feasts; Pharisees; Chief Priests)

¹As time for the Passover approached, crowds of people were coming to Jerusalem from the countryside[6]. They were going through purification ceremonies in preparation for the Passover.

²All the people were looking for Jesus, and as they stood around in the temple[7], they were saying things like, "What do you think? Do you think he'll come to the feast at all?"

³Meanwhile, the chief priests and Pharisees had given orders that whoever knew where Jesus was should report to them so that they could arrest him.

Preparing for the Triumphal Entry – Saturday, Nisan 9 Matthew 21:1-7; Mark 11:1-7; Luke 19:29-35; John 12:12a, 14-15
(Glossary articles: Biblical Chronology; Immediately / Quickly; Jerusalem; Prophecies and Fulfillments; Triumphal Entry)

⁴Then five days before Passover[1], Jesus and his disciples approached Jerusalem they came to a place near Bethany[2] at the Mount of Olives.

---

[1] 37:61-Literally, "five talents," "two talents," and "one talent." Another time Jesus told this same story with different details. (See Money in the Bible in the Glossary for more information on talents, minas, and the differences between the stories as told by Jesus two different times.)

[2] 37:62-Rome was sensitive to the wishes of the people to be governed up to a point. If they believed that placing a particular non-Roman in authority might threaten the peace of the empire, they'd deny that man his kingdom.

[3] 37:65-In Matthew's account of the similar story, Jesus has the master tell his slave, "I'll make you ruler over many things." Compared to the reward of ten cities or being made a ruler, the servant had been faithful in a relatively small stewardship. God's rewards for faithfulness are huge! Jesus consistently taught that the person who's faithful with the small things of this world will be put in charge of much greater things in eternity.

[4] 37:73-If you don't use what God's given you in ways that are profitable for his kingdom, whatever you do have will be taken from you and you'll be cast out. Stewards are required to be faithful.

[5] 37:75-This served as a warning to the religious authorities: Get with the program or suffer the consequences—and the consequences are terrible beyond description!

[6] 38:1-In fact, for the Passover, people would come from all over the Roman Empire and even from areas outside of the empire.

[7] 38:2-People would have to stand in lines at the temple for various reasons such as purification ceremonies. There weren't enough priests to keep lines from forming.

⁵When they arrived there, Jesus sent two of his disciples with these instructions:

⁶"Go to the village just ahead of us. There you'll quickly find a donkey along with a colt on which no one has ever sat. They'll be tied up, but you'll release both of them and bring them to me.

⁷"If anybody asks what you're doing, tell them, 'The Lord needs them,' and he'll send them right away."

⁸(All this happened to give fuller meaning to what the prophet said,

⁹Tell the daughter of Zion,

"Fear not!

"Behold, your King's coming,

"Lowly and sitting on a donkey—

"A colt, the foal of a donkey[3].")

¹⁰So these disciples did as Jesus had told them. They found the animals tied outside near a doorway, and they released them.

¹¹The owners were standing nearby and said, "What are you doing?"

¹²The disciples responded as Jesus had instructed and the owners allowed them to take the animals.

¹³Then the disciples brought the animals to Jesus and laid their cloaks on them, and Jesus sat on the colt[4].

The Triumphal Entry – Saturday, Nisan 9 Matthew 21:8-11; Mark 11:8-11; Luke 19:36-44; John 12:12b-13, 16-19
(Glossary articles: Biblical Chronology; Common Gender; Herod's Temple; Immediately / Quickly; In the Name of...; Jerusalem; Jewish Feasts; Lazarus; Pharisees; Prophecies and Fulfillments; Triumphal Entry)

¹⁴Enormous crowds who'd come for the Passover feast heard that Jesus was about to ride into Jerusalem and spread their clothes on the road. Others cut down leafy branches from the trees and spread them on the road in front of him.

¹⁵As Jesus came near the point where the road dropped down the Mount of Olives into the valley[5], there were crowds in front of him who'd come out from Jerusalem and more crowds following him who'd gathered from those staying around Bethany.

¹⁶(Among those who were following Jesus were some who'd been with him when he called for Lazarus to come out of the tomb, and they'd spread the word throughout the area and into the city. The crowds from the city came out because they'd heard about that miracle.)

¹⁷All the crowds started praising God for all the things they'd seen and rejoicing at the top of their voices, "Son of King David, bring us salvation[6]!" they shouted, and "'Blessings on the one who comes with the authority of[7] God himself[8]!' The king of Israel! We pray for salvation with all our might! Peace in heaven and glory in the highest! Blessings on the kingdom of David, our father!"

¹⁸Seeing the parade and hearing the shouts, the Pharisees said to each other, "See, we haven't accomplished anything in our opposition to him. Look! The whole world's turned to him!"

¹⁹Then some of the Pharisees near Jesus called to him, "Teacher, rebuke your disciples!"

²⁰But Jesus replied, "I promise you: if these were to be quiet, right away the stones themselves would start shouting!"

²¹As they reached the point where Jesus could see the city, he wept over it saying, "If you had only known, especially on this day that should've been your day, the things needed for your peace! But you're blind to these things.

²²"Because of your blindness, the time's coming when your enemies will build fortifications around you, surround you, and close you in on every side.

²³"They'll level you to the ground with your children in you. They won't leave one stone resting on another, because you didn't realize when God himself came to you."

---

[1] 38:4-Literally, "the next day" (John 12:12), but this was the next day after six days before Passover (John 12:1). Since Passover was on Thursday, this would've been Friday, the 9th of Nisan. That means that Jesus was cleansing the temple on a Sabbath. This certainly doesn't match traditional timelines, but it does match the Bible better than traditional timelines.

[2] 38:4-Literally, "to Bethphage and Bethany." The exact location of Bethphage isn't known. This may have been two towns that had grown together. Bethphage isn't mentioned in the Bible except in connection with this account. The reason it's mentioned here could be because the donkeys were actually in Bethphage.

[3] 38:9-Zechariah 9:9.

[4] 38:13-Matthew mentions both the colt and the colt's dam (mother) to show how closely events matched the prophecy in Zechariah. John's Gospel has the quotation from Zechariah but leaves out any mention of the dam. The other Gospels focus on the colt, because that was the animal Jesus rode. The dam was probably needed to calm this unbroken colt. Some translations of Matthew's account say that Jesus "sat on them," which might be mistaken to mean that he sat on both the colt and the dam at the same time. In fact, common gender (masculine) pronouns are used for the donkeys, while "them" in that phrase is neuter, which matches with "cloaks." People put their cloaks on both animals, and Jesus sat on the colt.

[5] 38:15-This was Kidron Valley, located between the Mount of Olives (where Bethany was located) and Temple Mount in Jerusalem.

[6] 38:17-Often translated "Hosanna." Many in America don't know the difference between "hosanna" and "hallelujah." "Hallelujah" means "praise to God" while "hosanna" is a prayer for rescue or salvation.

[7] 38:17-Literally, "in the name of…"

[8] 38:17-Psalm 118:26.

²⁴As Jesus entered Jerusalem, people in the city were asking, "Who is this?" and the crowds responded, "This is Jesus, the prophet from Galilee[1]."

²⁵(At the time, Jesus' disciples didn't really understand what was going on, but when Jesus ascended back to his glory in heaven, they recalled the prophecies that had been written about him and how people had fulfilled those prophecies.)

²⁶Then Jesus entered Jerusalem and went directly to the temple where he looked carefully at everything that was going on. By then it was getting late in the day, so he and his twelve disciples returned to Bethany where they were staying.

Cleansing the Temple Again – Sunday, Nisan 10 Matthew 21:12-13, 18-19a; Mark 11:12-17; Luke 19:45-46
(Glossary articles: Biblical Chronology; A Fig Tree Cursed; Herod's Temple)

²⁷Leaving Bethany the next morning on the way to the city, Jesus was hungry.

²⁸Along the road he saw a fig tree already in leaf some distance ahead, and he walked to it to see if there might be any figs on it. When he came to it, there was no fruit because it wasn't the season for figs, so he said, "May fruit never grow on you again," and the disciples heard what he said.

²⁹Then Jesus and his disciples continued on into Jerusalem where Jesus headed straight for the temple and started driving out all the vendors buying and selling things on the temple grounds.

³⁰He knocked over the tables of the moneychangers and the seats of those who sold doves. He wouldn't let anybody even carry their goods through the temple grounds.

³¹"The sacred writings say[2], 'My house shall be called a house of prayer for all nations[3],'" Jesus voice rang out, "but you've turned it into a 'thieves' lair[4].'"

More Teaching in the Temple Matthew 21:14-17; Mark 11:18-19; Luke 19:47-48; 21:37-38
(Glossary articles: Chief Priests; Herod's Temple; Scribes)

³²Then people who were blind and lame came to him in the temple, and he healed them.

³³But when the chief priests, scribes, and religious leaders saw the wonderful things that he did, heard the children shouting out, "Son of King David, bring us salvation!" in the temple, and heard what Jesus was teaching, they were furious and wanted to find some way to destroy his influence.

³⁴(These "religious leaders" were afraid of Jesus because all the people were so enthralled by what he was teaching them.)

³⁵They came to Jesus and said, "Don't you hear what these children are saying?"

³⁶Then Jesus answered them, "Of course I can hear them. Haven't you ever read in the sacred writings[5], 'Out of the mouths of infants and nursing babies you've perfected praise[6]'?"

³⁷By then it was late, so Jesus left with his disciples, going back to Bethany where they were staying. And Jesus established a pattern of teaching in the temple daily and then returning to Bethany on the Mount of Olives every night. Every morning the people came to the temple early just to hear Jesus teaching.

The Withered Fig Tree – Monday, Nisan 11 Matthew 21:19b-22; Mark 11:20-24
(Glossary articles: Belief / Faith; Biblical Chronology; Immediately / Quickly; A Fig Tree Cursed)

³⁸The next morning as they were traveling to Jerusalem and passed the place where Jesus had cursed the fig tree, the disciples saw that the tree had dried up from its roots.

³⁹When they saw this they were amazed, and Peter said, "Teacher, look! How did the fig tree you cursed yesterday wither away so quickly?"

⁴⁰"You need to entrust your entire life to God." Jesus replied, "I'm telling you the absolute truth: if you put that kind of faith in God and never doubt him when you pray, you'll get whatever you ask for.

⁴¹"What I did to that fig tree is nothing compared to what you'll be able to do. You could even tell this mountain, 'Get up and throw yourself into the ocean,' and it would be done.

⁴²"Once you have your life that dedicated to God, whatever you ask, trusting fully in God, will be done[7]."

---

[1] 38:24-Literally, "from Nazareth in Galilee."
[2] 38:31-Literally, "It is written…" but the sacred writings are clearly implied.
[3] 38:31-Isaiah 56:7.
[4] 38:31-Jeremiah 7:11.
[5] 38:36-'In the sacred writings' isn't present but is clearly implied.
[6] 38:36-Psalm 8:2.
[7] 38:42-An important point is too often overlooked here. If your life is dedicated to God and you're fully trusting in God, what you pray for will always be consistent with who God is and what he wants. Prayers like that are very powerful indeed, but they aren't selfish, they aren't done for show, and in most cases they are focused on spiritual matters, not the things of this world.

Two Days to Passover – Tuesday, Nisan 12 Matthew 26:1-5; Mark 14:1-2; Luke 22:1-2
(Glossary articles: Biblical Chronology; Jewish Elders; High Priest; Jewish Feasts; Chief Priests; Scribes; Son of Man)

⁴³Then Jesus told his disciples, "You know that it's just two days until the Passover feast begins. That's when I as a human[1] will be turned over to the authorities for crucifixion."

⁴⁴It was also about that time that the chief priests, scribes, and elders of the people got together at the palace of the high priest[2] to develop a plot to take Jesus by some treachery and kill him.

⁴⁵"But," they said, "not during the Passover feast, because that could lead to rioting among the people[3]."

Chapter 39 – Teaching in the Temple Again – Part 1

A Pharisee and a Tax Collector Pray in the Temple Luke 18:9-14
(Glossary articles: Herod's Temple; Pharisees; Sin / Rebellion; Tax Collectors and "Sinners")

¹Then Jesus told another story aimed at those who put their faith in their own self-righteousness and despised others who didn't live up to their standards:

²"Two men went to the temple to pray. One was a Pharisee and the other was a tax collector.

³"The Pharisee stood in the temple and prayed like this to himself[4]: 'God, I thank you that I'm not like other men: con men, dishonest, adulterers—or even like this tax collector! I fast twice a week. I give ten percent of everything I earn to you.'

⁴"The tax collector stood off to the side where he wouldn't be noticed. He wouldn't even look up to heaven. Instead, he beat his chest in the agony of his guilt and prayed, 'God, be merciful to me, I've rebelled against you[5]!'

⁵"I tell you, this tax collector went home justified, but not the Pharisee. You can be sure that, in the end, those who exalt themselves will be humbled and those who humble themselves will be exalted."

Jesus Asks Religious Leaders about John's Immersion Matthew 21:23-27; Mark 11:27-33; Luke 20:1-8
(Glossary articles: Baptize / Immerse; Belief / Faith; Herod's Temple; Jewish Elders; John the Immerser; Chief Priests; Scribes)

⁶Jesus was walking in the temple, teaching the crowds and bringing the good news of the kingdom, when some of the chief priests, scribes, and elders of the Jews confronted him.

⁷"What right do you have to be here in the temple teaching these things?" they asked. "Who do you think gave you this authority?"

⁸"I'm going to ask you something too," Jesus replied, "and if you answer my question, I'll tell you who gave me the authority to do these things.

⁹"So, the immersion taught by John—where did he get the authority to do that? Was this by God's authority, or was this something that he came up with on his own? You answer me!"

¹⁰At this the chief priests and elders who'd challenged Jesus began whispering among themselves.

¹¹"If we say, 'By God's authority,'" they murmured, "he'll ask us, 'Then why didn't you have faith in his message?'

¹²"But if we say, 'he came up with it on his own,' this crowd may riot, and we could be stoned, because they all think John was a prophet indeed."

¹³At last they replied to Jesus, "We don't know."

¹⁴"Then I'm not going to tell you," Jesus answered, "where I got the authority to do what I'm doing.

The Vineyard Keepers who Killed the Son Matthew 21:33-46; Mark 12:1-12; Luke 20:9-19
(Glossary articles: Pharisees; Chief Priests; Herod's Temple; Repentance; Sacred Writings; Scribes; Slaves)

¹⁵"Here's another story," Jesus told the temple crowd.

¹⁶"There was a landowner who planted a vineyard and built a wall around it with a lookout tower. Then he dug a winepress in the vineyard grounds, and he leased the vineyard to experienced keepers who could care for the vineyard.

¹⁷"When the vineyard was done, the owner went to live in a distant country for a long time.

¹⁸"Then when it was time for the grapes to be harvested, the landowner sent a slave to the vineyard keepers to get his share of the harvest. But the keepers grabbed the slave, beat him, and sent him away with no payment.

¹⁹"The landowner then sent another slave, but this time the keepers threw stones at him, wounding him in the head and then treating him shamefully. In the end they sent that one away with nothing, too.

²⁰"When the landowner sent a third slave, the keepers killed him. And when the landowner sent several slaves, they beat some and killed others, never sending any payment to the landowner.

---

[1] 38:43-Literally, "the son of man…"

[2] 38:44-Caiaphas.

[3] 38:45-The Feast of Unleavened Bread was a seven-day event beginning on Nisan 15. There was a major feast on the first day and again on the seventh day. The Jewish authorities didn't want to kill Jesus during the initial feast day (which was the day when the Passover meal was eaten—a special Sabbath in which no work was to be done), and they stuck to their plan.

[4] 39:3-Notice that, although this Pharisee's prayer starts by verbally addressing God, Jesus said that he was really just praying to himself.

[5] 39:4-Remember, sin is always treason—rebellion against God.

²¹"The landowner was perplexed, wondering, 'What can I do?' He had only one son, and he cared deeply for this son. Finally he decided to send this son to collect his share, thinking, 'Surely they'll respect my son!'

²²"But when the vineyard keepers saw the landowner's son, they said to each other, 'This is the fellow who's supposed to inherit the vineyard. If we kill him, we can take everything for ourselves.'

²³"So they grabbed him, threw him outside the vineyard, and murdered him.

²⁴"So," Jesus asked, "When the owner comes to the vineyard, what do you think he'll do to the keepers?"

²⁵Some in the crowd responded, "He'll see that they die in misery, and then he'll lease the vineyard to other keepers who'll pay his share at the proper time."

²⁶The chief priests and scribes who'd been listening knew that the point of this story was about them, and they replied, "Don't even think that!"

²⁷"And haven't you read in the sacred writings[1]," Jesus responded, "where it says, 'The stone that the construction crew decided not to use has become the first stone in the building[2]—the stone that establishes where all the other stones go.' and,

²⁸"'This is what God's done, and it's awesome to behold[3]!'?

²⁹"It's for this reason," Jesus said, "I'm telling you that the kingdom of God will be taken away from you and given to a nation that will produce the fruit of the kingdom.

³⁰"And anybody who falls down[4] on that stone in worship shall be broken[5], while anybody on whom the stone falls shall be crushed to dust."

³¹When the chief priests, scribes, and Pharisees heard these stories, they knew he was talking about them. They wanted to arrest him, but the huge crowds in the temple believed him to be a prophet, so they didn't dare arrest him for fear of starting a riot.

Jesus Questioned about Paying Taxes to Rome Matthew 22:15-22; Mark 12:13-17; Luke 20:20-26
(Glossary articles: Caesar; Herod; Pharisees; Romans and Jews)

³²Then the Pharisees got together with some who were political allies of Herod's family, trying to come up with a question that would trap Jesus in what he said so that they could turn him over to the Roman governor for execution.

³³They sent some of their group as spies, pretending to go along with what Jesus was teaching.

³⁴These men approached Jesus saying, "Teacher, we know that you're always true and that you teach the truth about what God wants from us. You don't turn aside from that truth for anyone, and you aren't impressed by any human authority.

³⁵"So what do you think—is it proper by God's laws to pay taxes to the emperor[6] or not? Should we pay or should we refuse to pay?"

³⁶Of course Jesus saw their evil intentions. "Why are you trying to test me, you fakes?" he responded. "Show me a coin that you would use to pay your taxes[7]."

³⁷One of those near him handed him a coin, and then Jesus held it up and asked, "Whose image is on this coin, and whose name's written on it?"

³⁸"The emperor's[8]," they responded.

³⁹"OK," Jesus said. "Then give the emperor what belongs to the emperor[9] and give God what belongs to God."

⁴⁰Those who'd questioned him were astonished by his reply, and they backed away into the crowd, unable to get him tangled up in his words.

A Woman with Seven Husbands? Matthew 22:23-33; Mark 12:18-27; Luke 20:27-40
(Glossary articles: Abraham; Agent / Angel; Moses; Sacred Writings; Sadducees; Scribes)

⁴¹After this some Sadducees came to Jesus with another question. (Now the Sadducees taught that there's no resurrection for those who die.)

⁴²"Teacher," they said, "Moses wrote that if a man dies without having children, his brother should marry the widow and raise up children for the brother who died.

---

[1] 39:27-Literally, "the writings," but "sacred writings" is clearly implied.
[2] 39:27-Literally, "the chief corner." In New Testament times, a single stone was placed at one corner as the first stone for a building and all other stones were lined up according to that stone. Jesus was making the point that while the religious leaders were rejecting him, God was going to make him the standard by which everything else would be measured.
[3] 39:28-Psalm 118:22-23.
[4] 39:30-The word here is often translated as "stumbles" or "falls," but the most common usage of this word in the Bible relates to falling down in worship. The options are between falling down in worship or having the stone fall on you and crush you.
[5] 39:30-"Broken" in the sense of repentant—the old life put to death and a new focus begun for all of life.
[6] 39:35-Literally, "Caesar."
[7] 39:36-Literally, "a denarius."
[8] 39:38-Literally, "Caesar's."
[9] 39:39-Literally, "Then give Caesar what belongs to Caesar."

⁴³"Now, as it happens, we know a case where there were seven brothers. The first of these brothers got married, but he died without having any children, leaving his widow for one of his brothers to marry.

⁴⁴"But the same thing happened to the second of the brothers, and the third, and so on until all seven had died without leaving any children. Then, last of all, the woman herself died.

⁴⁵"So, in this resurrection you talk about, which of the seven brothers will be her husband? After all, they were all married to her here on earth."

⁴⁶"You're so mistaken!" Jesus responded. "You don't know the sacred writings[1] and you don't know the power of God.

⁴⁷"In this world people get married and are given in marriage.

⁴⁸"But for those who are counted worthy to attain the resurrection, marriage contracts would be as useless for them as for God's agents in heaven[2].

⁴⁹"They don't die anymore because they're children of God and of the resurrection, and as such they're equal to God's agents.

⁵⁰"But as to the reality of the people rising from the dead, haven't you ever read in the sacred writings[3] how, when Moses was at the burning bush, God said to him, 'I AM[4] the God of Abraham, the God of Isaac, and the God of Jacob[5]'?

⁵¹"Now, God isn't the God of the dead, but the God of the living, for everybody who's ever lived is alive to him. So you're truly mistaken!"

⁵²When the crowds standing around heard this, they were amazed. Then some of the scribes said, "Teacher, that was a very good answer!"

⁵³After that none of the Sadducees dared to question Jesus again.

Chapter 40 – Teaching in the Temple Again – Part 2

The Greatest Commandment Matthew 22:34-40; Mark 12:28-34a
(Glossary articles: Caring Love; Law of Moses; Pharisees; Sadducees; Scribes)

¹When the Pharisees heard that Jesus had shamed the Sadducees so thoroughly that they refused to even try to challenge him again, they got together to plan their own attack on him.

²They sent a scribe who was an expert in the Law of Moses to test him. "Teacher," their expert asked, "which of the laws Moses gave us is the greatest commandment?"

³"The first commandment is this:" Jesus replied, "'Listen, people of Israel! Jehovah our God—Jehovah is one! And you shall care for Jehovah your God with all your heart, with all your soul, with all your mind, and with all your strength[6]!' That's the first and the most important commandment!

⁴"The second commandment is similar to it: 'You shall care for your neighbor as you care for yourself[7].' There are no commandments greater than these, and these two commandments cover everything in the Law of Moses and the writings of the prophets."

⁵"Well said, teacher!" the scribe responded. "You've certainly hit the nail on the head, because there's only one God, and there's no other god except him.

⁶"And to care for him with all your heart, understanding, soul, and strength and to care for your neighbor as you do for yourself is more important than all the burnt offerings and sacrifices you could ever offer!"

⁷When Jesus heard this scribe's response, he told him, "You're not far from being in the kingdom of God."

How Can Christ Can Be David's Son? Matthew 22:41-46; Mark 12:34b-37; Luke 20:41-44
(Glossary articles: Christ; Herod's Temple; Pharisees)

⁸While the Pharisees were still around him there in the temple, Jesus asked them, "About the Christ, whose son would you say he is?"

⁹"The son of David," they replied.

---

[1] 39:46-Literally, "the writings," but "sacred writings" is clearly implied.

[2] 39:48-This verse is often terribly misused. Jesus didn't say that we wouldn't know our spouses in heaven. He didn't say that we wouldn't have a strong love bond with our spouses in heaven. For those who have shared their lives as Christians in a bond of ever stronger Christian love, at least initially, that bond will surely be the strongest bond they feel. But the things that make the bonds of marriage exclusive in this world won't apply in heaven, so we will be able to form similar bonds with others without stirring up jealousy and bitter feelings on the part of our first love. The question Jesus didn't address here or at any other time as far as we know is this: "How will God make it alright if I reach heaven and someone I dearly loved doesn't?" For questions like that we simply need to trust that God does understand the issue, and he's got a plan to let us see how this is right and as it must be.

[3] 39:50-"In the sacred writings" isn't present but is clearly implied.

[4] 39:50-The "I AM" here is very emphatic, with echoes of Exodus 3:14 where God identified himself to Moses as "I AM."

[5] 39:50-Exodus 3:6.

[6] 40:3-Deuteronomy 6:5.

[7] 40:4-Leviticus 19:18.

¹⁰"Well, then," Jesus asked, "how is it that David, writing in the psalms as the Holy Spirit led him, called the Christ¹ 'Lord' when he wrote, 'Jehovah said to my Lord, "Sit at my right hand until I make all your enemies into a footstool for your use²!"'?

¹¹"If David called the Christ 'Lord,' how can the Christ be his son³?"

¹²After this none of the religious authorities dared ask Jesus any such questions. But the people in the crowds rejoiced to hear him.

A Widow's Coin Offering Mark 12:41-44; Luke 21:1-4
(Glossary articles: Herod's Temple; Money in the Bible)

¹³Later Jesus was across from the treasury area in the temple watching people as they left their offerings.

¹⁴As he watched, several wealthy people left large offerings. Then a destitute widow came up and threw in two tiny brass coins⁴ worth about 75 cents.

¹⁵At this Jesus called his disciples over and told them, "I'm telling you the absolute truth: that widow in her poverty has put more into the treasury than anyone else, because they all put in what they could easily afford, but she in her poverty has put in all she's got, leaving herself with nothing to live on."

Wise and Foolish Girls Matthew 25:1-13
(Glossary articles: Jewish Marriage Customs; Son of Man)

¹⁶Later Jesus said, "Understand this! The kingdom of heaven's like ten teenage girls⁵ who were going to walk in a wedding procession, escorting the groom by night to the wedding feast⁶.

¹⁷"Five of these girls were smart, and the other five were rather foolish. All of them had brought battery operated lanterns, but the smart ones brought extra batteries while the foolish ones didn't.

¹⁸"As it happened, the bridegroom wasn't able to leave on time, and the girls were dozing with their lanterns on while they waited.

¹⁹"Then in the middle of the night they heard the head of the procession calling out, 'Look here! The groom's coming! It's time to go out and join him!'

²⁰"At this these teenage girls got up and checked their lanterns. 'Give us some of your spare batteries,' the foolish ones said to the smarter ones, 'because our lanterns are about out.'

²¹"But the smarter girls replied, 'Not a chance. If we do that, there might not be enough for all of us and we'd all be lost in the dark. Go find an open store and buy some.'

²²"So while these foolish girls were running to the store, the groom showed up. The girls who were ready joined the procession and went into the feast with him, and once they were in, the gates were barred.

²³"Later the other girls showed up too. 'Lord, Lord!' they called. 'Open the gates!'

²⁴"But the groom replied, 'I'm telling you the absolute truth—I don't know you!'

²⁵"So the lesson here is this: Be alert, because you don't know either the day or the time of day when I'll return as a human⁷.

The Standard of the Judgment Matthew 25:31-46
(Glossary articles: Agent / Angel; Caring Love; Gentiles / Nations; Heaven; Hell; Satan; Son of Man)

²⁶"When I return in my radiant glory as a human⁸ along with all the sacred agents of God, then I'll sit as king on my judgment throne⁹ and all the nations will be assembled in front of me.

²⁷"I'll divide them as a shepherd separating his sheep from his goats. I'll have the sheep on my right side, but the goats will be sent to my left side.

---

¹ 40:10-Literally, "called him," but "called the Christ" is obviously implied. In this verse and verse 11, each reference translated as "the Christ" is actually "him" or "he," with "the Christ" clearly implied.
² 40:10-Psalm 110:1.
³ 40:11-In New Testament culture, "Honor your father and your mother" was understood as meaning that a son could never be lord over his father or any ancestor.
⁴ 40:14-Literally, "leptons," often translated "mites."
⁵ 40:16-Literally, "virgins," but in New Testament times that would indicate teenage girls. The fact that they were virgins isn't important to this story.
⁶ 40:16-This was common practice in New Testament Jewish culture.
⁷ 40:25-Literally, "when the son of man will return." Those who insist on predicting the date of Christ's return call him a liar, and those who try to determine the date of his return waste their time.
⁸ 40:26-Literally, "the son of man returns in his radiant glory…"
⁹ 40:26-This is the only time that Jesus told his disciples exactly what the judgment would be like—and he varied the details while repeating the same theme four times in a row for a level of emphasis exceeded only by his teaching that God's way is Christian love rather than law. This is certainly one of the most important lessons Jesus taught, and the standard of judgment described is the practice of Christian love.

²⁸"Then I'll tell those on my right side, 'Come, you who've found overwhelming joy in my Father[1], take over the kingdom we've been preparing for you since the creation of the world.

²⁹"It's yours because when I was hungry you gave me food, when I was thirsty you gave me something to drink, when I was a homeless stranger you took me in, when I was naked you clothed me, when I was sick you came to check up on me, and when I was in prison you visited with me[2].'

³⁰"But these righteous ones will reply, 'Lord, when did we ever see you hungry and feed you or thirsty and give you something to drink? When did we ever see you a homeless stranger and take you in or naked and clothe you? When did we ever see you sick or in prison and come to care for you[3]?'

³¹"'I tell you the absolute truth,' I'll reply: 'as sure as you did this for just one of the very least of these who are my brothers, you did it for me.'

³²"Then I'll tell those on my left side, 'Get out of here[4], you who are doomed to the eternal fire prepared for Satan and his agents.

³³"This doom is yours because when I was hungry you didn't give me any food, when I was thirsty you didn't give me anything to drink, when I was a homeless stranger you didn't give me any place to stay, when I was naked you didn't provide any clothing for me, and when I was sick and in prison you never came to check on me.'

³⁴"'Lord,' they'll ask, 'When did we ever see you hungry or thirsty or a homeless stranger or naked or sick or in prison and not care for you?'

³⁵"'I tell you the absolute truth,' I'll reply: 'as sure as you failed to care for one of the very least of these who are my brothers, you failed to care for me.'

³⁶"So those on the left will be condemned to eternal punishment, but those who did right will be welcomed into life everlasting.

"If I Am Lifted Up" John 12:27-43
(Glossary articles: Agent / Angel; Christ; Belief / Faith; Heaven / Sky; Isaiah; Jesus and Temptation; Law of Moses; Pharisees; Son of Man)

³⁷"Now I'm distressed down to the very depths of my soul!" Jesus continued. "What should I pray for? 'Father, save me from this?' But this is what I came for! 'Father, demonstrate the glory of who you are!'"

³⁸At this a voice came from the sky, "I've already demonstrated that glory, and I'll do so again."

³⁹Some of the people around him thought the voice was the rumble of thunder. Others in the group said, "One of God's agents spoke to him."

⁴⁰"This voice didn't come for my benefit," Jesus responded, "but for yours. The time's come for this world to face judgment and for the ruler of this world to be tossed out.

⁴¹"As for me, if[5] I'm lifted up[6], I'll draw everyone to me." (Jesus said "lifted up" to indicate exactly how he'd die.)

⁴²Some of the people around him responded, "We thought that the Law of Moses predicts that the Christ would live forever, so how can you say, 'I as a human[7] must be lifted up?' What do you mean by 'I as a human[8]?'"

⁴³"The light's only going to be with you for a little while longer," Jesus replied. "You need to get started on your journey while you still have the light.

⁴⁴"If you don't, the darkness will overtake you; and if you travel in the dark, you won't know where you're going.

⁴⁵"So while you've got the light, put your faith in the light and become children of the light."

⁴⁶After saying these things Jesus left there, and they couldn't find him. And although he'd done so many miraculous signs right in front of them, they still wouldn't put their faith in him.

⁴⁷This gave full meaning to the words written in the prophecies of Isaiah: "Lord, who's had faith in what we've reported? To whom has Jehovah's arm been revealed[9]?"

⁴⁸And this is further explained since Isaiah said, "He's caused their eyes to be blind and their hearts to be hardened. Otherwise they'd use their eyes to see and they'd understand so that their hearts would turn back to me and I would certainly heal them[1]."

---

[1] 40:28-Those who find God in this world are certain to find overwhelming joy in him, no matter how much they may suffer physically.
[2] 40:29-Here's what Jesus defined as the standard of God's judgment—"I was in need, and because you chose to be my servant, you cared for my need." This shouldn't be a surprise. That's Christian love for others, and it's the second of the two great commandments according to Jesus. In fact, to a large degree it's how we obey the first of the two great commandments, and Jesus made that clear in this passage.
[3] 40:30-For both the righteous and the wicked, the pattern of life they'd established became so natural that they didn't see it.
[4] 40:32-These are words you don't want to hear from God. If you were to hear those words from God, where could you go?
[5] 40:41-By using the word "if" here, Jesus implied that he in his humanity still had the choice to stop the process. How thankful we should be that he chose to carry out this plan.
[6] 40:41-"Lifted up" was obviously a phrase commonly recognized as meaning crucifixion.
[7] 40:42-Literally, "the son of man?"
[8] 40:42-Literally, "the son of man?"
[9] 40:47-Isaiah 53:1.

⁴⁹(This last is what Isaiah said when he saw God's glory and spoke with him.)

⁵⁰On the other hand, even among the Jewish rulers many did put their faith in him.

⁵¹But those leaders who put their faith in Jesus wouldn't openly admit it for fear the Pharisees would get them kicked out², because these men cared about hearing other people praise them more than having God praise them.

Judas Arranges the Betrayal Matthew 26:14-16; Mark 14:10-11; Luke 22:3-6
(Glossary articles: Judas; Chief Priests)

⁵²Then Satan took over in Judas' heart. (He was, of course, one of Jesus' twelve closest disciples) He went to the chief priests and the captains of the temple police asking, "What would you pay me if I betray Jesus so you can arrest him quietly."

⁵³The chief priests considered this great news. They paid him thirty silver coins for his help in catching Jesus at a time when there wouldn't be any crowds around.

⁵⁴Judas agreed to do his part, and from that time on, he looked for a way to betray Jesus.

Chapter 41 – Questions about the End
The Questions Matthew 24:1-4; Mark 13:1-5; Luke 21:5-8a
(Glossary article: Andrew; Herod's Temple; James; John; Peter; Slaves)

¹Then Jesus and his disciples left the temple grounds, and as they were walking away, his disciples pointed out the buildings of the temple compound.

²"Teacher," they exclaimed, "look at the awesome stones in the temple buildings and the beautiful things that have been given to the temple!"

³"You think these great buildings are so impressive?" Jesus asked, "I'm telling you the absolute truth: the time's coming when there won't be one stone of these buildings still left on top of another, and if one is found, it will be knocked down."

⁴As they were walking up the Mount of Olives, Jesus stopped and sat down to rest.

⁵Then Peter, James, John, and Andrew came to him while they were by themselves and asked³, "When will the things you were talking about happen? What's going to be the sign that you're coming? And what'll be the sign of the end of the world⁴?"

⁶"Beware!" said Jesus. "Don't let anybody mess with your minds on this one.

Predictions of the Fall of Jerusalem Matthew 24:15-22, 32-35; Mark 13:14-20, 28-31; Luke 17:31-32; 21:20-24, 29-33
(Glossary articles: Gentiles / Nations; Herod's Temple; Jerusalem; Judea; Sabbath; Slaves)

⁷"When you see Jerusalem surrounded by armies and that which is truly foul coming with the destruction of war (what Daniel the prophet called the 'abomination of desolation⁵') and standing in the very heart of the temple, you'll know that Jerusalem is about to be destroyed.

⁸"Then if you're in Judea, hide out in the mountains. If you're in the middle of the city of Jerusalem, get out! If you're out in the countryside, don't go into the city!

⁹"That will be the time of God's vengeance when everything the prophets wrote about the judgment of Jerusalem will be fulfilled⁶."

¹⁰(If you're reading this, you need to understand what this is telling you!)

¹¹"Don't hesitate when you see it coming!" Jesus continued, "If you're relaxing on your housetop and everything you own is in the house, don't try to go back into your house to get anything! If you're in the field, don't try to go home even to get your clothes! Remember Lot's wife⁷!

¹²"There'll be terrible anguish for women who are pregnant or nursing babies and great distress in the whole land as God's wrath comes on the people of this land! Some will be killed by armed men, and others will be dragged away into slavery in distant lands.

¹³"Pray that your time to escape won't come in the winter or on a Sabbath when the length of your journey is supposed to be limited!

---

¹ 40:48-Isaiah 6:10.

² 40:51-We don't know whether this was a threat to be kicked out of worship center or just to be kicked out of leadership in some way. Of course, being kicked out of worship center would include being kicked out of leadership.

³ 41:5-The disciples asked three questions: 1) when the destruction of Jerusalem would occur, 2) when Jesus' coming in power would occur, and 3) when the end of the world would occur. We don't know whether Jesus intentionally mingled his answers or whether his answers got mingled in the accounts because the disciples thought that they were just asking one question. This translation separates Jesus' answers for each of these questions based on what we know now that the authors of the New Testament couldn't have known.

⁴ 41:5-The temple in Jerusalem was one of the most fabulous building complexes in the world at that time. In the disciples' minds, the destruction of this temple had to be connected with the end of the world.

⁵ 41:7-Daniel 11:31; 12:11. For every two scholars there are probably at least three opinions about what this meant.

⁶ 41:9-This prophecy was fulfilled in 70 AD when the Romans thoroughly destroyed Jerusalem and massacred thousands.

⁷ 41:11-See Genesis 19:26.

[14]"This will be a time of terrible suffering—suffering like no one's ever seen before since the beginning of the creation of the world, and there'll never be a time so awful again.

[15]"If God weren't going to limit how long this lasts, not a single person in Jerusalem would escape the destruction.

[16]"But, for the sake of God's chosen ones, that time will be limited. Then Jerusalem will be occupied by the other nations until the time of this non-Jewish occupation is complete."

[17]Then Jesus gave this illustration: "Take a lesson from fig trees and indeed any of the trees: when you see that the tree's branches are already tender and budding and that leaves are growing on the branches, you know that it's almost summer.

[18]"In the same way, when you see these things happening, you'll know that this destruction is about to happen—that it's knocking on your doors. Then you'll know that God's kingdom is indeed here!

[19]"Now, I'm telling you the absolute truth—the people of this generation will still be alive when these things happen. But remember, even if the whole earth and sky were to be destroyed, my message will always apply for all time!"

Predictions of Jesus' Coming in Power Matthew 24:5; 9-14, 23-31, 37-51; Mark 13:6, 21-27, 33-37; Luke 12:35-48; 17:22-30, 34-37; 21:8b, 25-28, 34-36
(Glossary articles: Agent / Angel; Belief / Faith; Christ; Heaven; Immediately / Quickly; Miracles; Preaching / Proclaiming; Satan; Slaves; Son of Man)

[20]Then Jesus told his disciples, "The time's coming when you'll long for just one of the days when I was with you as a human[1], and you won't get it[2].

[21]"Then there'll be many who'll come claiming, 'I AM the Christ[3]!' and 'The time of his return is near!' Don't go to see them or follow after them!

[22]"There'll be false christs and false prophets, and sometimes they'll perform great 'miracles' in order to deceive God's own chosen ones (if that were possible).

[23]"Many people will be tricked by their messages—don't you be tricked.

[24]"So if anyone tells you, 'Look here! This man's the Christ!' or 'Look, there he is in the desert!' don't go into the desert looking. Or if they say 'Look here in these secret rooms,' don't even listen to such claims.

[25]"Now I've told you before it happens.

[26]"When I come back as a human[4] it will be like lightning that flashes in the east and is seen in the west—there'll be no doubt that it's me, as sure as vultures gather for carrion!

[27]"During that time many among you will get tripped up by Satan, betraying each other and even hating each other.

[28]"And because there'll be times of extreme lawlessness, the hearts of many will turn cold and they'll stop caring. People will turn you over to the authorities for prosecution—they'll even kill some of you, but the one who endures to the end will be saved.

[29]"Not long after the oppression of those days the sun will be hidden from sight, the moon will no longer provide light, the stars will fall from the sky, the waves of the sea will roar, and the powers of the heavens will be shaken[5].

[30]"All nations will be sent into distress and confusion! Everyone will be terrified because of the things happening to the earth.

[31]"When that happens, the sign of my return will appear in the sky, and people all over earth will be in anguish as they see me returning on the clouds of the sky, coming with awesome power and brilliant glory.

[32]"Then the final trumpet will sound, and I'll send my agents to gather those whom I've chosen from all over the earth—as far as the sky extends. But first the good news of the kingdom that I've brought must be proclaimed to every nation on earth before the end can come.

[33]"When these things start happening, it's time to look up, because your redemption is coming! But first I've got to experience great suffering and be rejected by the people of this generation.

[34]"And when I come back, it'll be like it was in Noah's time. Everybody was going about life as usual—eating, drinking, and getting married—until the very day that Noah got into his boat.

[35]"They weren't even thinking about disaster until the flood actually came and washed them all away.

[36]"Or it will be like it was in Lot's time. Everybody was going about life as usual—eating, drinking, buying, selling, planting, and building.

[37]"But the day Lot left town[6], fire and burning sulfur started coming down like rain from the sky to destroy them all.

---

[1] 41:20-Literally, "with the son of man…"
[2] 41:20-When the disciples asked about Jesus' coming, they were thinking of his taking over earthly power and chasing out the Romans—but he talked about his coming back to earth after a delay of thousands of years.
[3] 41:21-Literally, a very emphatic "I AM," as claiming to be The I AM—Jehovah God!
[4] 41:26-Literally, "when the son of man returns…"
[5] 41:29-This may be understood as symbolic language for earthly rulers falling from their positions of power or it may be taken more literally as in some sort of calamity coming from space.
[6] 41:37-Sodom.

³⁸"So that's how it'll be when I come back: Two men will be working in a field—one will be taken and the other will be left behind.

³⁹"Two women will be grinding flour for their bread—one will be taken and the other will be left behind.

⁴⁰"Two people will be asleep in bed—one will be taken and the other will be left behind[1].

⁴¹"And understand this—if the owner of the house had known what time the thief was coming, he'd have been on the alert, and he wouldn't have allowed the thief to sneak into his house.

⁴²"In the same way, you need to be ready because I'll show up at exactly the time you don't expect me[2].

⁴³"So pay attention! Stay alert and keep on praying that you'll be found worthy to escape all the trials that are coming and to stand in my presence[3], because you don't know when I'll be coming.

⁴⁴"It's like a man who leaves home and goes to a distant land, leaving his slaves in charge of the house with each one knowing his assigned duties and the doorkeeper standing guard.

⁴⁵"Like the doorkeeper, you need to be on guard, because you don't know when the owner of the house will return from the wedding, whether in the evening, at midnight, just before dawn when the rooster crows, or sometime up in the morning. When he returns, you'll need to answer his knock quickly. There'll be great joy for those that the master finds watching and ready!

⁴⁶"If you don't stay on guard at all times, suddenly he'll be back and you'll be sleeping.

⁴⁷"So who is this faithful and wise steward who's been put in charge of the master's staff to see that they get fed at the proper times?

⁴⁸"There's great joy for the slave[4] who's been put in charge when the master comes home and finds he's doing his job well. I'm telling you the absolute truth: that slave will be put in charge of everything the master owns[5].

⁴⁹"But if that evil slave who's been entrusted with such responsibility thinks, 'My master won't be back for a long time,' then he may start beating the other slaves and stuffing himself with their food while he hangs out with a bunch of drunkards.

⁵⁰"Then the master will show up when that slave isn't expecting him and will catch that slave unprepared. He'll have that slave cut in two[6] and thrown out with the fakes and those who are unfaithful, and there'll be great weeping and grinding of teeth in anguish!

⁵¹"So be sure you don't let your hearts get focused on partying, drunkenness, and the troubles of this world, because if you do, you won't be ready for the day of my return when it comes.

⁵²"That day will come for everyone on earth like a trap closing on an unsuspecting animal, so stay alert!

⁵³"Always keep your sleeves rolled up for work[7] with your lights on. Act like men who are expecting their master to return from a wedding at any moment.

⁵⁴"Then when the master arrives, you'll be ready to open the door for him right away.

⁵⁵"There's great joy for those slaves who are alert when the master arrives. I'm telling you the absolute truth: he'll have them sit down around the dining room table while he rolls up his sleeves and serves their meal[8]!"

⁵⁶At this Peter asked Jesus, "Lord, are these teachings just for us, or are they for everyone?"

⁵⁷"I'm not just saying this to you who are here," Jesus replied, "the message is for everybody to be alert!

⁵⁸"Any slave who knows what his master wants and doesn't get prepared or do what the master wants will be punished severely. But a slave who does wrong without knowing what the master expected will only be punished lightly.

⁵⁹"If you've been given a lot, you'll be expected to do a lot; and if you've been entrusted with a lot, you'll be expected to pay back even more.

Predictions of the End of Time Matthew 24:6-8; 36; Mark 13:7-8, 32; Luke 21:9-11
(Glossary articles: Agent / Angel; Immediately / Quickly; Son of God)

⁶⁰"And when you hear of wars and rumors about possible wars, don't let that scare you.

---

[1] 41:40-These verses provide one of the strongest passages used to support the idea that there'll be a time when God's people will be taken from the earth and those who aren't God's people will be left behind on earth. That's certainly a possible understanding of this passage, but "left behind" could also mean "left behind to wind up in hell" at the same time that God's people are taken to their reward. These are matters about which God has not given us clear information because we don't need that information in order to do our jobs. Our job is to spread the love and grace of God in any way we can. It's God's job to deal with when and how the end will come.

[2] 41:42-One thing we can know about the Lord's return—if a great many people are expecting his return at a certain date or time, that's when he's least likely to return.

[3] 41:43-Literally, "stand before the son of man..."

[4] 41:48-When it comes to God's business, we need to think of ourselves as his slaves.

[5] 41:48-Jesus made it clear that our service in this world will bring great responsibilities in heaven—responsibilities that we will love and that will bring us great joy.

[6] 41:50-This wasn't an idle threat in New Testament times. By Roman law, if a master killed his slave, he wasn't guilty of any crime. Normally, slaves were considered too valuable to be killed, but a slave could cross the line and suffer the consequences.

[7] 41:53-The literal wording here involves having your robes tied up out of the way for work.

[8] 41:55-The master serves a meal to his slaves! This was a drastic switch for people who'd grown up in New Testament times!

⁶¹"Wars are going to happen, but these wars aren't the sign that the end of the world will come right away. Nations will go to war against other nations and kingdoms against other kingdoms.

⁶²"There'll be powerful earthquakes in many different areas.

⁶³"Sometimes people will be starving to death, sometimes people will be dying of epidemic diseases, sometimes you'll see things that will terrify you, sometimes there'll be awesome sights in the sky and many other troubles, but all of these things are just the beginning.

⁶⁴"The bottom line is that nobody knows the actual day and time when the end will come. God's agents in heaven don't know. I as the very son of God don't know. Only the Father knows when that will be[1]."

Judgment Based on Jesus' Message John 12:44-50
(Glossary article: Belief / Faith)

⁶⁵Then Jesus called out, "If you put your faith in me, you're actually putting your faith in the one who sent me. And if you truly see who I am, you'll see the one who sent me.

⁶⁶"I've come into the world to bring light, so that anyone who has faith in me won't live in darkness.

⁶⁷"If you hear what I'm saying and don't put your faith in what I say, I won't need to condemn you. I didn't come into the world to condemn the world but rather to save the world.

⁶⁸"But if you reject me and don't put your faith in what I say, you'll still have to face judgment—the very message I've given you will be your judge when the end comes.

⁶⁹"After all, I didn't just make this stuff up—the Father who sent me gave the orders, telling me what I should say. And I know that his orders bring eternal life, so whatever I say is just what the Father told me to say."

Chapter 42 – Passover Preparations and the Meal

People Who Aren't Jews Seek Jesus John 12:20-24, 26
(Glossary articles: Andrew; Jewish Feasts; Slaves; Son of Man)

¹Some people who weren't Jews came to Philip and said, "Sir, we want to meet Jesus[2]." Philip went to Andrew and then they went to Jesus with this request.

²"The time's come," Jesus responded, "for me as a human[3] to be glorified[4].

³"I tell you the absolute truth: unless a grain of wheat goes into the ground as if dying and being buried, it's just a single grain of wheat. But if it gets buried, it grows a whole new stalk with many grains of wheat.

⁴"If you want to serve me, follow me! If you follow me because you want to serve me, you'll be able to get in wherever I go. And if you serve me, my Father will honor you."

Preparing for the Passover – Thursday, Nisan 14 Matthew 26:17-19; Mark 14:12-16; Luke 22:7-13
(Glossary articles: Biblical Chronology; Jerusalem; Jewish Feasts)

⁵The day festivities began for the Feast of Unleavened Bread[5]—the day that the Passover lamb was to be sacrificed—finally came.

⁶Jesus sent Peter and John saying, "Go prepare the Passover for all of us."

⁷Peter and John asked him, "Where do you want us to prepare the feast?"

⁸"Go to Jerusalem," Jesus replied, "and when you enter the city, you'll meet a man carrying a pitcher of water.

⁹"Follow him, and whatever house he enters, tell the man who manages the house, 'The teacher says, "My time has come, and I'll eat the Passover at your house with my disciples. Where's the guest room where we can do this?"'

¹⁰"Then the manager will take you upstairs to a large room all furnished and prepared. That's where you'll get everything ready for the feast."

---

[1] 41:64-The sign of the end of time is no sign. The end comes at a time when people don't expect it. If people are expecting it, that's almost certainly not the time. Prophecy was never meant to tell us exactly what's going to happen or when it's going to happen—it is intended to let us know that God knows, and that's all we need to know. We need to focus on shining the light of God's love in this world and forget about trying to figure out what's God's business and none of our business. Those who focus on trying to understand what Jesus said no one would know except God himself effectively call Jesus a liar.

[2] 42:1-Why did these non-Jews need to come to Jesus' disciples in order to make contact with Jesus? For one thing, Jesus' disciples served as a barrier between the crowds and Jesus both to allow him to teach effectively and to allow him to get rest when he needed it. It's also possible that Jesus was teaching in an area of the temple where non-Jews weren't allowed to go.

[3] 42:2-Literally, "the son of man…"

[4] 42:2-The Bible doesn't tell us if Jesus met with these people. But when Jesus heard that people from far away were asking for him, he knew that it was time for him to culminate his ministry.

[5] 42:5-The official start of Passover according to the Law of Moses was at twilight on the 14th of Nisan (called Abib in the Torah). Then sundown marked the start of Nisan 15 which was the first day of the Feast of Unleavened Bread, and most of the actual Passover feast occurred during the night on Nisan 15. However, it's clear from the Bible that Jews in New Testament times would speak of Nisan 14 (Passover) as "the first day of unleavened bread" and they'd also refer to the Feast of Unleavened Bread as "Passover."

¹¹So the disciples went into the city and found everything just as Jesus had described, and they got everything ready for the Passover meal.

<u>The Last Supper – The Betrayal Predicted – Friday, Nisan 15</u> Matthew 26:20-25; Mark 14:17-21; Luke 22:14, 21-23; John 13:2, 18-19, 21-30
(Glossary articles: Biblical Chronology; Dining Customs; Hell; Immediately / Quickly; Jewish Feasts; John; Judas; Peter; Sacred Writings; Satan; Son of Man)

¹²Just before sunset[1], Jesus and his twelve disciples reclined to eat their Passover feast.

¹³As they were eating, Jesus' breathing got choked up[2] and he said, "I'm telling you the absolute truth: one of you who's eating with me now is about to betray me."

¹⁴At this the disciples were seriously distressed and looked at each other in confusion, not sure what Jesus was talking about. Some of them began to ask him, "Lord, am I the one?"

¹⁵Jesus heard them and said again, "One of you twelve who's dipped bread in the dish with me will betray me[3].

¹⁶"I'm not talking about all of you. I know my chosen followers well, but this betrayal will give full meaning to what the sacred writing[4] said: 'The one who's eating my bread has lifted up his heel to crush me[5].'

¹⁷"I'm telling you this before it happens so that when it does happen, you'll know that you can be confident that I AM[6] exactly who I've claimed to be.

¹⁸"I must suffer and die as a human[7] just as it's predicted in the sacred writings[8], but how terrible it will be for the man who betrays me! It would indeed have been better for him if he'd never been born[9]."

¹⁹As it happened, John[10] (the disciple) was right next to Jesus. Simon Peter motioned to him to ask Jesus who he was talking about. So leaning back against Jesus, John asked, "Lord, who is it?"

²⁰Jesus answered, "It's the one to whom I'm about to give a piece of bread when I've dipped it." Then he dipped the bread and gave it to Judas, Simon's son.

²¹Then Judas (the one who was about to betray him) asked, "Teacher, am I the one[11]?"

²²Jesus responded, "You've said it yourself[12]."

²³Then Judas took the bread from Jesus' hand. After he received the bread, Satan took control of Judas[13].

²⁴Then Jesus told him, "Right now is the time to do what you're going to do." At this Judas abruptly left the meal, going out into the night.

²⁵None of the other disciples understood why Jesus had said this to Judas. Some thought that because Judas was in charge of the group's funds, Jesus was telling him to buy something for the feast or to give something to the poor.

<u>The Last Supper – The New Commandment – Friday, Nisan 15</u> John 13:31-35
(Glossary articles: Biblical Chronology; Caring Love; Disciples; Immediately / Quickly; Son of Man)

²⁶When Judas had left, Jesus said, "Now it's time for me as a human[14] to be glorified so that God may be glorified through me. And just as God will be glorified in what I do, so God will soon glorify me.

²⁷"Little children, I won't be with you much longer. You're going to look for me, but—do you remember when I told the Jews 'I'm going where you can't come with me'? Well that's what I have to tell you now.

---

[1] 42:12-The lamb for the Passover feast was selected on the 10th of Nisan and killed on the 14th at twilight, just before sundown. Sundown officially started a new day (the 15th of Nisan), and that was the official start of the Feast of Unleavened Bread.

[2] 42:13-This is often translated to say that Jesus became troubled in spirit. But how would the disciples know that he was troubled in spirit? The word "spirit" also meant "wind" or "breath." The word "troubled" also indicated a disturbance. What the disciples could see was Jesus getting choked up by the thought that one of his beloved disciples was about to betray him.

[3] 42:15-This statement refers to a practice of dipping bread in a dish of oil, but didn't clarify who the betrayer would be since they all would've been dipping from one or two dishes of oil. What Jesus said simply reaffirmed that one of the twelve would betray him.

[4] 42:16-Literally, "the writing," but "sacred writing" is clearly implied.

[5] 42:16-Psalm 41:9. In biblical times, sharing a meal, even just some bread, was looked on as forming a sacred bond between those who shared in the meal. Only the worst people would share a meal and then turn against the very person who provided the meal.

[6] 42:17-The "I AM" here is very emphatic.

[7] 42:18-Literally, "the son of man must suffer and die…"

[8] 42:18-Literally, "just as it is written," but "predicted in the sacred writings" is clearly implied.

[9] 42:18-Note the clear message here that for the guilty, there's indeed judgment and torment after death.

[10] 42:19-Literally, "the disciple whom Jesus cared about," but this is John's reference to himself.

[11] 42:21-Note that while the other disciples addressed Jesus as "Lord" when they ask this question, Judas addressed him only as "teacher."

[12] 42:22-In their language, the only distinction between the question, "Am I the one," and the statement, "I am the one" is an introductory word that makes this a question. Jesus threw Judas' words back in his own face. All Jesus' efforts with Judas had failed. Judas appears to have been next to Jesus at the meal, and this was a quiet word to Judas that only one or two others would've heard.

[13] 42:23-It seems that as soon as it was clear to Judas that Jesus knew exactly what he'd agreed to do, rather than repenting as Peter later did, Judas chose to turn even more strongly against Jesus, turning himself over to Satan's will.

[14] 42:26-Literally, "the son of man…"

²⁸"At this point I'm giving you a new commandment—a commandment that you care deeply for one another just like I've cared for you[1].

²⁹"From this time on you're to care for each other's needs. This is the very way that people will know that you're my disciples, if you truly care for each other."

The Last Supper – The New Covenant – Friday, Nisan 15 Matthew 26:26-30; Mark 14:22-25; Luke 22:15-20; John 13:1
(Glossary articles: Biblical Chronology; Caring Love; Jewish Feasts; Sin / Rebellion)

³⁰Even before the Passover feast came, Jesus knew that the time had come for him to leave this world and return to the Father.

³¹While he'd been in this world, he'd always cared deeply for his disciples, and now this caring love guided him to the very end of his life.

³²"Oh how I've looked forward," Jesus said, "to eating this Passover feast with you before I suffer. I'm telling you: I won't eat another Passover meal until the Passover is fulfilled in God's kingdom."

³³Then during the Passover meal, Jesus took a cup of wine, prayed a prayer of thanks for it, and gave it to the disciples.

³⁴"All of you drink from this," he said, "for I assure you that I won't drink any of this fruit of the vine from now on until the day when I drink it new with you in my Father's kingdom[2]."

³⁵Later he took a loaf of bread, prayed a blessing on it, broke it into pieces[3], and gave it to the disciples.

³⁶"Now each of you are to take this bread and eat it," Jesus said. "And from now on, whenever you do this, you're to remember me—this is my body which is being given for you."

³⁷Then he took the cup of wine that comes after the meal, prayed a prayer of thanks for it, and gave it to the disciples.

³⁸"All of you drink from this," Jesus told them, "for this is my blood establishing a new covenant with God—blood that's being shed for many to provide forgiveness of their sins[4]."

The Last Supper—Who's the Greatest? – Friday, Nisan 15 Luke 22:24-30; John 13:3-17
(Glossary articles: Belief / Faith; Biblical Chronology; Biblical Judges; Disciples; Judas; Peter; Slaves; Third Person Commands)

³⁹After supper some of the disciples began to argue about which of them would be considered the greatest.

⁴⁰Jesus (even though he knew that his Father had given everything to him and that he'd come from God and that he was soon to return to God) got up from the meal, laid aside his outer garments, and wrapped a towel around his waist.

⁴¹Then he poured some water into a basin and began to wash the disciples' feet[5] wiping them with the towel at his waist.

⁴²When Jesus got to him, Simon Peter said, "Lord, what's going on? Are you going to wash my feet?"

⁴³"Right now," Jesus told him, "you don't understand what I'm doing, but the time will come when you'll understand."

⁴⁴Peter replied, "Not in all eternity would I let you wash my feet!"

⁴⁵So Jesus told him, "If I don't wash your feet, you have no part in me or what I'm doing."

⁴⁶At this Peter responded, "Lord, don't stop with just my feet—wash my hands and my head too[6]!"

⁴⁷"If people have already bathed," Jesus answered, "they only need to wash their feet to be completely clean—and you're indeed clean (though not all of you)."

⁴⁸(Jesus said this last because he knew that Judas had turned against him and would soon betray him.)

⁴⁹When he'd finished washing their feet, dressed, and returned to the table, he said to them, "Do you understand what I just did to you?

---

[1] 42:28-This command is the very heart and soul of Christianity. Keeping it is how people will know that we are Jesus' disciples. Keeping it is how we mature in the image of our heavenly Father. Keeping it is how we prepare for heaven where that kind of caring love will be what makes heaven a paradise. Keeping it is how we're to attract the world to the good news. Keeping it is the evidence that the God who is love has given us his Holy Spirit to live in us. If we're not at least trying to do this, we're just not Christians.

[2] 42:34-Only Luke mentions two different cups of wine during this meal. The Passover traditions have different cups of wine to be taken at different points during this meal. The final cup of wine was known as "the cup after supper," and that's the cup mentioned in all four Gospels as commemorating the blood Jesus would shed in his sacrifice. In saying that he wouldn't drink any wine again until he shared it with his disciples in God's kingdom, Jesus wasn't pointing to heaven, but to the coming of God's kingdom at his resurrection. He did drink wine with his disciples not long after his resurrection.

[3] 42:35-Since the Passover feast occurred mostly on the 15th of Nisan (the first day of the Feast of Unleavened Bread) the bread used for the Passover meal would've been a relatively flat circle of bread, like a tortilla. The early Christians who continued this custom took this symbol so seriously that they were sometimes accused of cannibalism.

[4] 42:38-Sin is always treason—rebellion against God.

[5] 42:41-People normally walked either in open sandals or barefoot, and many animals traveled through the streets. The proper greeting for guests included washing this filth off of the guests' feet, and this was done by the lowest-ranking slave in the household. So Jesus was taking on the role of that slave, the Lord washing the feet of those who were supposed to be his servants.

[6] 42:46-Jesus had just gently but firmly scolded his disciples' worldly ambitions. They didn't need a bath; they didn't need to go back and be immersed again; they just needed a course correction.

⁵⁰"You call me 'teacher' and 'Lord,' and you're right to do so because that's indeed what I am. So, if I, your Lord and teacher, have washed your feet, in the same way you should be ready to wash each other's feet.

⁵¹"I've just given you an example, and you should practice the same kind of behavior. I'm telling you the absolute truth: a slave isn't greater than his master, nor is a messenger greater than the one who sends him out with a message.

⁵²"The kings and rulers of this world boss their people around while calling themselves, 'friends of the people.'

⁵³"But if you want to be my people, you must not behave like that, trying to boss each other around.

⁵⁴"In fact, it must be just the opposite with you—if you're the greatest among your brothers, act as if you're the most junior; and if you manage the team's affairs, do so as if you were a servant of all those in the team[1].

⁵⁵"Normally wouldn't you say that the one who's served food at a meal is greater than the one who serves him? Yet I've acted as the lowest of servants.

⁵⁶"Now, don't misunderstand. There's greatness in store for each of you.

⁵⁷"You're the ones who've been right there with me through all of my trials. And because you've been faithful to me, I grant you a kingdom just as my Father has granted a kingdom to me.

⁵⁸"When I come in my final power, you'll eat and drink at my table[2] in my own kingdom. And you'll sit on thrones as rulers[3] of the twelve tribes of Israel.

⁵⁹"And there's great joy for those who not only know these things but also put them into practice."

Chapter 43 – After Supper in Jerusalem
Being Prepared – Friday, Nisan 15 Luke 22:35-38
(Glossary articles: Biblical Chronology; Disciples; Prophecies and Fulfillments; Sacred Writings; Third Person Commands)

¹Then Jesus asked them, "When I sent you out with no money or luggage or even an extra pair of sandals, did you lack for anything?"

²"Nothing," they answered.

³"But right now," Jesus continued, "I'm telling you that things have changed.

⁴"If you've got money or luggage, take it with you when you travel. If you don't have a weapon, sell some of your clothing to get one[4].

⁵"The sacred writings say[5], 'He was counted as a law-breaker[6],' and that saying must find its full meaning in me. This is all coming to its final end."

⁶"Look here, Lord. We've got two swords," the disciples said.

⁷"That'll do[7]," said Jesus.

About Faith – Friday, Nisan 15 John 14:1-14
(Glossary articles: Belief / Faith; Biblical Chronology; Common Gender; In the Name of...)

⁸Then Jesus told them, "Don't worry. Just put your faith in God and in me[8].

⁹"There's lots of room in my Father's household[9]. If that weren't true, would I have told you that I'm going away to prepare a place for you[10]?

¹⁰"You can be certain that if I go away to prepare a place for you, I'll definitely come back to bring you there so that we can be together.

¹¹"You know where I'm going, and you know how to get there."

¹²"Lord," Thomas replied, "we don't know where you're going, so how can we know the way there?"

¹³"I AM[5] the way." Jesus said. "I AM[5] the truth. I AM[11] the life.

---

[1] 42:54-These are third person commands in the Bible. See Third Person Commands in the Glossary.
[2] 42:58-If you routinely get invited to eat with the President of the United States, you'll almost certainly have opportunity to influence his thinking, and you'll be considered a person of authority on the basis of that fact alone.
[3] 42:58-Literally, "judges," but in biblical times every judge was a leader with some level of executive authority.
[4] 43:4-These are third person commands in the Bible, but they've been converted to second person commands for English readers. The meaning is the same, but it doesn't come through as strongly in many other translations.
[5] 43:5-Literally, "It is written," but the sacred writings are clearly implied.
[6] 43:5-Isaiah 53:12.
[7] 43:7-Jesus had a plan for these swords. If he'd wanted to win the world by force of human arms, two swords wouldn't have been enough, and these disciples would've needed military training. The purpose of these swords can be found below in Good News 46:26-29.
[8] 43:8-There are several minor variations in how this simple sentence could be translated, but they all boil down to Jesus telling his disciples to have the same kind of faith in him that they have in God.
[9] 43:9-The word "mansions" sometimes used here isn't a valid translation. There's nothing in the Bible about us having mansions. The phrase sometimes translated "in my Father's house" can also mean "in my Father's household," which would refer to the family. Jesus wasn't talking about a house where God lives. He was saying that there's plenty of room in God's family for all who'll serve him.
[10] 43:9-This is a case where the words could be either a question or a statement. As a question, it assumes that Jesus had been telling his disciples that he was going away (we know he was doing that) and that he was going to prepare a place for them.
[11] 43:13-The "I AM" here is very emphatic.

¹⁴"You can't come to the Father unless you come through me. If you'd really known me, you'd have known my Father too, and from now on you do know him, and you've seen him[1]."

¹⁵At that point Philip spoke up: "Lord, show us the Father and that'll be enough for us."

¹⁶Jesus replied, "Come on, Philip. Have I spent all this time with you and you still don't really know me?

¹⁷"Anyone who's really seen who I am has seen the Father. How can you ask for what you've already got?

¹⁸"Don't you have faith that I'm in the Father and the Father's in me? I haven't said a single word on my own—the Father is alive in me and does the things you've seen me do.

¹⁹"Trust me when I say that I'm in the Father and the Father's in me, or else trust me because you've seen what he's done through me.

²⁰"I'm telling you the absolute truth: anyone who puts his faith in me will do the things I've been doing. In fact those who put their faith in me will do even greater things, because I'm going back to my Father.

²¹"And I'll grant you anything you ask for that's consistent with my nature[1] so that people will glorify the Father. I promise you: I'll grant you anything you ask for as long as it's consistent with my nature[2].

The Spirit of Truth – Friday, Nisan 15 John 14:15-31
(Glossary articles: Belief / Faith; Biblical Chronology; Common Gender; Satan; Third Person Commands)

²²"If you really care for me, keep my commandments[3].

²³"When you do that, I'll ask the Father, and he'll give you another powerful aide. I have to leave you, but he'll stay with you always[4]. He's the very Spirit of Truth.

²⁴"People whose lives are focused on this world can't receive this Spirit because they can't see him or comprehend him.

²⁵"You know him because he lives with you now[5] and will be in you. I'm not going to leave you on your own like a bunch of orphans—no, I'll come to you.

²⁶"In a little while people whose lives are focused on this world won't see me anymore, but you'll still perceive me.

²⁷"Because I'm living, you'll also go on living. When you experience my presence in you, you'll understand that I'm one with my Father and you're one with me as I become one with you.

²⁸"The person who truly cares for me is the person who knows my commandments and keeps them—and my Father will care for those who care for me in that way. I'll care for and reveal myself to anyone like that."

²⁹Judas (not the Judas who betrayed him) asked him, "How are you going to do that, Lord? How can you reveal yourself to us and not to the rest of the world?"

³⁰"If anyone really cares about me," Jesus replied, "then that person will live by what I've taught, and my Father will care for anyone who does that. We'll come to and dwell in such a person.

³¹"Anyone who doesn't really care about me won't live by the things I've taught. And you know that my message has come from the Father who sent me.

³²"I've given you these teachings while I've been present here with you, but the powerful aide that the Father's going to send you as my representative, the Holy Spirit—he'll teach you everything you need to know and help you recall all the things I've told you.

³³"Now I'm going to leave you with a special peace—a peace that's nothing like anything the world could give. Don't worry! Don't be afraid[6]! You know that I told you that I'm going away, but I'll come back for you.

³⁴"If you really cared about me, you'd be glad to hear me say, 'I'm going to the Father.' After all, there's much more to God than just what you've witnessed in me[7].

³⁵"I've told you all of this before it happens so that when it does happen, you'll put your faith completely in me.

---

[1] 43:14-Jesus was telling his disciples that if they'd really known him (God), they'd have to have known the Father (God) as well, and now that they'd spent years learning about him and coming to know him, in that same process they had, whether they realized it or not, come to know God.

[2] 43:21-Literally, "in my name…," but with the meaning of "consistent with who I am…"

[3] 43:22-Jesus intentionally emphasized that these were his commandments, not the commandments of Moses. He was saying that the only commandments from the Law of Moses that they'd be required to keep were the ones he'd taught—the commandments of caring love for God and for each other. By doing this, they'd meet the entire intent of Moses' Law.

[4] 43:23-The word Jesus used for this powerful aide implied a companion who'd be at your side in a battle or contest. It was also used for someone who'd be with you and represent your interests before the rulers if you were charged with some crime—the ideal lawyer who truly cares about you.

[5] 43:25-By telling his disciples that this Spirit of Truth was already living with them and would be in them, Jesus made it clear that he's that Spirit of Truth—that the Spirit of God living in him is the same as the Holy Spirit who'd live in them (though in a more limited way due to human sinfulness).

[6] 43:33-These are third person commands in the Bible, but they've been converted to second person commands for English readers. The meaning is the same, but it doesn't come through as strongly in many other translations.

[7] 43:34-This is often translated as "the Father is greater than I," but that implies that the Father's a greater God and Jesus is a lesser god. While God (who is spirit) lived in Jesus, his presence in Jesus was limited to what we could stand and what would be helpful for us. There's much more to God than we need to know about now, but everything we could stand to know about God was present in Jesus.

³⁶"I won't be able to talk to you much more about these things because the ruler of this world, Satan, is coming for me even though he has no right to me at all. The only reason he can come for me is so that the world may understand how much I care about the Father.

³⁷"I'm going to do exactly what the Father has commanded.

³⁸"Now let's get up and leave here."

The Desertion Predicted – Friday, Nisan 15 Matthew 26:31-35; Mark 14:26-31; Luke 22:31-34, 39; John 13:36-38
(Glossary articles: Belief / Faith; Biblical Chronology; Peter; Sacred Writings; Satan)

³⁹After that they sang a hymn and then they left the house headed for the Mount of Olives. As they were walking, Simon Peter asked him, "Lord, where are you going?"

⁴⁰Jesus responded, "Where I'm going, you can't come with me now, but later on you'll come after me.

⁴¹"The fact is," Jesus told his disciples, "tonight every one of you will fail to stand up for me.

⁴²"After all, the sacred writings say[1], 'I'll strike the shepherd, and the whole flock of sheep will be scattered[2].'

⁴³"But after I've been raised, I'll go ahead of you to Galilee."

⁴⁴Peter responded, "Lord, why can't I come with you now? Even if all the others fail to stand up for you, I'll never do that! I'd lay down my life for you!"

⁴⁵Jesus just shook his head and said, "Simon, Simon! Satan's actually demanded to have you so that he can sift you like wheat. But I've prayed for you that your faith in me may not fail[3].

⁴⁶"When you've turned back to me, you'll need to strengthen these, your brothers[4]."

⁴⁷Peter protested, "Lord, I'm ready right now to go anywhere with you, even if it's prison or death."

⁴⁸Jesus replied, "Would you really lay down your life for me? I'm telling you the absolute truth: before this night's over—before the rooster crows a second time[5] for the dawn, you yourself will have denied me three times."

⁴⁹Peter got agitated and said, "Even if I have to die with you, I'll never deny you!" And all the other disciples declared the same thing.

Chapter 44 – On the Way to the Garden

The Vine and the Branches – Friday, Nisan 15 John 15:1-8
(Glossary articles: Biblical Chronology; Common Gender)

¹"Think of it this way:" Jesus continued, "I AM[6] the vine and my Father's the one who takes care of the vine.

²"Every branch in me that doesn't bear fruit gets cut off and thrown away.

³"He doesn't cut off the branches that do bear fruit, but he does prune them so they'll bear more fruit.

⁴"You've already been purified by putting into practice the things I've taught you. Just stick with me and I'll stick with you.

⁵"A branch can't bear fruit by itself—it has to stay connected to the vine. In the same way, you can't bear fruit for God unless you stick with me.

⁶"Remember, I AM the vine, you're the branches. If you stick with me, I'll stick with you, and you'll be able to bear a great deal of fruit[7]—but without me you won't be able to bear fruit at all.

⁷"Anyone who doesn't stick with me will be cut off and thrown out like a branch withering away on its own. Those will be like the branches cut off from a vine, gathered up and thrown into the fire where they'll be burned up.

⁸"As long as you stick with me and live by the things I've taught you, you can ask whatever you wish and it'll be done for you.

⁹"When you live by the things I've taught you, you'll truly be my disciples, the Father will truly be glorified, and you'll bear a great deal of fruit indeed.

---

[1] 43:42-Literally, "it is written," but the sacred writings are clearly implied.
[2] 43:42-Zechariah 13:7.
[3] 43:45-The difference between Judas and Peter was where their hearts were focused. Judas didn't just betray Jesus—Judas had actually turned his heart against Jesus, putting the focus of his life on himself and on the things of this world rather than on God. Peter betrayed Jesus out of human weakness.
[4] 43:46-We need the Peters who fail in their human weakness but never really turn away from God. They can give us strength to overcome our failures.
[5] 43:48-Only Mark's Gospel mentions the rooster crowing twice. The other Gospel writers didn't consider this detail to be important, but Mark was working with Peter when he wrote his Gospel, and Peter would certainly have remembered every detail.
[6] 44:1-The "I AM" here (and wherever these words are in all capital letters) is very emphatic.
[7] 44:6-The fruit Jesus was talking about is the fruit of the Spirit described in Galatians 5:22-23. That fruit is Christian love, joy, peace, patience, kindness, goodness, faithfulness, gentleness, and self-control. When a person exhibits those things in his or her life, that person exhibiting the presence of God's Holy Spirit. A person who doesn't exhibit those things exhibits that God's Holy Spirit isn't working in his or her life.

The Commandment to Care – Friday, Nisan 15 John 15:9-17
(Glossary articles: Biblical Chronology; Caring Love; Common Gender)

[10]"I've cared for you unconditionally just as the Father cares for me unconditionally—now live in my caring love.

[11]"If you live by the things I've commanded, you'll experience life in my caring love just as I've kept my Father's commandments and live in his caring love.

[12]"I'm sharing this with you so that you may always experience the joy you've found in me.

[13]"This is my ultimate commandment—that you truly care for each other just as I've cared for you.

[14]"You can't care more deeply than in giving your life for your friends, and you are indeed my friends if you keep my commandments.

[15]"Up until now you've been my servants. Since I've been your master, you've had no right to ask what I'm doing. But now you've become my friends, and I've told you everything just as I've received it from my Father.

[16]"Remember, you didn't choose me—I chose you. I've given you the responsibility to go out and produce fruit that will last forever.

[17]"If you do that, my Father will give you anything you ask for that's consistent with my nature.

[18]"This is my commandment to you: Truly care for each other.

The Coming Spirit of Truth – Friday, Nisan 15 John 15:18-27 16:1-11
(Glossary articles: Belief / Faith; Biblical Chronology; Caring Love; Prophecies and Fulfillments; Sacred Writings; Satan; Sin / Rebellion)

[19]"If you experience the hatred of those whose lives are focused on this world, you can be sure they hated me before they came to hate you.

[20]"If you were part of their crowd, they'd care for[1] you as one of their own. But because the focus of your life isn't on this world (though you were part of this world when I chose you), that change in focus has caused worldly folks to hate you.

[21]"Remember when I told you, 'A servant isn't greater than his master'?

[22]"People like those who've persecuted me will always be around to persecute you. On the other hand, people like those who've lived by my teachings will also be around and will live by your teachings, too.

[23]"People whose lives are focused on this world may talk about God, but they've never known him or understood that he sent me, so they'll persecute you because you live according to what I've practiced in my life and what I've taught.

[24]"If I'd never come to tell them about God, they wouldn't be guilty of sin[2]; but now they have no excuse for their rebellion, because they've seen my Father in what I've said and done, and they've turned against me and against my Father.

[25]"This has given full meaning to what's in their own sacred writings[3]: 'They hated me without a cause[4].'

[26]"But when your powerful aide comes, the Spirit of Truth I'm going to send to you from the Father, he'll act as a witness for me. And you, too, will act as witnesses for me because you've been with me from the very beginning.

[27]"I've told you all this so that you won't get tripped up in your faith.

[28]"Indeed, they'll shut you out and they'll even kill you, thinking that they're serving God. They'll do these things because they've never really known me or the Father.

[29]"When these things happen, remember that I warned you.

[30]"Up until now I didn't need to warn you because I was with you to protect you. But now I'm going away to the one who sent me, and this time none of you is asking me, 'Where are you going?' because your hearts are so filled with sorrow at what I'm telling you.

[31]"Yet I'm telling you the absolute truth: it's actually to your advantage for me to go away. If I don't go away, your powerful aide cannot come to you, but if I do go away, you can be sure I'll send him to you.

[32]"When he comes, he'll bring a message to those whose lives are focused on this world: convincing them of the reality of human sin, of the importance of righteousness, and of the coming judgment.

[33]"He'll convince them of their sin because they don't focus their lives on me, of righteousness because I'm returning to my Father and they'll no longer have me to show them what righteousness means, and of judgment because Satan, the ruler of this world[5], has been condemned.

---

[1] 44:20-The word here is for the caring love that is Christian love.
[2] 44:24-Remember, sin is always treason—rebellion against God.
[3] 44:25-Literally, "what's written," but the sacred writings are clearly implied.
[4] 44:25-Psalm 69:4.
[5] 44:33-It's important to realize that Jesus very clearly taught that Satan is the ruler of this world. Yes, God can control him and God does have the final authority, but he's allowed us to choose Satan over him by our refusal to live by his commandments of caring love, and he's honored the fact that all of us have chosen Satan at least some of the time, and most people have chosen Satan's way to some degree all of the time. When things go wrong in this world, it's not because of God, it's because we've empowered Satan to rule in this world. In the end God will make all things right for those who serve him, but for now we must live in this world ruled by Satan and his forces.

Not Ready for the Whole Story – Friday, Nisan 15 John 16:12-15
(Glossary article: Biblical Chronology)
   ³⁴"I've still got a lot to tell you, but you're not ready for the rest of it right now.
   ³⁵"When the Spirit of Truth comes, he'll guide you to the truth in every situation, because he won't talk about himself. He'll simply pass along what he hears, and he'll reveal to you things yet to come.
   ³⁶"He'll bring honor to me because he'll take what's mine and pass it along to you. Understand, everything the Father has is mine. That's why I said he'll take what's mine and pass it along to you.

Leaving and Coming Back – Friday, Nisan 15 John 16:16-24
(Glossary articles: Biblical Chronology; In the Name of...)
   ³⁷"The time's coming shortly," Jesus continued, "when you'll not see me, but not long after that you'll see me again."
   ³⁸The disciples were confused and began whispering among themselves, "What's he talking about—'very shortly you'll not see me' and 'it won't be long until you'll see me again' and 'I'm going to the Father'? What does he mean by 'it won't be long'? We don't get it."
   ³⁹Jesus knew what they wanted to ask him, so he asked them, "Are you whispering among yourselves because of what I said about 'it won't be long'?
   ⁴⁰"I'm telling you the absolute truth: you're going to be sobbing while those whose lives are focused on this world will be rejoicing. But that sorrow's going to be turned into joy.
   ⁴¹"When a woman's about to bear a child, the labor pains may bring her to tears; but as soon as the baby's born, she forgets the anguish because she's so happy to have brought a new life into the world.
   ⁴²"In the same way, you'll have sorrow now, but I'll see you again, and you'll be filled with joy—a joy no one will be able to take from you.
   ⁴³"When that time comes, you won't need to ask me for anything. I'm telling you the absolute truth: the Father will give you whatever you ask that's consistent with my nature¹.
   ⁴⁴"Until now, you haven't asked for anything in that way. Now you'll be able to ask with the assurance that you'll get what you ask for, just so you'll experience the fullness of joy the Father wants you to have.

The Disciples Get It—Or Do They? – Friday, Nisan 15 John 16:25-33
(Glossary articles: Belief / Faith; Biblical Chronology; Caring Love; Disciples; In the Name of...)
   ⁴⁵"I've been talking to you as if in symbols and figures, but it won't be long before I'll stop using such symbols and figures and tell you very plainly about the Father.
   ⁴⁶"When that time comes, you'll ask for things that are consistent with my nature². And when you do, it won't be me asking the Father on your behalf—the Father himself cares deeply for³ you because you've cared so deeply for me and have put your faith in the fact that I came directly from God.
   ⁴⁷"I came into this world directly from the Father, and I'll leave this world to return to the Father."
   ⁴⁸His disciples responded, "Now you're talking plainly, not in figures and symbols.
   ⁴⁹"Now we're certain that you know everything, and there's no need for anybody to question your authority. Because of this we've put our faith and trust in you as the one who's come directly from God."
   ⁵⁰"So you think you're finally ready to put your faith fully in me?" Jesus replied, "In fact, the time's actually come now when you'll be scattered, each returning to his own things and leaving me by myself. Yet I won't be alone because the Father's always with me.
   ⁵¹"I've told you all of this so that you may have genuine peace. In this world the tribulation you'll have will make it look like you don't have peace, but cheer up, I've already conquered this world."

Chapter 45 – The Lord's Prayer
Glorified to Bring Glory to God – Friday, Nisan 15 John 17:1-8
(Glossary article: Biblical Chronology)
   ¹Then looking up into the sky Jesus prayed¹, "Father, the time's come for you to glorify me so that I in turn can bring glory and honor to you.

---

[1] 44:43-Literally, "in my name," but with the meaning of "consistent with who I am." For American Christians, "in my name" doesn't carry the real significance of those words. To pray in Jesus name meant to pray a prayer that would be consistent with who Jesus is and what he wants. It's fine to pray a selfish prayer, as long as you sincerely include that you want God's will to be done in the matter. It's fine to pray for even the smallest matters--like a perfect parent, God wants to hear about all our concerns. It's fine to pray about almost anything, but the primary focus of our prayer lives should be on God's kingdom and God's goals.
[2] 44:46-Literally, "in my name," but with the meaning of "consistent with who I am."
[3] 44:46-The word here is for the caring love that is Christian love.

²"To do this you've given me authority over all humanity to give life everlasting to all those you've given to me. And this is the path to life everlasting, coming to really know you by coming to really know me.

³"Up to now I've brought glory and honor to you in this world, but now I've finished that part of the work you gave me to do.

⁴"So now the time's come to bring glory and honor to yourself by giving to me the glory that I had with you before the world was ever created.

⁵"I've revealed who you are, your very character, to these men that you gave me, men who've now been taken out of their worldly environment. They were truly yours from the start, you gave them to me, and they've remained faithful to your message.

⁶"Now these disciples have realized that everything you've given me came from you. I've given them the message that you gave me, and they've accepted your message. They've come to understand that I came from you, and that you really did send me.

Prayer for the Disciples – Friday, Nisan 15 John 17:9-19
(Glossary articles: Belief / Faith; Biblical Chronology; Disciples; In the Name of...; Prophecies and Fulfillments; Sacred Writings; Satan)

⁷"I'm praying for these disciples. I'm not praying for those whose lives are focused on this world, but for these disciples you've entrusted to me, because they truly are yours.

⁸"Indeed, all those who follow me are yours and all those who trust in you are mine—and they give glory and honor to me.

⁹"Now I'm leaving this world and coming to you, but these followers will still be in the world. Holy Father, keep these whom you've given me through your authority² so that they may be united as one just as we are one.

¹⁰"While I was here with them in this world, I kept them by your authority³ as those you had entrusted to me, and only one of them (the very child of destruction) has been lost, so that what was foretold in the sacred writings⁴ might be given full meaning.

¹¹"But now I'm coming to you, and I'm bringing these prayers while I'm still in this world so that they may experience in themselves the joy I've experienced.

¹²"I've given them your message, and because they've focused their lives on you instead of the things of this world, the people whose lives are focused on things in this world despise them.

¹³"Yet I'm not asking that you take them out of this world, but that you keep them safe from the one who's the embodiment of evil.

¹⁴"They're not part of this world, just as I'm not part of this world, so Satan has no authority over them. Sanctify them by your message which is absolute truth.

¹⁵"Just as you sent me into this world, I've also sent them into the world.

¹⁶"For their sakes I've kept myself pure so they could see what that's like and themselves be purified by that same truth.

Prayer for Future Disciples – Friday, Nisan 15 John 17:20-24
(Glossary articles: Belief / Faith; Biblical Chronology; Disciples; Maturity / Perfection)

¹⁷"I'm not just praying for these men who are with me now, but also for those who'll put their faith in me through their message, so that all of them may be united as one, just as you and I are united as one⁵.

¹⁸"I'm praying that they may be united as one with us so that those whose lives are focused on this world may come to realize that you actually did send me⁶.

¹⁹"The glory that you gave me I've given to them also, so that they may be united as one just as we are united as one—I in them and you in me.

²⁰"I've done all this so that they may all reach maturity¹, united in us, and so that the world may know for sure that you really did send me and that I care for them just as you've cared for² me.

---

¹ 45:1-We're all familiar with the model prayer that Jesus taught his disciples, and that prayer is often called "the Lord's prayer." However, many Christians have pointed out that the prayer in this passage would more appropriately be called "the Lord's prayer." As you read this prayer, notice Jesus' selfless attitude and his heart-felt prayer for his disciples to be united in their commitment to God through him.
² 45:9-Literally, "through your name."
³ 45:10-Literally, "in your name."
⁴ 45:10-Literally, "the writings," but sacred writings is clearly implied.
⁵ 45:17-This prayer for unity among his followers, given just before his arrest, has been terribly neglected. And it's not a prayer for unity in form—it's a prayer for unity in spirit. Meeting in a common building with common leaders but with no common understanding of Christianity isn't what Jesus prayed for. Christian love and full faith in God must be the foundation of our unity if we're ever to live up to this prayer.
⁶ 45:18-This is God's plan for evangelism. When the world sees Christians united in living for the Lord and demonstrating the fruit of the Spirit in their lives, they'll see God in action and they'll know that he's real and that his ways are right and true.

²¹"It's also my desire, Father, that those you've given to me may be with me wherever I am and that they may witness the glory you've given me, just as you cared for me before the world was created.

Conclusion to the Prayer – Friday, Nisan 15 John 17:25-26
(Glossary articles: Biblical Chronology; Caring Love)
²²"Those whose lives are focused on this world don't know you at all, righteous Father, but I do and so do these disciples whom you've given me.
²³"I've revealed you to them, and I'll keep on revealing more about you, so that the caring love[3] you have for me will also be in them, just as I'll be in them."

Chapter 46 – In the Garden
Jesus' Prayer in the Garden- Friday, Nisan 15 Matthew 26:36-46; Mark 14:32-42; Luke 22:40-46; John 18:1-2
(Glossary articles: Agent / Angel; Biblical Chronology; James; Jesus and Temptation; John; Peter; Sin / Rebellion; Son of Man; Third Person Commands)
¹After all these teachings and this prayer, Jesus and his disciples crossed over a brook[4] and entered a grove of olive trees[5].
²Judas (the one who betrayed Jesus) also knew about this place because Jesus often went there with His disciples.
³Jesus told his disciples, "Sit here. Pray that you may not be overcome by temptation. Meanwhile, I'm going over there to pray."
⁴He took James and John[6] as well as Peter with him and became deeply distressed and sad.
⁵Then Jesus told them, "My very soul is so sad and distressed that I could die. Stay right here on watch with me."
⁶Jesus then went farther into the grove—about the distance you could throw a stone. Then falling on his face he prayed,
⁷"Abba[7], my Daddy, all things are possible for you. If it's at all possible, take this cup away[8]—nevertheless I want your will to be done, not mine[9]."
⁸After struggling in prayer for some time, Jesus returned to find the disciples asleep and said to Peter, "What's this, Simon? Couldn't you stand watch with me for even one hour?
⁹"Stay alert and keep praying so that you won't be tempted.
¹⁰"Yet I understand that your spirits are indeed willing, but your flesh is weak[10]."
¹¹Then Jesus left them again to pray saying, "O my Father, if the only possible option for this cup is for me to drink it, do it your way."
¹²Once again after some time struggling in prayer, Jesus came back to the disciples and found them sleeping—they just couldn't keep their eyes open. Again he reprimanded them, and they didn't know what to say.
¹³So Jesus went back to anguished prayer a third time, and his sweat became like great drops of blood falling to the ground. An agent of God from heaven appeared to him to give him strength.
¹⁴When he finally returned to his disciples for the third time and found them sleeping again, he said, "Are you still sleeping?
¹⁵"Look, the time's come and I as a human[11] am now being betrayed into the hands of sinners. Get up! Let's go! My betrayer's almost here!"

---

[1] 45:20-This is an important aspect of Christianity. We don't start out perfect or mature. We grow toward maturity. And maturity in one person may look very different from maturity in another, but it will always include the fruit of the Spirit and the unity of purpose for which Jesus prayed.
[2] 45:20-The word used twice here is for the caring love that is Christian love.
[3] 45:23-The word here is for the caring love that is Christian love.
[4] 46:1-Kidron Creek. The word used here is for a stream that would normally be dry in the dry months and a raging torrent in rainy weather.
[5] 46:1-Gethsemane.
[6] 46:4-Matthew says, "the two sons of Zebedee."
[7] 46:7- "Abba" is the Hebrew word for "father," but it was also the first word a Hebrew baby would be encouraged to say. "Abba" in Hebrew would be like "daddy" in our culture.
[8] 46:7-This is a third person command in the Bible, but it's been converted to a second person command for English readers. The meaning is the same, but it doesn't come through as strongly in many other translations.
[9] 46:7-Note that Jesus has just prayed a prayer that is basically self-centered, but that he emphasizes that what he wants most is God's will to be done. Selfish prayers are fine, as long as we keep our focus on God's will and our willingness to accept his answers.
[10] 46:10-These men had been up all night, and it was getting very late. By this time it was probably around 1:00 am, and the day had been filled with heavy activity and traditional observances including a feast.
[11] 46:15-Literally, "the son of man is now…"

The Arrest – Friday, Nisan 15 Matthew 26:47-56; Mark 14:43-52; Luke 22:47-53; John 18:3-11
(Glossary articles: Biblical Chronology; Jewish Elders; High Priest; Immediately / Quickly; Judas; Peter; Pharisees; Chief Priests; Prophecies and Fulfillments; Sacred Writings; Son of Man)

[16]While Jesus was still speaking, Judas (who'd received a battalion[1] of policemen[2] and their officers from the chief priests, the scribes, the Pharisees, and the elders of the people) arrived at the olive grove with a mob[3] armed with swords and clubs and carrying various lanterns and torches.

[17]Judas had told this mob, "I'll greet one of them with a kiss. He'll be the one you want. Seize him, place him under guard, and take him away."

[18]Arriving where Jesus stood with his disciples, Judas rushed straight up to Jesus and kissed him, saying, "Good to see you, teacher!"

[19]"Judas, my friend," Jesus said. "What are you doing here? Are you betraying me as a human[4] with a kiss?"

[20]Of course Jesus knew what was coming, so he stepped forward and asked, "Who are you looking for?"

[21]The people with Judas answered, "Jesus of Nazareth."

[22]Then Jesus said, "I AM[5]!"

[23]When Judas and the crowd heard him say, "I AM[6]!" they drew back and fell to the ground. Then Jesus asked them again, "Who are you looking for?"

[24]Once again those with Judas responded, "Jesus of Nazareth."

[25]"I've told you," Jesus replied, "I AM[7]. So if you're looking for me, just let these others be on their way." He said this in order to bring full meaning to what he'd said: "I've lost none of the ones you gave me[8]."

[26]When the disciples realized what was going on, they asked Jesus, "Lord, is this the time we should draw our swords and attack?"

[27]Meanwhile, Simon Peter drew his sword and cut off the right ear of the high priest's slave[9].

[28]Jesus then told the disciples, "Put your swords away!

[29]"Anybody who wants to use weapons will wind up killed by those weapons[10]. Or don't you get it?

[30]"Right now I could ask my Father, and he'd send an army of more than 50,000[11] of heaven's soldiers. But then how would the prophecies of these things in the sacred writings[12] be fulfilled?

[31]"Don't you understand that I'm going to drink the cup my Father's given me? For now you've got to allow these men to take me."

[32]At this Jesus touched the slave's ear and healed him.

[33]Then he turned to the mob (including the chief priests, the elders, and officers of the temple policemen[13]) and asked, "What do you think you're doing, coming out here with swords and clubs as if you were after a thief?

[34]"Every day I've been sitting in the temple teaching and you didn't arrest me then. But of course this is your time with the power of darkness. And all of this is happening so that the sacred writings of the prophets may be fulfilled."

[35]At this point all the disciples ran for their lives.

[36]As it happened, there was a young man who'd followed Judas. He was wearing nothing but a linen cloth thrown around his body. Then some of the young men in the mob tried to grab him, so he left the cloth behind and ran away naked[1].

---

[1] 46:16-The word used here is for a military group of about 500 men, but this probably indicates a contingent of at least more than 100. The Jewish authorities didn't want to take any chances in arresting Jesus.

[2] 46:16-Literally, "soldiers," but the role of temple soldiers was basically that of modern policemen.

[3] 46:16-The "mob" would've consisted of the soldiers armed with swords plus others armed with clubs.

[4] 46:19-Literally, "the son of man…"

[5] 46:22-Literally, the "I AM" here is very emphatic. When Moses asked God what his name is, God's reply was, "I AM!" In some Bibles this is translated as "Jehovah" or "the LORD" (with LORD in all capital letters). Later God commanded the Israelites to never use his name as profanity. Jews decided this name was so sacred that it should never even be spoken. By the time of Jesus' ministry people no longer remembered exactly how to pronounce the Hebrew word God used. The response of the crowd shows that at this point Jesus spoke his divine name—I AM. Hundreds of years of superstition about this name and its power caused the crowd to fall back, but when no bolt of lightning came from the sky, they were encouraged to come forward again.

[6] 46:23-The "I AM" here is very emphatic.

[7] 46:25-The "I AM" here is very emphatic again. However, while Jesus probably used Hebrew in the previous case, he probably reverted to Greek at this point to again emphasize that he was surrendering quietly (though the words in the Bible are in Greek for both cases).

[8] 46:25-See Good News 45:10 above in Jesus' prayer.

[9] 46:27-The slave's name was Malchus. He was probably the leader of the mob sent to arrest Jesus. Of course, Peter wasn't aiming for this man's right ear. Peter thought he saw an opportunity to draw his sword and take off this man's head in one sweeping motion, but as a fisherman he had no training for sword fights and didn't understand how difficult that act would be—so all he got was an ear.

[10] 46:29-This is the very reason Jesus wanted the disciples to have at least a couple of swords with them. He wanted to make this point in a way that they'd never forget.

[11] 46:30-Literally, "twelve legions…" It's worth noting that the word used for the soldiers who came out to the garden indicates about 500 men, while the words Jesus used indicate a hundred times that many from heaven's army. That wouldn't be much of a contest!

[12] 46:30-Literally, "the writings," but "the sacred writings" is clearly implied.

[13] 46:33-Literally, "soldiers," but the role of temple soldiers was basically that of modern policemen.

Chapter 47 – Three Jewish Examinations and Peter's Denial

The First Two Examinations – Predawn Friday, Nisan 15 Matthew 26:57-75; Mark 14:53-72; Luke 22:54-65, 69; John 18:12-27

(Glossary articles: Biblical Chronology; Christ; Jewish Elders; High Priest; Immediately / Quickly; Jesus' Trials; Judeans / Jewish Authorities; Peter; Chief Priests; Supreme Court; Scribes; Son of Man and Son of God)

¹Then these Jewish policemen[2] and their officers arrested Jesus, bound him, and led him away[3].

²Their first stop was at the palace of the father-in-law[4] of the man who was high priest[5] that year. (It was this high priest who'd advised the Jewish authorities that it would be expedient for one man to die for the people.)

³Peter had followed some distance behind and initially stood outside the gate to the courtyard of the palace.

⁴Another disciple[6] had also followed, but since he was known to the high priest, he was allowed to enter the courtyard. Then that other disciple spoke to the woman in charge of the gate, and she allowed Peter to enter the courtyard.

⁵Later the servant girl who kept the gate looked closely at Peter and asked him, "You're not one of that man's disciples, are you?"

⁶Peter replied, "Woman, I don't know what you're talking about. I certainly don't know that guy[7]."

⁷At that point a rooster crowed. Then Peter found a place to sit with the servants so he could see how things would work out.

⁸Later, since it was cold, Peter got up and walked over to where some of the servants and officers had started a fire, and he stood there trying to get warm.

⁹Meanwhile the high priest's father-in-law[8] was asking Jesus about his disciples and about his teachings.

¹⁰"I always spoke openly," Jesus said, "so that anybody in the world could hear what I was teaching. I always taught in worship centers and in the temple—wherever Jews typically meet. I've never said anything in secret, so why are you asking me?

¹¹"If you're really looking for the truth, you should ask those who heard me to tell you what I said to them. They certainly know what I said."

¹²When Jesus said this, one of the officers who was standing nearby slapped Jesus with the palm of his hand and said, "That's no way to speak to the high priest!"

---

[1] 46:36-Mark is the only Gospel that tells of a young man's naked escape from the Garden of Gethsemane when Jesus was arrested (Mark 14:52), and many believe with good reason that the young man who escaped was Mark himself.

Mark 14:13-15 tells us that Jesus' last supper earlier in that night had been in an upper room and that the disciples had been led to this room by a young man carrying a pitcher of water. It was very unusual for a man to carry a pitcher of water, though a widowed mother might send her young son for water, especially if she were very busy with other responsibilities.

Acts 1:13 tells us that after Jesus' ascension to heaven, his disciples were meeting in an upper room in Jerusalem. Acts 12:12 tells us that when Peter was miraculously released from prison, he went to the house that belonged to Mary, the mother of John Mark, where many of the Christians were gathered to pray for him. The fact that Mary is named as the owner of the house implies that she was a widow, and the fact that there was a room where so many could meet implies something like a large room that could be rented to guests for various purposes (weddings, feasts, etc.).

If all these references are to the same upper room in Mary's house, then it's likely that John Mark was the young man carrying the jug of water. (It's certainly possible even if they weren't all the same room.) After Jesus and his disciples left for Gethsemane and the room had been cleaned up, it's reasonable to conjecture that Mark might have gone to bed with only a linen cloth over his body. After all, it was Passover, the weather was warm, and it would've been very late at night.

It's also reasonable to conjecture that Judas, who'd left during the meal, brought his mob to this house first in his search for Jesus. As a young man, Mark might well have grabbed his linen sheet around his naked body to follow the mob and see what was happening. The mention of this young man who ran away naked may well be Mark's way of saying, "I was there—I witnessed this."

No one has ever come up with another reason to include this brief account, and it adds one more layer of evidence (though not proof) that John Mark actually was the author of this Gospel. Given all the other evidence, there's no good reason to doubt this as fact. We have testimony from Christians from the late first century on that John Mark was the author, and that he'd worked with Peter in Rome to write this Gospel. That testimony certainly fits with the facts.

[2] 47:1-Literally, "soldiers," but the role of temple soldiers was basically that of modern policemen.

[3] 47:1-Jesus was taken to the Jewish authorities, but they carefully saw to it that for various reasons these examinations wouldn't qualify as actual trials.

[4] 47:2-Annas.

[5] 47:2-Caiaphas.

[6] 47:4-The name of this disciple who was known to the high priest will probably never be known. Nicodemus and Joseph of Arimathea come to mind immediately, but there was no hesitation among the authors of the Gospels to use those names, so this probably wasn't one of them.

[7] 47:6-Peter was indeed ready to die for Jesus if it meant that he'd die fighting. He proved that in the olive grove when he drew his sword to fight 500 armed men. He just wasn't ready to die for Jesus without a fight.

[8] 47:9-Annas. This man was still considered by some to be the real high priest.

[13]Jesus responded, "If I've said something wrong, speak up and say what it is. But if what I've said is true, why would you slap me?"

[14]Then the high priest's father-in-law[1] sent Jesus, still bound, to the official high priest[2]. The Jewish elders were already assembled at his house[3], along with the scribes, the chief priests, and members of the Jewish Supreme Court[4].

[15]They brought in several "witnesses" who were willing to testify for money, trying to find testimony that would justify a death sentence against Jesus, but they couldn't find two who agreed on evidence that would actually support condemning Jesus[5].

[16]Finally those examining Jesus found two false witnesses who said, "We heard this guy say, 'I can destroy the temple of God and raise it back up without human hands in three days.'" (Even then the testimony of these two didn't fully agree.)

[17]At this, the high priest stood up and said to Jesus, "OK, what about the accusation these men are making? Don't you have any response at all?"

[18]Jesus gave no reply, so the high priest said, "I'm putting you under oath by the living God. Now tell us whether you're indeed the Christ, the son of God."

[19]Jesus responded, "I AM[6] exactly as you said[7]. But I'm telling you: the time's coming when you'll see me sitting as a human[8] at the right hand of the power of God and coming in clouds of the sky."

[20]Then the high priest tore his clothes saying, "That's lying about God! Why do we need any more witnesses? You yourselves have heard his lies about God. So what do you think now?"

[21]The leaders who were present responded, "He deserves to die."

[22]Then some of them blindfolded him, spit in his face, beat him, and said, "If you're the Christ, prophesy and tell us who it was that hit you." And even some of the officers slapped him with their palms. This went on until dawn.

[23]Meanwhile, as Simon Peter stood by the fire warming himself, a servant girl said, "You're one of his disciples too, aren't you?"

[24]This time Peter denied with an oath, saying, "I am not!"

[25]About an hour later one of the servants of the high priest who was kin to the man whose ear Peter had cut off said, "Didn't I see you in the garden with him? I can tell by your accent that you're a Galilean too."

[26]Now Peter began to curse and swear as he denied for the third time, and while he was still speaking the rooster crowed for the second time.

[27]At that point Jesus turned and looked at Peter, and Peter recalled Jesus saying to him, "Before the rooster crows the second time, you'll deny me three times."

[28]At this Peter went out and sobbed as if his heart would break.

The Third Jewish Examination – After Dawn Sunday, Nisan 17 Matthew 27:1-2; Mark 15:1; Luke 22:66-68, 70-71; 23:1; John 18:28a
(Glossary articles: Biblical Chronology; Christ; Jewish Elders; High Priest; Jesus' Trials; Chief Priests; Supreme Court; Scribes; Son of God)

[29]As soon as it was officially day[9], the elders and chief priests assembled quickly (along with the scribes[10]) and led Jesus into their Supreme Court[11] chamber. At this point they asked only one question: "If you're the Christ, tell us."

[30]But this time Jesus responded, "If I tell you, you won't believe anything I say, and if I question you, you certainly won't answer any of my questions or let me go."

[31]Then they all insisted that he answer their question, "Are you the son of God?"

[32]Jesus responded, "I AM[12] exactly as you've said."

---

[1] 47:14-Annas, who was the real power behind the high priesthood. He'd been deposed from the high priesthood by the Romans, but he managed to keep family members in this office.

[2] 47:14-Caiaphas.

[3] 47:14-In the middle of the night, the elders and some witnesses who were to testify against Jesus were already at Caiaphas' palace. That reveals the level of planning for this event.

[4] 47:14-Often translated "Council" or "Sanhedrin," but this body was the highest Jewish court and the highest Jewish authority religiously and politically.

[5] 47:15-The problem these leaders faced was that the Jewish law required two witnesses whose testimony agreed before a guilty verdict could be given. Either they hadn't adequately prepared the witnesses, or the witnesses weren't good enough actors. However, this passage does make it plain that there were those on the Supreme Court who seriously questioned the witnesses. Nicodemus and Joseph of Arimathea were probably two who did so.

[6] The "I AM" here is very emphatic.

[7] 47:19-Jesus' response turned Caiaphas' question into a strong statement.

[8] 47:19-Literally, "the son of man sitting…"

[9] 47:29-In this translation, officially day is assumed to be the first non-Sabbath after Jesus' arrest which would be Sunday, Nisan 17.

[10] 47:29-The scribes were there to keep a record of what happened.

[11] 47:29-Often translated "Council" or "Sanhedrin," but this was the highest Jewish court.

[12] 47:32-The "I AM" here is very emphatic.

³³"What more do we need?" they asked. "We've heard it ourselves from his own mouth[1]."

³⁴At this they had Jesus bound again and the whole crowd led him from the high priest[2] to the Roman headquarters building for trial before the governor, Pilate.

Chapter 48 – Trials before Pilate and Herod

First Trial before Pilate – Sunday, Nisan 17 Matthew 27:11; Mark 15:2; Luke 23:2-7; John 18:28b-38a
(Glossary articles: Biblical Chronology; Caesar; Herod; Jesus' Trials; Jewish Feasts; Judea and Galilee; Judeans / Jewish Authorities; Pilate; Chief Priests)

¹It was early in the morning when the Jews came to Pilate, but they wouldn't enter Pilate's headquarters lest they become ceremonially unclean and be prohibited from observing the Feast of Unleavened Bread[3].

²Then Pilate went out to the crowd and asked them, "What's this man accused of doing?"

³The Jewish authorities replied, "If he weren't a criminal, we wouldn't have brought him to you."

⁴"You take him and judge him by your own laws," Pilate responded.

⁵To this the Jewish authorities replied, "It's against your law for us to put a man to death.

⁶"We've found out he's been misleading our whole nation, telling people not to pay their taxes to the emperor[4] and saying that he himself is the Christ—a king."

⁷(Getting the Romans to execute Jesus assured that Jesus would die by crucifixion, just as he'd predicted.)

⁸Then Pilate went back into his official headquarters and called for Jesus. He asked Jesus, "Are you the king of the Jews?"

⁹Jesus responded, "Are you asking this on your own, or did someone else put you up to this?"

¹⁰"Am I a Jew?" Pilate responded. "Your own people and even the chief priests have turned you over to me, so what have you done?"

¹¹"I have no interest in a worldly kingdom," Jesus responded. "If my kingdom were of this world, my servants would fight, and I would never be in the hands of these Jewish authorities. But my kingdom isn't here in this world."

¹²"Are you a king, then?" Pilate asked.

¹³"Those words are true," Jesus replied. "I was born and came into this world to carry a message of truth. Everybody who's serious about being truthful listens to me."

¹⁴Pilate scoffed: "What is truth?"

¹⁵After examining Jesus further, Pilate went out again and told the chief priests and the mob, "I can't find any fault with this man."

¹⁶At this, the Jewish leaders got angrier than ever. Among the things they said was, "He's an agitator! He started spreading his message in Galilee, and now he's carrying it throughout this city and the whole province of Judea."

¹⁷As soon as Pilate heard them mention Galilee, he asked if Jesus were a Galilean. When he determined that Jesus was indeed a Galilean and belonged to Herod's[5] jurisdiction, he sent Jesus to Herod, who was also in Jerusalem at that time[6].

The Trial before Herod – Monday, Nisan 18 Luke 23:8-12
(Glossary articles: Biblical Chronology; Herod; Chief Priests; Jesus' Trials; Miracles; Scribes)

¹⁸Now Herod[7] was very glad to see Jesus. He'd heard a lot about Jesus and for a long time he'd wanted to see one of Jesus' miracles.

¹⁹Herod himself questioned Jesus every way he could, but he couldn't get Jesus to give him any response at all. Meanwhile the chief priests and scribes stood around strenuously accusing him of all kinds of things.

²⁰Finally, Herod and his soldiers began to treat Jesus with contempt. They made fun of him, dressing him in a kingly robe.

---

[1] 47:33-Note that there's no indication of how many on this Supreme Court agreed with this decision. It was certainly a majority, but we learn in Good News 49:46 that Joseph of Arimathea was at least one member who didn't agree, and Nicodemus certainly wouldn't have agreed. The account of the examination by Caiaphas in Good News 47:15-16 indicates that there were people on the Supreme Court seriously questioning the witnesses against Jesus. But when Jesus claimed to be the son of God, those who wanted to support him were out-voted. This was just too huge a claim to support.

[2] 47:34-Caiaphas.

[3] 48:1-This feast was a seven-day feast. Technically, it was the Feast of Unleavened Bread, but since it started with the Passover meal, it was often referred to as Passover. Any Jew who entered the home of anyone who wasn't Jewish would be considered ceremonially unclean until sundown. These leaders worked in the temple and performed religious rites, but if they were ceremonially unclean from entering Pilate's home, they'd be barred from their work for a whole day during the busiest time of the year and from sharing in the feast. Since a large number of the chief priests were apparently involved in the Sunday trial, having them all unclean would've been a real problem.

[4] 48:6-Literally, "Caesar."

[5] 48:17-This was Herod Antipas, son of Herod the Great.

[6] 48:17-The Roman provinces of Galilee and Judea were territories where the majority of the population were Jews, though northern Judea was Samaritan territory and separated the Jews in southern Judea from those in Galilee. Jerusalem was the Jewish capital of Judea (but not the Roman capital). Galilee was considered a rather unimportant area politically, but Judea and especially Jerusalem represented potentially serious political dangers for Pilate.

[7] 48:18-This was Herod Antipas, son of Herod the Great.

²¹At last they sent him back to Pilate, and from that time on Pilate and Herod (who'd been at odds with each other until then) became friends.

The Second Trial before Pilate – Tuesday, Nisan 19 Matthew 27:12-31; Mark 15:3-20; Luke 23:13-25; John 18:38b-40; 19:1-16
(Glossary articles: Bar-Abbas; Biblical Chronology; Caesar; Crucifixion Timing Issues; Jewish Elders; Herod; Jesus' Trials; Jewish Feasts; Judeans / Jewish Authorities; Pilate; Chief Priests; Romans and Jews; Third Person Commands)

²²Outside Pilate's headquarters the chief priests and elders just kept accusing Jesus of crimes, but Jesus wouldn't respond to their accusations[1].

²³Pilate asked Jesus, "Don't you have anything to say? Just listen to all the things they're saying about you!" But Jesus wouldn't say a word, and that astonished the governor.

²⁴Then Pilate went out to the mob and told them, "You've brought this man to me as someone who's misleading the people. Now I've examined him in your presence, and I've found nothing to support the charges you've made against him.

²⁵"Herod also examined him as you know. I sent you back to Herod to hear his verdict yourselves, and he found nothing that would justify a death sentence. Based on that, I'm only going to punish him[2]."

²⁶Meanwhile, the crowds outside began to chant for Pilate to release a prisoner as was the custom each year at Passover, so Pilate spoke to the crowd. "You've got a custom that I should release someone of your choice from prison at the Passover. So, I've got this 'king of the Jews' and I've got this man called Bar-Abbas. Which one of these two do you want me to release, Bar-Abbas or Jesus?"

²⁷Now Bar-Abbas was a well-known leader in the fight against the Roman occupation. He and his companions were chained together in prison because they'd committed murder and robbery in their efforts to rebel against the Roman authorities.

²⁸Pilate gave the Jews this choice because he knew that the reason the authorities had delivered Jesus to him for trial was that they envied the influence Jesus had on the people.

²⁹But the chief priests and elders persuaded the crowds[3] to call out, "Release Bar-Abbas!"

³⁰"Then what do you want me to do with this Jesus that you call the king of the Jews?" Pilate responded.

³¹"Crucify him[4]!" the crowd called out.

³²"Why?" exclaimed Pilate. "What's he done wrong?" But the crowd just kept chanting for his crucifixion.

³³Then Pilate ordered that Bar-Abbas should be released and he sent Jesus to have him whipped.

³⁴The soldiers led Jesus into the headquarters building, calling the whole garrison together. After whipping him, they clothed him in a robe of royal purple and twisted some thorns together as a crown that they forced onto his head.

³⁵Then they bowed in mockery before him and shouted, "Hail, king of the Jews!" They hit him on the head with a reed, spit in his face, and slapped him with their hands.

³⁶Finally Pilate came back out to the mob, saying, "I want you to know, after examination under torture[5], I can still find no fault in this man."

³⁷At this he brought Jesus out still wearing the crown of thorns and the purple robe. Pilate, wishing to release him, cried out, "Just look at this man!"

³⁸When the chief priests and their temple policemen saw him, they started chanting, "Crucify him! Crucify him!"

³⁹Pilate said, "You go crucify him! I can't find any fault in the man!"

⁴⁰Some of the Jewish authorities responded, "We have a law, and according to that law he should die because he claimed to be God's own son."

⁴¹When Pilate heard these words, he was even more frightened of this situation and rushed back into the headquarters building[6].

---

[1] 48:22-This was Tuesday, and the crowd of chief priests and their allies that had been at Pilate's headquarters early Monday morning had been largely replaced by this time with the normal Passover crowds.

[2] 48:25-The word used here that's translated "punish" could mean anything from a gentle rebuke to a severe whipping or worse. While it's hard to know what Pilate actually had in mind, it would've been something he hoped would satisfy these Jewish authorities, so rather severe but not deadly.

[3] 48:29-The people in this crowd would've included very few if any of the people who surrounded Jesus when he entered Jerusalem. The crowds then were made up largely of people from Galilee who were in Jerusalem for the Passover, people from the area around Bethany who were aware of Jesus having raised Lazarus from the dead, visitors to Jerusalem for the Passover who got caught up in the excitement, and some from Jerusalem with ties to Bethany who'd have known about Lazarus. Remember, when Jesus entered Jerusalem that day, the people in the city were asking who this man was. The crowd in front of Pilate's headquarters would've been made up mostly of people who lived in Jerusalem.

[4] 48:31-This is a third person command in the Bible, but it's been converted to a second person command for English readers. The meaning is the same, but it doesn't come through as strongly in many other translations.

[5] 48:36-The Bible doesn't actually say "under torture," but that's clearly implied and was standard procedure for such "examinations."

[6] 48:41-Today a person making such a claim to a powerful ruler would probably bring a response of scornful laughter, but in New Testament times this was something the pagan world took very seriously. They had many stories of gods having children and the terrible

⁴²"Where are you really from?" he asked, but Jesus wouldn't answer him. "Are you refusing to answer me?" Pilate demanded. "Don't you know that I've got the power to crucify you and the power to release you?"

⁴³Jesus responded, "You wouldn't have any power at all against me unless God gave it to you. That's why the ones who brought me to you are guiltier than you."

⁴⁴From that point on, Pilate got serious about trying to get Jesus released, but the response of the Jewish leaders was, "If you let this man go, you're no friend of the emperor[1]. Anybody who claims to be a king is speaking out against the emperor[2]."

⁴⁵After hearing this, Pilate brought Jesus out and sat on the judgment seat in a place called The Pavement. This was the Preparation Day[3] for the final Passover feast, and it was around noontime[4].

⁴⁶While Pilate was on the judgment seat, his wife sent a message to him: "Don't do anything to hurt that innocent man! I've had a terrifying dream about him."

⁴⁷Then Pilate said to the Jewish leaders, "Behold! Here's your king!"

⁴⁸But the mob began chanting, "Kill him! Kill him! Crucify him!"

⁴⁹"Why?" the governor asked for the third time. "What's he done wrong?"

⁵⁰But the crowd just kept chanting louder and louder: "Crucify him!"

⁵¹Pilate then asked, "Shall I crucify your king?"

⁵²To this the chief priests responded, "We have no king but the emperor of Rome[5]!" And the people in the mob were insistent, demanding at the top of their lungs that Jesus be crucified. And the voices of the chief priests and their supporters drowned out anything Pilate could say.

⁵³When Pilate realized that he wasn't going to be able to win this argument and that further efforts could bring on a riot, he called for a basin of water and washed his hands in front of the crowd saying, "You see, I'm innocent of the blood of this good man[6]."

⁵⁴Then the crowd responded, "We accept on ourselves and on our children any guilt for shedding his blood."

⁵⁵So Pilate sentenced Jesus to death. When his soldiers had whipped Jesus again and mocked him, they took the purple robe off of him and dressed him in his own clothes.

⁵⁶Then Pilate formally turned Jesus over to the soldiers for crucifixion, and the soldiers led him away.

The Death of Judas Matthew 27:3-10; Acts 1:18-19
(Glossary articles: Judas; Chief Priests; Herod's Temple; Jewish Elders; Law of Moses; Prophecies and Fulfillments; Sin / Rebellion)

⁵⁷Then Judas (the one who betrayed him), when he realized that Jesus would be condemned, was filled with remorse.

⁵⁸He took the thirty silver coins back to the chief priests and elders and told them, "I've sinned against God[7] by betraying an innocent man."

⁵⁹"What do you want us to do?" they asked. "That's your problem."

⁶⁰Then Judas threw the money down in the temple and left.

⁶¹The chief priests discussed what to do with the money and decided it would violate the Law of Moses to put it in the temple treasury since it was blood money.

⁶²In the end, Judas went out and hanged himself in a field called the potter's field. When his body was finally cut down, it fell to the ground and broke open with all of his guts spilling out onto the ground.

---

things that happened to those who hurt these children of the gods. What the Jews considered criminal blasphemy, Pilate considered a very dangerous possibility.

[1] 48:44-Literally, "no friend of Caesar's." We might think that some local Jewish authorities wouldn't have much influence with the emperor of Rome when compared with the Roman governor of the province, but the emperors were very sensitive the local concerns, especially in provinces as prone to insurrection as this one. There's historical evidence that Pilate was reprimanded more than once by the emperor because he offended the local authorities.

[2] 48:44-Literally, "Caesar."

[3] 48:45-The day before any Sabbath was known as Preparation Day. Since no work was allowed on a Sabbath, it took much of the day on Preparation Day to get ready. This was especially true for the women. All food had to be ready, and supplies of water had to be filled, so that people could have enough to eat and drink without preparing food or carrying water. Every Saturday was a Sabbath, so almost every Friday was a Preparation Day. For feast days that the Law of Moses defined as Sabbaths, the day before the feast day was an extra Preparation Day. If such a feast came on a Friday, there'd be two Sabbaths in a row, and Thursday would be a very busy Preparation Day.

[4] 48:45-Mark's Gospel is clear that Jesus was crucified about 9:00 am. John's Gospel is equally clear that Pilate set up his judgment seat around noon. And a lot happened after this noontime event before Jesus was crucified. This provides clear biblical evidence that there were days between the arrest and the crucifixion. According to the chronology used here, this Preparation Day was on a Wednesday.

[5] 48:52-Literally, "We have no king but Caesar."

[6] 48:53-Some have translated this as if Pilate were telling the Jews to deal with Jesus' crucifixion, but the verb isn't in the form of a command, nor would Pilate have done that in any case. If Jesus were to be crucified, he'd have to be crucified by the Romans—a crucifixion by Jews wouldn't be tolerated.

[7] 48:58-Remember, sin is always treason—rebellion against God.

⁶³The Jewish leaders then took the coins and purchased the field where Judas had died as a place to bury strangers. For these reasons that field came to be known as the Field of Blood.

⁶⁴All of this gave full meaning to what Jeremiah the prophet had written: "They took the thirty pieces of silver, the price set on him by the children of Israel, and gave the coins for the potter's field, just as Jehovah directed[1]."

Chapter 49 – The Crucifixion and Burial

The Walk to the Cross – Wednesday, Nisan 20 Matthew 27:32-33; Mark 15:21-22; Luke 23:26-31, 33a; John 19:17
(Glossary articles: Biblical Chronology; Jesus' Crucifixion)

¹In the morning, the soldiers led Jesus away, forcing him to carry the beam for his own cross.

²Along the way they came on a man named Simon[2] coming into the city, and they forced him to carry Jesus' cross the rest of the way.

³A large crowd of people followed Jesus including women who mourned and wept over him, but Jesus turned to these women and said, "Daughters of Jerusalem, don't cry for me. Weep for yourselves and your children!

⁴"I promise you: it won't be long before people will say, 'How good it is for the women who've never had a baby and the breasts that have never nursed a child.'

⁵"At that time people will cry out to the mountains, 'Fall on us!' and to the hills, 'Cover us!'

⁶"After all, if they do these things when the wood's green, what will happen when the wood's dry?"

⁷Then they continued to a place called "The Place of the Skull[3]."

The Crucifixion – 9:00 am Wednesday, Nisan 20 Matthew 27:34-36, 38; Mark 15:23-25, 27-28; Luke 23:32, 33b-34; John 19:18, 23-24
(Glossary articles: Biblical Chronology; Jesus' Crucifixion; Prophecies and Fulfillments; Romans and Jews)

⁸When they arrived at the place, they gave Jesus vinegar[4] mixed with a bitter perfume[5] to drink, but when he tasted it, he refused to drink it.

⁹The soldiers nailed Jesus to the cross. Then they separated his clothing into four parts, one for each soldier, with his tunic separate from the rest.

¹⁰The tunic had been woven in one piece from top to bottom, so they said, "Let's not tear it. Instead, let's gamble for it to decide who gets it."

¹¹This happened to fulfill what the prophet had written: "They divided my garments among themselves and gambled for my clothing[6]."

¹²Then they sat around to guard the scene.

¹³It was 9:00 in the morning when they crucified Jesus along with two thieves who'd rebelled against the Romans[7]—one on his right hand and the other to the left. (This gave full meaning to the sacred writing[8] that says, "And he was counted as one with lawbreakers[9].")

¹⁴As they were crucifying him, Jesus prayed, "Father, forgive these men. They don't know what they're doing."

The Sign on the Cross Matthew 27:37; Mark 15:26; Luke 23:38; John 19:19-22
(Glossary articles: Pilate; Chief Priests; Jesus' Crucifixion)

¹⁵Pilate had a sign posted on the cross that said, JESUS OF NAZARETH, KING OF THE JEWS. It was written in Hebrew, Greek, and Latin, and since the place of the crucifixion was close to the city, a lot of the Jews were reading the sign.

¹⁶Then the chief priests went to Pilate and said, "Instead of 'King of the Jews,' we want you to write 'He said, "I'm king of the Jews."'"

---

[1] 48:64-Jeremiah 32:6-9.
[2] 49:2-Matthew wrote that Simon was from Cyrene and that he had two sons named Alexander and Rufus. Simon and his sons were probably well known to those who first read Matthew's Gospel.
[3] 49:7-In America today, the most common name for this place is "Calvary," which is a Latin term for "Place of the Skull." In the Bible it's "Golgotha," but the meaning is the same. Today, there's no clear evidence for the exact location of this place.
[4] 49:8-Literally, "sour wine."
[5] 49:8-The vinegar (or sour wine) is described in Mark as mixed with something like myrrh, which is a bitter tasting substance with a pleasant smell. In Matthew the vinegar is described as mixed with gall (something bitter). There were two words for myrrh in the Greek: "*myrrha*" and "*smyrna*." The word Mark used was "*smyrnidzo*," meaning something kind of like myrrh. For gall, Matthew used the word "*cholays*." That word could mean literally the bitter gall fluid that comes from the gall bladder, or it could figuratively apply to something bitter. The point seems to be that this vinegar had something in it that made it extra bitter.
[6] 49:11-Psalm 22:18.
[7] 49:13-For the Jews, these criminals would've been heroes except for the fact that they used robbery to support their insurrection against Rome. To the Romans, as long as these men weren't stealing from Romans, their actions as thieves would've been a local matter, but their insurrection against Rome is what got them crucified.
[8] 49:13-Literally, "the writing," but "the sacred writing" is clearly implied.
[9] 49:13-Isaiah 53:12. Many of the ancient manuscripts don't include the part in brackets, but this is a valid comment.

[17]But Pilate responded, "What I've written, I've written."

People at the Cross Matthew 27:39-44, 55-56; Mark 15:29-32, 40-41; Luke 23:35-37, 39-43; John 19:25-27
(Glossary articles: Belief / Faith; Chief Priests; Jewish Elders; Jesus' Crucifixion; John; Mary Magdalene; Mary-Mother of Jesus; Scribes; Son of God Third Person Commands)

[18]Not too far from Jesus' cross stood his mother, Mary, Mary's sister, Mary Magdalene, another woman named Mary[1], and many other women from Galilee who'd taken care of Jesus' needs during his ministry and followed him to Jerusalem.

[19]These women were standing well away from the cross, but when Jesus spotted his mother and John, he said to his mother, "Woman, this man is now your son." Then he said to John, "This woman is now your mother." So from that time on, John took Mary into his home.

[20]Some of the chief priests, scribes, and elders were standing nearby sneering and mocking him saying, "You saved so many others, now save yourself[2] if you're really 'the Christ,' the 'chosen one of God,' the 'king of Israel'" and "Get off that cross so we can see for ourselves and believe all your claims."

[21]Others passing by shook their heads in mock disbelief and said, "So you were going to destroy the temple and build it back in three days? Now let's see you save yourself. If you're really the son of God, come on down from that cross!"

[22]Still others said, "He claimed to trust in God, so let God rescue him now—if he'll have him. After all, he said, 'I'm the son of God.'"

[23]The soldiers also made fun of him, offering him vinegar[3] to drink and calling out to him, "If you really are the king of the Jews, let's see you rescue yourself from this!"

[24]Then one of the men who were being crucified with him ridiculed him too, saying, "If you're really the Christ, save yourself and us."

[25]But the other man who was crucified with Jesus rebuked him, saying, "Don't you fear God, now that you're about to die just as he is?

[26]"You know that we deserve this punishment because of the things we've done, but this man hasn't done anything wrong."

[27]Then turning to Jesus he said, "Lord, remember me when you come into your kingdom[4]."

[28]"You can be sure of this," Jesus responded, "this very day you'll be with me in paradise."

On the Cross – Noon to 3:00 pm, Wednesday, Nisan 20 Matthew 27:45-54; Mark 15:33-39, 42b; Luke 23:44-49, 54; John 19:28-37
(Glossary articles: Belief / Faith; Biblical Chronology; Crucifixion Timing Issues; Elijah; Herod's Temple; Immediately / Quickly; Jerusalem; Jesus' Crucifixion; Sabbath; Sacred Writings)

[29]From noon to about 3:00 clouds covered the sky[5] as far as the eye could see.

[30]Around 3:00 Jesus screamed, "God! God! Why have you left me?" Some of the people standing around commented, "He's calling for Elijah[6]!"

[31]Then, to give full meaning to what's in the sacred writings[7], Jesus said, "I'm so thirsty."

[32]The jar of vinegar was still there, so one of the people near the cross quickly took a sponge soaked with vinegar and, putting it on the end of a branch, held it to Jesus' mouth for him to drink.

[33]Others standing near the cross jeered, "Let him alone! Let's see if Elijah will really come to rescue him."

[34]Then Jesus cried out again, "It's done! Father, I'm entrusting my spirit to you," and he stopped breathing.

[35]About this time there was an earthquake that split the bedrock[8] of the mountains, and the curtain in the temple that separates the Holy Place from the Most Holy Place was torn in two from top to bottom.

[36]Graves were opened by the earthquake and several bodies of saints who'd died were raised from the dead. After Jesus' resurrection these resurrected saints were seen in Jerusalem by many people.

---

[1] 49:18-The third Mary was "the mother of James the Younger and Joses" (Matthew and Mark) and also "the wife of Clopas" (John). Another woman listed among the group was Salome (Mark), "the mother of Zebedee's sons," James and John (John).

[2] 49:20-This is a third person command in the Bible, but it's been converted to a second person command for English readers. The meaning is the same, but it doesn't come through as strongly in many other translations.

[3] 49:23-Literally, "sour wine."

[4] 49:27-Notice that this man had more faith in Jesus than any of his disciples. It's very likely he had contact with Jesus at some point in the past. See Jesus' Crucifixion in the Glossary.

[5] 49:29-Literally, "the sky was dark..." Often people try to claim that this was a supernatural darkness in which all light was taken away, like being deep in a cave with the lights all off. Such a darkness would've been the subject of a lot of conversation and many written reports. People paid a lot of attention to any such event that they couldn't explain. Since no such event has been found in any of the records from that time, it's far more likely this was cloud cover.

[6] 49:30-Jesus cried out in the Aramaic language, and the word for "God" was pronounced a lot like the name "Elijah."

[7] 49:31-Literally, "the writings," but "sacred writings" is clearly implied. See Psalm 22:15.

[8] 49:35-Literally, "rocks were split," but the word used for "rocks" is the word for bedrock.

[37] When the Roman commander[1] and the soldiers guarding Jesus witnessed the earthquake and its effects; they were struck by fear and said, "Surely this man really was the son of a god."

[38] Because it was a Preparation Day[2], the Jewish leaders went to Pilate and asked to have his soldiers break the legs[3] of the men being crucified so that their bodies could be removed before the start of the Sabbath. (That Sabbath was an important Sabbath[4]).

[39] So the soldiers broke the legs of the two men who'd been crucified with Jesus, but when they came to Jesus they found that he was already dead, so they didn't bother breaking his legs.

[40] However, one of the soldiers took a spear and ran it through his side just to be sure, and right away blood and water[5] came gushing out.

[41] (I, John[6], saw this myself and my testimony is the truth. I tell you this so that you'll have faith.)

[42] All these things happened so that what's in the sacred writings[7] could be given full meaning: "Not a single bone in his body will be broken[8]," and "They'll look on the one they've pierced[9]."

[43] But the crowd that had come out to see the execution beat their chests with pride[10] and returned to the city.

[44] Meanwhile Jesus' followers and the women from Galilee who'd stood by him during the crucifixion stayed some distance from the cross, watching.

The Burial – About 6:00 pm, Wednesday, Nisan 20   Matthew 27:57-61; Mark 15:42a, 43-47; Luke 23:50-53, 55-56; John 19:38-42
(Glossary articles: Biblical Chronology; Jesus' Crucifixion; Jesus' Resurrection; Judeans / Jewish Authorities; Law of Moses; Mary Magdalene; Nicodemus; Pilate; Sabbath; Supreme Court)

[45] Now there was a wealthy Judean man named Joseph[11]—a prominent member of the Jewish Supreme Court[12] who was a good man and a disciple of Jesus looking forward to the coming of God's kingdom (but secretly for fear of the other Jewish authorities who opposed Jesus).

[46] Joseph hadn't agreed with the Supreme Court's condemnation of Jesus. Now he screwed up his courage and went to Pilate to ask for Jesus' body.

[47] Pilate was amazed that Jesus was already dead, so he summoned the commander from the crucifixion site to verify that he'd been dead long enough to be certain of the death.

[48] When the commander verified that Jesus was definitely dead; he gave Joseph permission to take the body.

[49] Joseph took Jesus' body down. Then he and Nicodemus (the man who'd once come to Jesus by night) placed the body in Joseph's own tomb.

[50] This tomb was in a garden not far from where the crucifixion had taken place. The tomb had been freshly cut into the rock, and Jesus was the first to be laid in the tomb.

[51] Nicodemus had brought along about a hundred pounds of a mixture of fragrant spices[13] for the body, and Joseph had obtained some fine linen to wrap the body according to Jewish burial customs.

[52] By the time they finished wrapping the body with the linen and the spices, it was almost sundown and the start of the Sabbath, so they rolled a large stone in front of the entrance and left.

[53] Mary Magdalene and another Mary[14] who'd stayed with Jesus all the way from Galilee, tagged along and, sitting across from the tomb, saw where his body was placed.

---

[1] 49:37-Literally, "the centurion."

[2] 49:38-Literally, "it was Preparation." Used this way as a proper noun, the word "day" wasn't included. Every Friday was known as "Preparation" because of all the activities that had to be done to prepare for the regular Saturday Sabbath, but the day before any other Sabbath would also be called "Preparation," and this is such a case.

[3] 49:38-There's a common belief that breaking the legs of a person being crucified would cause fluid build-up in the lungs, resulting in death by drowning. The evidence from people who've had themselves crucified to experience the suffering indicates that this isn't the case at all. It's likely that breaking the legs wasn't done gently, and that this caused severe internal and likely external bleeding, hastening death.

[4] 49:38-That Sabbath wasn't the weekly Sabbath, but the Sabbath that occurred on the seventh day of the Feast of Unleavened Bread.

[5] 49:40-"Water" means a clear fluid, not necessarily H_2O.

[6] 49:41-John didn't actually give us his name here, but he did clearly indicate his role as an eyewitness. The fact that John's name never appears in John's Gospel while it's clear that the author was part of Jesus' most inner circle of disciples is one of the strongest pieces of evidence that John was indeed the author.

[7] 49:42-Literally, "the writing," but "the sacred writings" is clearly implied.

[8] 49:42-Psalm 22:17.

[9] 49:42-Zechariah 12:10.

[10] 49:43-"With pride" isn't literally in the Bible, but that seems the most likely meaning here. Those who beat their chests were clearly not Jesus' followers.

[11] 49:45-Joseph of Arimathea.

[12] 49:45-Often translated as "Council" or "Sanhedrin," but this was the highest Jewish court.

[13] 49:51-Myrrh and aloes.

[14] 49:53-This Mary was the wife of Clopas and mother of Joses.

⁵⁴Then the two women returned to their lodgings.

⁵⁵All the women rested on the Sabbath[1] in accordance with the commandment in the Law of Moses, but as soon as they could, they started preparing some additional spices and fragrant oils for his body.

Chapter 50 – Resurrection Events
Guards at the Tomb – Thursday to Sunday, Nisan 21-24 Matthew 27:62-66, 28:2-4, 11-15
(Glossary articles: Agent / Angel; Biblical Chronology; Jesus' Resurrection; Pilate; Chief Priests; Pharisees)

¹On the day after Jesus was crucified[2], some of the chief priests and Pharisees got together with Pilate and told him, "Sir, we remember that when this liar, Jesus, was still alive, he said, 'I'll rise from the dead after three days.'

²"Because of that, we want you to command that the tomb where he's buried be made secure until the three days are past.

³"Otherwise some of his disciples might come by night and steal the body, claiming, 'He's risen from the dead.'

⁴"If that happened, the resulting deception would be worse than what we had when he was alive."

⁵"I'm giving you some soldiers[3] to guard the tomb," Pilate told them. "Go make the tomb as secure as you know how."

⁶So these Jewish leaders sealed the stone covering the entrance to the tomb and had the Roman soldiers stand guard at the tomb[4].

⁷The soldiers remained on guard twenty-four hours a day.

⁸Then sometime after sundown Saturday, there was a great earthquake and an agent of God wearing clothing of purest white and surrounded by brilliant light descended from the sky. He rolled the stone away from the entrance and sat down on it[5].

⁹Seeing this display of power, the soldiers shook with fear and fell to the ground as if they were dead. Then they ran from the scene, and some of them continued into the city and told the chief priests everything that had happened.

¹⁰The chief priests and other leaders got together to decide what to do.

¹¹Then they gave the soldiers a large bribe and said, "Tell everybody, 'His disciples came at night while we were asleep and stole his body out of the tomb.' And if the governor hears about this, we'll take care of him for you[6]."

¹²So the soldiers took the bribe and did as the Jewish leaders had suggested, and many of the Judeans came to accept this account.

Women Come to the Tomb – About 6:00 am, Sunday, Nisan 24 Matthew 28:1, 5-10; Mark 16:1-11; Luke 24:1-10; John 20:1-2
(Glossary articles: Biblical Chronology; Crucifixion Timing Issues; Jesus' Resurrection; Mary Magdalene; Sabbath; Sin / Rebellion; Son of Man)

¹³After the Sabbaths[7], early Sunday morning just before the sun rose, Mary Magdalene and some other women[8] headed for the tomb with some spices for Jesus' body.

¹⁴On the way they were discussing who they could get to roll the stone away from the entrance to the tomb[9].

¹⁵As they approached the tomb, they saw that the stone had already been rolled away—and it was a huge stone.

¹⁶When the ladies entered the tomb, they couldn't see Jesus' body anywhere. At this Mary Magdalene ran from the tomb alone[10].

---

[1] 49:55-The Sabbath had already started by the time Jesus' burial was completed.

[2] 50:1-This was the second feast for the Feast of Unleavened Bread. This was a Sabbath, so these Jewish authorities shouldn't have been doing this "work" on the Sabbath, but they felt it was too important to put off. Interestingly, one of their most frequent complaints about Jesus was that he broke the Sabbath rules.

[3] 50:5-Literally, "You have a guard." It's clear from other information in the account that these were Roman soldiers Pilate assigned to this duty.

[4] 50:6-The Jewish authorities would've gone to Pilate with this concern as early as they could on Thursday, so the soldiers were on guard and the tomb was sealed that day—probably before noon—and the soldiers would've assured that the body was in the tomb before sealing it.

[5] 50:8-Sitting on the stone was like saying, "So there!"

[6] 50:11-The response of the Jewish authorities shows that they knew Jesus had actually risen from the dead. Their assurance of dealing with the governor (Pilate) makes it clear that the soldiers were Roman. Roman soldiers who let a prisoner escape were subject to the punishment due to that prisoner—in this case crucifixion. That's why these soldiers came to the Jewish authorities for a bribe and for assurance that they wouldn't be in danger if Pilate found out. But the fact that the Jewish authorities did bribe the soldiers to say that the body was stolen is clear evidence that they believed the soldiers' story.

[7] 50:13-Matthew clearly says "after the Sabbaths" (though it's generally not translated to show that the word "Sabbaths" is plural). This supports the idea here that there were actually two Sabbaths between Jesus' death and his resurrection.

[8] 50:13-Mary the wife of Clopas, Salome, and Joanna are named, and then the Bible says there were also others.

[9] 50:14-These women were unaware of a guard having been placed at the tomb.

[10] 50:16-When Mary Magdalene ran from the tomb, she hadn't seen the heavenly agents or heard their message. What she knew was that the stone was rolled back and the tomb was empty.

¹⁷Standing in the tomb, the other women were astonished when suddenly they saw two young men wearing shining white robes and sitting on the right side of the tomb, and the women bowed their heads.

¹⁸Then one of the young men calmed them saying, "Don't be afraid. You're looking for Jesus[1] who was crucified. But why would you look for the living among the dead?

¹⁹"He's not here—he's risen from the dead. Come take a look at the place where he was lying.

²⁰"Don't you recall what he told you when you were in Galilee? He said, 'I must be turned over to sinful men and crucified as a human[2], but on the third day I'll rise again.'

²¹"So you must go quickly and tell his disciples—including Peter[3]—that he's going ahead of you into Galilee, and you'll see him there.

²²"After all, isn't that what he told you was going to happen? Now I've told you." And the women recalled what Jesus had indeed said.

²³Overwhelmed by awe and joy, the women left the tomb and ran to find the disciples to tell them what had happened. Meanwhile Mary Magdalene had gone to find Peter[4].

²⁴As they were hurrying to find the disciples, Jesus met the group of women, saying, "Good morning!"

²⁵On seeing him, the women came and held him by the feet and worshipped him.

²⁶But Jesus reassured them, saying, "Don't be afraid. Just go tell my brothers to head for Galilee—they'll see me there[5]."

²⁷Meanwhile Mary Magdalene found Peter and John[6] and said, "They've taken the Lord out of the tomb and we don't know what they've done with his body[7]!"

The Disciples' Reactions – About 7:00 am, Sunday, Nisan 24 Luke 24:11-12; John 20:3-10
(Glossary articles: Biblical Chronology; Disciples; Jesus' Resurrection; Mary Magdalene; Sacred Writings)

²⁸When the group of women told the disciples[8] what they'd seen, it sounded to them like a made-up story and they didn't believe a word of it.

²⁹But responding to Mary Magdalene's report of the missing body, Peter and John[9] set out for the tomb, running[10].

³⁰John[11] reached the tomb first and stood at the entrance to the tomb looking in.

³¹He could see the linen cloths that had been wrapped around Jesus' body just lying where the body had been, but he didn't enter the tomb.

³²When Peter got to the tomb, he went right in and saw the linen strips of cloth just lying where Jesus' body had been.

³³The facecloth was neatly folded and lying by itself a little way from the linen strips of cloth.

³⁴Then John[12], too, entered the tomb, and when he saw the evidence, he believed that Jesus had risen, but Peter simply wondered what had happened[13].

³⁵(At this point they still didn't understand what was in the sacred writings[14] predicting that the Christ[15] must rise from the dead.)

³⁶Then these two disciples went back to Jerusalem.

---

[1] 50:18-Literally, "Jesus of Nazareth who was..."

[2] 50:20-Literally, "the son of man must be turned over to rebellious men and crucified…"

[3] 50:21-The mention of Peter as separate from the disciples is a clue that Peter separated himself from the others after his denial of Jesus. This disciple who'd been ready to die with a sword in his hand hadn't been ready to face a serving girl's scorn, and that had to cause him to question whether he had any right to be among Jesus' disciples. But he may also have been questioning himself and how he could've given years of his life to someone who was now dead.

[4] 50:23-We don't know why Mary Magdalene had gone to find Peter, but for some reason that's what she'd done.

[5] 50:26-The disciples didn't respond well to this instruction. It took more prodding from Jesus to get them to return to Galilee.

[6] 50:27-Literally, "the disciple whom Jesus cared about," but this is how John referred to himself. Apparently John had gone to see Peter, perhaps to try to convince him to come back to the group.

[7] 50:27-Mary Magdalene had left the tomb before seeing the agents or hearing their message that Jesus was alive, and she hadn't been with the other women when Jesus appeared to them, so her message to Peter and John was just that the tomb was empty. Peter and John had no trouble believing that the tomb might have been emptied by the owners.

[8] 50:28-Peter and John weren't with these disciples. Since his denial of Jesus, Peter had apparently removed himself from the group, and John was apparently trying to bring him back into the group. So the women were reporting to just nine of the twelve plus any other disciples who were with them at this point.

[9] 50:29-Literally, "the other disciple," but this is John referring to himself.

[10] 50:29-Here we see where Peter's heart really was. When he heard that Jesus' body was missing, he ran to the tomb. He may have denied the Lord in a time of weakness, but he was still a disciple.

[11] 50:30-Literally, "the other disciple," but this is John referring to himself.

[12] 50:34-Literally, "the other disciple," but this is John referring to himself.

[13] 50:34-Peter wasn't ready yet to believe that Jesus had risen from the dead, but he couldn't come up with anything that made sense. John saw the grave wrappings lying in the tomb, and resurrection was the only thing that made sense. Jesus had told them that he'd rise from the dead, and nobody would've removed the body and left the grave wrappings behind.

[14] 50:35-Literally, "the writing," but "the sacred writings" is clearly implied.

[15] 50:35-Literally, "he," but "the Christ" is clearly implied.

Mary Magdalene Meets Jesus – Sunday, Nisan 24 John 20:11-18
(Glossary articles: Agent / Angel; Biblical Chronology; Jesus' Resurrection; Mary Magdalene)

³⁷Meanwhile Mary Magdalene returned and was standing outside the tomb crying.

³⁸She stooped down to see inside the tomb, and through her tears she saw the two agents from God, one sitting at the head and the other at the foot of where Jesus' body had been lying.

³⁹Then one of God's agents said to her, "Lady, why are you crying?"

⁴⁰"Because," Mary replied, "They've moved my Lord's body and I don't know where they've taken him."

⁴¹Then she turned away from the tomb and saw Jesus standing nearby, but through her tears she didn't recognize him.

⁴²"Lady," said Jesus, "Why are you crying? Who are you looking for?"

⁴³Mary assumed this man must be in charge of keeping the garden so she turned away from him and said, "Sir, if you've moved his body, tell me where you've laid him and I'll take him away."

⁴⁴At this Jesus simply said, "Mary!"

⁴⁵"Teacher!" Mary exclaimed, turning quickly back to him.

⁴⁶"Don't cling to me," Jesus told her, "because I haven't yet gone back up to my Father. Just go tell my brothers, 'I'm going back up to my Father and your Father, to my God and your God.'"

⁴⁷When Mary left, she went to see the disciples. She told them that she'd seen the Lord, and she reported on what he'd told her[1].

Chapter 51 – Jesus Is Alive and Appears to Followers

Two Disciples Meet Jesus – Afternoon, Sunday, Nisan 24 Mark 16:12-13; Luke 24:13-35
(Glossary articles: Agent / Angel; Biblical Chronology; Christ; Chief Priests; Dining Customs; Disciples; Jerusalem; Moses; Sacred Writings)

¹Later that day, two disciples[2] were walking to a town[3] about seven miles from Jerusalem.

²As they walked, they were talking about all the things that had happened, and while they were deep in conversation, Jesus came up and started walking with them, but God kept them from recognizing him.

³Jesus said, "What are you talking about? I saw you walking, and you looked so sad."

⁴Then one of the disciples[3] replied, "You must be the only visitor to Jerusalem who hasn't heard what's been going on the past few days."

⁵"What things?" Jesus asked.

⁶"The things about Jesus of Nazareth!

⁷"He was a powerful prophet before God and all the people—both in the things he did and in the things he taught.

⁸"We were actually hoping that he'd be the Christ[4] who'd rescue Israel from bondage.

⁹"But the chief priests and the rulers of our people condemned him to death and turned him over to the Romans for crucifixion.

¹⁰"Now it's been three days since he was killed.

¹¹"And to top it off, some women who've traveled with us and who went to the tomb early this morning shook us all up because they didn't find his body in the tomb.

¹²"They came back saying they'd had a vision of heavenly agents who told them that he was alive[5].

¹³"Then some of the men went to the tomb, and they found it just as the women had said, but they didn't find Jesus[6]."

¹⁴"Oh you foolish, foolish men, so slow to accept the things written by the prophets!" Jesus replied. "Wasn't it appropriate for the Christ to go through this suffering before entering into his full glory?"

¹⁵Then beginning with Moses and continuing through all the prophets, Jesus explained all the things written in the sacred writings[7] about himself.

¹⁶As they were getting close to their destination[8], Jesus acted as if he were planning to continue on beyond that village, but they insisted that he stay with them.

---

[1] 50:47-At this point the disciples weren't ready to believe. We talk about doubting Thomas, but there was really no difference between his response and the response of the others.

[2] 51:1-These weren't two of the remaining eleven disciples. They were two of the many disciples who followed Jesus around and were serious about listening to his teachings.

[3] 51:4-Cleopas.

[4] 51:8-Literally, "the one," but "the Christ" is clearly implied.

[5] 51:12-This passage tells us that the disciples to whom the women reported what they'd seen included more than just the nine members of the inner group of twelve (minus Judas, Peter, and John).

[6] 51:13-This passage indicates that Peter and John had gone to the rest of the group to tell them what they'd seen, but they hadn't seen agents of God or Jesus himself at this time.

[7] 51:15-Literally, "the writings," but "the sacred writings" is clearly implied.

[8] 51:16-Emmaus.

¹⁷"Spend the night here with us," they said. "It's already getting late in the day¹."

¹⁸So Jesus agreed to spend the night with them.

¹⁹When they'd arrived at their lodgings and a meal had been prepared, Jesus reclined with them around the food. He took some bread, blessed it, and broke it, giving it to them.

²⁰At that point, God opened their eyes, and they realized that they'd been walking with Jesus. But as soon as they realized this, Jesus vanished from sight.

²¹In their excitement they said, "How could we have been so blind? Didn't he set our hearts on fire while he was talking with us as we walked, showing us what the sacred writings² really mean?"

²²So they got up from the meal and immediately left for Jerusalem. There the eleven disciples and the others who were with them told these two, "The Lord has truly risen from the dead! He's appeared to Simon³!"

²³At this the two disciples recounted all that had happened while they were walking and how they'd recognized Jesus when he was breaking the bread for them.

Meeting with the Disciples – Evening, Sunday, Nisan 24 Mark 16:14; Luke 24:36-48; John 20:19-25
(Glossary articles: Biblical Chronology; Disciples; Forgiveness; Jerusalem; Law of Moses; Preaching / Proclaiming; Prophecies and Fulfillments; Repentance; Sacred Writings; Sin / Rebellion)

²⁴While these disciples were still describing their experience, Jesus himself suddenly appeared among the group⁴.

²⁵"Peace to you," he said.

²⁶But instead of peace, the disciples were shocked and terrified, assuming he was a ghost. After all, the doors were shut tight in fear that the Jewish authorities would come after them.

²⁷So Jesus said, "Why are you so troubled—and why these questions in your hearts?

²⁸"Take a good look at my hands and my feet and see that it's really me⁵. Touch me and see for yourselves, because a ghost wouldn't have flesh and bones—and you can see for yourselves that I do."

²⁹Then Jesus let them examine his hands and his feet, but they were still struggling to believe it and blown away by what they were experiencing.

³⁰So Jesus asked, "OK, if that's not enough⁶, do you have any food here?"

³¹The disciples gave him a piece of broiled fish and some honeycomb, and he ate it as they watched.

³²Then he said, "Didn't I tell you all of this while we were together earlier?

³³"I told you that everything written about me in the Law of Moses and in the writings of the prophets and in the psalms had to be fulfilled."

³⁴Then he gave them the gift of understanding so that they'd understand what was in the sacred writings⁷.

³⁵"So you see," Jesus told them, "that's what's in the sacred writings⁸, and that's why it was necessary for me as the Christ to suffer crucifixion and death and to rise from the dead the third day.

³⁶"Now, as the Father sent me, in the same way I'm sending you, so that the message will be proclaimed to everyone in the world, starting at Jerusalem—the message that God wipes out the sins of those who change their lives to focus on living for him⁹.

³⁷"You're to be the witnesses to what's happened."

³⁸When he'd said this, he breathed on them and said, "Receive God's Holy Spirit.

³⁹"If you forgive anyone's sins, that person's sins are indeed forgiven, and if you don't forgive someone's sins, that person's sins aren't forgiven."

⁴⁰At this point the disciples were all convinced except Thomas (also called The Twin), who wasn't present when the Lord appeared.

⁴¹So when the other disciples told him, "We've seen the Lord!" he replied, "Unless I see the nail scars in his hands and put my own finger into the scars and my hand into his side where the spear went in, I'll never believe¹."

---

¹ 51:17-For a person traveling on foot, "late in the day" could easily mean late enough that if you walked to another town, you might have difficulty finding lodgings. This may have been as early as 3:00.

² 51:21-Literally, "the writings," but "the sacred writings" is clearly implied.

³ 51:22-The appearance of heavenly agents and the message they brought—to which several women testified—wasn't convincing to these people, but the appearance to Simon—a man—was convincing. It was a male-dominated society. (The Bible doesn't tell us any more about Peter's meeting with Jesus.)

⁴ 51:24-While Jesus was flesh and bone, and while the scars of the nails and spear were still there, something was different about him. One obvious difference was that he could enter a room without using a door or window.

⁵ 51:28-Literally, "I AM," and the "I AM" here is very emphatic. This passage uses what is technically poor English grammar, but since most Americans use this grammatical construction, that's what's used in this translation.

⁶ 51:30-First Jesus had them examine the wounds to prove that he wasn't a ghost, but when they still doubted, he ate some food to prove that he wasn't a ghost.

⁷ 51:34-Literally, "the writings," but "the sacred writings" is clearly implied.

⁸ 51:35-Literally, "that's what's written," but "written in the sacred writings" is clearly implied.

⁹ 51:36-Often translated "repentance."

Thomas Meets Jesus – Monday, 8 days after the Resurrection John 20:26-29
(Glossary article: Belief / Faith)

⁴²Eight days later the disciples were all together (including Thomas this time) with the doors shut tight[2].

⁴³Then suddenly Jesus was standing there with them, saying, "Peace to you."

⁴⁴Then Jesus walked over to Thomas and said, "Here, reach out and put your finger into my hands and then put your hand into my side. Stop doubting and put your faith in me."

⁴⁵"My Lord," Thomas responded, "and my God!"

⁴⁶"Oh, Thomas!" Jesus replied. "Do you have faith now that you've seen me? What joy is in store for those who haven't actually seen me and have still put their faith in me."

Chapter 52 – Appearances in Galilee

In Galilee – Jesus Questions Peter John 21:1-23
(Glossary articles: Caring Love; Galilee; Immediately / Quickly; James; John; Peter)

¹Later, Jesus appeared to the disciples again at the Sea of Galilee[3], and this is how it went:

²One evening Simon Peter, Thomas (who was also called "The Twin"), Nathan[4] (the one from Cana in Galilee), James and John[5], and two others[6] were together.

³Simon Peter said, "I'm going fishing." and they said that they'd go with him. They went out to the shore and quickly got into the boat, spending the whole night fishing without catching a thing.

⁴As the sky was just getting light, they saw Jesus on the shore but didn't realize who it was[7]. Jesus called to them, "Children, don't you have any fish?"

⁵"No," they responded.

⁶"Then throw your net out on the right side of the boat," he called to them, "and you'll get some."

⁷So they threw the net out on the right side, and then they couldn't pull it back in for all the fish.

⁸Realizing what had just happened, John[8] said to Peter, "It's the Lord."

⁹When Simon Peter heard that, he put on his outer garment (which he'd taken off while they were fishing) and jumped into the sea to swim to shore.

¹⁰The other disciples stayed with the boat dragging the net[9] to shore. (They'd only been about a hundred yards from shore.)

¹¹As soon as they reached shore, they found that Jesus had already started a charcoal fire and he had a fish and some bread cooking.

¹²"Bring some of the fish you just caught," Jesus called to them.

¹³Simon Peter stood up and dragged the net filled with fish (a hundred fifty-three fish when they were counted) onto the shore. And even though there were so many fish, the net wasn't damaged.

¹⁴"Come, eat some breakfast," Jesus said.

¹⁵None of the disciples dared ask him, "Who are you[10]?" because they knew it had to be the Lord.

¹⁶Then Jesus brought them some of the bread and fish to eat. (This was the third time Jesus had appeared to his disciples as a group since the resurrection.)

¹⁷After breakfast Jesus said, "Simon, son of John, do you truly care for me more than these things[11]?"

¹⁸"Yes, Lord," Simon replied, "you know how much I love you[12]."

---

[1] 51:41-We call him "doubting Thomas," but in fact he did exactly what the others had already done. None of the disciples were ready to believe without proof.

[2] 51:42-The Bible doesn't say whether this meeting was in Jerusalem (as seems to be implied) or in Galilee (where Jesus had told the disciples to go).

[3] 52:1-Literally, "the Sea of Tiberius," but that was another name for the Sea of Galilee. (See John 6:1.)

[4] 52:2-Literally, Nathanael.

[5] 52:2-Literally, "the sons of Zebedee" rather than "James and John."

[6] 52:2-These "two others" probably weren't from among the twelve.

[7] 52:4-If it had been broad daylight, they would already have come to shore. This was just as the sky began to lighten, when it would've been hard to make out someone on the shore.

[8] 52:8-Literally, "the disciple whom Jesus cared about," but this is John's way of referring to himself.

[9] 52:10-The Bible uses a term for the boat that indicates it was a relatively small boat. This may have been smaller than the usual fishing boat, making it impossible to haul the net into the boat.

[10] 52:15-The disciples were still down by the sea, and Jesus was at least several yards away in the dim morning light.

[11] 52:17-The word Jesus used here is the word for the caring love that's the very nature of God and the love that all Christians are commanded to practice. The word for "these" may be either masculine (meaning "more than these other disciples") or neuter (meaning "more than these fish and fishing in general"). In the language of the New Testament there's no way to tell which was intended.

[12] 52:18-In responding, Peter didn't use the word for Christian caring love but instead used a term for a family type love. This implied a love that didn't include the commitment implied by the caring love Jesus indicated.

¹⁹"Feed my lambs." Jesus told him.

²⁰Later Jesus again said, "Simon, son of John, do you truly care for[1] me?"

²¹"Yes, Lord," Simon replied, "you know how much I love you[2]."

²²Jesus said, "Take care of my sheep."

²³After a short time Jesus asked him for the third time, "Simon, son of John, do you love me[3]?"

²⁴Peter was upset that this third time Jesus asked, "Do you love me," so he replied, "Lord, you know everything. You know how much I love you[4]."

²⁵Jesus responded, "Feed my sheep.

²⁶"I'm telling you the absolute truth: when you were younger, you dressed yourself and went wherever you wanted, but when you're old, you'll stretch out your hands[5] and someone else will dress you and take you where you don't want to go."

²⁷Jesus said this to indicate the kind of death by which Peter would bring glory to God. When Jesus had said this, he told Peter, "Follow me[6]."

²⁸Peter looked around and saw John[7] following behind them and asked Jesus, "OK, Lord, but what about him?"

²⁹"If I want him to hang around until I return," Jesus responded, "What business is that of yours? You follow me[8]!"

³⁰(Some of Jesus' followers heard about what Jesus said, and they got the idea that John[9] wasn't going to die. But Jesus didn't tell him that he wouldn't die; he just said, "If I want him to hang around until I return, what business is that of yours?")

The Great Commission Matthew 28:16-20; Mark 16:15-18
(Glossary articles: Baptize / Immerse; Belief / Faith; Evil Spirits; Disciples; Galilee; The Great Commission; In the Name of...; Preaching / Proclaiming)

³¹Jesus told his disciples to meet him on a specific mountain while they were in Galilee.

³²When they saw him, they worshipped him, but some doubted[10].

³³Then Jesus stepped forward and told them, "All authority's been given to me in heaven and on earth.

³⁴"Therefore, as you go throughout the world[11], proclaim the good news to everyone.

³⁵"Make disciples in every nation, immersing[12] them into the nature of[13] the Father and the son and the Holy Spirit, teaching them to live by all the things I've commanded you[14].

³⁶"Those who put their faith in me and are immersed[15] shall be saved, while those who don't put their faith in me will be condemned[16].

³⁷"Those who truly put their faith in me will do marvelous things.

³⁸"Some will cast out evil spirits, some will speak in foreign languages, some will handle serpents with no harm to themselves, some will be unhurt even when they drink poison, and some will lay hands on the sick and bring healing[1].

---

[1] 52:20-Again Jesus used the word for caring love.

[2] 52:21-Again Peter used the word for a family type of love, not caring love.

[3] 52:23-This time Jesus used the word for a family type love that Peter had been using, not the word for caring love. This probably came across as, "Do you really even like me?" Notice that Jesus asked for Peter's allegiance three times to mirror the three times Peter had denied even knowing him. Peter probably realized this.

[4] 52:24-Peter still used the word for a family type love, possibly afraid that if he used the word for caring love, Jesus would ask how Peter could've denied knowing him.

[5] 52:26-This was a clear indication to Peter that he'd be executed for serving Jesus.

[6] 52:27-Jesus' ministry began with him saying, "Follow me," to Peter, and now it was ending with the same challenge.

[7] 52:28-Literally, "the disciple whom Jesus cared about," but this is John's way of referring to himself.

[8] 52:29-Jesus wanted Peter to stop worrying about what he demanded of others. He was giving Peter an awesome job even after Peter had denied him three times. He'd questioned Peter's loyalty three times to remind Peter of his three denials.

[9] 52:30-Literally, "this disciple."

[10] 52:32-None of the eleven disciples would've doubted by this time, so this meeting involved more than just the eleven. This may be the time Paul mentioned in 1Corinthians 15:6 when Jesus was seen by more than 500. The instructions Jesus gave here weren't just for the eleven.

[11] 52:34-This is often translated as a command to "go," but in the Bible the word is a participle and should be translated "going," "as you go," or "wherever you go."

[12] 52:35-Translating this word as "immersing" brings out how Christians are immersed into the very nature of God. It's an immersion in water, but it's also a spiritual immersion into the nature of God.

[13] 52:35-Literally, "into the name of..."

[14] 52:35-Too often Christians have focused on immersion or some other ritual with water when this Great Commission focuses on a discipleship commitment and on training. The only actual imperative verbs here are the command to proclaim the good news (Mark 16:15) and the command to make disciples (Matthew 28:19). There are two participles (immersing and teaching) that follow the command to make disciples, and these carry the force of that command. If you accept getting wet without accepting the responsibilities of discipleship and training, you're not a Christian. The word "Christian" means "slave of Christ."

[15] 52:36-Remember, this "immersion" also implies cleansing as a result of the immersion.

[16] 52:36-Since putting your faith in Jesus involves making him Lord, there's reason to question the faith of anyone who knows that Jesus wants his followers to be immersed and either refuses or intentionally puts off being immersed.

³⁹"And I promise you this: I'll be with you always, even to the end of time."

Chapter 53 – Final Events
Jesus Returns to Heaven Mark 16:19; Luke 24:49-53; Acts 1:2b-17, 20-26
(Glossary articles: Baptize / Immerse; Jesus' Resurrection; Heaven / Sky; Jerusalem; Judea; Sacred Writings; Third Person Commands)

¹After giving his final commandments and instructions about the kingdom of God to his disciples, having repeatedly and clearly demonstrated to them over a period of about 40 days that he actually had come back from the dead, Jesus got together with them for the final time in Jerusalem.

²As they were eating a meal, Jesus told them, "Understand, I'm getting ready to send you exactly what my Father promised.

³"John truly immersed people in water, but in a few days you'll be immersed[2] in God's Holy Spirit himself.

⁴"I want you to stay here in Jerusalem until you're given that power from God."

⁵At this, the disciples asked, "Lord, has the time come for you to restore Israel as the ruler over all the nations of the world?"

⁶"It's none of your business," he responded, "to know the timing for things that the Father has kept as his business[3].

⁷"But you'll certainly receive power when God's Holy Spirit comes to you.

⁸"Then you'll testify about me in Jerusalem, in all parts of Judea and Samaria, and even to the farthest reaches of the world."

⁹As he talked with them, Jesus had led them out onto the Mount of Olives close to the town of Bethany.

¹⁰Then raising his hands, he blessed them. While he was in the act of blessing them, he was taken up into the sky as they watched, and finally a cloud blocked their view of him.

¹¹While the disciples stood staring into the sky watching him go up, two men appeared beside them in dazzling white clothing.

¹²"You Galileans," the men said, "why are you standing here gazing into the sky. This Jesus, who's been taken up into the sky, will come back in much the same way as you saw him go."

¹³Then the disciples returned to Jerusalem—about a half mile away—filled with joy.

¹⁴When they got back to the city, they went to the upper room where they were staying.

¹⁵Then the eleven disciples continued in prayer, united as one, along with the women (including Jesus' mother, Mary) and Jesus' brothers.

¹⁶During this time, Peter got up in front of the disciples (about one hundred twenty altogether) and said, "Fellows, what the sacred writings[4] said about Judas (as David wrote while inspired by God's Holy Spirit[5]) had to come to pass.

¹⁷"That happened when he became a guide to those who arrested Jesus. He was counted as one of us, and he had a part in our ministry.

¹⁸"So as it's written in the book of Psalms, 'Make the place where he lived desolate with none to live in it[6],' and, 'Have somebody else take over his job[7].'

¹⁹"So I think we need to select one of the men who's been with us during Jesus' entire ministry, from the time John immersed him to the day he was taken up into the sky, to take Judas' place as a witness to Jesus' resurrection."

²⁰So they proposed two men: Joseph the Just[8], and a man named Matthew[9].

²¹Then they prayed saying, "Lord, you know everyone's inner heart.

---

[1] 52:38-Jesus didn't say that all Christians would be able to do all of these things. He didn't make any of these things a test of one's salvation. But he did indicate that such capabilities will be available to his followers as God sees fit.

[2] 53:3-Translating this as "immersed" clarifies that Christians would be immersed in the very Spirit of God and live in his presence constantly.

[3] 53:6-This is an important principle that Christians too often ignore. We may discuss when Jesus will return and how things will go at the end, but we must never fight about matters we don't really know and were never meant to know.

[4] 53:16-Literally, "the writing," but "the sacred writings" is clearly implied.

[5] 53:16-The Holy Spirit hadn't come on these men yet, and it's not obvious that the passages Peter quoted should really have applied here. It's possible that Peter was again trying to run ahead of God, and that God's choice for a replacement was Saul of Tarsus who became the Messenger Paul. The Bible tells us nothing else about either of the men involved in this action.

[6] 53:18-Psalm 69:25.

[7] 53:18-Psalm 109:8. These are third person commands in the Bible, but they've been converted to second person commands for English readers. The meaning is the same, but it doesn't come through as strongly in many other translations.

[8] 53:20-"The Just" was also used with the names of two other men in the New Testament (Acts 18:7 and Colossians 4:11). This man was also called "Barsabas" which means "son of Sabas."

[9] 53:20-There's a slight difference between this man's name and the other Christian messenger named Matthew. This man's name meant "Gift of God," while the other Matthew's name meant "Gift of Jehovah." Most translations call this one "Matthias," but most Americans aren't familiar with that name and "Matthew" works much better.

²²"Show us which of these two you've selected for this ministry as a messenger to replace Judas who went where he belonged after turning against the Lord."

²³Then they rolled the dice to select who was to take Judas' place, and Matthew was selected.

²⁴From that time on he was counted as one with the other eleven messengers.

A Preview of the Work of the Messengers Mark 16:20
(Glossary article: Preaching / Proclaiming)

²⁵What follows from here is the story of how they went everywhere proclaiming the news and how the Lord worked with them and confirmed their message with miraculous signs.

TO BE CONTINUED...

GLOSSARY

Abraham

For those unfamiliar with Abraham, his name is normally pronounced AY-brah-ham. Abraham is one of the key figures in Jewish history. The Bible tells us that, because of his faith in God, he was accepted as righteous even though he wasn't sinless. (In Romans 4, Paul makes a strong case that God has always saved people because of their faith, not because of their actions—but he also makes it clear that the kind of faith he was talking about affects what people do.)

God changed the name of one of Abraham's grandsons to "Israel." Israel then had twelve sons, and they were the ancestors of "the twelve tribes of Israel." It was to these tribes that God gave the Law of Moses as recorded in Genesis, Exodus, Leviticus, Numbers, and Deuteronomy.

God gave Abraham the commandment to circumcise his descendants, and to this day this is a distinguishing characteristic of his descendants. In New Testament times, many Jews equated circumcision with salvation. Paul made a strong argument that the real children of Abraham in God's sight were those who have faith rather than physical descendants (See Galatians 3). Jesus made a similar point to the Pharisees (Good News 33:21-31).

Agent / Angel

The word in the Bible normally translated "angel" wasn't a religious word limited to heavenly beings. It was actually the common word for a messenger or agent authorized to act on behalf of another, whether that agent were heavenly or earthly. In fact, using the word with the meaning it had in New Testament times, it would be appropriate to call US Marshalls "federal angels." At least one time Jesus used this word to refer to a human agent of God, and there are other places in the Bible where the word is used of human messengers.

Often God's agents are described as being "men dressed in white," or "radiant white." Each translator has to choose how this word should be translated from the context. In the Bible, God's agents (angels) are never referred to as having wings or as being female. In ancient culture, female agents could not have implied authority.

From the information in the Bible, it appears that God assigns tasks to his agents and then gives them the power, authority, and ability to carry out their tasks on their own. The message of the Bible makes it obvious that God likes to delegate tasks to his creations, just as he's delegated to us as humans the task of carrying the message of Christianity to the world. This is an important clue to some of the things God may have us doing in his creations once we graduate from this world.

Andrew the Disciple

Andrew was a fisherman (Good News 8:25-30), he was Simon Peter's brother (Good News 6:5), and he was one of the twelve disciples (Good News 14:3), but he wasn't one of the close inner circle of three (Peter, James, and John). His brother, Simon Peter, is normally mentioned first, which probably means that Peter was older than Andrew. Before meeting Jesus, Andrew was a disciple of John the Immerser (Good News 6:1-5), as were some other members of Jesus' twelve disciples.

Andrew—though he wasn't part of the inner circle of three—felt comfortable in bringing people to Jesus when some of the other disciples may not have. It would certainly be nice to know more about this man. But beyond what the Bible tells us, there are only stories written down long after the events—stories that may or may not be true.

Anointing Jesus

The Gospels tell of two occasions when a woman came into a house where Jesus was a dinner guest to anoint Jesus. Both occasions happened in the town of Bethany, and in both cases the host was named Simon, a very common name in those times. Besides those similarities, there are some clear differences, including the fact that either the hosts for these meals were two different men named Simon or that Simon had undergone a dramatic change between the two events.

The First Anointing (Read Good News 23:1-20)

Note the following about this case: 1) Simon obviously disapproved of Jesus; 2) the woman had a bad reputation; and 3) the woman washed and anointed Jesus' feet, dirty from the filth on ancient roads. Simon should've had a slave or servant to wash the feet of his guests, but he had not done so. Simon hadn't greeted Jesus with a customary kiss, but this woman was kissing Jesus' feet as she washed them. Simon hadn't anointed his guest's head with oil as was customary, but this woman was anointing Jesus' feet with perfumed oil. This woman took on the job of the lowest household slave and did it using her own tears and her own hair. Then, at her own expense, she even perfumed his feet. It's no wonder that Matthew, Mark, and Luke all wrote about what she'd done.

The Second Anointing (Good News 37:50-58)

There's a similar event that occurred just before Jesus and his disciples celebrated their last Passover supper together. In this later case, the woman is identified as Mary, the sister of Lazarus and Martha—not as a woman with a bad reputation. Mary anointed Jesus' head instead of his feet, and she didn't use her hair in any way. The host was again named Simon, but the Simon who hosted this meal is described as a former leper who'd been healed by Jesus. Matthew, Mark, and John all include the story of this anointing by Mary. Mary would've been aware of the woman who'd anointed Jesus at an earlier occasion, and that may well have inspired her to do what she did when she had an opportunity.

The fact that Matthew and Mark both wrote about both of these incidents makes it clear that they were, indeed, two separate incidents with a few common details.

Augustus Caesar

Augustus Caesar was the first emperor of Rome. Augustus was the nephew and adopted son and heir of Julius Caesar. He established what became known as "the Roman Peace." Augustus Caesar was the ruler who ordered the registration that took Joseph and Mary to Bethlehem just before Jesus was born (Good News 2:6). From historical records, it appears that this registration was the one done in his 25th year (between January, 3 BC, and January, 2 BC) during which the whole empire was required to sign an oath of allegiance to Augustus.

Baptize / Immerse

The Issue

This translation uses the word "immerse" rather than baptize as a matter of clarity and honesty and in order to communicate important aspects of how the Bible uses this word. The word "baptize" has a very long history that includes at least some level of intentional concealment of the meaning of the word used in the New Testament.

The New Testament was written entirely in a version of Greek used very commonly throughout much of the Roman Empire in New Testament times. People in the empire had grown up with hundreds of different languages and dialects, but most could read and speak this form of Greek.

As Christianity gained more and more influence in and around Rome, more and more of the New Testament was translated into Latin.

Errors and Results

First error: During this early period, there were various errors in understanding Christian doctrine that influenced the early translations into Latin. One error was thinking that a ritual in water caused all of a person's previous sins to be forgiven, but that any sins committed after that ritual would have to be dealt with some other way. In the minds of many Christians, the ritual was a necessary element in gaining this initial forgiveness. In reality, the biblical teaching was that a person's faith brings justification. The ritual in water is simply a first expression of that faith and a means of impressing on people by a physical ritual what was happening spiritually. Thus, as long as a person remained faithful to God, all sins were covered, and God is the judge who knows whether a person has faith in him.

Second error: People began thinking that sins committed after this water ritual had to be paid for by acts of righteousness or by suffering of some sort. The Bible clearly teaches that neither acts of righteousness nor suffering can earn forgiveness for sins. God's grace is more than sufficient, and our efforts can do nothing to "un-sin" a sin. And suffering has no beneficial affect toward a person's forgiveness and justification. If suffering paid for sin, everyone in hell would eventually get out.

With these two errors in Christian teaching, it became logical for many who accepted Christianity as the true religion to decide not to go through this water ritual until the very last moment of life, thereby eliminating as many sins as possible just before dying. But that resulted in a need for a water ritual at a point in life when immersion could cause death. Some Christian leaders began to pour water over such candidates as a substitute for immersion. But if that practice was acceptable for a person who was close to death, logically it had to be acceptable for anyone else. And if pouring water on a candidate was acceptable, why not just sprinkling water on the candidate? Thus the errors in thinking about what this ritual really was motivated a movement away from immersion, especially in areas where Greek wasn't generally understood.

Third error: Even before the birth of Jesus, an idea developed that a child inherits guilt from his or her ancestors and is therefore condemned to hell from the moment of birth. In the eighteenth chapter of Ezekiel, God specifically denies that idea.

Fourth error: This error is closely related to the first error. People thought that this water ritual was some sort of magic that would cause God to accept a person whom he would otherwise have rejected. Since the water ritual was believed to remove all guilt from one's own sins and from the sins of ancestors, and since infant mortality was quite common, many parents wanted their infant children to experience this water ritual as early in life as possible. The problem was that immersing an infant in water, especially in the winter, could weaken the infant and contribute to the infant's death. Once again there was strong motivation to replace immersion with something safer.

More and more, Christian leaders moved from immersion of adults who had faith in God to pouring water or sprinkling water on someone who might or might not have faith. Obviously, infants couldn't have such faith. Peter specifically pointed out that it wasn't the washing in water that caused a person to be forgiven, but rather the proper response to God.

Effect on Translations

So as Christian leaders began translating the New Testament into Latin, the practice of pouring water or sprinkling water on a convert was becoming common. Therefore, it was convenient to make the immersion that had been practiced in New Testament times obscure.

Greek wasn't as common in Rome, or the continent of Europe as it was in the rest of the Empire. "Baptize" was a Greek term. Normally, a person speaking or writing in Latin would use *immergere* to talk about being dipped in water, but Christians translating the Bible into Latin instead *baptizo*, taking the Greek word and writing it in Latin letters. Using such a Greek carry-over word with no native meaning in Latin made it possible to teach water rituals that didn't involve dipping in water.

An "Official" Latin Translation

When the emperor of Rome declared that Christianity was legal and made Christianity his religion (about 313 AD), Christian leaders gained enormous influence in Rome, and over time, the need for an official Latin Bible became obvious. Toward the end of the 300s, that translation into Latin was authorized by the Christian leaders in Rome, and the translators chose to use the carry-over Greek word for this water ritual rather than the more commonly understood Latin word. This foreign-sounding word strengthened misunderstandings and made the ritual seem more mystical and magical. "Baptism" became a necessary ritual of initiation demanded by God rather than a first expression of faith—a means to act out physically the spiritual reality of putting the old person enslaved by sin to death and resurrecting a new person free in Christ.

That Latin translation of the Bible became the absolute standard throughout Europe to the point that most people weren't even aware of a Greek original. The church authorities in Rome insisted that only the Latin Bible could be used and that all religious writing must be in Latin. (It's significant to note that Christians in the Greek-speaking part of the empire east of Italy generally stayed with immersion for this water ritual.)

English Translations

About a thousand years after that official Latin translation was done, men started translating the Bible into English, but they had to work from the Latin Bible. (It was about a hundred years before Greek manuscripts of the New Testament were available in Europe.) By then the errors mentioned above had become ingrained in European Christianity, and the Latin words borrowed from Greek for the water ritual involved in becoming a Christian had come into use in English, but without any reference to the real meaning in the New Testament.

The original English translators probably had no intention of obscuring the meaning when they used these borrowed Greek words in their English translations—they probably didn't know the history of the words used for this ritual.

After the earliest translations, almost all translators working on English translations followed their example. Both Roman Catholics and Protestants practiced the water ritual of Christianity almost exclusively by either sprinkling water on a convert or pouring water over a convert's head. And performing the ritual for infants was also almost universal. (There were some scholars as early as the 1500s or before who insisted that these practices weren't consistent with biblical teaching and that immersion of converts who chose on their own to put their faith in God was the only correct biblical practice, but these were a small minority.)

Why the Change in This Translation?

For the purposes of this translation, the important point is that something was lost in not actually translating the Greek words into clearly understood English. In the New Testament there is a secondary meaning to being "immersed into Christ"—a meaning that, beyond being immersed in water, the convert was being immersed into the very nature of Christ. (Being "immersed in the Holy Spirit" also takes on similar and important added meaning.)

The fact that besides "dunking," the Greek word for immersion implies washing or cleansing is another case of something that can be lost in translation. And, sadly, there's no English word that can carry all of the implications of the Greek, but it seems dishonest not to try to actually translate the concept. So this translation uses "immerse" with footnotes to point out any additional meaning implied.

Is John No Longer a Baptist?

The John who served as the forerunner for Jesus is shown in most translations as "the Baptist." Some members of the Christian denominations known as "Baptists" consider John to be the first "Baptist." In keeping with actually translating this word and its relatives, this translation identifies him as "the Immerser." As Acts 19:1-12 makes clear, the immersion taught by John wasn't Christian immersion, so John clearly wasn't a Christian (he died before Christ's resurrection, before Christ's commission to his disciples, and before the coming of the Holy Spirit). John was certainly not a "Baptist" in the sense of any modern Christian denomination using that name. Giving him a name that better describes his identifying characteristic takes nothing away from Christians who are called Baptists and does add at least some clarity related to what John was doing.

New Testament Teaching about Immersion

In the New Testament, immersion (baptism) is never presented as some sort of magic. God isn't into magic, and he's definitely not impressed by a human getting wet. God isn't interested in rituals if a person's heart and life aren't dedicated to following his ways. The same is true for Christian immersion. Peter clarified what really matters when he said that Christians are saved in being immersed, not because they get washed in water, but because they are immersed as a result of their decision to respond appropriately to God in all aspects of life. It's not getting wet that saves us as Christians; it's our willingness to do God's will (which includes immersion).

A good illustration of the biblical function of Christian immersion may be found in a John Wayne movie called *The Alamo*. In this movie, a relatively small group of men fighting for the independence of Texas from Mexico are defending a mission building in San Antonio called "The Alamo." A huge Mexican army is approaching to drive them out. The leader of the independence fighters, Colonel Travis, is depicted in the movie as using his sword to make a line in the dirt of the Alamo courtyard. He then tells his followers that they can still escape the Mexican army if they leave immediately, but if they cross this line they are committing themselves to live, fight, and die for the cause of independence with the assurance that they will die in this fight.

In the same way, Christian immersion is acting out a commitment to live and die in the service of Christ Jesus. It's the convert's way of dramatizing the fact that he or she has put the old self to death and is now living a whole new life, no longer focused on self and on worldly possessions, but now focused on God and his kingdom.

But beyond that, Christian immersion is also a symbolic representation of being immersed not just into water, but also into Christ himself—to be one with him and have his spirit living in you. In addition, Christian immersion is a symbolic representation of having your sins washed away by Jesus' death. For most people, those intentional extra meanings to immersion are masked when translators use a word like "baptize" instead of "immerse" and immersion is replaced with other rituals.

Other Issues

In order to reinforce the authority of the Christian leaders in Rome, the church also taught that salvation could only be provided by priests authorized by Rome, so no one but priests could "baptize" anybody. When the protestant reformation occurred, this practice wasn't re-examined by the reformers, and the routine practice to this day is that only the professional leaders "baptize" converts.

In the Bible, there's no hint that professional leaders play any special role in Christian immersion. Anyone can immerse a new Christian. In fact, there's evidence that when they brought Christianity to a new community, early Christian leaders turned the practice of immersing new converts over to the people they'd converted as quickly as possible. (See 1Corinthians 1:14-17.) In the Bible, the only requirement for Christian immersion is that the person being immersed must have decided to give his or her life to serving God. The person who immerses the convert need not even be a Christian. After all, if it were necessary for that person to be a real Christian in God's eyes, how many times would you need to be immersed to be sure you were OK? All Christians are empowered by Jesus to spread the good news of Jesus' message and to immerse and train converts.

It's still important to get the pattern of when to immerse right, because if we get it wrong, this practice doesn't have the effect that God intended. Jesus gave us the pattern in the great commission (Good News 52:33-39). Our job as Christians is to lead people to make a discipleship commitment first. As soon as they make that commitment to accept Jesus as Lord, they are proper candidates for immersion—not before. Then once they are immersed, our job is to train them in the way of life that Jesus taught, and their job is to learn how to live as Jesus taught.

<u>What about Those Who Don't Know?</u>

It's worth noting that in Romans 2, Paul makes the point that if an uncircumcised person lives up to the moral requirements of God's law, God will view that person as circumcised; and if a circumcised person doesn't live up to those same requirements, God will view that person as uncircumcised. Both Jesus and Paul made it very clear that in God's eyes, a person is justified by his or her willingness to serve God to the best of that person's understanding. That's the meaning of Christian faith. If a person doesn't understand the significance of Christian immersion, God wouldn't require that person to do what he or she doesn't know to do. But if a person comes to understand God's intent, at that point he or she becomes responsible to do God's will.

Some are concerned that if they accept immersion as adults, they somehow condemn their parents or ancestors who didn't know this biblical teaching. On the contrary, the strong message of Jesus and the New Testament is that God's grace can cover anything we lack once we turn our lives over to him. A person who doesn't do what he or she doesn't know to do isn't guilty of sin. (See Good News 34:35-37; Romans 7:5-10; James 4:17; etc.)

The issue for a person who's not immersed is really the issue of Lordship. If the failure to be immersed is due to lack of knowledge or the result of intentional false training, and if that person sincerely tries to live for God, there's nothing in the Bible that would indicate that person is at risk. But if a person knows that the Lord intended his followers to practice immersion of converts and all that this symbolizes, and yet that person refuses to do what he or she knows the Lord wants, the problem isn't the failure to get wet; it's the failure to accept Jesus as Lord.

<u>The Bottom Line</u>

Christian immersion is therefore important for two reasons. First, it's important because we, as humans, need this way to act out the commitment we're making. God knows us, and he knew that we need this as a means to establish a strong memory of our decision to follow him. Second, Jesus clearly taught that those who became disciples should be immersed, and if we refuse or intentionally delay doing what Jesus taught, this is obviously evidence that there's something lacking in our acceptance of him as Lord—and that's very dangerous!

Bar-Abbas

His name is normally pronounced bar-AB-us. This is one of the names that must be present in the main body of the translation.

There are three things worth noting about Bar-Abbas (Good News 48:26-33):

1. <u>The Name</u>: "Bar-Abbas" literally means "father's son" or "daddy's boy." Note that Jesus was the ultimate son of the Father, but Bar-Abbas was probably a common nickname.
2. <u>The Crime</u>: As a rebel against Rome, Bar-Abbas probably didn't want his real name known lest his family suffer reprisals. It's not unusual for rebels to use an alias and to support their rebellion by stealing. And it's not unusual for rebels to commit murder in support of their cause. From a Roman perspective, the crime of rebellion would've been the charge against this man and the reason he was awaiting execution. From a Jewish perspective, rebels against Rome were heroes, so the crimes of stealing and murder would've been emphasized as the charges against him. Based on Pilate's suggestion of Bar-Abbas, it's likely that the murder and theft carried out by him and his band had affected the priestly class, and that Pilate hoped the priests would choose Jesus in the interests of their own security if nothing else.
3. <u>The Sentence</u>: Bar-Abbas and at least some of his fellow rebels had been captured and would certainly have been scheduled for crucifixion—that was the Roman punishment for non-Romans who rebelled against the empire. It's quite likely that it was two of Bar-Abbas' companions who were crucified with Jesus.

Belief / Faith / Trust

The failure to communicate the real meaning of biblical faith is really inexcusable, so this translation brings out that real meaning which is masked in many other translations.

<u>A Confusing Factor</u>

In the Bible, there's absolutely no difference between the word for "faith" and the word for "belief," and that same word often carries the meaning of "trust." It's the translator's choice whether to use "faith," "belief," "trust," or some other similar word or phrase to translate the Greek term. How to translate this word should be determined from the context in every case.

For the King James Version of the Bible, the translators chose to translate the verb form of this word as "believe" and the noun form as "faith," though those translators did have access to Greek manuscripts of the New Testament, and it should've been clear that the noun and the verb were variations of the same word (noun-*pistis*, verb-*pisteuein*). The translators had to know that their practice would mask the real connection between these words. With that approach, people were saved by grace through their "faith" (noun) while a person had to "believe" (verb) in order to be saved. If nothing else, this created some confusion.

The Bible makes it very clear that saving faith involves focusing your life on living for God. (See Discipleship 1: Fundamentals of Christianity for a clear discussion of the evidence for this.) But translating the Greek verb as "believe" tends to give the impression that saving faith involves just believing certain things to be true, thus eliminating the need for a changed life. This is definitely contrary to the message Jesus taught.

A Danger Related to Proper Translation

The danger in translating this to clarify that saving faith involves focusing one's life on God is that some will understand this as works salvation—the idea that you have to somehow earn forgiveness for sin. That's quite impossible. It's not an issue of what we do that brings salvation; it's an issue of the heart. When we want what God wants, God is willing and eager to have us in his eternity. That desire to live as God wants will affect how we live and what we do, but it's the desire, not the actions, that makes us fit for his kingdom. Even in the Jewish sacred writings we can find God's repeated emphasis that it's not the outward actions that please him, but the obedient heart. We can't be part of his kingdom until we accept God as king. We don't have saving faith unless we're trying to be faithful. Two people may live very much the same way outwardly—one for show and one based on faith in God. The first is lost and the second is saved.

In this translation, the word generally translated as "faith" or "belief" has instead been translated to emphasize focusing your life on living for God or as trusting in God whenever it has to do with saving faith.

Prayer and Believing

Many people think Jesus taught that the power of belief in yourself, or in some magical effect of strong belief itself, would accomplish miracles. If that were what he taught, it should be obvious that the teaching was wrong, because it just doesn't work. A drug addict may jump off a tall building convinced that he can fly, but his absolute belief doesn't save him from falling to his death.

What Jesus and his followers taught isn't belief in belief or belief in self. The "belief" involved in prayer as Jesus taught it actually has to do with trusting God to the point that every thought you have is influenced by that trust. That kind of faith affects what answers and what miracles a person can expect from God.

If you've entrusted control of your life to God and you're focused on doing his will (which is the definition of saving faith), what you ask of God will obviously be consistent at least with what you think would bring glory to him and success to his kingdom. When we get our lives that focused on God, he does put power we can't even conceive at our disposal. Those who'd use this power selfishly will never have access to it. And as you might expect, this power isn't focused on the worldly, because God's kingdom isn't of this world—it's focused on the spiritual (which can certainly affect the physical world in awesome ways).

Putting This into English

In English we have an idiom: "You've got to have something to believe in." When we say that, we're talking about some idea or principle that guides your life—something you wouldn't intentionally violate by what you say, what you do, or even what you think. That's a good example of the English word "believe" used in the way Jesus used the word. Therefore, this translation consistently seeks to bring out this real meaning of saving faith, the need to shape your life around God and what he teaches.

God can't take us to heaven if we don't accept his authority, because he knows that we'd bring our rebellion with us. When we end our rebellion, God knows he can trust us in heaven, so he's willing and eager to forgive whatever would keep us out.

Bethabara

The name is normally pronounced Beth-A-bar-a and means "house of the ford." This town was near where John the Immerser was proclaiming his message when he immersed Jesus (Good News 5:28). A town of Bethany is mentioned as being close to Bethabara, but that was a different Bethany from the one where Mary, Martha, and Lazarus lived on the Mount of Olives not far from Jerusalem. The exact location of either Bethabara or this other Bethany is unknown. Bethabara was on the east side of the Jordan River and near a ford of the Jordan River closer to Galilee than to Jerusalem.

Bethlehem

The name is normally pronounced BETH-leh-hem and means "house of bread." The town is located about six miles south of Jerusalem in the mountains of Judea.

The great King David, who became king of Israel about 1,000 years before Jesus was born, was from Bethlehem. The prophet Micah prophesied that the Christ would be born in Bethlehem (Micah 5:2). About 700 years later, Jesus was born in Bethlehem (Good News 2:6-3:17).

The New Testament tells us that Joseph, who was Jesus' earthly father, was descended from King David (Good News 1:16), and that his hometown was Bethlehem (Good News 2:7). Mary's hometown appears to have been Nazareth in Galilee. We don't know why Joseph was in Nazareth or how he came to know Mary, but from what the Bible tells us, it seems that Joseph may have planned to stay in Mary's hometown after the marriage until circumstances changed their plans.

Shortly after Mary and Joseph were married, Joseph was forced to return home to Bethlehem due to an imperial registration requirement. Once he returned to Bethlehem, what the Bible tells us indicates that Joseph and Mary were probably planning to stay there and make Bethlehem their home. But when King Herod the Great heard about a new Jewish king being born in Bethlehem, he was determined to kill the child, so Joseph and Mary had to flee to Egypt (Good News 3:13-17).

After Herod the Great died, Joseph and Mary left Egypt, apparently planning to move back to Bethlehem. But when Joseph heard about Herod's son (Archelaus) who'd taken over as ruler in Judea, they decided instead to return to Mary's hometown (Good

News 3:19-20). Apparently they lived there until Joseph died, and Mary seems to have stayed on there until after Jesus' move to Capernaum.

If Jesus ever went back to Bethlehem, there's nothing in the Bible about such a visit.

Bethsaida

The name is normally pronounced Beth-SIGH-i-dah and means "house of fishing." The Bible tells us that Philip, Peter, and Andrew were from this town (Good News 6:5-6). Both Capernaum and Bethsaida were on the northern shore of the Sea of Galilee near the point where the Jordan River flows into the Sea of Galilee, with Bethsaida east of Capernaum. We don't know why Peter and Andrew had moved from Bethsaida to Capernaum, but it wasn't a long move.

Biblical Chronology

General Issues

The assigning of dates and putting things in order according to date and time was far less important for biblical cultures than for us today. Biblical authors were far more likely to focus on topic rather than on chronology. And even when biblical authors did try to show dates, translating to modern dating involves some level of guesswork.

We don't know for certain the actual year of almost any event in the Bible. Probably the best documented date is the year John the Immerser began his ministry, but even that's open to some speculation.

Biblical Years

Biblical authors didn't have anything like our calendars. Years were generally numbered by how long a ruler had been ruling. For most biblical rulers, there's some level of guess-work involved in identifying when a ruler did start ruling. While we have good information about the Roman emperors and governors who might matter in dating New Testament events, there are still some important questions. For example, we don't know for sure what year Herod the Great died, and that information happens to affect our guesses about the year Jesus was born.

Luke gives more information about chronology than the other Gospel authors. For example, Luke wrote that John the Immerser started his ministry in the fifteenth year of the reign of Augustus Caesar. That tells us that John started his ministry between September of 28 AD and September of 29 AD.

But when it came to dating Jesus' birth, Luke only recorded that it was at the time of a registration of some sort that occurred during Augustus' reign while Quirinius was in charge in Syria. From historical records, we know that Quirinius wasn't the governor of Syria until long after Jesus was born, but we also know that he was in Syria and had significant authority over certain matters around the time Jesus was born because Augustus didn't fully trust the man who was governor. We also know that there was a registration that took place about the right time.

Jews were more focused on keeping track of years than many other cultures, but even among Jews, there are many difficulties. What we know from the Gospels is that none of the Gospel writers wrote their accounts in strictly chronological order.

When Jesus was born isn't important; when his ministry started isn't important; when he rose from the dead isn't important; how long he ministered as a human isn't important. What's important is the message he brought and the fact that he did rise from the dead. But we'd still like to know these dates to help fill in the picture of Jesus' life. This translation, based on extensive research and the latest available information, assumes that Jesus was born in September of 3 BC, that he started his ministry in 30 or 31 AD, and that he died and rose from the dead in April of 34 AD.

Months and Dates

For Jews, months and the dates of a month were maintained fairly accurately in Israel. Every new moon began a new month, so some months were 29 days long and some were 30 days long, and a month that was 29 days long one year might be 30 days long the next. The actual date of the new moon was determined by visual observation, so sometimes a month might get an extra day or be a day short based on human error or guesses when clouds hid the moon, and with very limited communication systems, Jews living outside of Israel might celebrate a new moon a day before or after those in Israel.

There were normally twelve months in a Jewish year, so a typical year would be about 356 days long rather than 365. With this error of about 9 days a year, the months would've kept appearing in different seasons if there were no adjustment, but every year in the month before Passover, the Jewish authorities would determine whether the barley crop would be ready for harvest by the middle of the next month. If not, that month would be repeated to make sure the barley would be ripe by Passover. This was done because the Feast of First Fruits began immediately after the Passover Sabbath. Using this technique, some years had thirteen months, and the calendar stayed accurate enough for the needs of the culture.

Days of the Week

Jews observed a seven-day week at least from the time of Moses (about 1400 years before Jesus was born), but the Bible doesn't mention specific names for any of the days except Friday and Saturday, the sixth and seventh days of the Jewish week. Saturday was called "the Sabbath," meaning "rest," because it was a sacred day of rest ordained for the Jews by God. Friday was known as "Preparation" because no one was to do any physical work of any sort on a Sabbath, so everything needed for that day had to be prepared the day before the Sabbath.

The thing that could be confusing was that while every Saturday was a Sabbath, so was any sacred day of rest. For example, each of the three annual feasts ordained by God for the Jews included at least one Sabbath, and the Feast of Unleavened Bread (closely associated with Passover and generally even called Passover) had two Sabbaths, one on the first day of the feast and one on the last day (the seventh day). And each of these Sabbaths also had a day called Preparation just before the Sabbath.

As far as can be determined from the Bible, any day of the week could be referred to by its number (first day, second day, etc.). There's no indication in the Bible or in presently available secular information that other names were used for other days of the week.

For the Jews, each day began at sundown, and that's still true today. Each village or city had someone or some group responsible for identifying the beginning of the day, especially when that day was a Sabbath. The restriction on manual labor started at sundown and lasted until the next sundown. (This is important in understanding the "three days and three nights" of Jesus' burial.)

Hours of the Day

The daylight period of each day was divided into twelve hours. However, while a village might have a sundial in the market area and wealthy people might have a sundial in a courtyard, knowing the exact hour (let alone minute) was unimportant for most people in biblical times. In the Bible we find references to "the third hour," "the sixth hour," "the ninth hour," and "the eleventh hour." This tells us that for most purposes, the day was divided into four periods of about three hours, with the eleventh hour referring to that last hour just before sunset and the start of a new day. Closer timekeeping than that was rarely needed. Hours grew longer in the summer and shorter in the winter to maintain twelve hours in a day.

While nights were technically twelve hours long, for most purposes they were divided into four "watches." The Bible has references to the second, third, and fourth watches of the night. These "watches" were important for military operations, but most people wouldn't have paid much attention to the nighttime divisions.

Thus a 24-hour day was divided into eight periods of approximately three hours, and people could handle most of the needs of their culture with that level of accuracy. Some scholars who studied the stars were interested in exact hours of the night, and sometimes there was a need to know the hour of the day, but most people wouldn't be concerned about actual hours, let alone minutes or seconds.

Chronology of the Birth of Jesus

This is addressed in the article Birth of Jesus – The Date below.

Chronology Issues: Calling the First Disciples and the Wilderness Temptation (Good News 6-8)

If you read the accounts of Jesus calling his followers in the four different Gospel accounts (especially about calling Peter and Andrew) you may be troubled by what at first appears to be two conflicting stories, one told by John and the other by Matthew, Mark, and Luke. You may also find a difficulty with when Jesus' temptation in the wilderness occurred. In John's Gospel, we read how the day after Jesus' immersion, John the Immerser pointed Jesus out to some of his own disciples, and how, as a result of this, Andrew and Peter came to meet Jesus for the first time. John's Gospel makes it clear that John the Immerser introduced Andrew to Jesus and Andrew followed Jesus and introduced Peter to Jesus the day after Jesus was immersed, and that Jesus took his disciples to a marriage feast in Cana the next day. But John doesn't say who the disciples were that Jesus took with him to Cana or how many there were.

Matthew, Mark, and Luke all tell how Jesus called Peter and Andrew to follow him while they were busy at their work as fishermen. These three Gospel accounts all tell us that after being immersed by John, Jesus went to the wilderness for forty days where he was tempted by Satan, and that following this temptation, he called Andrew and Peter to be his followers. But none of these three Gospels tells us how long it was between Jesus' immersion and his temptation. (Mark uses a word generally translated as "immediately," but see the article on "Immediately" in the Bible below to understand the biblical use of that word.) The events recorded in John's Gospel make it clear that some days must have come between the immersion and the temptation.

This translation assumes the following: Andrew and another of John the Immerser's disciples heard John call Jesus "the lamb of God," and they followed Jesus to see where he went. Andrew got his brother, Peter, to come meet Jesus. The Bible doesn't say that they began to accompany Jesus regularly at that time. Then Jesus took some disciples to the marriage feast, but we don't know how many disciples or who they were. Following the wedding feast, Jesus went to the wilderness to be tempted for forty days, and after the wilderness temptation, he started calling men to accompany him as his full-time disciples. He started this process of selecting his twelve closest disciples with Peter, Andrew, James, and John—four fishermen.

Chronology Issues: The Second Cleansing of the Temple and a Fig Tree Cursed (Good News 38:27- 42)

Matthew, Mark, and Luke each record at least part of the events involving the second time Jesus acted against vendors in the temple and his cursing of a fig tree, but some of the details are different between the three accounts, and there's no way to determine the exact order of events. This is a case where we have what we should expect—witnesses who recalled the events but who remembered some of the details differently. Mark's chronology is used in this translation because it has more details.

Both Matthew and Mark indicate that Jesus cursed a fig tree in the morning on his way into Jerusalem. The main difference between the accounts is that Matthew indicates that the fig tree "immediately" withered, but Mark tells us that it was on the way into town the next morning that Jesus and his disciples observed that the tree had withered. As mentioned above, "immediately" didn't have the same meaning in New Testament times as our word "immediately" does for us today.

Another difference is that Matthew says that Jesus cursed the fig tree after cleansing the temple, while Mark says that Jesus cleansed the temple between cursing the fig tree one morning and seeing it withered the next morning. Yet another difference is that Matthew and Luke read as if Jesus cleansed the temple on the same day he made his triumphal entry into Jerusalem, but Mark makes it clear that it was the next day.

However, when we take into consideration the use of the word "immediately" in that culture and the fact that neither Matthew nor Luke specifically says that Jesus cleansed the temple on the same day as his triumphal entry, the chronology given by Mark works to blend all three accounts.

Chronology of the Final Events of Jesus' Life on Earth

This is covered in the articles on Jesus' Trials, Jesus' Crucifixion, Jesus' Resurrection, and Crucifixion Timing Issues below.

The Length of Jesus' Ministry

If Jesus' death was in April of 34 AD (see Crucifixion Timing Issues below) we can calculate the approximate length of his ministry. We know that John the Immerser started his ministry sometime between September of 28 AD and September of 29 AD. Jesus' ministry started in the spring, so it must have started in the spring of either 29 (when Jesus was 30), 30, or 31 AD. (Anything after 31 AD wouldn't work well with Luke's statement that Jesus was "about 30" when he was immersed. See Good News 2:15.)

We know from Acts that John's fame spread into parts of Egypt and what is today Turkey, so it seems likely that John had a fairly strong ministry before he died. If John ministered for about two years before Jesus was immersed and about one year after that, that would work with the fame he achieved, and that would place the start of Jesus' ministry at 31 AD when Jesus was 32 years old. That would mean that Jesus was immersed in the spring of 31 AD at the age of 32 ("about 30") and that he died three years later in the spring of 34 AD. However, these same facts would work just as well with John immersing Jesus after one year of ministry and then continuing to minister for two years after that, making Jesus' ministry four years long.

What's important about Jesus' ministry is the content. And for those who accept him, his ministry continues today and has never ended.

Biblical Judges

Biblical government was very different from what we have in America. In America, we have separation of powers built into our constitution, dividing our government into executive, legislative, and judicial branches. In biblical times, judges were always political authorities, whether a judge was the emperor, the governor of a province, or a village elder. Kings and emperors could make up the laws, judge those accused of doing wrong, and act as chief executive for implementing the laws. Even in a village, those who ran the village came up with the rules and passed judgment on those who broke the rules.

Knowing this gives a different meaning to passages like 1Corinthians 6 where Paul told the Christians in Corinth that Christians will judge the world and judge agents of God. In Paul's mind, this meant leadership with the necessary implication of the ability to show good judgment in a leadership role.

Biblical Names

As much as possible, this translation avoids using the difficult names of people and locations that appear in most Bible translations except in footnotes or the Glossary. As American Christians, these names mean nothing to us. Instead of naming people, this translation refers to "a man," "a woman," "a priest," and so on, providing any additional information about the person that may be useful. Then the actual name is provided in a footnote for anyone interested in knowing the name. (In the case of Jesus' lists of ancestors, the actual names appear in this Glossary under Genealogy of Jesus.) Instead of naming cities or provinces whose names might be difficult to pronounce, this translation refers to "a city," "a village," "a province," and so on, providing something about the location if that's known and would be helpful with actual names in footnotes.

Nobody really knows how biblical names were pronounced. There were no recording machines. And pronunciation differed from area to area just as it often does today. The Bible records a time when Peter was recognized as a Galilean just by the way he talked (Good News 47:25).

Just as a side note, none of the biblical languages actually had a J sound. In Greek, Jesus' name would've been pronounced something like yay-SOUS, and in Hebrew it would've been pronounced something like yeh-HOE-shoe-ah. And the best information we have indicates that the "ch" sound as in Christ wasn't pronounced like the "k" sound we give it.

The bottom line is this: no one should ever be embarrassed by an effort to pronounce biblical names, and no one should ever be proud of pronouncing them "correctly."

Birth and Childhood of Jesus – Events

An Innkeeper? (Good News 2:7-8)

The traditional view of Jesus' birth involves an innkeeper who gave the couple permission to stay in his stable for the birth of their son, but this isn't really what the Bible says (though many translations make it appear so). In biblical times, the traveler's inn was no place to have a baby. The traveler's inn would be the place where travelers could find a place to sleep, wine to drink, and a prostitute. Joseph and Mary were in Bethlehem, Joseph's family home. It makes no sense that he'd even have tried to take her to a traveler's inn.

The word Luke used that's generally translated "inn" is also the word for the guest room in a home. In fact, it's the word used for the guest chamber where Jesus and his disciples ate the Passover before his crucifixion. Since Joseph was a member of the kingly family descended from David, he and his bride would've been welcome in town and could surely have found lodgings in a family guestroom.

In New Testament times, middleclass homes often had attached stables, and this was probably the case for the house where Joseph and Mary were staying with Joseph's family. With the Roman registration going on, the family guest chambers would've been full enough that having a baby born there would've been awkward, and the stable would've been a good choice for the birth. Women from Joseph's family would've been with Mary in the stable as she gave birth. Joseph would have been in the house with the other men. Joseph would've joined his wife after the birth, and that's consistent with what the Bible says.

We normally picture Jesus being born the first night Mary and Joseph were in town, but the Bible doesn't say that. In fact, they may well have been staying in the house for a few days before the birth, but when Mary's labor started, they would've moved to the stable for some privacy.

This doesn't change the fact that Jesus was born in a stable and spent his first night in an animal's feeding trough. But it does clarify that Joseph was surely providing for his wife the best way he could.

<u>Swaddling Clothes</u> (Good News 2:7-8)

We often see pictures of the infant Jesus in the manger with his arms and legs free, but according to the Bible the infant Jesus was wrapped in "swaddling clothes." It was customary in this period for a newborn to be wrapped in cloth to keep the child's arms and legs still, making it easier for a new mother to handle the baby safely.

<u>The Shepherds</u> (Good News 2:9-14)

If Jesus was born in September, it would be very reasonable for shepherds to be in the fields at night with their sheep. For December that's much less likely. The winter weather would've made this unpleasant at best, and archeological records we have make it clear that shepherds didn't normally pasture their sheep outside the fold at night in the winter.

What had been a typical, calm night for the shepherds was dramatically interrupted. One of God's agents brought the very brilliance of the glory of God, and that was more than enough to terrify these shepherds. But this agent quickly calmed their fears and gave them wonderful news—the Christ all Jews had longed for had been born in Bethlehem. Then this agent was joined by a huge crowd of others, all praising God. The Bible tells us that there were at least two shepherds, but it doesn't tell us how many there were. (The Bible says nothing about a drummer boy.)

We have a tradition that these agents of God were singing, but the Bible doesn't really say that—though I suspect their speech was sweeter than any music we've ever heard. We also have a tradition that the "angels" were female and had wings, but that's not the case with any of God's agents mentioned in the Bible. His agents are always referred to with masculine words.

The words of the agents to the shepherds about peace on earth have been variously translated as meaning a blessing of peace to men who practice good will toward others, a blessing of peace to men who are especially favored by God, or as a blessing of peace to all mankind because all mankind was being favored by God in this event. The reality is that all of these are appropriate at least to some extent, and the wording in this passage could support any of them.

<u>Other Christmas Traditions</u>

There are many traditions associated with Christmas that have nothing to do with the biblical account of Jesus' birth. Most people know that Christmas trees, Christmas lights, snowmen, jolly elves, and Santa Claus have nothing to do with the birth of Jesus. Another tradition involves the donkey Mary rode on their trip to Bethlehem. In the Bible, the donkey is never mentioned. As poor as she and Joseph were at that time, it's much more likely that she walked.

What we as Christians could do, in light of the information we now have, would be to celebrate Jesus' birth on September 11th with a strictly Christian focus and then let December 25th be the worldly season of jolly elves, tinsel, evergreen trees, gift exchanges, and the like.

<u>Jewish Birth Rituals</u> (Good News 3:1-3)

Joseph and Mary did some things after Jesus' birth that were requirements in the Law of Moses (Leviticus 12). A woman was to be ceremonially purified 33 days after the birth of a son, and if the son were her firstborn child, that son was to be considered God's property, because God destroyed the firstborn sons of Egypt and saved alive the firstborn sons of the Israelites. God demanded that every Israelite firstborn son be redeemed by a sacrifice. The sacrifice was specified as a lamb and either a turtledove or a young pigeon, but this was followed by a provision for those who couldn't afford a lamb to bring either two turtledoves or two young pigeons.

From this we learn that Joseph and Mary weren't wealthy enough to afford a lamb at this time. The fact that they couldn't afford a lamb a month after Jesus' birth makes it clear that the scholars from the east hadn't yet arrived in Bethlehem.

<u>Simeon's Blessing on the Baby Jesus</u> (Good News 3:4-6)

It's quite possible that Mary, a girl from Galilee, had never been to the temple before this. All Jewish males were to try to get to the temple three times each year (though by this time many Jewish men living far from Jerusalem couldn't fulfill this requirement), but Jewish women were not required to go. What a shock it must have been when an elderly man named Simeon, about whom Mary and Joseph knew nothing, began talking about their son. But for this man to say that this child would bring understanding to the nations—that was astonishing! Most Jews would never have considered that God's Jewish Christ would also be the Christ of non-Jews.

<u>Scholars from the East</u> (Good News 3:9-17)

The word translated "scholars" in this translation has been variously translated as "wise men," "magi," "astrologers," "astronomers," etc. This word was a term used by Persians, Babylonians, and Medes for their highly trained scholars. From about 587 BC until about 538 BC, the Jews had been exiled to these eastern areas. Some like Daniel and his companions became high-ranking leaders in these foreign lands and stayed there when other Jews were returning to their ancestral homeland. These scholars were probably descendants of those who stayed behind either in Persia or Babylon or somewhere in that area.

There's no doubt that these scholars were Jewish—at this point in history no one who wasn't Jewish would've made such a trip to worship and bring gifts to a newborn Jewish king. The fact that they showed absolutely no doubt about this king having been born indicates that they had in their possession some form of prophecy or a revelation from God linking the birth of the Christ to the specific sign they'd seen in the sky.

You'll see many pictures and manger scenes where scholars riding camels are shown as present in the stable for Jesus' birth, but according to the Bible, they actually arrived in Bethlehem months after Jesus was born. When they arrived in Jerusalem looking for the child, they referred to him as "the one who's been born to be king of the Jews" (Good News 3:9). They were quite confident he'd been born when they first saw the star that indicated his birth. When they arrived in Bethlehem, the Bible says that they went to the house where the young child was. The Bible doesn't say that they went to a stable, and the word for "young child" is the word for a toddler, not an infant.

As has often been noted, the Bible doesn't say that there were three of these scholars—there were just three kinds of gifts mentioned as brought by them. They may even have brought other gifts not mentioned in the Bible, and there may have been anything from two to several scholars. And while Roman authorities tried to keep the roads as safe as possible, these men wouldn't have traveled with such precious gifts without some group of armed servants to protect them.

Assuming Jesus was born in September of 3 BC (see Birth of Jesus – The Date below), travel from Persia to Israel right away would've become very difficult before such travelers could've reached Jerusalem. Winter rains would wash out roads, and there'd be cold temperatures and possibly snow or ice to deal with. These wealthy scholars would've waited until spring brought better traveling conditions, which would be consistent with their arrival in May of 2 BC.

The fact that these scholars went to Jerusalem first makes it clear that they weren't daily following a star, and that fits with the idea of the astronomical conjunction described below (see Birth of Jesus – The Date). If they started around April, arrival in May wouldn't be unusual. When they left Jerusalem headed for Bethlehem, the Bible indicates that they saw the heavenly sign again, apparently after an extended period of not having seen it, which would be consistent with the astronomical conjunction suggested below.

When they got to Bethlehem, they would've had no problem finding this child. The word spread by the shepherds when he was born would still be fresh in the memories of these townspeople. After all, this was the City of David. This was the home of the kingly line. This was the place where the prophet Micah had said the Christ would be born. Of all the Jews, these people more than any others would've been expecting the Christ. And whether they believed the shepherds or not, they wouldn't have forgotten what the shepherds said.

Like so many Jews, these scholars clearly expected an earthly king born to great wealth and political power. That's why they started looking in Jerusalem. Imagine their surprise when they found the child of these humble parents.

Herod's Reaction to Jesus' Birth (Good News 3:9-17)

First, contrary to what some have said, the scholars from the east didn't start their questioning at the palace. According to the Bible they started their questioning before getting to Herod. They may well have started their questioning at the temple, or they may have simply started at the city gate or in the streets. What we do know is that before they got an answer to their question, Herod heard about their quest and called them into his presence for interrogation.

Herod was extremely jealous of his throne. He'd killed his favorite wife, various sons, and other relatives whom he considered threats to his authority. Herod had done much for the economy of his realm and specifically for the Jewish temple, but when it came to any threat to his authority, he wouldn't hesitate to kill. So when Herod was troubled, all Jerusalem would've been truly troubled.

When one of God's agents warned Joseph about Herod's intent to kill the child, Joseph didn't hesitate. The way the Bible passage reads, it appears that Joseph left with his family the same night that he had the dream. That's not unreasonable. In fact, if the scholars told him about their visit with Herod, it's hard to see why he was still in Bethlehem. In any case, the agent apparently didn't have a hard time convincing Joseph to get out of town with his family. Herod's response should've been predictable.

Joseph and Mary may well have been in their own house by this time, and they probably would've left without telling his family anything. That way, if Herod's men came looking for him, the family could honestly say that they knew nothing about the location of this child. With the wealth the scholars had left them, Joseph and his little family could afford to escape quickly.

There was a large Jewish community in Egypt at this time, so Joseph and Mary could've found friends and probably even relatives there. Herod's people would've had no authority at all in Egypt. And as a carpenter, Joseph would've had no trouble finding work. Egypt was an economic powerhouse during this time.

When Herod realized that these scholars had tricked him, the Bible says that he sent soldiers to kill all male children in or around Bethlehem from birth to two years old "based on the time he'd learned from the scholars." We can be certain that Jesus wasn't yet two years old. The Bible says that Herod questioned these scholars carefully about when the star had first appeared, so he would've known just how old the child was. But knowing Herod, he'd take no chances. He would've added some amount of time to be sure he got the child he was after. Assuming that the "star" was the astronomical conjunction described below, that Jesus was born in September of 3 BC, and that the scholars arrived around May of 2 BC, Jesus would've been 7 or 8 months old when they arrived in Egypt. It would be reasonable for Herod to round that to one year and then double it, and it's likely that his soldiers didn't take chances if a child even looked like he might be in that age range.

However, Bethlehem wasn't a large city. While it was a terrible tragedy to the area, the total number of children killed was probably less than twenty. At the time this was written, a gunman in Connecticut had recently killed that many children in an elementary school. We can be glad that Jesus told us that their heavenly agents have direct access to God, and we can trust God to deal with this in his love and grace and mercy in a way that will bring us even more joy when we see what he's done.

Joseph and Mary Return to Israel (Good News 3:19-20)

We know that Herod the Great died in the winter, after an eclipse of the moon but before Passover. There was a total eclipse of the moon in January of 1 BC. If the scholars left Bethlehem in May of 2 BC, Joseph and Mary's stay in Egypt could've been as short as 8 months and would certainly have been no more than a year. The trip back wouldn't have been as rushed as the trip to Egypt.

From what the Bible says, Joseph probably intended to return to his family home in Bethlehem until he heard who'd taken Herod's place. Herod's son, Archelaus, was now ruling Judea and that included Bethlehem, and Archelaus was even more jealous of his throne than his father had been. But Archelaus hadn't been given authority in Galilee where Mary's family apparently lived. When Joseph heard that news and had another dream warning him, he changed his plans and returned to Mary's hometown.

While Archelaus had the strong jealousy that his father had before him, he lacked the political skills of his father, so if he remembered the stories about another king born in Bethlehem, he would've been a very dangerous threat. It's likely he hadn't paid a lot of attention to his father's efforts to kill a child in Bethlehem, but Joseph didn't want to take any chances. So while it would've been a significant detour, it was possible to bypass Judea on the way to Galilee, and that appears to be what Joseph did in order to avoid any risk to the young child.

Going to Jerusalem when Jesus Was Twelve Years Old (Good News 3:21-29)

No record has been found of a bar mitzvah ceremony in Judaism in New Testament times. Today the bar mitzvah is a ceremony where a 13-year-old Jewish boy takes on the responsibilities of manhood. The word means "son of the covenant," and the ceremony marks the point when a Jewish boy is considered fully responsible for living according to the Law of Moses. In New Testament times, this age would have been about when a young man would be expected to start as an apprentice for whatever job he was expected to do for the rest of his life, whether there was a special ceremony or not. It's likely that at twelve years of age Jesus had recently reached the age where his community considered him to be a man, and it's possible that Joseph and Mary arranged some sort of ceremony at the temple during Passover to mark this transition—or maybe just taking Jesus with them to Jerusalem was the sign that he was now an adult and therefore expected to attend the feasts.

In any case, Jesus certainly seemed to consider this the right time for him to emphasize a transition from being Joseph's son (apprenticed to Joseph as a carpenter) to being God's son (apprenticed to God as the Christ). Given what the Bible says, Jesus' childhood was probably not all that unusual, and Joseph and Mary may have started thinking that the rest of Jesus' life might follow this normal pattern. In this event, Jesus was clearly letting them know that while he was only twelve years old, he was well aware that his life wouldn't be normal. Jesus appears to have been saying quite emphatically, "My real Father is God, and now that I'm considered an adult, it's time for me to get busy doing God's work."

Passover occurs in the evening of the day before the start of a seven day Feast of Unleavened Bread, so the family had been in or near Jerusalem for a little over a week. On the trip, Joseph and Mary would've traveled with a group of family, friends, and neighbors from Galilee, and the walk to Jerusalem would've been like a traveling social event. Joseph and Mary weren't wealthy, and lodgings in Jerusalem during the feast were expensive, so it's likely they would've camped outside the city with this same group. It would've been normal for children and young people to have their own activities during the trip and at the campsite, separate from the adults, though whatever adults were near the children would've kept an eye on what was happening. By this time Mary and Joseph surely had other children, and if those other children were along for the trip, Mary would've been busy looking after the younger children. Joseph and Mary would've considered Jesus old enough to take care of himself during the day, both while traveling and at the campsite. If this trip did indeed mark Jesus' transition to adulthood, this may well be the first trip Jesus was allowed to attend the adult Passover functions even if he'd come to Jerusalem on other trips.

The three days Mary mentioned as looking for Jesus could mean one day of travel away from Jerusalem (when they weren't seriously looking), one day or a little more than a day of travel back to Jerusalem while checking other groups to see if Jesus had joined some other group bound for Galilee, and one day of hunting for Jesus (mothers can exaggerate when they're upset), or it could mean three days of looking after returning to Jerusalem. However, it's hard to see why the temple wouldn't have been among the places that they would've looked first, so this was probably the third day after the Passover feast. The trip back to Jerusalem may have been somewhat slower than the trip leaving Jerusalem since they would've been searching every group heading out of Jerusalem toward Galilee, so Mary and Joseph may have found Jesus very shortly after they actually got back to the city.

An interesting point here is that this happened at the end of Passover, about the same time of year as Jesus' resurrection. In fact, it's likely that the date of Jesus' resurrection (Nisan 24) was the same as the date that Joseph and Mary found Jesus in the temple.

Growing in Favor with God (Good News 3:29)

How could Jesus, God in the flesh, increase in favor with God? This is evidence of the very real humanity of Jesus. As Jesus himself said, "God is Spirit." It was the unlimited presence of that divine Spirit that caused Jesus to be God in the flesh. It was a lot like God's Holy Spirit living in us, but with a vastly stronger connection. And of course Jesus was born without our natural inclination to the selfishness and self-interest that first draws us into the rebellion of sin. It's important to understand that Jesus as a child and as an adult had real choices, and that he had to make the right choices in spite of Satan's temptations. He had all the temptations every child faces. But in his humanity, Jesus grew in ways that pleased the God-presence within him in every case. As Paul said (Romans 5, 1Corinthians 15), Jesus was the second Adam. He walked this world in innocence, and God was with him and in him. But unlike Adam, when Satan tempted Jesus (and he tempted him over and over), Jesus didn't yield to his temptations.

Birth of Jesus – The Date

Matching Herod's Death with Jesus' Birth

From a combination of the details that Luke and Matthew provide, accounts from ancient historians, and what archeologists and astronomers can tell us about the New Testament period in history, it's not clear exactly when Jesus was born, but the evidence for September 11, 3 BC seems to work best at this time, so that's what this translation assumes.

We know that Herod the Great (the Herod who was king when Jesus was born) died in the spring of either 4 BC or 1 BC, and this translation assumes his death was in 1 BC. While the ancient historical accounts aren't entirely reliable, their information would have to be rejected with no good reason to do so in order to go with the 4 BC date. In this case, the biblical information supports these ancient accounts.

Luke provided detailed information about the date of the start of John's ministry, and we now know that the date was between the fall of 28 AD and the fall of 29 AD—probably spring of 29 AD. Luke says that Jesus was "about 30" when he started his ministry (Good News 2:15). If Jesus was born in September of 3 BC, he would've been exactly 30 years old when John began his ministry. Allowing two years for John's ministry before Jesus' immersion, Jesus would've been 32 when he was immersed by John, and that works with "about 30." (It's possible John only ministered for one year before Jesus was immersed, in which case Jesus would've been 31 when he was immersed.)

On the other hand, if Herod died in the spring of 4 BC and Jesus was born before his death, then Jesus would have to have been born no later than the spring of 5 BC. With that date, he'd have been 33 in the spring of 29 AD when John the Immerser began his ministry. If we allow even one year for John's ministry before Jesus' immersion, Jesus would've been 34 when Luke says that he was "about 30," and that's at least a stretch.

So given Luke's date for the beginning of John the Immerser's ministry and his estimate of Jesus age when Jesus was immersed by John, the 1 BC date for Herod the Great's death works best both from the information in secular sources and from the biblical information.

The Registration and Quirinius' Role (Good News 2:6-7)

Luke tells us that Jesus was born around the time that an official registration was ordered by Augustus Caesar. In this case it's important to understand not only what Luke said, but also what he didn't say.

The King James Version of the Bible says, "And it came to pass in those days, that there went out a decree from Caesar Augustus, that all the world should be taxed. (And this taxing was first made when Cyrenius [Quirinius] was governor of Syria.) And all went to be taxed, every one into his own city" (Luke 2:1-3). But there are problems with this translation and with how we, as Americans, understand it.

First, "all the world" seems to imply to us that Caesar ordered something that affected all the people in the Roman Empire. The problem here is that historical records of such empire-wide taxations have been found, but they indicate no such empire-wide taxation in or near 3 BC. However, as we'll show, that doesn't mean that Luke was wrong.

Second, Luke didn't actually say "taxed." The word Luke actually used was for a registration. Normally that would indicate a census. However, we also know that Augustus Caesar did order that everyone be required to sign an oath of allegiance at about the right time for Jesus' birth, and this would've been the "registration" Luke mentioned. (There are a couple of other possibilities, but the oath of allegiance seems to work very well. This oath was to be required in celebration of the 25th year of Augustus' reign. Augustus began his reign on January 16th of 27 BC. The 25th year of his reign would therefore have begun in January of 3 BC, which works well with Jesus being born in September of 3 BC.)

Third, Luke didn't actually write, "when Cyrenius [Quirinius] was governor of Syria." There was an official word for governors, but Luke chose not to use that word. Instead, Luke used a word that indicates that Quirinius was in charge (at least of the registration) in Syria. We also know that at least some activities that affected Judea under Herod the Great were run by Roman authorities in Syria. We know from historical records that Quirinius wasn't governor of Syria when Jesus was born, but we also know that the man who was governor was a political appointee and that Augustus didn't trust his administrative skills. We also know that Augustus sent Quirinius into that area with some level of authority during the right time period. We don't know how much authority Quirinius exercised, but it's reasonable that Augustus might have put him in charge of something as important as this registration.

Fourth, the words, "And all went to be taxed, every one into his own city," along with Joseph's return to Bethlehem, may seem to us to imply that every man in the empire was required to return to his ancestral home. However, this more likely meant that people had to go to their hometown where the local authorities could keep track of who did come and who didn't. We know of at least some cases where transient workers were required to go home for such activities, and the Bible doesn't tell us whether Joseph had made Nazareth his permanent home or whether he might have been on a contract job. It's quite possible that Joseph's permanent home was in his parents' home in Bethlehem when he was between contract jobs. Matthew's account of Joseph and Mary's return from Egypt seems to imply that Joseph was planning to return to Bethlehem until he found out who'd taken Herod's place ruling over that area, at which point he took his family back to Mary's hometown—Nazareth. This may imply that Joseph had very little connection with Nazareth before their marriage.

The bottom line is that events around the time suggested for Jesus' birth in this translation do fit with the historical records as long as we pay attention to what the Bible really does and doesn't say.

Matching the Star (Good News 3:9-13)

Traditionally, we've pictured the star that the eastern scholars followed as a very bright star or comet, but if that were the case, there'd be historical records of such an event that we could find in ancient documents other than the Bible, and no such records have been found. This star must have been something that was very impressive to these eastern scholars but hardly noticeable to the average person—either that or a vision only the scholars could see. The fact that these scholars said that they'd seen the star "at its rising" and the fact that the star seems to have gone away and to have reappeared when they left Jerusalem, both seem to imply an actual event they saw in the sky rather than a vision God gave them that no one else could see, but an event that the average person wouldn't have noticed.

Astronomers today know that there was an interesting event between September of 3 BC and May of 2 BC that could account for the star the eastern scholars saw. Planets with orbits farther from the sun than earth's orbit appear from earth to move backward at certain times. In ancient times, planets were known as "wandering stars" because their apparent movement in the sky doesn't match the real stars, and on September 11 of 3 BC the planet Jupiter (known to ancients as the kingly planet) appeared from earth to be so close to the star Regulus (known to ancients as the king star) in the constellation known as Virgo (the virgin) that the two would have appeared as one object. Jupiter then appeared to move away, but it "reversed course" and the two objects appeared to pass almost that close to each other in the constellation Leo (the lion) again on February 17th and May 8th of 2 BC.

The biblical account reads as if the initial appearance of the "star" caused these scholars to decide to head for Judea and as if the "star" then went away for a time and reappeared as they neared Bethlehem. This could fit well with the first conjunction of Jupiter and Regulus. This would have been something these scholars would have noticed while most people wouldn't have paid much attention.

If this is the case, Jesus would've been born on September 11 of 3 BC, and the scholars would've arrived in Jerusalem around late April or early May of 2 BC. (Arrival in February wouldn't work for two reasons: 1) These scholars wouldn't have traveled in winter if they could avoid that. And, 2) it's very unlikely that Herod would've been in Jerusalem in February since Jerusalem was in the mountains and colder than his official capital in Caesarea on the Mediterranean seacoast. Passover was in March that year, and Herod might well have moved to the mountains then and stayed for the hot summer months.)

Since the scholars believed that the king had already been born when they first saw this "star" and that therefore they couldn't have attended his birth, and since travel in winter would've been hazardous and uncomfortable at best, the scholars would probably have waited until spring to leave their homes and travel to Jerusalem. That would also allow time to make preparations for such a trip. A September date for Jesus' birth certainly fits better with shepherds in the field than a December date.

However, neither such a conjunction of "stars" nor any other similar event in the night sky would've sent these scholars to Jerusalem unless they knew some prophecy predicting what they observed as the sign of the Christ's birth. Daniel and many other Jews apparently remained in the capital of Persia when other Jews were returning to their homeland, and it would be possible that Daniel left a written prophecy that these men relied on—a prophecy now lost in history.

Matthew's record says that "After hearing what the king had learned about Bethlehem, they left Jerusalem, and the star that they'd seen when they were in the east went ahead of them. When they saw the star again, they were overjoyed, and it stood over the place where the toddler was" (Good News 3:13). For us, this seems to imply that the star led them to Bethlehem (especially the way it appears in most other translations), but if the "star" was that conjunction, then it wouldn't have been in the right part of the sky to lead them from Jerusalem to Bethlehem. However, Matthew's wording could simply mean that the star "went ahead of them" in the sense that they saw it again when they reached Bethlehem—in other words, it was already there so it must have preceded them. After all, these scholars had already received clear direction about where to go, so they didn't need a star to guide them.

If this conjunction of Jupiter and Regulus is the right answer, the "star" didn't point out the actual house where Joseph and his family were living. But the message of the shepherds would still have been fresh in people's minds, and just a few questions would've led these scholars to Joseph's home.

We sometimes get the impression that these scholars traveled primarily at night, but that's unlikely. When they left their homeland, they knew that they were looking for the king of the Jews, so they headed for Jerusalem. When they left Jerusalem, they knew that they were heading for Bethlehem. Roads were dangerous at night, especially if you were unfamiliar with the roads. In the dark, you or your pack animals could easily suffer a broken leg or a bad fall. Travel was bad enough in daylight.

The bottom line is that, in this world, we may never know what the star really was, but there's no reason to doubt Matthew's account. The dates shown in this translation have been selected to be consistent with the astronomical conjunction. Even if that wasn't the "star" that these scholars followed, the dates must be close to right in order to match the start of the ministries of John and Jesus and the timing of Augustus' registration and Herod's death.

Caesar

The emperors of the Roman Empire were known as "Caesar." This term started with Julius Caesar, a Roman from a prominent family. He was working toward making himself emperor when he was assassinated. His adopted son and heir, Octavian, managed to accomplish what Julius had not, and took on the name "Augustus Caesar" as the first emperor of the Roman Empire. (He didn't actually use the title "emperor," but he did establish the role of emperor.) From the time of Augustus on, the emperors of Rome were known as "Caesar."

In the New Testament, "Caesar" is used to refer to Augustus, Tiberius, Claudius, and Nero. (The emperor Caligula reigned for about four years between Tiberius and Claudius, but there's no reference in the New Testament that can be connected to his reign.)

Augustus was emperor when Jesus was born, and he ordered the registration that forced Joseph and Mary to move to Bethlehem in time for Jesus' birth (Good News 2:6). In 14 AD, Augustus died and his nephew, Tiberius, became emperor. He was emperor during Jesus' entire ministry, and references to Caesar relative to taxation (Good News 39:35-39) and during Jesus' trials (Good News 48:6, 44, and 52) would all have been to Tiberius. Claudius is mentioned in Acts as having forced all the Jews to leave Rome at one point in his reign (Acts 18:2). And Nero was the emperor to whom Paul appealed when the Jewish authorities were trying to get him executed (Acts 25:11). (At the time of Paul's appeal to Caesar, Nero hadn't yet started persecuting Christians.)

Capernaum

For those unfamiliar with Capernaum, this name is normally pronounced cap-ER-nee-um. Jesus was born in Bethlehem and reared in Nazareth, but during his ministry, Capernaum was his base of operations. Capernaum was a fishing village on the north shore of the Sea of Galilee. This was the home of Peter, Andrew, James, and John, and may well have been the home of Matthew and possibly some of the other disciples. It's possible that Jesus' mother and the mother of James and John were sisters. (See Jesus' Crucifixion under Crucifixion Events and Issues below for the evidence that this might be the case.)

The Bible seems to indicate that Jesus' mother didn't follow him when he first moved to Capernaum, but later she seems to have been traveling with his group. If her sister lived in Capernaum, moving there at some point after Joseph died might have been attractive with her eldest son, Jesus, living there.

Christ / Messiah

The word "messiah" (borrowed from Hebrew) means "anointed one." When applied to a person, anointing could involve something as simple as oiling down one's hair or as special as a ceremony dedicating a person to the office of king, priest, or prophet. In its ceremonial use, it came to represent a person being anointed with God's Spirit.

By New Testament times, this term was used as a title for the one God had promised to send as the savior of Israel—and indeed of the whole world. Used in that sense, the word is generally capitalized in English (Messiah). (In biblical times there were only capital letters.)

The word "Christ" was the Greek word for "Messiah." In the Gospels, the words "Christ" and "Messiah" were used interchangeably, but "Christ" was used more often than "Messiah." Every use of either term in the New Testament is a reference either to the expected Jewish savior or to Jesus as that savior. In this translation, with only one exception the word "Christ" is used for any reference to "Messiah" or "Christ."

With the expectation of an earthly ruler who'd take over the whole world, it's not hard to see why the Jewish leaders would've scoffed at this wandering rabbi with no political power who said he was the Christ.

However, it wasn't long after Jesus' ministry that his disciples began to use the word "Christ" as a proper name for the Lord. Throughout the Gospels, the way people use the word "Christ" is consistent with the Jewish concept of the earthly leader, though a shift in this concept can be detected even during Jesus' ministry, but as early as Peter's sermon on the day of Pentecost opening the invitation for people to accept Jesus, we find the word "Christ" used as a name for Jesus. Outside the Gospels, "Christ" is used exclusively as a name or title for Jesus.

Christian Love / Caring Love

Jesus commanded his followers to have Christian love for God, for each other, for those in need, and even for their enemies. That fact makes it clear that Christian love isn't what we normally think of when we hear the word "love." In fact, there isn't a good word in English at this time that really carries the meaning of Christian love.

The New Testament was written in Greek, and in New Testament times there were at least four Greek words for various concepts of love. Three of these words dealt with emotional situations that people can't control. But the word that Jesus and his followers used most often and the one that always means Christian or godly love is actually a word that wasn't used that much before Jesus used it and gave it his own definition. Many know this word as "*agape*." This is a love that's a matter of personal choices, having no necessary emotional content (though it can lead to emotional attachments)

Before the birth of Jesus, the Jews had used this word in translating passages in their sacred writings from Hebrew into Greek, including the passages in Leviticus and Deuteronomy that deal with loving God and loving others (the great commandments). Jesus took that and showed his followers how this kind of love is at the heart of what God wants from us.

Jesus described Christian love by telling the story we call "The Good Samaritan." When he told that story, those listening would've understood one important background fact—Samaritans and Jews had detested each other for hundreds of years. Samaritans and Jews both claimed to be the true Israelites, the true people of God, and the keepers of the true sacred writings of the Israelites. Jews and Samaritans each claimed that the other group had mixed ancestry while their group was the true Israel. With these groups living next to each other, each claiming to be the true people of God, the true children of Abraham, and the keepers of the true sacred writings of Moses, the animosity between these groups just festered over the years.

In Jesus' story illustrating Christian love, a Jew traveling down the mountain road from Jerusalem to Jericho is attacked by thieves and left for dead (Good News 22:21-35). A Jewish priest and a member of the Jewish tribe of Levi both happened by this man and avoided any contact with him. Both of these men were especially involved in the religious practices of Judaism, but both of them failed to care for this fellow Jew. Then a Samaritan came on the scene. Given the animosity between Jews and Samaritans, if anything, this man might've been expected to utter a curse. Instead, he stopped to help the Jew. But something that may be missed is that he had to start with forgiveness—turning over to God the responsibility for retribution for anything this Jew and his relatives had done to Samaritans. Once he'd done that, he was able to focus on the man's needs and do what he could to help. So from Jesus' story we find these characteristics of Christian love:

1. <u>Forgiveness</u>—the willingness to turn retribution over to God and focus on the needs of others. This doesn't mean that we establish some friendly relationship or that we say that what someone else did to hurt us is OK, but that we won't seek revenge or retribution. We leave that to God and trust him to do that job.
2. <u>Caring</u>—seeing the needs of others and truly caring about those needs, even when the "others" are enemies. They may still be enemies, but we choose to care about their needs.
3. <u>Active</u>—this Samaritan got his hands dirty and bloody binding up the Jew's wounds and treating them for infection.
4. <u>Unselfish</u>—this Samaritan had to put aside his plans and focus on the needs of a man who was his enemy.
5. <u>Generous</u>—when the Samaritan left the Jew at an inn, he paid for the Jew's lodging and care, he left additional money for future care, and he promised to pay any other costs the innkeeper might have in caring for this Jew. Even before reaching the inn, the Samaritan had used his oil, his wine, and his fabrics to medicate and bandage the Jew's wounds according to the best medical practices of the time.

(Some may find additional aspects of Christian love, but most of them are implied in these five.)

So Christian love involves looking for needs and then doing what you can to meet those needs. All five of the aspects of Christian love listed above are things we can control. Commanding a person to forgive in the sense of turning retribution and vengeance over to God, to care about the needs of others, to get active in meeting those needs, to be unselfish in meeting those needs, and even to be generous in caring for those in need is reasonable, even though it may go against our human inclinations. In other words, Christian love is an act of the will. While it may lead to an emotional connection over time, Christian love doesn't necessarily involve any emotions. You can practice Christian love toward someone you hate. In fact, Jesus commanded his followers to do so!

For these reasons, in this translation, the word "love" is generally not used, or if it is used, it's modified as "caring love" to clarify that this isn't what we Americans generally think of as love.

The Roles of Christian Love

Jesus also told us that Christian love is the greatest commandment—first love for God and then love for each other—and that this commandment sums up everything else God ever told us (Good News 40:1-7). He said that our Christian love would be the standard by which others would recognize us as Christians (Good News 42:29). In other words, if we aren't serious about practicing Christian love, either we aren't Christians or we certainly fall short of being the people Jesus commanded his followers to be.

According to the Bible, Christian love is the very nature of God, and Jesus instructed his followers to mature in the nature of God (1John 4:8, 16; Good News 9:69). Jesus emphasized throughout his ministry that for us as his followers, God is our Father, and we're to grow up in God's likeness. No one can be a true follower of Christ without growing in this characteristic.

Christian love is also God's tool for evangelism (Good News 9:23). As people see us practicing Christian love, they'll be drawn to us and to the God who taught us to live that way. It's in practicing Christian love that we show God's love to the world—the people of this world see God living in us.

Christian love is what will make heaven a true paradise, because everyone who's allowed into heaven will be looking for ways to make life better for the others around them. There'll be no need for fear. There'll be no greed. As we serve God in his creations, the bond of love between us will cause us to work together with joy.

It shouldn't be a surprise that Christian love is also the standard of the judgment. The only time Jesus specifically described the judgment day, he described the standard of the judgment as "I was in need, and you met my need." (See Good News 40:26-36.) And, he went over this same theme four times in a row, showing an emphasis on this message unequaled in anything else he taught except the fact that the kingdom is about a person's heart, not his or her external actions.

Finally, Christian love is how we can always experience God's presence. God is that kind of love, so when we practice that kind of love, we sense the power of his Holy Spirit in our lives.

When God's Holy Spirit works in you, and your life is focused on the God who is love, you'll see the needs around you, and you'll respond to meet those needs. When your life is focused on yourself and the things of this world, you'll never even see the needs of others, and if you do notice someone in need, you won't care enough to seriously help unless helping that person would in some way benefit you.

Common Gender

The Fourth Gender

We who speak English generally think of words as having a potential for three genders: masculine, feminine, and neuter. These apply to males, females, and things that are neither male nor female. But there's a fourth gender often overlooked, and that's common gender—a gender that applies to both males and females. In English we have no separate words to specifically refer to anything as common gender. Instead, we use the masculine gender words for common gender. For example, we speak of "mankind," meaning both males and females.

A Recent Shift from Common Gender

In recent times, we as a culture have tried to move away from the use of masculine words to cover both men and women. We've started using both masculine and feminine terms instead of just the masculine as common gender. For example, where once we'd have said, "If anyone has trouble with this problem, he should review the last lesson," today we'd say, "If anyone has trouble with this problem, he or she should review the last lesson." But this is a rather recent development, and most existing translations of the Bible haven't seriously addressed the issue.

Biblical Languages and Jesus' Words

Biblical languages also used masculine gender terms as common gender terms. So when Jesus said, for example, "If any man hears my voice..." we generally understand that he was using a masculine gender word in a common gender mode, and that we could legitimately translate, "If any person hears my voice..." He wasn't intentionally discriminating against women—the language he used already did that.

The Practice in This Translation

Because of our cultural shift away from using masculine terms in a common gender application, this translation avoids common gender applications wherever it's possible to do so without affecting the readability of the passages involved. But the use of masculine terms as common gender terms is so ingrained in our language that this isn't always possible.

References to God

One special example of this is references to God. God is the creator of everything in this world, including both men and women. As Jesus told us so clearly, God is spirit. While God can embody any physical form he chooses to embody, he has no defining physical form. The Bible is very clear about this from the beginning to the end. There are references to God that mention arms or feet or hands or sitting on a throne, etc., but these are clearly not to be taken literally. They are ways to express in physical terms that which isn't physical and can't be fully expressed in human language. Thus God isn't sexual. He has no need of sex organs, and he's the source of both everything that's male and everything that's female. In biblical times, the cultures were all male dominated, so to speak of God as anything but male would've necessarily implied a god who wasn't dominant. To a significant degree, that's still true in our culture today, and for that reason, this translation always refers to God with male pronouns, even though the God revealed in the Bible is neither male nor female.

Crucifixion Events and Issues

This article is divided into four main headings:
1. Crucifixion Timing Issues
2. Jesus' Trials
3. Jesus' Crucifixion
4. Jesus' Resurrection

The first topic deals with the timing of events and why this translation assumes a timing that's not compatible with what's become the common traditional view—that Jesus' arrest and crucifixion both occurred on the same day—a Friday. Each of these topics is addressed in this order below.

1. Crucifixion Timing Issues

This topic addresses timing issues with the arrest, the examinations and trials, the crucifixion, and the resurrection of Jesus. The Bible provides us with the following information that affects how we understand the timing of these events:

1. Jesus' arrest and trials took place close to Passover (Easter timeframe), so sunset would've been around 6:00 pm and sunrise would've been around 6:00 am and the narrow streets of Jerusalem would've been jammed with visitors from all over.
2. Jesus' arrest took place during the night in an olive grove on the Mount of Olives the same night that Jesus and his disciples had shared a Passover feast.
3. Before dawn, Jesus was questioned twice—once by Annas (father-in-law of the high priest and a former high priest himself), and once by Caiaphas (the official high priest) along with a group of Caiaphas' associates.
4. The questioning by Annas and Caiaphas took place on a Passover feast day which was like a Sabbath and therefore it was against Jewish law, because it should've been considered work, which was forbidden on any such day.
5. Following the questioning by Caiaphas, Jesus was ridiculed and abused by Jewish temple guards.
6. Jesus was questioned briefly by the whole Jewish Supreme Court at Caiaphas' palace just after sunrise—but the Bible doesn't say which sunrise. There's no credible way the authorities could have got away with a Supreme Court trial on a holy day, so this would not have been the same day. Since the next day was the normal weekly Sabbath, the court could not have met that day either.
7. Jesus was taken under guard from the site of the trial by the Jewish Supreme Court to the Jerusalem headquarters of Pilate, the Roman governor. Since we don't know where the Supreme Court met and we don't know where Pilate's headquarters were, we can't know how far this trip was. However far this was, the trip would have been slow through the crowded streets of Jerusalem.
8. After a brief examination by Pilate, Jesus was sent to Herod's palace. We do know where Herod's palace was, but since we don't know where Pilate's headquarters were, again we don't know how long the trip was. Herod then questioned Jesus more extensively.
9. Herod turned Jesus over to his soldiers who spent some time mocking him.
10. Herod sent Jesus back to Pilate.
11. Pilate questioned Jesus more carefully and tried to avoid executing him.
12. Pilate set up his judgment seat outside the headquarters building about noon.
13. Pilate gave the Jewish crowd a choice between releasing Jesus or a criminal named Bar-Abbas, and the Jewish authorities got the crowd to choose Bar-Abbas.
14. Apparently in an effort to gain Jewish sympathy for Jesus, Pilate turned Jesus over to his soldiers to have him beaten and abused.
15. Pilate finally condemned Jesus to crucifixion while trying to shift the blame to the Jewish authorities.
16. A crucifixion detail was assigned and set out for a site outside the city.
17. Jesus and two insurrectionists would've walked slowly as they had to carry the crossbeams for their own crosses.
18. At some point, Jesus fell under the load of the crossbeam, and another man was forced to carry it.
19. Jesus was nailed to the cross about 9:00 am on Preparation day for a Passover Sabbath.
20. The sky was heavily overcast from about noon until about 3:00 pm.
21. Jesus died that afternoon, sometime around 3:00 pm.
22. Joseph of Arimathea walked from the cross through town to Pilate's headquarters to request Jesus' body.
23. Pilate sent a soldier from his headquarters to the crucifixion site outside of town to verify that Jesus was dead.
24. The Roman commander in charge of the crucifixion walked through town to Pilate's headquarters to report that Jesus was, indeed, dead.
25. Pilate agreed to let Joseph have the body, and Joseph walked back to the crucifixion site, somehow arranging to get the supplies he'd need for the burial.

26. The Jewish authorities convinced Pilate to have Roman soldiers guard the tomb around the clock to see that the body wouldn't be stolen.
27. There were two Sabbaths between Jesus' burial and Jesus' resurrection (though this isn't clear in most English translations).
28. Women came to the tomb on a Sunday morning and found the stone rolled away and the tomb empty.

There's no way to make all these pieces of information from the Bible fit what has become the traditional idea of the timing of events related to Jesus' crucifixion, so either the Bible's wrong or the traditional idea is wrong. This translation assumes that the Bible is right and the traditional idea is wrong. The Bible doesn't give enough information to determine what events happened on which days or even how many days it took from Jesus' arrest to his burial, but as will be shown, the timing suggested in this translation meets all the biblical criteria with one possible exception that presents difficulties in all translations and in the original. We'll start by addressing the issues that demonstrate why the traditional timeline can't work.

The Issue of 9:00 am and Noon

First, Mark says that Jesus was crucified at 9:00 am (the third hour of the day—Mark 15:25). John clearly says that Pilate set up his judgment seat at 12:00 noon to pass judgment on Jesus (the sixth hour of the day—John 19:14). Yet, the traditional idea of the timing has Pilate passing judgment on Jesus the same day that Jesus was crucified.

If Mark and John are both right, then Jesus wasn't crucified the same day that he was arrested—and nothing in the Bible says that he was crucified that same day. The fact that the Gospel authors don't mention the passage of days during the period of Jesus' trials only means that they were focused on the topic of Jesus' crucifixion, not on chronology. That's typical of biblical writers in both the Old Testament and the New Testament, and it's important to remember when studying the Bible.

Three Days and Three Nights?

Second, Jesus said that he'd be in the tomb three days and three nights (Good News 17:13). He was buried the evening of the day he was crucified (Good News 49:38-52). But if that was a Friday, he wasn't in the tomb for three days and three nights or anything even close to that.

By the traditional timing, Jesus was in the tomb for a very small part of Friday evening, all day Saturday, and Sunday until sometime before dawn—basically just over one day and two nights. Many Christian leaders have claimed that in New Testament times, "three days and three nights" would be understood as meaning any part, no matter how small, of three different days. However, there's no historical or archeological evidence that anyone else ever said anything like this and meant something so different from what had been said.

If Jesus actually meant what he said, and if he was right (and it's the position of this translation that he did and he was), then we have another case where the traditional idea doesn't work.

Multiple Trips through Crowded Streets before 9:00 am

A third problem is that the traditional idea of how things happened doesn't hold up to simple common sense when we consider everything that had to happen.

Jerusalem was an ancient city with narrow streets. Jesus was arrested and crucified during the week of the Passover and the Feast of Unleavened Bread. That was the most significant of all Jewish holidays, and Jews came from all over the Roman Empire and surrounding countries to celebrate this feast each year. During this feast, the streets of Jerusalem were packed so tightly that even an individual would've had difficulty hurrying through the streets, and a group of soldiers moving a prisoner would've been that much slower. (Think of traffic at rush hour in a major city, and then assume it was at least that bad.)

According to the Bible, Jesus was examined briefly by the Jewish Supreme Court just after dawn, but the Bible doesn't tell us if this was at the temple, at Caiaphas' palace, or somewhere else. Jesus was then taken under guard to Pilate's headquarters building. After Pilate had examined him, Jesus was taken under guard to Herod's palace. There he was extensively questioned and then mocked and abused. Then he was taken under guard back to Pilate's headquarters for further examination by Pilate.

We know that the narrow streets of Jerusalem would've been crowded and that soldiers transporting this prisoner wouldn't have been in a rush, especially after Jesus was turned over to the Romans. We don't know for certain how far each of these trips would have been or how long each trip would have taken, but travel would have been slow.

By the time Jesus was taken from Herod back to Pilate, Pilate was trying to drag his feet. He didn't want to condemn Jesus. As a delaying tactic, he had Jesus examined under torture. He then sought to gain sympathy for Jesus by bringing him out with the wounds of torture clearly visible, but the crowds still called for his crucifixion. He tried to substitute a murderer for Jesus, but that didn't work either. Finally, Pilate gave in and issued orders to have Jesus crucified.

At that point, a squad of soldiers had to be organized and equipment had to be gathered to crucify Jesus and two insurrectionists. Finally, the whole group walked through the crowded streets of Jerusalem to a place outside the city gates. And for this final trip, William Barclay[1] says that it was normal to have these men paraded through as much of the city as possible to heighten the effect of the crucifixion on the local population.

There's no conceivable way that between 6:00 am (dawn) and 9:00 am Jesus could've been moved under guard so many times and been examined so many times and even tortured—especially with the Roman governor, the supreme authority in Judea, trying to delay or derail the process.

The Problem of Passover Sabbaths

A fourth issue has to do with Passover Sabbaths. To understand this point, according to Leviticus, the Passover lambs would've been sacrificed in the evening on the 14th of Nisan, with a requirement to start the Feast of Unleavened Bread at sundown and to eat

---

[1] Page 379 of *The Daily Study Bible: The Gospel of Mark*, Second Edition, by William Barclay, copyright 1956, published by The Westminster Press, Philadelphia.

all the meat of the Passover lamb and burn any remains prior to dawn. In Jewish culture, each day begins at sundown, so Passover officially began shortly before sundown on the 14th of Nisan, and the meal continued through the night of the 15th of Nisan. According to Leviticus, the 15th of Nisan was the start of a seven-day feast called the Feast of Unleavened Bread, and it was to be considered a Sabbath. For 34 AD the Feast of Unleavened Bread began on Friday, the 15th of Nisan, and continued for seven days through Thursday, the 21st of Nisan. There was a second great feast on the 21st, and that was also a special Passover Sabbath. (See Leviticus 23:5-8.)

Every week the Jews observe a Sabbath (a day in which no work is to be done) on Saturday, but special feast days are also Sabbaths including the feast on the first day and on the seventh day of the Feast of Unleavened Bread. The day before a Sabbath was known as "Preparation" because of all the preparation that had to be done so that everything would be ready for the Sabbath. If two Sabbaths occurred very close to each other, the preparation work was that much more challenging. In 34 AD, the first day of the Feast of Unleavened Bread was on a Friday, so there were two Sabbaths together (that Friday and the normal Saturday Sabbath). Then the final day of the Feast of Unleavened Bread was on a Thursday with one day for additional preparation between that Sabbath and another regular Saturday Sabbath. Since food couldn't be refrigerated, preparations for Sabbaths involved a lot of work for women.

Matthew 26, Mark 14, and Luke 22 all tell us that Jesus celebrated the Passover with his disciples just before he was arrested, but John 19:31 and 19:42 tell us that Jesus was crucified sometime on a preparation day associated with the Passover feast. If Jesus was arrested the night of the first Passover feast and crucified that same day, then the day he was crucified couldn't have been a Preparation day for a Passover feast. Most Christian scholars avoid this topic, and those who consider it tend to try to explain away either the passages in Matthew, Mark, and Luke or the passage in John. None of the explanations that attempt to support the idea of Jesus being crucified the same day he was arrested can provide a reasonable explanation of this conflict. Some scholars maintain that this cannot be resolved, but it can.

There's also the problem that Matthew says that the women came to the tomb early Sunday morning "after the Sabbaths" (plural, Good News 50:13, though most English translations change the word to singular). Matthew's account indicates that there was a normal Sabbath and a special Sabbath between Jesus' burial and his resurrection. That, too, doesn't work with burial happening Friday evening—the same day as the arrest.

Now, technically the Passover was on the 14th and the Feast of Unleavened Bread was the 15th through the 21st, but in the minds of Jews these two were so linked that long before the time of Jesus, the prophet Ezekiel referred to them both as a unit he called Passover (Ezekiel 45:21). There are many Jews today who, when they speak of Passover, include both of these feasts in that one word. So it's not surprising to find that both of the feast days associated with the Feast of Unleavened Bread are referred to in the Gospels as "Passover" feasts.

If we assume that Jesus and his disciples celebrated the actual Passover feast on the 15th, and then that Jesus was crucified the day before the feast on the 21st, there's no disagreement here between the Gospels.

<u>The Solution</u>

Once we accept that there are two feasts associated with Passover, and that Jesus celebrated the first and was crucified the day before the second, there's plenty of time between those two feasts for all of the examinations and trials to take place, even allowing time off for observing Sabbaths.

This translation assumes that explanation is correct. The bottom line is that Jesus was arrested on the day we consider "Good Friday," but that Resurrection Sunday was a week after the traditional "Easter."

But what about the three days and three nights? The day of the week for the start of Passover and the Feast of Unleavened Bread varies from year to year. In 34 AD, Passover (the 14th) came on a Thursday at twilight. During the night (the 15th since it was after sundown) Jesus and his disciples celebrated the Passover feast and then went to the garden where he was arrested. Taking several days for examinations by the Jews and trials before Roman authorities, Jesus was then finally condemned on Tuesday afternoon (the 19th). He was then crucified on Wednesday (the 20th, a Preparation day for the Passover Sabbath on the 21st).

According to the Bible, Jesus died sometime around 3:00 pm, and Joseph of Arimathea went from the cross to Pilate to request Jesus' body. Pilate sent a messenger through the crowded streets back to the cross to see if Jesus were already dead, and the Roman commander in charge returned and confirmed the death. With permission from Pilate to take the body, Joseph returned to the cross, gathering burial supplies somewhere along the way. Then he and Nicodemus took the body to Joseph's new tomb and buried Jesus there. But with four trips between Pilate's headquarters and the cross (two by Joseph and two by Roman soldiers), it had to be very close to sundown before the stone was rolled in front of the door where Jesus' body lay.

Three days and three nights later would've been around sunset on Saturday evening. But doesn't the Bible say that Jesus rose on Sunday morning? Actually, the Bible doesn't say that. It says that the women came to the tomb to anoint Jesus' body and found it empty on Sunday morning (Good News 50:13-16). The Bible doesn't say when Jesus rose from the dead.

While Matthew's account of the Roman guards who were supposed to be guarding Jesus' tomb reads almost as if those soldiers were still present when the women arrived, a careful reading will show that Matthew didn't actually say that, and it's unreasonable to think that the Roman soldiers standing guard would've been frightened away while some Jewish women stood there watching. It's much more reasonable to understand that the agent of God rolled the stone from the door during the dark of night, and that the guards and Jesus were long gone when the women arrived.

But isn't that more than three days and three nights from Wednesday just before sundown to just after Saturday's sundown? A little, yes, but Jesus didn't say "exactly three days and three nights." This wasn't a technical conversation between scientists. Jesus did say that he'd rise "after three days (Good News 29:12)," and that's exactly what he did.

So this translation assumes the following chronology:

- Friday, Nisan 15 – Jesus is arrested and questioned by Annas and Caiaphas at their respective homes
- Friday & Saturday, Nisan 15 & 16 – No further events due to Sabbaths
- Sunday, Nisan 17, just after dawn – the Jewish Supreme Court finds Jesus guilty
- Sunday, Nisan 17, still early morning – Jesus delivered to Pilate for a first trial where Pilate learns that he's a Galilean, so Pilate sends him to Herod
- Monday, Nisan 18 – Herod questions Jesus extensively and joins his soldiers in mocking Jesus, then sends Jesus back to Pilate
- Tuesday, Nisan 19 – There's an extended trial before Pilate with the final verdict coming in the late afternoon
- Wednesday, Nisan 20 – Jesus and two others are crucified about 9:00 am: Jesus dies about 3:00 pm and is buried just before sunset
- Thursday, Nisan 21 – early in the morning, the Jewish authorities get Roman soldiers to guard Jesus' tomb around the clock
- Friday & Saturday, Nisan 22 & 23 – Jesus remains in the tomb
- Sunday, Nisan 24, just after Saturday's sundown – Jesus rises from the dead, an agent of God rolls the stone away, and the Roman soldiers flee
- Sunday, Nisan 24, about sunrise – women come to the tomb and find it empty

If we accept what the Bible says and don't read into the account things that the Bible doesn't say, we can find a solution that works in practically every way.

One Possible Exception

There's one exception to this neat resolution of the timing of events, and it involves a problem in John's Gospel that's a problem no matter what the other Gospels say. John 19:13-14 says that Pilate set up his judgment seat to deliver his final verdict on Jesus about noon, and that this was a Preparation day for Passover. Then John 19:31 and John 19:42 both say that Jesus was crucified on a Preparation day. John 19:31 points out that this was a Preparation day for a very special Sabbath. Even without considering the other Gospels, this would seem to indicate that Jesus was crucified well after noon on that Preparation day, and that just won't allow time for the events that followed.

When we consider the other Gospels, the problem gets worse. Matthew says that Pilate had a message from his wife after he sat on the judgment seat, and that the attempt to substitute Bar-Abbas for Jesus and an incident of abuse by Pilate's soldiers both occurred after Pilate set up his judgment seat. That means that Jesus couldn't have been crucified until well into the afternoon if we accept Matthew's order as accurate. And then we have Mark's statement that Jesus was crucified at 9:00 am.

This translation assumes that one of two things must be true:

- When two Sabbath's occurred close together (as would've been the case in 34 AD), there were two preparation days before the first of these Sabbaths to allow extra time for the needed preparations. This would allow for the day Pilate passed judgment to be a Preparation day as well as the next day when Jesus was crucified, but at this time there's no evidence that this was actually the case.
- The phrase "the Preparation day of the Passover, and..." in John 19:14 is in error. Any reference to Preparation day should apply only to the day of the crucifixion, not to the time when Pilate set up his judgment seat, but whoever originally put this information together for John made a mistake in calling the day Jesus was condemned a Preparation day. As with the first option, there's absolutely no evidence to say that this is the case.

Either of these assumptions would be difficult to justify since there's no clear evidence to suggest that either of these is true, but any other solution is significantly more difficult to resolve. Just looking at the information in John, it appears that some solution is needed, but there's nothing to say what that solution should be.

2. Jesus' Trials

Jewish Examinations – Not Trials

There were three Jewish examinations of Jesus. At least two of these would've been in violation of Jewish laws against work on a Sabbath.

Sabbath Violations

The only way to make the chronology of the four gospels work is to assume that these events took place in 34 AD. In that year the first day of the Feast of Unleavened Bread (which was a Sabbath) was on a Friday. According to the Bible, Jesus was arrested during that night (which was certainly a violation of the Sabbath laws). The Bible says that after being examined by Annas and Caiaphas, "when it was morning" the Jews brought Jesus to their Supreme Court. It's likely that the "morning" mentioned here was a couple of days later on Sunday morning, which wouldn't have been a Sabbath, but the examinations by Annas and Caiaphas occurred on Friday, which would've been a violation of Sabbath laws. However, since these examinations were relatively private matters that took place behind locked doors and were done by the top Jewish officials, the risk of being penalized was small.

Why "Examinations," Instead of Trials

If any of these "examinations" had been considered Jewish trials, then a verdict of death should've resulted in stoning, not crucifixion. But if none of them was considered an actual trial, then the Jewish leaders couldn't have Jesus stoned. For a Jewish trial involving a capital offence, at least two days were required for Supreme Court arguments—one for the prosecution and one for the defense. And by Jewish law, a unanimous verdict was assumed to be a false verdict. However, these problems would go away if the Jewish leaders didn't consider any of these examinations to be an official trial, and if the official trial and the actual execution were to take place at the hands of the Romans.

In addition, by arranging for the Romans to carry out the execution, the Jewish leaders might hope to deflect any backlash away from themselves and onto the Romans. That was an ingenious political maneuver (though it eventually backfired).

Examination by Annas (Good News 47:2-13)

Jesus was arrested in the middle of the night and taken to Annas, the father-in-law of Caiaphas and the power behind the office of High Priest. Caiaphas held the title of High Priest, but even though he'd been deposed by the Romans, Annas still had that title, too. Apparently Annas wanted first crack at examining Jesus. Since Annas wasn't the official High Priest, his examination of Jesus was brief, involved no witnesses, and carried no official weight.

Examination by Caiaphas (Good News 47:14-22)

When Jesus was taken to Caiaphas, there were witnesses prepared to testify against him. The presence of witnesses against Jesus at Caiaphas' home during the night that Jesus was arrested implies that preparations for examination by Caiaphas took place even before Jesus was arrested.

The fact that discrepancies were repeatedly found in the testimony of the witnesses implies that someone must have been acting as Jesus' defense council if only to try to find weaknesses in the case against Jesus. The authorities didn't want to be accused of having Jesus killed without just cause. The Law of Moses required at least two witnesses who agreed on their evidence against a defendant.

This nighttime examination was a dry run. According to the Law of Moses, no trial was to be held at night. But an examination where the accounts of witnesses could be checked, while certainly against the intent of the law, might be considered not a technical violation of that part of the law. (This was still a clear violation of the Sabbath laws.) These men wanted to have the coming official examination by the Jewish Supreme Court carefully orchestrated before it started.

Two witnesses were finally found who agreed on a claim that Jesus said something about destroying the temple, though the details of their accounts didn't match. Since it was considered illegal to speak against the temple, this looked like the first chance to find any accusation against Jesus that might hold up.

Jesus had told some Jewish leaders, "Destroy this temple and in three days I'll raise it up again" (Good News 15:6-8), but at the time he said this, he was talking about the temple of his own body which they'd later destroy on the cross only to see it raised back up in three days. Given Jesus' words with no explanation, it's possible that an accusation of speaking against the temple would've held up, but when Jesus wouldn't comment on the accusation, Caiaphas knew he was going to need something more than this to get consensus to execute Jesus. Perhaps as a measure of desperation, he used terminology that effectively required Jesus to reply under oath as to whether he were the Christ and the son of God. It's quite likely that he had no idea that this would give him exactly what he needed. Having been put under oath before God to answer, Jesus emphatically stated that he was indeed the Christ.

It seems likely that there were some, perhaps several, who'd up to this point resisted a death sentence for Jesus, but his own testimony that he was the Christ was considered incredible. In their minds, the Christ would come from the ruling class and would come as a ruler. This itinerant, homeless rabbi couldn't possibly be the Christ.

Even if his only crime were the insanity that caused him to make such a claim, the political risk represented by people who claimed to be the Christ was great enough to support elimination of this threat. After all, he did have a major following, and if he tried to use that following to drive out the Romans, unless he was a very powerful ruler, these men couldn't comprehend that he could succeed. Caiaphas' had said earlier that it would be expedient for one man to die to protect the nation.

Immediately after Caiaphas got what he wanted, the Bible tells us that "some of them" began to abuse Jesus. However, the way it's presented implies that the abusers were some of the temple soldiers (policemen) who'd been involved in arresting Jesus. The statement that "even some of the officers" joined in clearly implies that this wasn't the Jewish elders hitting Jesus; it was the soldiers and possibly some of the mob who accompanied them when they arrested Jesus.

The interesting thing about these two examinations is the fact that these men, who had so often criticized Jesus for healing people on a Sabbath, now clearly violated the Sabbath laws in their efforts to condemn Jesus.

Examination by the Jewish Council (Good News 47:29-34)

This is not a critical issue, but there are a couple of reasons why this translation puts the examination "after dawn" on the Sunday after two consecutive Sabbaths rather than the morning of the arrest. First, the day of Jesus' arrest and the next day were both Sabbaths. Private examinations at night in the walled compounds of Annas and Caiaphas might not draw much attention, but it would look very bad to have the Supreme Court meeting on a Sabbath. Second, the Jewish leaders had responsibilities related to the feast. Since Jesus was already in custody and sure to be condemned, this examination by the Supreme Court wouldn't have been important enough to take these religious leaders away from their responsibilities.

Because of the pre-trial by Caiaphas, the authorities didn't need a lot of time to get the decision they wanted from the Supreme Court. All they had to do was place Jesus under oath and ask one question. Yet Supreme Court members like Nicodemus and Joseph of Arimathea still didn't want to see Jesus condemned.

The Bible mentions no witnesses for this final examination by the Supreme Court. Instead, they immediately demanded that Jesus tell them if he were the Christ. When Jesus again emphatically stated that he was the Christ, the Supreme Court decided that he deserved to die. Jesus was then bound and delivered to the Roman Governor, Pontius Pilate.

First Trial before Pilate (Good News 48:1-17)

Pilate's Situation

At the time of Jesus' arrest, Pilate had been governor of Judea for about four years. Even if all we knew about Pilate were what we have in the Bible, we could tell that he was an educated man who saw Jesus as a good man and no threat to the Romans, but Pilate was too threatened by political forces to risk releasing Jesus.

Pilate had been appointed as governor by the emperor, Tiberius, with the understanding that his primary job was to keep this province under control. A Roman emperor couldn't and wouldn't tolerate any hint of rebellion, and Pilate's ties to Emperor Tiberius didn't provide him with confidence that the emperor would trust his judgment if a bunch of Jewish leaders claimed that Pilate had released a dangerous rebel. If Jesus never did anything that threatened the peace, these Jewish leaders could organize riots. The empire was vast, and the only way to control it was to stop any hint of trouble before it got out of hand. Since the Jews were notorious for their rioting and rebellion, Pilate wouldn't want any risk of a riot just to save one man's life, no matter how much he respected the man.

Appearing before Pilate—The Initial Jewish Mistakes

Because of the Passover activities, the Jewish authorities wouldn't enter Pilate's headquarters building. Entering the home of anyone who wasn't Jewish would've made them ceremonially unclean, so Pilate had to come out just to communicate with the Jewish authorities.

The Jewish leaders had been very busy with Passover functions, and at first they came to Pilate without a good plan; it seems they thought Pilate might execute Jesus just because they told him to. They'd probably never delivered a Jewish prisoner to Pilate before. When Pilate asked what the accusation was against Jesus, the first response of the Jewish authorities was just that they wouldn't have turned Jesus over to Pilate if he weren't a criminal. The Jewish authorities knew that Pilate wouldn't execute Jesus for blasphemy against a Jewish God or just because he claimed to be the Christ, but apparently they hadn't thought through what charge they needed to use to get Jesus crucified.

They quickly modified the charge to add that Jesus had claimed to be a king—something that would get Pilate's attention. But Pilate saw through what they were doing. They wanted this man dead, but they didn't want to kill him themselves. So Pilate simply told them to take Jesus and put him on trial according to their own laws.

The response of the Jewish authorities—that they didn't have the authority to execute a prisoner—was actually a rather lame response. Pilate knew that these authorities wouldn't hesitate to execute someone by stoning if they weren't concerned about who'd get the blame. (See Acts 7:54-60 where these same men stoned to death a Christian named Stephen.) Pilate knew that the Jewish authorities just wanted to shift the blame for Jesus' execution.

The Jewish authorities slipped up again by telling Pilate that Jesus' efforts had started in Galilee. As soon as Pilate heard that Jesus was from Galilee, he grabbed on the idea of sending him to Herod Antipas, who was then the Roman ruler for Galilee. That ended the trial activities for Sunday.

It's interesting to note that Pilate did no harm at all to Jesus during Jesus' first appearance before him. At the time of this first trial, there's no hint of abuse by his soldiers, beatings of any sort, or even insults.

The Crowds

Sometimes people talk about the crowds present at Jesus trial as if they were the same people as the crowds that welcomed Jesus to Jerusalem on what we now call "Palm Sunday." While some who criticized Jesus during that celebration may also have been among the crowds for the trial, those who celebrated Jesus' arrival wouldn't have been present in the crowd demanding crucifixion. The majority of the crowds on Palm Sunday were visitors to Jerusalem camped outside the city. A lot of those people would've been from Galilee where Jesus had spent most of his ministry. Even those from the city who joined in the celebration wouldn't have been among the friends of the Jewish authorities who made up the crowd outside Pilate's headquarters.

We also need to remember that, in the city, there wouldn't have been room in the streets for large crowds to gather in front of Pilate's headquarters. The crowds present for the trials were made up of the chief priests, the members of the ruling Jewish council who'd voted to have Jesus condemned, and those who owed allegiance to these authorities. It wouldn't have been hard for the Jewish authorities to gather a crowd of their supporters that would fill the available space.

Trial before Herod Antipas (Son of Herod the Great) (Good News 48:18-21)

Herod had been appointed by the Romans as the ruler of Galilee and three other territories, but his family claimed Jewish roots. It was important for Herod to emphasize his Jewish roots in order to bolster his authority in Galilee, so he'd come to Jerusalem to observe the Passover at the temple. (Pilate's capital was in Caesarea, but he came to Jerusalem because Passover was a time when crowds of Jews from all over the empire might cause rioting or even start an insurrection against Rome.)

Herod had already heard a lot of things about Jesus (Good News 25:32-34), and he was eager to examine this man. Herod had killed John the Immerser, but there'd been rumors that Jesus was John come back from the dead, and Herod was superstitious enough to want to verify that this wasn't John. Herod had talked with John, and his meeting with Jesus must have quickly provided assurance that this man was indeed not the man he'd executed.

Some of the Jewish authorities appeared before Herod with accusations against Jesus. Since Herod claimed Jewish ancestry, they had no problem with entering Herod's palace where they vehemently pressed their accusations against Jesus, but none of their accusations worked.

The Bible tells us that Herod also hoped to get Jesus to perform some miracle—a command performance like a magic act, but Jesus wouldn't go along with that. Herod took enough time to be sure that Jesus wasn't John and that Jesus would do no miracles for him. Then he decided to get some fun out of the event by joining his soldiers in mocking Jesus. At last, Herod—apparently tired of this game—sent Jesus back to Pilate.

It's worth noting that according to the Bible, Herod didn't do anything to seriously injure Jesus. He and his soldiers mocked Jesus, but they didn't beat, whip, or torture him. This was Pilate's prisoner, and if he were going to send this prisoner back to Pilate, he wanted to send him back unharmed.

Second Trial before Pilate (Good News 48:22-56)

This second trial occurred on Tuesday, the 19th of Nisan. (See Crucifixion Timing Issues above.) Once again the Jewish authorities refused to enter Pilate's headquarters.

At this second trial, Pilate questioned Jesus more closely about being a king, and Jesus assured him that his kingdom wasn't an earthly kingdom. To Pilate, this may have sounded like nonsense, but it certainly didn't sound like a threat against Rome. Pilate went back out to the crowd, pointed out that neither he nor Herod had found any reason to crucify Jesus, and then attempted to shift the sentence from crucifixion to some lesser punishment.

By this time it was about noon, and Pilate went out to a place where he could pronounce his official judgment. But before he could pass judgment on Jesus, he got a message from his wife concerning a terrible dream she'd had about Jesus and the danger of harming him. Once again Pilate was faced with his pagan past and its belief in the power of dreams, so he tried again to have Jesus released.

During the Passover festivities there was a tradition for the Roman governor to release one prisoner. While there's some question about the actual order of events here, it appears that about this time it occurred to Pilate that this custom might give him a way to get Jesus released. Pilate had a prisoner named Bar-Abbas (see the article on Bar-Abbas above) who'd tried to start an insurrection against Rome, and in his efforts to do this, he'd committed murder and theft. While the Jews looked on insurrectionists as heroes, Pilate seems to have thought that the Jewish authorities wouldn't want this man. We don't know who Bar-Abbas had robbed or who he'd killed, but we can guess that his crimes had hurt these Jewish authorities more than the Romans. So Pilate gave the crowd a choice between Jesus and this criminal named Bar-Abbas. To his surprise, the authorities convinced the crowd to call for the release of Bar-Abbas and the crucifixion of Jesus. Convincing the crowd to call for the release of an insurrectionist hero wouldn't have been difficult, but apparently Pilate didn't expect the Jewish authorities to want that.

Pilate's next tactic was to have Jesus tortured by whipping and abuse, including a crown made of thorns on his head. Then he brought Jesus out where the crowd could see him, hoping for sympathy for this Jew who'd been so badly beaten. But again the Jewish authorities and the crowd they'd gathered called for Jesus to be crucified. If anything, their insistence simply grew stronger.

In frustration, Pilate told the Jews to crucify Jesus themselves—he couldn't find any reason to crucify this man. At this the Jewish authorities slipped up again, saying that Jesus should die because he claimed to be God's son. For the Jews this was terrible blasphemy, but for Pilate, this was a whole different matter. As a pagan, Pilate grew up with stories about the children of gods and how much trouble a man could get into by going against such people. Pilate may have been skeptical about such stories, but these Jews had a very powerful religion that he knew he didn't understand. Pilate rushed back into his headquarters building, asking Jesus where he really came from. At first Jesus didn't respond at all, but when he did, his words were designed to ease Pilate's concerns at least a little. He said that those who'd turned him over to Pilate were guiltier than Pilate.

The Bible tells us that after this exchange, Pilate tried more than ever to get Jesus released. But at last the Jewish authorities hit on a tactic that would work. They told Pilate that if he let Jesus go, they'd let Tiberius Caesar know that he had released a man who called himself a king.

Finally, when he saw that continued resistance might lead to rioting, Pilate washed his hands in front of the crowd, blamed them for his judgment, and sentenced Jesus to die by crucifixion.

3. Jesus' Crucifixion

See the article on Crucifixion Timing Issues above for information on why the crucifixion is shown as being on a Wednesday, the sixth day of the Feast of Unleavened Bread (Passover), in 34 AD.

<u>Walking to the Cross</u>

Wednesday morning, the 20th of Nisan, 34 AD, the Romans in Jerusalem formed a crucifixion squad and gathered three prisoners who were to be crucified. Three sets of cross-beams were brought out, and the prisoners who were to be executed were given these heavy beams (about 100 pounds each) to carry to the place where they'd be executed. (Various sources indicate that the uprights would've weighed about 200 pounds each, so these were carried to the site separately.) Each man wore a sign declaring the crime for which he was being executed—a means of warning others against committing the same crime.

There were two crimes that would get a person crucified 1) some form of rebellion against Roman authority; or 2) running away from your master if you were a slave. In fact, slavery was such an important institution in the empire that running away from your master could be considered a form of rebellion against the empire. All three of these men were to be crucified for rebellion against the empire, though Pilate didn't consider the charge to be justified in Jesus' case.

By the time the procession got close to the city gate, Jesus was having enough difficulty carrying the cross-beam that the soldiers commandeered a man named Simon (a visitor to Jerusalem) to carry the cross. Under Roman law, a Roman soldier could have any non-Roman carry a burden for one mile. Simon was a Jew from Libya and, as such, a good candidate to carry this burden. Since Simon was just coming into the city, the place of execution must have been no more than a mile outside the city gates.

It's interesting that the Bible names Simon's two sons, and one of them was mentioned by Paul when he wrote to the Christian team in Rome. At the time Paul wrote that letter, at least one of Simon's sons appears to have been a leading Christian in Rome.

<u>Nailed to a Cross</u> (Good News 49:8-14)

The soldiers led their prisoners to a place known as "The Place of the Skull." The Bible gives the Hebrew name of this place as "Golgotha," but after Latin became the official language of the Roman church, Europeans tend to refer to the location by the Latin name, "Calvary." No one knows for sure exactly where this was, but we know that it was outside of the city of Jerusalem and near a well-used road into the city.

We know that Jesus' hands and feet were nailed to the cross, but there may also have been ropes used to assure that the person crucified couldn't pull away from the cross. Unlike many depictions of the crucifixion, those who were crucified would have been entirely naked. The Romans wanted this punishment to be as degrading as they could make it. The victims were clothed for the trip to the site of the crucifixion and then stripped naked for the actual crucifixion, thus making their clothing loot for the soldiers.

A commonly accepted theory is that the person crucified would have so much trouble breathing due to his lungs being compressed by his position on the cross that he'd die of asphyxiation or by drowning in his own body fluids. This theory holds that the victim could delay his death by using his legs to lift his body and relieve the pressure on the chest until his legs gave out. However, the evidence from modern cases of people having themselves crucified to imitate Jesus' suffering shows that this theory is incorrect. Victims died of blood loss, infected wounds, dehydration, and/or starvation. Sometimes victims of crucifixion survived on the cross for several days. Breaking the victim's legs did result in a quicker death due to traumatic shock and additional internal (and possibly external) bleeding. There's one case recorded where a person survived crucifixion when he was taken down and treated for his wounds, though two of this man's companions who were also taken down died of their wounds.

The Bible tells us that Jesus was nailed to the cross about 9:00 am, and that's a very reasonable timeframe for the process of taking prisoners from Roman headquarters to an execution site and getting them onto the crosses while the streets of Jerusalem were packed with Passover crowds. The Bible tells us that the sign on Jesus' cross announcing his crime simply read, "Jesus of Nazareth, the king of the Jews." As was probably common practice, the sign was written in Latin (the language of the Roman rulers), in Hebrew (the language of the Jews), and in Greek (the language used most commonly by much of the Roman Empire).

People at the Cross (Good News 49:18-23)

In the crowd following Jesus to the cross were several women who were in tears. In spite of his suffering, Jesus took time to warn them that the real need for mourning was yet to come. Thirty-two years later the Jews rebelled against Rome, and within four years the temple and almost all of the city of Jerusalem had been torn to the ground and leveled. There was a report that well over a million people died in the fighting.

Each of the Gospels mentions some of the women who were at the cross by name. Matthew, Mark, and Luke mention Mary Magdalene. Matthew and Mark mention Mary the mother of James the Less (one of the twelve disciples) and a brother named Joses, and John mentions someone who may be that same woman but whom he names as Mary who was the wife of Clopas. Only John mentions that Jesus' mother was present. John also mentions that Jesus' aunt (Mary's sister) was present, while Matthew mentions the mother of James and John (Zebedee's sons) and Mark mentions a woman named Salome. (It's possible that Salome was the mother of James and John and was also Jesus' aunt. If so, then James and John would've been Jesus' first cousins, but that's just a guess.) Mark clearly tells us that many other women were present who'd followed Jesus to Jerusalem from Galilee.

(As a side note, if Salome was the mother of James and John and Mary's sister—and therefore, Jesus' aunt—that may offer some insight into why she's the one who asked that her sons be given the places of primary importance in Jesus' kingdom. See Good News 30:18-28.)

The soldiers would've remained at the site of Jesus' execution. It was their job to see to it that these men did die and that no one tried to rescue them. And since clothing was a valuable commodity, dividing the clothing among themselves and gambling for an especially valuable garment isn't surprising.

In the case of Jesus' crucifixion, there were two other groups present: some of Jesus' followers mourning his crucifixion, and some of the Jewish authorities ridiculing and taunting Jesus.

Paradise Promised (Good News 49:24-28)

The soldiers, the Jewish authorities, and even one of the men crucified with him all taunted Jesus, but the other man crucified with Jesus shows an astonishing contrast. All the people present at the cross, including Jesus' followers, believed that Jesus had been totally defeated—except this one victim. This man rebuked his fellow victim, saying that they'd earned their condemnation, but that Jesus had done nothing to deserve execution. That would be surprising enough, but this man then expressed full confidence that instead of being defeated, Jesus was actually the victor. "Lord," he said, "remember me when you come into your kingdom." The obvious question must be, "How did this guy come to understand what even Jesus' closest followers didn't get?"

The Bible tells us that this man was being crucified because he was an insurrectionist who'd tried to use armed resistance against the Roman rulers. That fact may give us some a clue:

As an insurrectionist, this man might have looked on Jesus as a possible leader for insurrection. Jews in general, and even Jesus' own disciples, expected the Christ to drive out their foreign rulers by force, so thinking that the rumors about Jesus being the Christ might be true, this man probably joined with Jesus' followers hoping to find the political leader who'd take on the Romans. While with Jesus, he apparently heard enough of what Jesus was teaching toward the end of his ministry to understand what the disciples refused to see—that Jesus wasn't bringing an earthly kingdom, that Jesus planned to die and rise again, and that in his death and resurrection Jesus planned to find victory. He came to have faith in Jesus' plan, accepting the message Jesus brought. But his past as an insurrectionist caught up with him, and he was arrested and condemned to death by crucifixion. At the cross he saw before his own eyes exactly what Jesus had been talking about, and that gave him the courage to express his faith in Jesus so strongly.

This man is often presented as someone who was saved without being immersed in water. That's a ridiculous argument. First, Jesus hadn't yet given the great commission. The Holy Spirit hadn't yet come. While Jesus was having his followers immersed, the full role of Christian immersion was still more than a month away. Furthermore, for this man to know and have faith in Jesus' plan to rise from the dead, he must have had very close contact with Jesus, and Jesus was having his followers immersed. The evidence certainly can't show that this man hadn't experienced that early immersion practiced by Jesus' followers. Since people hadn't yet been commanded to be immersed—even if he hadn't been immersed, this man would've been in the same position as men like Abraham and David.

The bottom line is this: understanding Christian immersion has nothing to do with this man. Christian immersion is effective because and only if a person has faith in Jesus. The critical factor is the faith (See the article on Baptize / Immerse above), and this man obviously had more faith than anyone else at the crucifixion site.

Jesus' Death on the Cross (Good News 49:29-37)

From about noon until around 3:00 pm the Bible says that the sky was darkened. The passages literally say that "darkness" was "all over the land," and some have speculated that this was a supernatural darkness blocking all light, but the account itself is incompatible with that. None of the people at the cross (soldiers, chief priests, or others) seems to have been especially disturbed by this darkness. This was Passover time, in the heart of the rainy season. So much cloud cover for a three hour period at Passover would've had people remarking about the unusual weather, but not much more. On the other hand, complete darkness for that long would've resulted in so much comment that it would've shown up in secular records from that period—and it hasn't.

Then around 3:00 in the afternoon Jesus cried out, "God! God! Why have you left me?" There's no way around this. Jesus died as a man. God couldn't die, and God couldn't be present with such sinfulness as Jesus was bearing. We have no way of understanding what this meant or how terrible it was for Jesus. He'd never rebelled against God—not even once. The weight of sin and rebellion that we bear from childhood and to which we have become so accustomed that we rarely even think of it was unknown to Jesus before this time—then suddenly he was bearing all the sins of the entire world.

On the other hand, he'd never known a time when God wasn't absolutely present with him and in him, but suddenly God wasn't there. It would do no good for God to die; a man had to die for our sins. And it would do no good for just any man to die; a perfect man had to die if there was to be any rescue. For the man who knew no sin or rebellion to suddenly become the essence of sin would've been traumatic beyond our imaginations. For the man who'd never known a moment without God to suddenly feel the complete absence of God would've magnified that trauma far more.

But for this man to die bearing our guilt and taking our punishment in hell—there's no human language that can express that trauma. And he did it for you! Your sins, your rebellion against God's commands to practice caring love, pounded the nails into his hands and then sent him to hell! Both the message of the New Testament and simple logic tell us that a man who dies bearing the guilt of so much sin and rebellion will go to hell. And Jesus knew that he had to go through that—something we can't begin to understand. No wonder he agonized so deeply in the garden as he prayed to have this cup taken away. Then after crying out in thirst, Jesus called out again to God, expressing his continued faith as he entrusted his spirit to God's care, and he died.

As Jesus died, an earthquake shook the mountains. Earthquakes weren't uncommon in this area. The Bible tells us that in this earthquake, some tombs were opened. Those families who were wealthy enough to afford it generally had a tomb that was either a natural or a man-made cave with the entrance blocked by a large stone. Having an earthquake break open some tombs wouldn't be that surprising, but the Bible tells us that this time some of those who'd lived for God were raised from the dead just as Jesus was dying.

During the earthquake, a curtain in the temple was torn from top to bottom. (See the article on Herod's Temple below for more information on the temple.) The curtain between the Holy Place and the Holy of Holies has been variously described as somewhere between 60 and 80 feet high. In any case, it was a massive curtain. The tearing of this curtain symbolized the opening of access to God for all Christians (who are described as "a royal priesthood"—see 1Peter 2:9). The fact that it was ripped from top to bottom shows that this was done by God—no human could've done this.

The soldiers at the cross experienced the earthquake when Jesus died, and the Bible tells us that the commander in charge of the soldiers said, "Surely this man really was the son of a god." This is often translated as if the commander said that Jesus was the Son of God—as if he realized Jesus' unique relationship with the God of Israel. The grammar here doesn't support that well. Normally, when God is mentioned in the New Testament the terminology is "the God" with a definite article before the word "God." And when Jesus is referred to as the Son of God, the terminology is "the son" with a definite article before the word "son." In the Bible, there's no definite article before either the word "son" or the word "god" indicating that this pagan soldier saw Jesus as more than human, which is about the best we should expect from such a man.

Cleaning Up the Scene (Good News 49:38-42)

According to the Law of Moses, no work at all could be done on a Sabbath, so the day before a Sabbath was referred to as Preparation Day. Normally a Preparation Day would be on Friday, because the normal weekly Sabbath took place on Saturday. However, the word "Sabbath" simply meant a cessation, to stop doing something, and any holy day on which the Israelites were to do no work was considered a "Sabbath." For any such Sabbath there had to be a Preparation Day to get everything ready so that no work would need to be done on the Sabbath. The preparation day on which Jesus died was on a Wednesday because there was a special Sabbath that occurred on Thursday. (Remember, Passover was linked to the Feast of Unleavened Bread, which was a seven-day festival with special feast days on the first day and the seventh day, both of which were Sabbaths—see Exodus 12:16.)

Because Jesus was crucified on a Preparation Day for the seventh day of the feast, which was a very special Sabbath (Good News 49:38), the Jewish authorities didn't want some dying criminals hanging on crosses on the main road outside the city gates. Moses' Law forbid leaving an executed person hanging overnight at any time, and this holiday period just reinforced the desire to keep that law. This was supposed to be a sacred and festive occasion. So the authorities petitioned Pilate to have the legs of these men broken, hastening their deaths.

Upon receiving their orders to break the victims' legs, the soldiers carried them out for the two criminals crucified with Jesus, but they found that Jesus was already dead. Rather than waste the effort on breaking his legs, one of the soldiers used his spear to make sure Jesus was really dead. If you were a Roman soldier assigned to execute a prisoner, you wouldn't take chances about the person's death, because if that person somehow survived, you could be executed in his place.

Burial (Good News 49:45-52)

Jesus died around 3:00 pm, but he wasn't taken off of the cross at that time. After Jesus was confirmed dead and pierced by a Roman spear, Joseph of Arimathea walked to Roman headquarters to get permission from Pilate to bury Jesus' body. Even with the order to have their legs broken, Pilate was surprised that Jesus was already dead, so he sent a soldier to the crucifixion site to have the officer in charge of the crucifixion come and confirm the death. The officer in charge of the crucifixion walked back to Pilate's headquarters to report that Jesus was indeed dead. When Pilate knew that Jesus was dead, he gave Joseph permission to take the body. Then Joseph had to return to the scene of the crucifixion. (There may have been more activities, but this article assumes that

Joseph had already coordinated with Nicodemus who was bringing spices for the burial and with a servant who gathered the burial cloth strips and the helpers for preparing the body.) The crowded streets of Jerusalem would've made these trips back and forth a slow process, and once Joseph had the body, there were still the preparations for burial that had to be observed before the actual burial. The deadline for the burial was sundown, because the Sabbath began at sundown. With all of this activity after 3:00 pm, it would have been tight getting Jesus' body into the tomb before sundown.

So Jesus was buried very close to sundown with only minimal and rushed burial preparation activities. The women who'd been at the cross followed Joseph and Nicodemus and saw where Jesus was buried and how the body had been prepared. Apparently they thought the preparations for burial weren't as thorough as they would've wanted, so they decided to return when they could with the things they'd need to complete the process properly.

4. Jesus' Resurrection
Preparing Spices for Jesus' Body (Good News 49:53-55)

The women needed spices and oils in order to properly prepare the body for burial. The Bible is very clear that it was almost sundown for the Sabbath when the stone was rolled in front of the tomb, and the women were there observing what was done. The Sabbath that began at sundown would've been on Thursday, Nisan 21, and the women couldn't have purchased the supplies they needed that day.

The next day was Friday, Nisan 22, and this was a Preparation day for the usual weekly Sabbath. The women needed to purchase and prepare the spices they would use on Jesus' body while they also made preparations for the Sabbath and took care of daily chores. The addition of getting things ready to anoint Jesus' body as well as the normal preparation for a Sabbath would've made this a very busy day. Jesus' body wasn't going anywhere, so with everything else that was going on, these women didn't try to get to the tomb that day.

Of course Saturday, Nisan 23, was another Sabbath, and they couldn't go to the tomb on that day, so they planned to get to the tomb as early as they could on Sunday, Nisan 24. But they wouldn't want to go in the dark. They'd go to the tomb just as the dawn sky was light enough to allow travel.

Guards at the Tomb (Good News 50:1-7)

Only Matthew tells about the Roman guards at the tomb. From Matthew's account you might think the guards were still present at the tomb when the women arrived, but that's not necessary or reasonable. Roman soldiers wouldn't have run away while Jewish women stood their ground. The fear of the Roman soldiers probably was a combination of at least four factors: 1) God's agent came in the dark of night, and people are always more prone to panic at night; 2) these guards were at a tomb—and in this tomb was someone who their leader had described as the child of a god; 3) the earth shook; and 4) an agent of God appeared and easily rolled back the very large stone that the guards had sealed. That combination could indeed terrify a first century soldier who'd have been rather superstitious anyhow! Furthermore, the commander wouldn't send his best soldiers to guard a tomb from Galilean fishermen.

The evidence from the Bible is consistent with Jesus having come out of the tomb shortly after Saturday's sunset. There are two possibilities here: 1) the earthquake, the heavenly agent's appearance, the opening of the tomb, and Jesus' resurrection all occurred just after darkness came, and the soldiers fled at that time, or 2) Jesus rose from the dead just after sunset and left the tomb without any fanfare, with the arrival of the heavenly agent and the opening of the tomb occurring shortly before the arrival of the women near dawn. In any case, the body, the soldiers, and God's agent were gone when the women first arrived.

When the Jewish authorities requested a Roman guard at the tomb, Pilate told them to make the tomb "as secure as you can." Pilate hadn't heard this resurrection claim before, but he'd received the commander's report and he'd been face to face with Jesus. He knew about the claim that Jesus was a son of a Jewish god, and he knew about his wife's dreams. Now, hearing that Jesus had obviously anticipated dying and that he'd claimed he'd rise from the grave, Pilate may have felt that the resurrection was inevitable. His words, "Make it as secure as you can," may express resignation to the coming resurrection. (Based on what happened later, the Jewish leaders may have had the same premonition.)

The Bible doesn't specifically say so, but since the threat mentioned by the Jewish authorities was for a grave robbery at night, these guards would've been stationed at the tomb twenty-four hours a day. The Jewish authorities didn't get to Pilate to request the guard until the morning after the crucifixion, but they were constantly on guard from that time until God's agent came and sent them running in terror sometime after Saturday sunset. (Any time after Saturday sunset would be the first day of the week, what we call Sunday.) And surely the soldiers verified the presence of the body before they sealed the tomb.

An Agent of God Arrives (Good News 50:8)

At some point after Saturday's sundown, an agent of God suddenly showed up at the tomb, rolled the stone away from the entrance, and sat on the stone as if to say, "So there! That's how much your seal and your soldiers mean to God!" Notice that the Bible doesn't tell us whether or not Jesus' body was still in the tomb when the agent of God arrived, nor does it tell us what time during the night the agent arrived. Jesus rose sometime very shortly after sunset, but the arrival of the heavenly agent could've been any time during the night. (From information provided in the Bible we know that walls were no obstacle for Jesus' resurrected body. See Good News 51:24-26 and 42-43.)

A Bribe for the Soldiers (Good News 50:9-12)

The guards at the tomb were Roman soldiers, but when the agent of God chased them off, they ran to the Jewish authorities. They knew that they were in trouble if the truth of what happened came out. They might be frightened off by an agent from God, but they weren't afraid of some Jewish priests. By coming to the Jewish authorities, they were in essence telling them, "This is your fault, now you'd better make it right, or you'll have to deal with us!" They knew that reporting what had actually happened to their officers would've resulted in punishment, possibly even death, for letting a condemned man escape. But by threatening the priests, they got money and assurance that these men would see that they weren't punished if Pilate heard about what had happened.

The fact that the Jewish authorities offered to protect these soldiers from punishment if Pilate heard what had happened shows that these had to be Roman soldiers. If they'd been Jewish soldiers, Pilate wouldn't have cared at all that they didn't do the job assigned to them. He would've considered this understandable for these poorly trained local troops. But if Roman soldiers failed to guard a dead body, that was a different matter. The danger was that people would hear of this and that Roman soldiers would be laughed at. For Pilate's authority to work, he needed the local population to be afraid of Roman soldiers.

If the Jewish leaders had thought that these Roman soldiers were lying, they would've reported them to Pilate, and the soldiers would've been subject to arrest and punishment. The fact that the Jewish authorities believed the soldiers and were willing to bribe them to lie is evidence that these Jews were among the first to believe the fact that Jesus had indeed risen from the dead, just as he'd predicted. We can only guess what panic filled the hearts of these Jewish leaders, but their actions show that they did believe that Jesus had been raised from the dead—though believing wasn't the same as putting their faith in Jesus. (See the article on Belief / Faith above.)

Women at the Tomb (Good News 50:13-27)

In the manuscripts of his Gospel, it's clear that Matthew used the phrase, "after the Sabbaths [plural]," (Matthew 28:1) to describe when the women arrived at the tomb (though most English translations show the word "Sabbath" as singular). The fact that Matthew mentioned "Sabbaths" fits well with the timing assumed in this translation: that there was one Sabbath on Thursday, the seventh day of the Feast of Unleavened Bread, starting at sunset of the day Jesus died, and then a day of preparation (Friday) was followed by the weekly Sabbath on Saturday. Jesus rose from the dead at the end of that second Sabbath, and when the women came to the tomb on Sunday morning after these two Sabbaths, he was already gone.

The Bible tells us when the women came to the tomb, not when Jesus rose from the dead. Based on Jesus' own words, he rose after Saturday's sundown. That would make a full three days and three nights in the earth, just as he'd predicted.

The Bible also tells us that, as the women approached the tomb, they were discussing who'd roll back the stone from the entrance for them. This conversation shows that these women weren't aware of the soldiers guarding the tomb. If they'd known, they would've known that they couldn't enter the tomb without Pilate's authority to have the tomb opened.

Finding the tomb open, the women entered. But when they found it empty, Mary Magdalene ran out of the tomb and headed off by herself. Meanwhile the other women remained in the tomb, and suddenly they saw two men wearing brilliant white garments inside the tomb. These men told the women in the tomb that Jesus had risen from the dead, just as he'd told them he would, and that they should tell Jesus' disciples.

In telling the women to carry the news to the disciples, the young men actually said, "Tell his disciples—including Peter..." After his denial of Jesus, apparently Peter didn't feel that he should be counted among Jesus' disciples, so he wasn't with the others. And from what the Bible says, John was apparently with Peter, probably trying to encourage him.

The Bible makes it clear that Jesus appeared to some of the women as they were on their way to tell the disciples what they'd seen, but that Mary Magdalene was no longer with that group—she didn't see Jesus until after Peter and John had come to the tomb.

On their way to find the disciples, Jesus suddenly met the other women with a greeting that's hard to translate. The word Jesus used is closely related to the word for grace or a gift. It implies a sense of sincere joy along with the gift. If you think about it, after three days in the tomb that we'll never fully understand but that had to be terrible beyond our ability to imagine, Jesus wasn't just wishing these ladies a good morning, he was expressing his joy at being out of that tomb.

Meanwhile, Mary Magdalene was running to get Peter and found John with him. Remember that Peter and John hadn't heard the report of the other women. And Mary Magdalene had only seen the empty tomb with the stone rolled back, so that's all she could tell Peter and John. When Peter and John heard Mary's report, they immediately set out running to the tomb to see for themselves what'd happened.

The Reactions of the Disciples (Good News 50:28-36)

After hearing Mary Magdalene's report, Peter and John ran to the tomb. John reached the tomb first, but he didn't go in until Peter arrived. When they did go in, they saw that the tomb was empty and that the linen wrappings that had been around the body were just lying where the body had been. The linen wrappings were an important clue. Had someone taken the body out of the tomb, they wouldn't have taken the linen wrappings off the body and then left them in the tomb. That made no sense at all. These two disciples didn't see Jesus or any heavenly agents, but seeing the evidence that was there, John immediately believed that Jesus had done what he said he'd do. Peter was more bewildered than anything else.

The rest of the disciples heard the report from the other women, telling about agents of God and a message that Jesus had risen from the dead and was now alive, and they just didn't believe it. That pill wouldn't go down. It sounded like a fantasy story.

Mary Magdalene Meets Jesus (Good News 50:37-47)

Mary Magdalene followed behind Peter and John and arrived back at the tomb after they left. Looking into the tomb again, this time Mary saw the two agents of God, but through her tears they just looked like men wearing white clothing. Mary was sobbing. She saw two men and assumed they might know where the body had been moved, though they might also have been workers who'd come to clean the tomb. After all, she knew that Jesus didn't own or have any right to this tomb, and she hadn't been talking with Joseph or Nicodemus, so she didn't know their plans. After a brief exchange with these "men" in the tomb, Mary turned away from the tomb and saw Jesus, but through her tears she didn't recognize him. There was a garden in front of the tomb, and Mary assumed that this man must be the person in charge of the garden.

When Jesus asked Mary why she was crying, she asked him to tell her where the body had been moved so she could take it away, intending to give the body a proper burial. (The fact that she seemed confident that she could do this indicates that she had some level of wealth.) At this Jesus spoke her name, and she recognized him. The word she used to address Jesus once she recognized him is hard to translate. First, the Bible was written in a language that was understood throughout the Roman Empire, but Mary and Jesus and the Jews in general grew up with a different language as the language of their homes and intimate lives. At this intimate moment, Mary reverted to this intimate language and used a word that means both "Master" and "Teacher." (In their culture, your teacher was indeed your master.)

<u>To Galilee and Back to Jerusalem</u> (Good News 52:1-30)

One of the first things the agents in the tomb told the women was that the disciples were to go to Galilee and meet Jesus there. They didn't. It took repeated appearances by Jesus before the disciples finally did go to Galilee. The Bible doesn't tell us why Jesus wanted time in Galilee, but we can guess. First, this would be away from the authorities who had him crucified. Jesus clearly had no desire to try to force them to see and accept his resurrection. Second, most of Jesus' disciples were from Galilee, and Paul tells us that Jesus was seen by more than 500 disciples at one time (1Corinthians 15:6), which would've been more likely in Galilee. Jesus probably wanted some serious time with his disciples without worrying about Jewish authorities, and Galilee would be the area where they could meet safely.

The Bible says nothing about the journey to Galilee or the trip back to Jerusalem. The Bible does tell us that Jesus met with his disciples while they were still in Jerusalem after the crucifixion, that he then met them in Galilee and delivered his great commission there, and that he and the disciples were back in the area of Jerusalem when he ascended into heaven. We can be sure the trips back and forth occurred, but we can't determine the exact timing.

Cursing, Swearing, and Profanity

Many people confuse cursing, swearing, and profanity as if they were all the same thing, but they are three different things. The Bible deals with all three, and as Christians we need to pay attention to what the Bible teaches about each of these.

<u>Swearing</u>

Jesus told his disciples not to swear at all (Good News 9:50). Swearing is an admission that you're a liar. Swearing involves taking an oath by something you respect or value to establish that what you're saying isn't a lie this time. For a person who's consistently truthful, such an oath is unnecessary. It's the person who has a reputation for lying who's most likely to use a lot of oaths to try to convince people that what he or she's saying is true this time.

The things Jesus pointed out as oaths that were inappropriate were common oaths among Jews at the time. Today we have other oaths, but the problem Jesus was addressing is two-fold and it's still around. First, when we use an oath, we generally have no ownership of or control over the thing we swear by—we really have no right to swear by such things. And second, as mentioned above, every time you use an oath, you imply that you're a liar. The oath is to establish the truth of what you're saying, but if you need an oath, it gives the impression that you don't consistently tell the truth. Jesus' solution is to simply and consistently tell the truth. Remember, since Satan is the father of lies, the need to use an oath comes from Satan and his influence. None of us can completely master this one, but we need to come as close as we can.

But the point Jesus was making wasn't just about using oaths to try to establish that you're telling the truth. Any emphasis used routinely to try to say that you're telling the truth this time is an indication that you can't be trusted to tell the truth without such emphases. Jesus wants his followers to be known for telling the truth and to talk in a way consistent with that reputation so that people will understand that Christians are truthful.

On the other hand, we shouldn't view this as another law. This is a principle. Jesus was dealing with the practice of using oaths casually. It wasn't uncommon for Jesus to use strong blanket statements to impress his listeners with what he was teaching and then later to demonstrate that there were exceptions to the blanket statement. This is such a case.

For example, this prohibition of swearing doesn't apply to being put under oath in court. In the Bible, Jesus allowed himself to be put under oath before Caiaphas (Good News 47:18-19). And God himself used oaths on rare occasions to impress people with the absolute certainty of what he was communicating (Hebrews 3:18; 6:13, 16; 7:21; etc.). There's even an occasion in the Bible when Paul felt it necessary to use an oath in order to communicate his point with adequate force (Galatians 1:20). And Jesus often used a phrase that's been translated different ways and is generally shown in this translation as "I absolutely assure you."

Jesus' point was that his followers should be so truthful that anyone who knew them would immediately trust their word. The situation Paul dealt with when he resorted to an oath was trying to communicate a truth to a pagan society where lying was all too common. The oath was needed not because Paul was a liar, but because those who read his letter lived in a culture where lying was common and an oath was more likely to cause people to accept something as true.

However, in reading the Bible we find that Christians very rarely used oaths, and that should be the way with Christians today. We should be known as people who consistently tell the truth so that when we tell people the message of salvation, they'll know that we're convinced of the truth of what we say. That was Jesus' real concern.

<u>Cursing</u>

Cursing is actually a prayer. It's a prayer that something bad will happen to someone or something. The Bible never says that it's wrong to curse. Jesus cursed the Pharisees for their legalistic approach to serving God (Good News 13:33-70). Jesus even cursed a fig tree to make a point. In writing to the Christians in Rome, Paul cursed wrong ideas repeatedly (Romans 3:4, 6, 31; 6:2, 15; 7:7, 13; 9:14; 11:1, 11), and we can also find Paul's curses in 1Corinthians and Galatians, including a curse on anyone who claims to teach Christianity but teaches legalism instead. And in Acts 8:20, Peter cursed a magician named Simon with a terrible curse, effectively condemning him to hell.

Cursing was used very carefully both by Jesus and his followers, but there are occasions where cursing is appropriate. For example, it's clearly appropriate to curse both the ideas and the people who push the ideas that pervert Christianity into legalism, libertarianism, or anything else inconsistent with Jesus and the message he brought. Normally, Christians shouldn't be known for cursing, but Christians do need to be known for taking a strong stand against those who claim to be Christian and yet who pervert the message.

Profanity

Profanity is a word made up of two roots: 1) "pro" meaning "for," and 2) "vanity" meaning emptiness or nothingness. Profanity is using words without meaning what you say. It's what Jesus was talking about when he said, "I tell you, in the judgment you'll have to give account for every single word of profanity you've ever spoken" (Good News 11:34).

In the Bible, you won't find a single case of profanity. Once again, this is part of the principle of having people accept what we say as trustworthy. If we use words and then excuse ourselves by saying that we don't really mean what those words mean, we tell people not to trust what we say. And saying something like "pardon my French" simply compounds that problem—profanity on top of profanity.

When Christians speak of hell, Jesus wants people to know that they're talking about a very real hell. When Christians speak of God damning people, Jesus wants people to know that they're serious about this coming judgment. Even if a Christian is talking about shit or crap, Jesus wants people to know that his followers only use these words when they are talking about the real thing or using these words to illustrate how defiling something is.

Dining Customs

In New Testament times, people would lie on low couches or on cushions on the floor arranged in a "U" with guests reclining on their sides with their arms on the cushions and their legs away from the center of the "U." The food items were placed in the middle of the "U."

This helps us understand various aspects of what the Bible says about some of the meals Jesus attended. For example, the woman who came to a meal and washed Jesus' feet with her tears had easy access to his feet since he was lying on cushions with his feet extended away from the food.

The fact that the disciples were reclining at the last supper also helps us understand that scene. The people sharing in the meal would've been lying relatively close to each other, so when John, who was next to Jesus, wanted to speak privately with Jesus, he leaned back against Jesus' chest. Some have speculated that Judas was on the other side of Jesus, but that's not clear—he was just in a position where Jesus could hand him a piece of bread.

When Jesus washed the disciples' feet (Good News 42:39-45), they were lying with their feet extended away from the food, making it easy for Jesus to access their feet. He probably started at one leg of the "U" and ended at the other leg.

It appears from the Bible that Peter was probably the last one Jesus came to (though that's not certain), and if so he was probably located at one tip of the "U." That was probably not his normal position at meals. We'd expect that Peter, James, and John would usually be with Jesus close to the center of the "U," but at this meal there was still an argument going on about who'd be Jesus' top adviser in his new kingdom. Jesus had entered Jerusalem like a conquering hero, and James and John had asked Jesus for the two top positions in his kingdom, effectively trying to cut Peter out. If James and John were Jesus' first cousins, that fact might have made matters look that even worse to Peter. This may have caused Peter to pout at the end of the "U."

When it came to dipping bread, there may have been only two or three bowls in which to dip bread. Jesus' statement that a person who dipped bread with him was going to betray him would've done little to clarify who the guilty party would be; it simply reaffirmed that it was one of the twelve. We can't be certain how clearly John understood that Judas was the one who was going to betray Jesus when Jesus handed a piece of bread to Judas, but if John did understand this, it seems clear that the other disciples didn't and that John didn't tell them.

DaVinci's painting of The Last Supper is definitely not an accurate representation of the event. DaVinci wanted to capture the look he imagined would be on the face of each of the disciples, and seating them on chairs on one side of a raised table worked much better than the reality of reclining on cushions around the food.

Disciples, Apostles, Messengers, and Missionaries

Disciples

The word "disciple" means "one who's accepting training from someone." It's the root for the word discipline, and it implies a disciplined learning process. In New Testament times, this wasn't a religious word; it applied to anyone who was in training to learn the ways of a master. A disciple's teacher was the disciple's master in a very real sense. If you wanted to be a disciple of this or that teacher, you had to be willing to do whatever that teacher told you to do. You could certainly leave and stop being a disciple, but you couldn't go against the master's instructions and remain a disciple.

For Christians, discipleship training continues for a lifetime. The purpose of Christian discipleship is to prepare you for an exciting and joyful life in a paradise that's just too great to describe. (See the article on Heaven later in this Glossary and the more extensive information in Discipleship 1: Fundamentals of Christianity.) The danger is that if you don't learn to fit into that paradise, you won't get in, because God knows that you'd ruin it if you did.

Jesus had disciples from the very beginning of his ministry. We know that he had disciples when he went to the marriage feast in Cana (Good News 6:15-22) before he called the four fishermen (Peter, Andrew, James, and John), though we don't know who they were or how many there were. Throughout his ministry he had a variety of disciples—some who followed him constantly even though they weren't part of the twelve (for example, the two who were put forward as Judas' replacements after having been with Jesus from the time of his immersion until the resurrection), some who accepted his teaching eagerly but who didn't follow him on a daily basis (for example, Nicodemus and Joseph of Arimathea), and some who came and went from time to time.

We don't know what Jesus did from the time he was 12 until the time he came to see John the Immerser at age 31 or 32, but the fact that he had disciples before he called the four fishermen is a hint that he may have been speaking in Galilean synagogues and gathering a following even before he was immersed. Also, the fact that John the Immerser said that he needed to be immersed by Jesus before John realized that Jesus was God's Christ indicates that Jesus was certainly living in a way that seriously impressed John.

We also don't know how Jesus and his disciples supported themselves early in his ministry. Feeding even a few extra men would've been expensive. We know that some women who had access to wealth became followers and provided significant support as Jesus' ministry developed (Good News 8:22-23), but early in Jesus' ministry, after the visit to a wedding feast in Cana, the Bible tells us that Jesus took his disciples with him to Capernaum for a few days. It's possible that these disciples were providing their own food and lodgings in Capernaum, but at some point the group transitioned to full-time ministry, and we don't know exactly how that transition worked.

In some passages, the Bible talks of Jesus and his disciples without making it clear whether the disciples mentioned were the twelve or some larger group of disciples. We know from the Bible that at one point Jesus sent out seventy disciples on a mission (Good News 31:1-12). And we know that often the crowds numbered in the thousands. Based on the way certain passages are worded, it seems likely that Jesus' disciples could be thought of as an inner circle of three, a slightly larger circle of twelve, an even larger circle of 70, and possibly an even larger group of over 100 who were serious about following Jesus.

We don't know how long Jesus took in selecting the twelve disciples of his inner circle. We know how he called the four fishermen and the tax collector, Matthew. The Bible also provides information about how Philip and Nathanael (Bartholomew) met Jesus and came to believe in him as the Christ, but the Bible doesn't tell us whether they became full-time followers of Jesus at that time or some later time. For the other five of the twelve disciples the Bible doesn't provide any information about when Jesus called them or what they were doing before Jesus called them. There are Christian accounts from history providing some details, but these were written long after the events, and we can't be sure how accurate they are. From the information the Bible provides about seven of the disciples, we learn what we really need to know. When Jesus knew that someone was ready, he simply said, "Follow me." And that's still what he does today. Once Jesus says this, he expects no hesitation and no turning back.

Apostles or Messengers

In New Testament times the word "apostle" was commonly used in secular conversations and simply referred to someone who was sent out to accomplish a particular task. An apostle was a messenger empowered to do his job. At some places in the New Testament, this word is translated "messenger" or something like that by most English translations. The English word "apostle" comes from a Greek word literally meaning "one sent out."

During Jesus' ministry, this word wouldn't have been used as a title for an office of leadership. Jesus was training these men for leadership, but they were still trainees. When Jesus sent them out on a specific mission, they were called "apostles," but that was just the name for what they were doing.

Once Jesus ascended to heaven, those who had been with him and trained by him naturally became the leaders, and as they moved out from Jerusalem, they became the ones sent out to guide in the development and expansion of the team. They traveled throughout the Roman Empire and beyond, carrying the message and establishing teams of Christians wherever they went. For these men, "apostle" came to be a title of authority among Christians.

We often think of twelve apostles (the eleven who didn't betray Jesus and another man named Matthew—also translated as "Matthias"—who joined the group after Judas died). Then the Bible tells of another apostle named Paul, so that would make thirteen. However, the Bible refers to various others as apostles (for example, Barnabas in Acts 14:14, a man named Andronicus and a woman named Junia in Romans 16:7, Jesus' brother, James, in Galatians 1:19, etc.). Some of these apostles (including Paul) had special powers that others appear not to have had, but it's not clear exactly how God worked this, and we get onto dangerous ground as soon as we try to say what God would or wouldn't have done when we don't have clear information in the Bible. (See the article on Miracles below.) For example, in 1Thessalonians 2, Paul speaks of himself along with Silas and Timothy, as "apostles of Christ," with a strong emphasis on being sent out by Christ rather than by any human agency.

It's worth noting that Paul (who was not one of the original 12 but who regularly referred to himself as an apostle) found it necessary at one point to rebuke Peter (who was one of the original 12), and James, one of the Lord's brothers who didn't put his faith in Jesus during Jesus' ministry, took on a role of leadership during a meeting with other Christian leaders including Peter.

Because of the false religious baggage that can give a wrong idea of what "apostle" means, in this translation the word "messenger" is used, and in the rest of the New Testament a choice is made between "messenger" and "missionary." "Messenger" and "missionary" have the meaning of the word used in the Bible without the false baggage.

Missionaries

The English word "missionary" doesn't appear in this translation of the Gospels or anywhere in most other translations. It's mentioned here because it comes from a Latin word with exactly the same meaning as the Greek word for "apostle" or "messenger" and it's used in this translation outside of the Gospels. It's worth remembering that in New Testament times, the Greek word wouldn't necessarily have had the strong religious implications "missionary" carries today, but in parts of the New Testament that implication is appropriate. While at least some of Jesus' original disciples had special gifts from God that aren't generally available to missionaries today, after Jesus ascended to heaven, the job of the Christian messenger was exactly the same as the job of the missionary is today. The power to do obvious public miracles is no longer needed in most cases. God hasn't sent a new revelation, and the miracles God wants on a daily basis today don't require those powers.

Elijah

For those unfamiliar with Elijah, his name is normally pronounced ee-LIE-juh. This is one of the names that must be present in the main body of the translation.

Elijah is the name of a Jewish prophet in the Old Testament. There's no book of Elijah in the Bible, but there is a fair amount of information about him in 1Kings and 2Kings. He's also mentioned a few other times in the Old Testament, with the final mention being in the writings of the prophet Micah, who lived and prophesied long after Elijah's time. Micah 4:5 records a message from God that Elijah would be sent back to the Jews to prepare the way for the Christ.

In New Testament times, Elijah was generally thought of as second only to Moses among the Old Testament prophets. None of the prophets who came after Elijah performed miracles like Elijah did, though his disciple, Elisha, came close. By the time of Jesus' birth, many Jews were very eagerly expecting the arrival of the Christ, and that meant that they were also looking for Elijah to come because of Micah's prophecy. That's why both John the Immerser and Jesus were thought of as possibly being Elijah (Good News 5:17 & 25:33).

In the New Testament, Elijah appears in two ways. First, as just described, people who witnessed the ministries of John the Immerser and of Jesus were speculating about whether one of them might be Elijah come back from the grave. Jesus made it clear that, while John wasn't literally Elijah come back from the grave, he was the fulfillment of that prophecy. In many ways, John's ministry was similar to that of Elijah. Second, when Jesus took Peter, James, and John to a mountaintop for them to witness his glory, Elijah and Moses appeared with Jesus, talking about Jesus' coming death and resurrection. At that time the two greatest prophets of the Old Testament talked with Jesus and recognized him as their Lord.

Elijah was also mentioned in connection with Jesus' words on the cross when Jesus cried out, "God! God! Why have you left me?" (Good News 49:30). The word Jesus used for "God!" sounded something like "El-o-ee," and some people thought he was calling for Elijah. In English, those words don't sound all that much alike, mainly because of the "j" in Elijah. However, there was no "j" sound in the languages familiar to New Testament people—it just wasn't a sound they used. In their languages, "Elijah" sounded more like "ay-lee-yaw." Given the fact that we don't know exactly how either one was pronounced, it's not that surprising that people might have mistaken one for the other in a crowd.

Evil Spirits, Unclean Spirits, and Demons
The Wrong Bias

In the Bible, evil spirits are also called "demons" or "unclean spirits." These terms are interchangeable in the Bible, and in this translation, all three of these have been translated as "evil spirits" to minimize confusion.

The Bible describes the role of evil spirits in people's illnesses in three ways: 1) those who clearly had evil spirits (demons) controlling one or more aspects of their lives—evil spirits with their own personalities; 2) those who clearly had an illness, injury, or handicap unrelated to spiritual powers; and 3) those whose symptoms didn't seem to match known diseases, injuries, or handicaps but who also provided no clear evidence of evil spiritual beings associated with their symptoms. The first of these categories would be a case such as in Good News 16:8-15 where Jesus allowed a large number of demons to enter some pigs. The second category would be a case such as in Good News 17:43-52 where Jesus healed a man with a withered hand. In that case, there was no indication of demons or evil spirits being involved. For the third category, we need to consider two examples. In Good News 31:28-38 we read about a young boy with epilepsy who was healed by Jesus. It's obvious that the father and those in the crowd blamed his condition on an evil spirit, and Jesus didn't try to correct their poor science. In Good News 16:63 we find a case where Jesus is described as healing a man who was mute due to a demon. In this case, the people clearly believed that the man's inability to speak was due to a demon, but there's no evidence of an evil spiritual power as Jesus heals the man.

Jesus didn't come to teach science or medicine. He came to bring a message of eternal salvation. When he chose to heal someone, he didn't go into details about what was wrong with the person, he simply healed that person. Are we to assume that every mention of demons and evil spirits in the Bible is an actual case of an evil spiritual power, or are we to assume that Jesus might sometimes have addressed a situation in a way the crowd could understand, commanding an infirmity to come out of a person in a way that the crowd would assume dealt with an evil spiritual presence? There's no absolute answer in the Bible, and the question doesn't matter. The testimony of the Bible is that there definitely are evil spiritual beings who can and do take over control of people. The closer we stay to God, the less likely we are to come under control of some evil spiritual power.

Modern Culture and Evil Spirits

Our modern culture largely discounts all references to evil spirits and demons. One of the reasons we're so biased to discount those references is our concept of an evil spirit. Our mental image of demons is at least somewhat shaped by art from the middle ages that shows nasty looking imps as demons.

In the Bible, there isn't a single case of an evil spirit being described as having any physical form at all. There isn't a single case of anyone having seen an evil spirit. When evil spirits speak as evil spirits, two things are obvious: 1) this isn't viewed by the biblical characters involved as normal—the normal behavior of demons or evil spirits is to act through the humans they possess, perhaps affecting what the human says, but not speaking as themselves (stealth mode if you will), and 2) they speak through the human's voice, not through a voice of their own. In the Bible, demons are spiritual powers, not physical beings.

The Distinction between Spiritual and Physical Ailments

In the Bible, there's also a clear distinction made between physical ailments and evil spirits. Now, biblical times were scientifically primitive times, so it shouldn't be surprising that in some cases this line could get blurred, but an ailment that clearly affected one's physical body was almost never attributed to evil spirits while one that affected one's spiritual nature was attributed to evil spirits. An example of something that blurred the lines would be something like the epilepsy mentioned above that showed no outward physical symptoms but seriously affected one's behavior.

Modern Concepts and Evil Spirits

In more recent times, as science has advanced the understanding of various disorders, most folks have come to discount the activity of evil spirits. We've learned that there are physical, chemical, and genetic reasons for many things once attributed to evil spirits. And we've given names to various things that we classify as mental or emotional disorders.

However, at least up until now, we have no idea why many of these things occur. We have no cause for a great many of the effects we've learned to name. No germ, virus, or genetic characteristic seems to be responsible for a lot of the things we classify as psychological illnesses. And for such things, even if we knew the cause, in most cases we wouldn't be able to say what caused the cause. In other words, if we find that a particular mental or emotional or spiritual problem is caused by an imbalance in some gland in the body, and if we find that this imbalance is caused by some genetic issue, and if we find that the genetic issue was brought on by some detrimental change in the person's DNA, we still couldn't rule out a spiritual cause for that initial detrimental change in the DNA. But at least for now, there are many, many issues that modern science can't trace to any physical root cause. It's silly to claim that evil spirits don't exist just because we've given names to some of the things they can do. Just because we don't want spiritual powers to be real doesn't make them any less real.

Jesus and Evil Spirits

During Jesus' ministry, though he did a lot of healing, the Bible gives no evidence that he ever advertised himself as a healer or exorcist. In fact, the Bible records many times when Jesus told those he healed not to spread the word about his healings. Jesus focused on his teaching, not his healings. This isn't to say that Jesus never intended his healings to draw attention to him and what he was doing—he knew that he couldn't avoid that and that these miracles would play an important role in establishing the fact that his teaching came from God—for no other power could do these things. (Nicodemus made that point when he spoke to Jesus.) Jesus also did the healings to demonstrate what God wants as opposed to what Satan, the prince of this world, wants.

Though the Bible doesn't ever tell us, it seems obvious that Jesus had at least two reasons for forbidding the testimony of the evil spirits who recognized him: First, he wouldn't want his reputation to be the result of the testimony of evil spirits. Second, the Bible makes it clear that, until after his crucifixion, Jesus didn't want the general public to know that he claimed to be the Christ. The closer he got to the crucifixion, the more it became obvious, but if he'd made these claims early in his ministry, it would've been hard to avoid one of two fates: 1) to be killed by envious Jewish leaders before he'd completed his ministry; or 2) to be forced into the role of an earthly king. Jesus had specifically selected followers who wouldn't be able to threaten either extreme, and he didn't want evil spirits to interfere, though he didn't mind his immediate followers hearing their testimony.

An Underlying Biblical Principle

The message of Genesis 3 is that everything bad in this world is here in one way or another because of the environment of sin and rebellion we humans have created. Before the first humans sinned, the world was a paradise. When the first humans rebelled by doing what Satan encouraged them to do, they voted to have Satan run their world instead of God. They put Satan in God's place, and God honored their decision. God's way is paradise, but Satan's way is anything but paradise. In fact, while the Bible never specifically says it, the implication is that without God's behind-the-scenes protection, this world would be far, far worse than it is.

Conclusion

So are there really evil spirits? To argue that the Bible is wrong about the reality of evil spirits is to argue based on opinion only. There's no evidence to prove the Bible is wrong. In fact, there's a lot of evidence to support the Bible's view of evil spirits. In this translation, the assumption is that evil spirits are real and that Jesus did demonstrate the power to do what psychologists still can't do—to get rid of these evil spirits.

For an additional insight, see the article on Wind, Breath, and Spirit.

Faith

See the article on Belief / Faith above.

A Fig Tree Cursed

Jesus destroyed a tree because it didn't have any figs on it (Good News 38:27-42), even though it wasn't time for trees like this to bear fruit. While the lesson Jesus later taught verbally from this incident is about faith, there's another lesson here. Normally, a fig tree in full leaf would have figs, (though just as normally a fig tree wouldn't be in full leaf at the time just before Passover when Jesus cursed the tree). The lesson is that, just as Jesus condemned a fig tree that gave every appearance of being ready to have fruit without actually bearing any fruit, so God would condemn those who gave an appearance of being ready to bear spiritual fruit without actually bearing any.

Forgiveness

Letting It Go

Forgiveness has different aspects, and that can lead to confusion about what Jesus wanted from his followers. Matthew 7 begins with the famous verse, "Judge not, that you be not judged." (In this translation it's Good News 11:1—"Don't condemn others for what they do so that you won't wind up being condemned.") Yet later in that same chapter, Jesus says that we shouldn't give holy things to "dogs" and that we shouldn't throw pearls out to the "swine" (Good News 11:5). Now, determining who the dogs and swine are requires judgment, so how should Christians deal with this?

What's clear when we seriously consider what Jesus taught is that we're never to do God's job of retribution; we're to simply turn retribution over to God and let him handle it. We're never to even try to "get even," because we don't know where "even" is, and we generally want to go well beyond getting even. And if we try to get "even," we always rebel against God's commandment to practice Christian love even to our enemies. Only God knows what retribution is proper, and he's told us, "Vengeance is mine! I will repay!" (Romans 12:19). We need to trust that promise and leave pay-back to God.

It's important to apply principles like this to ourselves. For example, this applies to road rage. It's not our job to get back at someone who drives in an offensive manner. Those who try to do so often wind up driving just as offensively or more offensively, making them as bad as the ones who offended them. This also applies to the person who gossips about you or who lies about you or who mistreats you. You may need to get away from such people, you may even need to report such people to the proper authorities, but you're not to try to get even. Trust God. He'll do the job right.

In Good News 10:14-17 we find Jesus' model prayer, and toward the end of that prayer Jesus included the words, "forgive us for the times we've hurt you, just as we forgive those who hurt us" (Good News 10:16). Then immediately after finishing this model prayer, Jesus further emphasized this point: "if you forgive people when they hurt you, your Father in heaven will also forgive you when you hurt him; but if you don't forgive people who hurt you, your Father isn't going to forgive the times when you've hurt him" (Good News 10:19). Jesus didn't often repeat a lesson three times in a row like this. He wanted to be sure we understood just how important this is.

Later Jesus told a story to illustrate why we should always forgive in this way (Good News 22:1-14). The story makes it clear that God's forgiven us of overwhelming guilt as rebels against and traitors to his kingdom, and since he's done that, we have no right to withhold forgiveness from those who hurt us. At the end of this story, a man who refused to forgive is condemned to torture. Jesus said, "And that's exactly what my heavenly Father will do to every one of you if you don't truly, from your heart, forgive your fellow disciples when they offend you" (Good News 22:15). Our sins sent Jesus to the cross. Each of us is an accessory to the murder of God's son. If God can forgive us for that, we have no right to withhold forgiveness.

None of us is perfect. All of us hurt others when we shouldn't, and generally the ones we hurt most and most often are those closest to us—the very ones we should be most careful not to hurt. Jesus calls on us to practice forgiveness, and in practicing forgiveness we will find forgiveness not only from God but often from others whom we've hurt.

In the television sitcom called *Reba*, the character named Van had a word for what God demands of us. That word was "letitgo." (In other words, "let it go.") Sometimes we don't want to turn loose of our anger and resentment, but God knows that we can only find peace when we do so, and that we can't be fully effective as his representatives in this world until we're willing to turn retribution over to him and truly "let it go."

Restored Relationships

Letting it go doesn't mean re-establishing a close relationship with someone who's likely to hurt you again and again. That's different from simply turning retribution over to God. There's another level of forgiveness that involves re-establishing a relationship with such a person. In Good News 22:3 Jesus taught his disciples to forgive repeatedly if a person confessed the wrong he or she'd done and repented (turned from) doing that wrong. This level of forgiveness is contingent on the person's changing in some way to stop hurting you or others. While Jesus doesn't specifically say so, the fact that he elsewhere repeatedly teaches forgiveness with no word about the forgiven person's repentance implies that the forgiveness he's talking about in Good News 22:3 involves more than just turning retribution over to God. This kind of forgiveness involves restoration of the relationship.

In this case we need to be sure that we're on both sides of the issue. In other words, we need to be ready to re-establish a relationship with someone who does express his or her desire to change, and we need to be willing to apologize and change when we see that something we're doing is hurting others. Jesus said that it's the peacemakers who are truly seen as the children of God (Good News 9:10).

Genealogy of Jesus

Similarities in Matthew and Luke

Matthew and Luke are the only Gospel accounts that give any details about Jesus' ancestors. Matthew details Jesus' lineage back to Abraham, the ancestor of all Jews. Luke details his ancestry back beyond Abraham to Adam, the first human. Thus Luke includes several generations that lived before the start of Matthew's list, so there's no disagreement between the accounts in that area. From Abraham to King David the ancestries overlap, so in this area there's still no disagreement between the accounts. But the two accounts diverge significantly after King David with the exception of two ancestors.

The table on the next page shows the areas where there are differences between Luke's account and Matthew's account as well as some names not shown in Matthew's list but included in the genealogies in the Jewish sacred writings (the Old Testament). There is a reason for why these lists are so different, but first we need to consider the differences.

In the list of people from David to Shealtiel, there's no common ground between Matthew and Luke, though they have about the same number of generations when we add in the people listed in 1Chronicles but skipped in Matthew's list. Then both Matthew and Luke list Shealtiel and his grandson Zerubbabel, but they both list these men as father and son, though 1Chronicles lists Pediah as Shealtiel's son and Zerubbabel's father. The fact that Ezra, Nehemiah, and Haggai (who lived during the time of these men) all repeatedly refer to Zerubbabel as the son of Shealtiel may indicate that, for some reason, Pediah's name got purged from their family tree during Zerubbabel's lifetime. 1Chronicles lists five or six sons for Zerubbabel, but none of them is named either Rhesa or Abiud in that list.

Given Matthew's willingness to leave out generations to fit his pattern of three sets of fourteen generations, and given the amount of time between Zerubbabel and Jesus, we can be sure that Matthew left out more names in that area, but we have no way of determining how many or what those names were. It appears that Luke may not have left out any generations (except Pediah).

The obvious question is this: "How can both be right, and how can these genealogies diverge after David and then reconnect for two generations before diverging again?" Among Jews, this was possible.

After King David, Luke follows the lineage of David's son Nathan. Nathan and his descendants didn't become kings of Judah. Matthew follows the lineage of David's son Solomon and his descendants who did become kings. The genealogies diverge from that time until right at the end of the time that descendants of David ruled Judah. At that point both Luke and Matthew include Shieltel. Following Zerubbabel, Matthew follows the lineage of a descendant named Abiud while Luke follows the lineage of another descendant named Rhesa. These are both presented as sons of Zerubbabel, but since neither is listed in 1Chronicles, there are 3 possibilities: 1) Zerubbabel had other sons after those listed in 1Chronicles; 2) Zerubbabel's sons listed by Matthew and Luke are in the 1Chronicles list, but under different names; or 3) Matthew or Luke or both may have skipped a generation and listed grandsons as sons.

Table of Genealogies

Matthew	Luke	Names Matthew Skipped
Solomon	Nathan	
Rehoboam	Mattathah	
Abijah	Menan	
Asa	Melea	
Jehoshaphat	Eliakim	
Joram	Jonan	
Uzziah (Ahaziah)	Joseph	
	Judah	Joash
	Simeon	Amaziah
	Levi	Azariah
Jotham	Matthat	
Ahaz	Jorim	
Hezekiah	Eliezer	
Manasseh	Jose	
Amon	Er	
Josiah	Elmodam	
	Cosam	Jehoiakim
Jeconiah	Addi	
	Melchi	
	Neri	
Shealtiel	Shealtiel	
		Pedaiah (Not in Matthew or Luke)
Zerubbabel	Zerubbabel	
?	Rhesa	
Abiud	Joannas	
Eliakim	Judah	
Azor	Joseph	
Zadok	Semei	
Achim	Mattathiah	
Eliud	Maath	The Old Testament genealogies don't address this period, so while we know that, given the number of years involved, he must have skipped several generations, we don't have any way to check either Matthew's or Luke's list against any earlier source.
Eleazar	Naggai	
Matthan	Esli	
Jacob	Nahum	
	Amos	
	Mattathiah	
	Joseph	
	Janna	
	Melchi	
	Levi	
	Matthat	
	Heli	
Joseph		
Jesus		

One suggestion to explain the differences in the genealogies has been that one Gospel gives the lineage of Mary while the other gives the lineage of Joseph. That doesn't work, because the accounts diverge after King David, come together again for two generations, and then diverge again. Once the lineage of Joseph diverged from the lineage of Mary, the lines shouldn't have been able to converge again at any point. It's possible that this explains the differences from Zerubbabel to Jesus' parents, but not the part from David to Shealtiel. But there is a viable explanation.

The Levirate Marriage Explanation

Shortly after the Gospels were generally circulated among Christians, the issue of these divergences became obvious, and one solution that seems to work was put forward at that time. According to the records we have available today, this solution was apparently suggested by members of Joseph's family who could've been familiar with details not given in the Bible. There is a practice ordained by God for Jews. In the law given to Moses, if a man died without children, his wife was to be given to her dead husband's brother (Deuteronomy 25:5-10). Using information from the book of Ruth, if there were no surviving brother, apparently the widow would be given to the closest relative of her deceased husband. Then the first son born to that couple would be considered legally the son of the deceased husband. In such a case, some would count the legal lineage through the deceased husband, while others could count the lineage through the biological father. Such a practice would've been especially important for the Jews when it came to the lineage of King David, because his family was considered the legitimate kingly line. And since Joseph was a descendant of David, this would've applied to his lineage.

So according to this explanation, Matthew strictly follows the line of kings descended from David through David's son, King Solomon, and lists the father of a man in that lineage as Shealtiel, son of King Jehoiachin (also known as King Jeconiah). King Jehoiachin and all his sons were taken into captivity in Babylon, and the Babylonians installed his uncle, Zedekiah, as ruler, but the Jews never accepted Zedekiah as an actual king, and his authority was very short-lived. Once King Jehoiachin and all his biological sons were in captivity, it's quite reasonable that a near relative of Jehoiachin (a man named Neri descended from David's son Nathan) who was left in Judah might have been given one of Jehoiachin's wives, and that the son of this couple (Shealtiel) would've been considered the legitimate heir to the throne. (This would fit with a passage in the Bible where Jeremiah cursed Jehoiachin and declared that none of his descendants would ever sit on the throne, but Shealtiel's grandson, King Zerubbabel, did sit on the throne. If Shealtiel wasn't Jehoiachin's biological child, then Jeremiah's prophecy would be true.)

Both Matthew and Luke list Shealtiel (who didn't become king) and his grandson, King Zerubbabel, in the lineage, but at that point they diverge again, with Matthew following the lineage of King Zerubbabel's descendant named Abiud while Luke follows the lineage of King Zerubbabel's descendant named Rhesa.

There are two possibilities for the remainder of the lineage: 1) one of them (probably Matthew) follows the lineage of Joseph while the other follows the lineage of Mary, or 2) the lineage re-converges at Joseph due to another Levirate marriage with Joseph's biological father being a man named Heli who was a descendant of Zerubbabel but not in the direct kingly line (as reported by Luke) while Joseph's Levirate father was Jacob (as reported by Matthew), a man in the direct kingly line who died without leaving a male heir. While either one of these is possible, the second is more likely because of the practice among Jews of tracking the ancestry only through fathers. (See Sons and Fathers in Biblical Thinking below for more information on the significance of this practice.)

Another point of significance is that Luke clearly indicated that Shealtiel was the son of Neri, while the 1Chronicles clearly lists him as the son of King Jehoiachin. We know that Luke was a careful researcher, so making such an obvious mistake would've been very unlikely unless he had strong evidence that wasn't recorded in the biblical writings we have today.

The Bottom Line

In the end, it doesn't really matter that much to us today. Both Gospels agree that Jesus was born to Mary and that Joseph served as his earthly father. Both agree that Jesus fulfilled the prophecies that the Christ would be of the lineage of Abraham, Judah, and David. That's really all that matters as far as genealogy is concerned.

Gentiles / Nations

Among the Jews in New Testament times, "gentiles" had become a term for people who weren't Jews. The word literally meant "nations," but for Jews it had come to mean "all the nations except us." For a translator, the two meanings of this word can present problems in cases where the context would support both meanings.

The term "Greek" is also sometimes used in the Bible for actual Greeks and sometimes as synonymous with "Gentile," not implying actual Greek ancestry. Greek was well established as the common language of the areas ruled by Rome.

A confusing factor is that sometimes the word "Greek" is a general term for any non-Jews, and sometimes it's used for Jews who grew up in Gentile areas. Jews who grew up in Gentile areas might learn Hebrew or Aramaic, but they would normally have been far more comfortable in Greek than in either Hebrew (the language of almost all of the Old Testament) or Aramaic (the everyday language of Jews in Palestine).

For Jews, any Gentile was considered religiously unclean, so eating with a Gentile or entering a Gentile's home would cause a Jew to be ceremonially unclean. When Peter carried the message of Jesus to the first Gentiles to accept Christianity, his Jewish Christian associates accused him of eating with Gentiles as if that were a crime.

While Jesus intentionally focused his ministry on the Jews, there were several occasions during his ministry when he made it clear that his message would be for both Jews and non-Jews.

In this translation, the words "gentile" and "gentiles" aren't used. Instead, this term is translated as "nations," "pagans," or "non-Jews," depending on the context. However, in reading any translation of the Bible, it's helpful to remember that the words "Greek" and "Gentile" have these different meanings.

The Gospels

The New Testament begins with four books known as Gospels that tell about the life and ministry of Jesus: Matthew, Mark, Luke, and John. (The word "gospel" actually means "good news," and these books are called "gospels" because of the good news Jesus brought.) But in his Gospel, Luke mentions that "many" other gospel accounts had been written. What happened to those other gospel accounts? Apparently, those gospels were considered unnecessary after the four we now have had been written, and no one was willing to spend the time and money to maintain copies of those earlier gospels.

Of the four Gospels, three of them (Matthew, Mark, and Luke) have very strong similarities. Mark is the shortest of the Gospels, and almost everything in Mark also appears in either Matthew or Luke. Various things that aren't in Mark's Gospel appear in both Matthew and Luke. Sometimes the different Gospels use exactly the same words in exactly the same order. This has led some to suggest that the authors of these Gospels copied from each other, but a closer look shows that this isn't the case. There are just too many differences that can't be explained if this were true. The fact that Matthew, Mark, Luke, and John each include things not covered by the others or covered differently makes it clear that none of them was working directly from any of the others, but the similarities between the Gospels (especially Matthew, Mark, and Luke) makes it clear that they all made reference to one or more common sources—one or more of those gospels that Luke mentioned and that we no longer have.

After the Christian team first started (as recorded in Acts chapter 2), there was an immediate and urgent need for a written account of Jesus' life and ministry—especially focusing on his death and resurrection and some of his main teachings. After all, the Christian team started on a major Jewish feast day. When the message was first proclaimed in Jerusalem, thousands responded, and some of those thousands came from far away and knew little or nothing about Jesus. If they were going home, they'd want some written information about Jesus to take with them. If they decided to stay in Jerusalem, they'd still need that same written information to send home to their families and friends.

Acts 6 tells of a time when the early Christian team leaders faced a problem and dealt with it. The solution was delegated to others saying, "It wouldn't be good for us to leave the word of God" to deal with the problem (Acts 6:2). Then they said, "We will give ourselves continually to prayer and to the ministry of the word" (Acts 6:4). Now, the "ministry of the word" they mentioned certainly included teaching and proclaiming the message, but it may also have referred to their work in recording the information so desperately needed by these new Christians.

No doubt the first gospels were very brief, even shorter than Mark's Gospel. But it's reasonable to assume that at least some of these men then began a serious effort to bring together everything they could about Jesus' life and ministry. They may have sent someone (possibly Matthew since he was probably better educated) to Galilee to get people to remember as much as possible of his teachings. As the Holy Spirit brought things to their memories, and as those who'd been disciples and others who'd become Christians gathered more and more accounts from witnesses, new editions of the message would've been written with the additional information being recovered. This is what would've led to the "many accounts" Luke wrote about. And there can be no doubt that all four of the Gospels we have today took advantage of that early material.

Historical evidence indicates that John's Gospel was written somewhere around 90 AD, while the internal evidence in Matthew, Mark, and Luke indicates that these Gospels were written around 65 AD, give or take a few years.

The names we associate as authors of these gospels were added long after the Gospels were written. From the evidence available, Mark, Luke, and John seem to be fairly well established as the authors of those Gospels (though that's not absolutely certain). Who wrote the Gospel we call Matthew is more open to speculation, but it's clear that the author was a faithful Christian with a Jewish background, that he wrote this Gospel very early in Christian history (before 70 AD), and that he was inspired by God's Holy Spirit. He may have been the disciple named Matthew, but the evidence for that is weak. We don't really need to know who wrote the book; we can be sure God inspired the author, whoever he was.

What follows here is a discussion of each of the gospels, starting with John and ending with Matthew.

1. John's Gospel

The author of this Gospel was the Messenger John, the brother of James and son of Zebedee, though he never gave us his name in the Gospel. Instead, he referred to himself as "the disciple Jesus cared for deeply." The evidence that supports naming him as John involves three things: 1) this author was clearly one of Jesus' closest three disciples; 2) this author names Peter but he never mentions himself or James by name; and 3) the Bible tells us that James was executed too soon in the history of Christianity to have written this Gospel. Historical evidence indicates that John lived much longer than any of Jesus' other messengers, and this Gospel appears to have been written to fill in important information not included in Matthew, Mark, or Luke.

There's no good way to treat any of the Gospels as a chronological account of Jesus' ministry, though some sections are clearly and carefully chronological. Where one of the Gospels provides chronological information, this translation follows that chronology. Where the chronology isn't emphasized, this translation organizes the materials topically along with materials from the other Gospels.

<u>Unique to John</u>

John's Gospel provides us with some awesome teachings from Jesus that aren't mentioned in the other Gospels. In some cases, these were difficult teachings at the time, and that may be one reason they weren't included in the earlier Gospels, but they are certainly important teachings.

Among the most important items in John and not the others would be John's introduction where he describes Jesus as the Logic of God behind the creation of this universe (Good News 4:1-5); the section on Jesus' conversations with a Samaritan woman when he clearly stated that God is spirit (Good News 24:19); and the extensive sections telling what Jesus said to his disciples just before he was arrested including information about the Holy Spirit (Good News 43:22-32 and 44:19-33). Christianity would be far poorer without this Gospel.

2. Luke's Gospel

The author of this Gospel was Luke, a physician who wasn't Jewish and who became a Christian when he met a Christian messenger named Paul. Luke makes it clear that he wasn't an eyewitness to the events of Jesus' ministry, but that he'd gained his information from those who were eyewitnesses. The link to Paul is also supported by the fact that in Paul's writings, every time he mentions something that is covered in the Gospel accounts, his reference is consistent with how that item is addressed in Luke's Gospel. There's no good reason to doubt that Luke wrote this Gospel, and he also wrote the book called Acts, though he never mentioned his name in either book.

<u>Luke's Motivation to Write</u>

Luke was a friend of the messenger, Paul, and traveled extensively with him. In that process, Luke had met many other Christians, including Christians who'd known Jesus personally, and he had many opportunities to get the details about who Jesus was and what he'd done from these eyewitnesses. We know from Luke's second book (Acts) that Paul was imprisoned while he was in Jerusalem. Paul was then transferred to an administrative center on the west coast of Galilee where he remained in prison for more than two years awaiting a final trial, and it's clear that Luke visited with him there during that time. Luke wasn't imprisoned, so he had excellent opportunities to talk with many of the Galileans who'd known Jesus.

Eventually, Paul demanded that his case be heard by the emperor, so he was transferred to Rome, and Luke accompanied him on that trip. While Paul was in prison in Rome awaiting trial before the emperor, he apparently converted an influential Roman called Theophilus. Apparently Luke met this man while visiting with Paul.

While we don't have records to prove it, it's unlikely that the emperor would've bothered to learn much about all the people who came before him for trial. This is especially true for Nero, who was the emperor while Paul was imprisoned in Rome, but who'd not yet turned against Christians. Instead, it's likely that Nero would've assigned some member of the Roman elite to research the details and provide him with a brief recommendation about how to deal with this or that case.

Luke dedicated each of his books to this man he called Theophilus, and the wording he used in addressing Theophilus would be consistent with Theophilus being a high-ranking Roman. It could be that he had been assigned by Nero to look into Paul's case and came in contact with Paul and the message of Christ through this chance assignment. Once he became a Christian, there was a golden opportunity. Theophilus wanted more information about Paul and about Christianity. Luke wanted to help his beloved friend, Paul, when the trial came before Nero.

Whether things actually happened that way or not, the man that Luke called Theophilus was willing to finance Luke's work while Luke wrote about Jesus and Paul. It would be reasonable to guess that Theophilus was one of those Paul mentioned in Philippians 4:22 as members of Caesar's household who'd become Christians because of Paul's imprisonment.

While Luke was aware of several books telling about Jesus' life, he felt that Theophilus and other people like him needed something else. Theophilus wasn't a Jew. Luke wasn't a Jew. But most of the other books about Jesus had been written by Jews and primarily for Jewish Christians. So with Theophilus' support, Luke wrote the story of Jesus specifically for those who weren't Jews, and he followed this with a book that explained Paul came to be on trial before Caesar.

From what's in Luke's books, it's clear that Luke wrote Acts as a defense of Christianity in general and of Paul in particular. The information in the early part of Acts gives the necessary background for anyone to understand how Christianity got started and how Paul came to be a Christian and a messenger to those who weren't Jews. Once the account in Acts starts following Paul's career as a missionary, the focus of Acts is entirely on Paul.

We know from Paul's writings that Luke didn't cover every occasion when Paul suffered for being a Christian messenger, but every incident Luke did record supports the view that whenever Paul was in trouble, if the source of the trouble was Roman, the issue was resolved in Paul's favor, but if the source of the trouble was Jewish, the issue escalated out of control. Luke carefully provided the step-by-step process that led from a relatively unimportant Jewish incident to Caesar's courtroom. If Theophilus was the person assigned by Nero to review Paul's case, then Acts would've been the ideal tool to convince a Roman court officer that Paul wasn't guilty of any crime against Rome.

<u>Unique to Luke</u>

The earliest part of the story of Jesus' birth was written by Luke. Matthew's Gospel gives details that Luke doesn't mention, but only Luke tells about the actual birth in Bethlehem.

Luke also includes some important things Jesus taught that aren't mentioned in the other Gospels we now have. One of the more important ones is the story we call the Good Samaritan (Good News 22:21-35). Another is the story of the juvenile delinquent son (Good News 20:17-36). Only Luke tells about a thief dying on a cross next to Jesus who, in those final hours, demonstrated a faith in Jesus stronger than any of Jesus' other followers (Good News 49:24-28). Only Luke tells us about the story where Jesus made it clear that none of us can ever do anything to pay for our own sins (Good News 21:1-4). These and other things provided by Luke show why this Gospel was so important to early Christians and remains important for us today.

3. Mark's Gospel

Mark's Gospel is the shortest and the most dynamic. It was written by a young man named John Mark, though he never gives us his name in the Gospel.

Clues to Mark as the Author

There are clues in the biblical accounts that make it likely that this young man was the man Jesus described to his disciples as carrying a water pitcher through the streets of Jerusalem (Good News 42:8-9). It's likely that the house where Jesus and his disciples kept their last Passover was owned by John Mark's mother. It's also likely that the young man described in Mark's Gospel as being present wearing only a bed sheet when Jesus was arrested and as running away naked when someone grabbed his wrap was John Mark.

We know several things from the Bible: 1) that John Mark was related to Barnabas, an early Christian leader and messenger who helped get Paul accepted by the Christian leaders in Jerusalem when Paul was converted; 2) that John Mark accompanied Barnabas and Paul when they traveled to Cyprus with the gospel message; 3) that John Mark left his uncle and Paul and went home while Barnabas and Paul continued their work in southern Galatia; 4) that this caused some contention between Paul and Barnabas before their next trip, with the result that Barnabas went one way with John Mark and Paul went another way with a Christian named Silas; 5) that John Mark later became a valued companion to Paul and that he also worked with Peter in Rome; 6) that John Mark's mother owned a fairly large house in Jerusalem where Christians gathered for prayer when Peter was imprisoned.

This last piece of information provides an interesting possible connection. If John Mark's mother owned the house as the Bible says, then she was probably a widow. Normally, young men didn't carry water through the streets of Jerusalem—that work was for the women. But a widow might send her young son to get water. If that did happen and the widow's young son was John Mark, then he would've been present when Jesus and his disciples ate their last Passover meal together. Judas left the meal before the others, so when he got the temple policemen and mob who'd arrest Jesus, Judas would have led them first to the house where they'd eaten. By the time he arrived at the house, Jesus was long gone, and the young John Mark might easily have gone to bed with just a single bed sheet for cover. Then young John Mark might easily have decided to grab his bed sheet around his body and follow the mob to see what would happen—and that could've led to his running naked from the garden. That's a lot of "maybe" and "if," but if that isn't what happened, why did the author of this gospel even mention the young man who ran away naked. If that young man was indeed John Mark, this incident would've been his way to say, "I was there for this event, and I saw what happened."

Ancient Christian accounts tell that John Mark wrote his Gospel while working with Peter in Rome, and that the information in his Gospel was largely based on Peter's memories. There's no reason to doubt that information.

Mark and "Immediately"

One interesting point about Mark's Gospel is his use of the word often translated as "immediately." (See "Immediately" as Used in the Bible below.) This word shows up thirty-six times in the sixteen chapters of Mark's Gospel. (It shows up about half that often in Matthew and Luke, and even less frequently in John.) Furthermore, Mark uses this word where it's obvious that the thing he's talking about couldn't have happened immediately (see Mark 1:21, 1:28, and 15:1 as examples). This was a word Mark liked to use—probably because he found the message so exciting, but a translator has to be careful to consider the real meaning in each case. Based on the evidence in the context, this translation often uses other words or phrases to translate what Mark intended.

Unique to Mark

Some of the things Mark mentioned that weren't mentioned in any other Gospel include 1) the account about Jesus healing a blind man in two steps (Good News 12:31-35); 2) the story Jesus told about a farmer who knows how to plant a seed and watch it grow but who has no idea why it grows (Good News 18:38-47); 3) the fact that Peter heard a rooster crow twice the night he denied knowing Jesus (Good News 43:48); and 4) the story of a young man fleeing naked from the garden when Jesus was arrested (Good News 46:36). But we can almost feel the impetuous Peter behind Mark's words. Mark also sometimes includes details not found in any of the other Gospels.

4. Matthew's Gospel

Who Wrote Matthew?

The traditional idea is that Matthew, who was one of Jesus twelve disciples, wrote this Gospel. There are two problems with this. First, early Christian history says that Matthew wrote his gospel "in the Hebrew dialect," and we know that the Gospel we call Matthew isn't in Hebrew and isn't a translation from Hebrew or any dialect of Hebrew. Second, throughout the New Testament, the authors did what Jesus told them to do—they bore witness to what they'd seen, heard, and experienced. Those who knew Jesus personally were adamant about having actually witnessed the events in the Gospels. Those who became Christians later made it clear that they wrote based on eyewitness accounts. Mark didn't claim to be an eyewitness, but he gave us one insight that almost has to be about his presence in the garden when Jesus was arrested. Luke told us plainly that he wasn't an eyewitness to Jesus' ministry, but in Acts he told us where he was an eyewitness to Paul's ministry. John told us that he was one of Jesus' closest disciples. Paul never claimed to be an eyewitness to Jesus' ministry, but he told us of the revelations he received from Jesus after his conversion, and his teachings are absolutely consistent with what Jesus taught. Peter specifically claimed to have been with Jesus. The author of Hebrews makes it clear that he wasn't an eyewitness, and neither James nor Jude claims to have been an eyewitness to Jesus' ministry. The question has to be, if the Matthew who'd been a disciple wrote the Gospel of Matthew, why is there not even a single claim that he was an eyewitness to these events? There's not even a single personal insight such as the one Mark gives about being in the garden when Jesus was arrested.

Matthew may have been the man best suited to put together accounts from eyewitnesses. The Gospel we call Matthew contains extensive materials that could have come from such eyewitnesses. This may be the reason Matthew's name came to be associated with this Gospel. And it's still possible that the Messenger Matthew did write this, and for some reason gave no indication that he was writing as an eyewitness. Whatever the case, this Gospel is and should be a part of the Bible, clearly inspired by God's Holy Spirit, and the matter of who actually wrote it shouldn't be a concern.

Unique to Matthew

The vast majority of the things Matthew recorded in his Gospel also appear in one or more of the other Gospel accounts, but Matthew gives us some insights and teachings not included in those other Gospels. The Golden Rule appears only in Matthew (Good News 11:15). Only Matthew gives us Jesus' description of the judgment and what the standard of the judgment will be (Good News 40:26-36). Matthew tells us about the guards at the tomb (Good News 50:1-12). And Matthew tells us some things about Jesus' birth not included elsewhere. We can be thankful that we have this Gospel, and we don't really need to know who wrote it because whoever wrote it, the author was obviously inspired by God.

The Great Commission (Good News 52:31-39)

Many translators show the great commission starting with a command to "go." That translation implies an imperative verb, but in the Bible the verb for "go" is a participle that should really be translated "going" or "as you go" or "wherever you go." Jesus wasn't interested in commanding people to go. The only commandment in this Great Commission is "make disciples." The other verbs in this passage ("immersing" and "teaching") are also participles, but since they follow the command to "make disciples," they carry the weight of that command, emphasizing two necessary parts of making disciples. (See Baptize / Immerse above.)

Note that in this passage Jesus called on his followers to first make disciples before immersing them, and then called on them to teach these new disciples all the things he'd commanded them to teach. Too often we see immersion as the key—the "end-all do-all." Too often people go through some water ritual called "baptism" before they become disciples. And too often such people are left with little if any real teaching after that ritual. These are like the seed falling on rocky soil and not having enough root to survive (Good News 18:18).

Some may ask, "What are we really supposed to teach people once they accept discipleship?" The reality is that Christianity has a lot of aspects, but all of them lead back to Christian love. Christian love is the very nature of God (1John 4:8 and 4:16). As Jesus said, if we can master Christian love, we will have mastered everything God ever told us (Good News 40:1-7). Christian love is the standard by which we will be judged (Good News 40:26-36). Christian love is what marks us as Christians (Good News 42:29), so if we don't practice Christian love, we're not even Christians. And Christian love is an important factor in what will make heaven a true paradise. (See Christian Love / Caring Love above.)

Heaven / Sky

In the Bible, the word "heaven" and the word "sky" are exactly the same word. The translator must choose which word to use based on the context. The meanings for this word include the atmosphere or sky, the universe or stars and planets, and the place where God is and where we will go at the resurrection. In this translation, there are some cases where the traditional choice of how to translate this word has been changed because another choice seemed more appropriate based on the context.

Finding the Real Heaven

With reference to our final reward as Christians, we Christians often get a very wrong impression of the biblical message of heaven. Christian songs about heaven and most sermons about heaven give us the impression that heaven involves an eternity of not much to do. We'll be singing God's praises for all eternity, telling him over and over how wonderful he is for what he did in the "good old days" back on earth. We'll be talking with each other—about the "good old days" back on earth. We'll all have crowns, so crowns won't mean much. We may work in gardens in a new world. But what if you're not into music and you don't enjoy working in gardens all that much? For many Christians—probably even most Christians—the idea of heaven sounds a lot like eternal boredom—and that would definitely not be paradise. In the movie *The Preacher's Wife* starring Denzel Washington, the strong implication over and over is that earth is vastly better than heaven (not Mr. Washington's fault). There's something very wrong with our message if that's the impression people have of our hope in heaven.

There's not a lot of detail provided in the Bible, probably because it would be very hard to express the detail in a way that would work well. But Jesus and his followers did provide some information that's important and that gives a very different picture of heaven.

We know that God's a creator, and if he found it worthwhile to create one time, it's likely he's found it worthwhile to create many, many times and in many, many different ways. The Bible tells us that his agents participated in this creation and continue to participate in this creation in many different ways. So if God's busy with many, many creations, then there'd be all kinds of opportunities for us to serve him in ways we'd find exciting and rewarding. With unlimited creations, God can certainly find something you'd love to do.

Jesus clearly taught that those who are faithful in this life will be given much greater responsibilities and authority in heaven (See Good News 20:50; Good News 37:60-74 with emphasis on verses 65, 67, and 73; and Good News 41:48). For some, their greatest joy may be in heavenly choirs and music ensembles. For others, their greatest joy may be in tending gardens of breathtaking beauty. But those aren't the only opportunities. Paul indicates that some of us will be leaders of teams of God's agents. There's no way to know what all we'll be doing, but the promises of our Lord indicate that we'll have good reason to be praising God forever, not so much for what he did in "the good old days," but for what we're getting to do in his service. In fact, we won't be able to shut up about how much we love him for what we're getting to do and experience. The one who knows us best and loves us most is the one who'll assign the tasks, and we can certainly trust him.

And beyond that there's more. There's a new world of awesome beauty, a sea of water so clear that the ripples sparkle like diamonds, mountains taller than any on earth, and everyone there is truly interested in making your day as good as it can be. That's paradise! Just think of anything you find good in this world, and then understand that the God who made that good thing can make something even better in a world where there's no sin.

Paul said that our hope of heaven should be the strongest motivating factor for Christians (1Corinthians 15:19). Yet Christians say things like, "I'm breathing, and that beats the alternative," or, "I woke up this morning, and any day I wake up is a good day." In doing that, they deny their faith. They clearly indicate that their primary hope is in this world, not in heaven. They openly admit that they don't trust God to do better there. But Jesus made it very clear that if our focus is on this world, we cannot be his disciples (Good News 10:30; 18:19; 29:14; 35:36; etc.). God's team can never accomplish what he intends until we have a concept of heaven that's inspiring and motivating, and the Bible provides that concept, but we've almost universally missed it.

Satan and Heaven

There are a couple of passages in the Bible that have been interpreted to indicate that Satan was once a leader of heavenly agents in God's realm and that he rebelled against God and was cast out of heaven. That may or may not be correct—the passages involved are certainly not clear on that point. Translators have tended to translate such passages so that they fit with that idea, and that's OK, but it injects the translator's opinion.

In doing this translation, that didn't seem to be the real intent of those passages, so this translation takes a different approach. For example, in the passage where Jesus speaks of seeing Satan falling from "heaven," this translation favors the idea that Jesus was saying that Satan had just suffered a catastrophic fall from his high power in this world. Indeed, the message Jesus brought was a mighty blow to Satan's power, and when Christians live as Jesus taught, that fall continues today.

Either approach is OK, but without better biblical evidence for the concept that Satan was a leader in heaven and was then cast out, it seemed inappropriate to reinforce what may be a false idea.

Hell

Most people—even those who claim to be agnostics or atheists—have some sense that this life isn't the end—that there'll be something else, and that this "something else" involves some sort of accounting for what we've done in this life. After all, if there's nothing beyond this life, then the most logical way to live is as a sociopath. If there's nothing beyond this life, then it would make sense for you to find all the pleasure you can in this life regardless of how much damage that did to others. If there's nothing beyond this life, then this is your one chance to get whatever you can and do whatever you can get away with as long as you're enhancing your pleasure in this life. But with a very few possible exceptions, people know that's a lie.

Jesus clearly taught that judgment is real and that unspeakable torment and anguish awaits those who don't learn to seek God's ways. A good example is Jesus' story of a wealthy man and a beggar named Lazarus (Good News 20:54-65). In this story Jesus told how the wealthy man died and how he was in torment, begging for just a hint of water to cool his tongue. We know that Jesus based all of his stories on reality, so we can be confident that this story reflects reality, whether it's an account of events that actually happened or a made-up story that shows how things typically happen. Over and over Jesus warned people of the garbage dump where those unfaithful to God would be consigned.

In fact, this story may not have been one of Jesus' made-up stories to illustrate a point. If it's a made-up story, it's the only one that mentions a person by name.

Jesus' word for "hell" was "Gehennah." Gehennah means "Valley of Hinnom," and this was actually the name of a valley on the south side of Jerusalem where the city's garbage was dumped. This garbage was always burning, and worms and rodents were always present in the garbage. The idea Jesus was conveying is that people can make themselves unacceptable for heaven, and that if they do this, they'll be thrown into the garbage dump of eternity.

Some Christians, including many Christian leaders, have taught that we can somehow pay for our sins by suffering and thereby escape hell. The Bible never says anything to support that idea. If suffering paid for sins, then eventually everyone in hell would get out. The truth is that no amount of suffering can pay for even one sin, and there's nothing else that we can do to pay for our sins or redeem ourselves after we've turned against God (Good News 21:1-4).

Here's the issue. God's prepared a wonderful and eternal life, filled with challenging and exciting activities, but it only works as a paradise if the people in that paradise aren't selfish, arrogant, greedy, and deceitful. So that's what this world is for—to teach us the evils of those attitudes, and to allow us to find God's way and thereby prepare ourselves to be a part of a real paradise. But there must be a garbage dump for those who refuse to hear the message and respond. That's what hell is.

Herod

For those unfamiliar with this name, it's normally pronounced HAIR-udd. This is one of the names that must be present in the main body of the translation.

There were three rulers named Herod in the Bible, and three others who aren't called Herod in the Bible but who were part of the family and who are sometimes referred to as "Herod" in secular books.

Herod the Great

This Herod was king at the time of Jesus' birth (Good News 3:9-18). More information about this Herod can be found in this Glossary under Bethlehem; Birth of Jesus – The Date; and Birth and Childhood of Jesus – Events. This Herod ruled three areas mentioned in the Bible where Jesus did most of his ministry (Judea, Samaria, and Galilee) plus several other areas. In the Bible, he's simply called "Herod."

Wikipedia quotes descriptions of Herod the Great as "a madman who murdered his own family and a great many rabbis," "the evil genius of the Judean nation," "prepared to commit any crime in order to gratify his unbounded ambition," and "the greatest builder in Jewish history." For the Romans, he was an ideal ruler. He had Jewish ancestry, which reduced the risk of insurrection; he cultivated strong ties with Roman officials at the highest levels; and he ran his kingdom in a way that maintained the peace and brought economic prosperity.

For the Jews, his work on the temple was his most significant contribution. By the time his construction work was complete, the temple in Jerusalem was considered by non-Jews to be possibly the finest temple in the world of that day.

There are questions about the exact date of his death. Most scholars favor 4 BC, but many others favor 1 BC and some suggest 5 BC. Using just the information in the Bible, 1 BC seems most likely, but that's open to challenge. The dates shown in this translation do assume the 1 BC date for his death.

Herod Archelaus

When Herod the Great died, Herod Archelaus was made "tetrarch" over the areas of Judea, Samaria, and Idumea, but his reign only lasted about 10 years because of his political incompetence. In the Bible, he's referred to simply as Herod's son, Archelaus. Archelaus' reputation was that he was crueler than his father without being as politically competent. This is the man who was ruler in Judea when Joseph and Mary came back from Egypt, and Joseph decided not to settle back in Bethlehem because of his reputation (Good News 3:19-20).

Herod Antipas

Herod Antipas was another son of Herod the Great. He was "tetrarch" of Galilee and Perea. The Bible mentions this Herod in connection with two events: 1) he was the Herod who executed John the Immerser (Good News 23:47; 25:21-34); and 2) he was the Herod who questioned Jesus when Jesus was on trial (Good News 48:17-21). In the Bible, he's simply called "Herod."

Apparently the Romans considered this member of the Herod family a good administrator. He ruled his territory for over 40 years, but when his nephew accused him of plotting against Rome, he was removed from authority and exiled. His role in the execution of John the Immerser was, according to the Bible, that of an unwilling participant.

Herod Philip

Herod Philip was a third son of Herod the Great who inherited part of Herod the Great's kingdom. In the Bible, this man is simply referred to as Herod's brother, Philip. He was made "tetrarch" of several smaller districts. In the Bible, he's only mentioned in connection with Herod Antipas having married Philip's wife. (See Good News 23:47.)

Herod Agrippa I

This Herod was a grandson of Herod the Great. He started his rule as "tetrarch" of Galilee and Perea after the exile of his uncle, Herod Antipas. After a couple of years in that role, he was made king of practically all the territory that Herod the Great had controlled, but he died three years later. In the Bible, he's simply called "Herod."

This Herod is mentioned in Acts as the Herod who had the disciple James, the brother of John and son of Zebedee, executed. Herod Agrippa then had Peter imprisoned, but God sent an agent to get Peter out of prison. Shortly thereafter the Bible tells how this Herod died "eaten by worms." (See Acts 12:20-25.)

Herod Agrippa II

This Herod was a great-grandson of Herod the Great and son of Herod Agrippa I. He ruled over Galilee and various territories near Galilee, but he was also given the right to control who'd be high priest at the temple in Jerusalem. In the Bible, he's simply called "Agrippa."

This is the Agrippa who heard the case against Paul shortly after Paul had made his appeal to Caesar. At that time, Herod Agrippa II commented that Paul could have been released had he not appealed to Caesar. (See Acts 25 & 26.) The rule of this Herod ended in 66 AD with the start of the Jewish insurrection against Rome. Herod Agrippa II sided with the Romans in that war, even though he was Jewish. He understood that the Jews had no hope of winning their battle against the empire, and in 70 AD the Romans totally destroyed Jerusalem.

Herod's Temple

Herod's Temple was a remodeling and expansion of the Second Temple built by the Jews after the Babylonian captivity. This expansion of the temple was planned and largely carried out by Herod the Great, though it wasn't completed until the time of Herod Agrippa II, Herod the Great's great-grandson. The temple complex was an architectural marvel with the temple building itself at the top of the mountain and terraced courtyards at lower levels. Anyone in one of those courtyards could always look up to see the temple at the top of the mountain. Even pagan visitors wrote about this temple as one of the most impressive in the empire.

The temple compound was almost a third of a mile long by almost two tenths of a mile wide, surrounded by a wall. Non-Jews could enter this outer wall into a courtyard where merchants sold animals for sacrifice and temple souvenirs, and where money changers exchanged various currencies for the currency accepted in the temple. (Roman coins were considered unfit for use in God's temple.)

Inside this temple compound was another wall that isolated the central area from this public courtyard. Signs were posted warning any non-Jew against entering this area on threat of death by stoning. The wall was low enough not to obstruct a person's ability to see the inner courtyards, but no gentile was to enter any area inside the low wall, and the Romans supported the right of Jews to kill any gentile who did enter that area. In this area, there was a large courtyard open to all Israelites (Jews), even lepers. This area was known as the Court of the Women, though it served as a popular area for Jewish families to gather.

Farther into the temple compound was a relatively small area known as the Court of the Israel. This area was restricted to only Jewish males. Beyond that was larger the Court of the Priests which was restricted to only those who were of priestly ancestry. The Court of the Priests surrounded the temple building itself. The temple building was a rectangle, three times as long as it was wide and nearly ten stories tall. Only priests could enter the Court of the Priests, and only a priest selected by lot could enter the temple itself. (See Good News 1:4 for example, and see the information under Zechariah below.) Twice a day, morning and evening, a priest was selected to enter the temple and offer incense to God on a golden altar. The area that the selected priest entered was known as the Holy Place, and it consisted of two-thirds of the area inside the temple. The other one-third was separated from the

Holy Place by a curtain about sixty to eighty feet high and was called the Holy of Holies or the Most Holy. Only the High Priest could enter that area, and he could only enter it once a year on the Day of Atonement. It was the curtain between the Holy Place and the Holy of Holies that was torn from top to bottom when Jesus died.

High Priest

By Jewish law, the high priest was to be a descendant of Moses' brother, Aaron. Once he became high priest, a man was to remain high priest until he either died or became unfit for the office (deformed, mentally deranged, etc.). But under the Romans, such high offices were auctioned to the highest qualified bidder, so the Jewish high priesthood changed hands from time to time. (It appears that, in order to avoid civil unrest, rulers—even including foreign rulers—appointed only men who were indeed descendants of Aaron.)

During New Testament times, a man named Annas pretty much controlled who got the office, and he kept it in his family. Caiaphas, the official high priest when Jesus was arrested and crucified, was a son-in-law to Annas. The Romans had deposed Annas himself from the high priesthood after he'd served about ten years in that office. However, everybody knew that Annas was the power behind the Jewish high priesthood, and he was still referred to as a high priest (see Luke 3:2).

When Jesus was arrested, he was taken first to Annas for questioning. Annas was the real power in Jewish religion and politics, and, there can be no doubt that Annas was heavily involved in planning for Jesus' arrest and crucifixion.

Immediately / Quickly

A word often translated "immediately" appears frequently in the Gospels and Acts, and especially in Mark's Gospel. From various passages it's clear that the real meaning in context is that something happened either quickly or not long afterward. In this translation, the context has been used to determine whether to translate as "immediately," "quickly," "right away," "soon," or something similar that would fit the context well.

In the Name of...

There are many places in the New Testament where the term "name" has special significance in a phrase like "in the name of..." In such cases, the meaning is much more than a literal name. In New Testament times, this term applied to the very character and authority of the person bearing that name.

Thus when Jesus told his followers that they'd receive what they asked for "in his name" (for example in Good News 44:43), he wasn't talking about adding the words "in Jesus' name" to the end of their prayers as if those words were some sort of magic incantation. The meaning was that the prayer would be granted if it was consistent with the character and authority of Jesus.

Someone may wonder whether promises like this have any value, since that means that praying in Jesus' name would be praying for what God wants, and God can do whatever he wants with or without our prayers. But there's actually enormous power in such prayers. Satan is the prince of this world (see Good News 40:40; 43:47; 44:33, and Ephesians 2:2). We've voted to make him ruler of this world by our refusal to do things God's way, and God's honored our vote. But when we ask God to do things in this world consistent with who he is and with his authority, he's promised to override Satan's authority.

Those who are good parents will know that as parents, we always want the best for our children, but when our children express a special desire, we'll give that special attention. We may not give them what they want in every case, but we'll often go beyond what we'd have done if they hadn't asked.

Similarly, when Jesus told his followers to immerse converts in the name of the Father, the son, and the Holy Spirit, he was using this meaning for "name" and the double meaning for "immerse." Jesus followers aren't just to be immersed into water, they are also to be immersed in the very nature and character of God as we have come to know him through Jesus and through his Holy Spirit within us.

This translation emphasizes the full meaning of this use of the word "name" wherever possible.

Isaiah

Isaiah was a Jewish prophet who wrote one of the longer books in the Old Testament. The book he wrote is sometimes called "the Gospel of the Old Testament" because it has so many prophecies about the Christ that were fulfilled in Jesus' ministry. Isaiah is one of the Old Testament books quoted frequently by Jesus.

James the Disciple

There were actually two of Jesus' twelve disciples who were named James, but the Bible doesn't tell us anything about the one called James the Younger other than his name.

The other James was the brother of John. They were sons of a man named Zebedee, and they and their family were fishermen in partnership with Peter and Andrew's family. James appears to have been the older brother since his name is generally mentioned first. He was part of the three disciples who were closest to Jesus (including Peter and John). Jesus called James and John the "sons of thunder," which indicates some lack of patience on their part.

Although James was one of the inner circle of three disciples, he was the first of Jesus' messengers to die. Shortly after the Christian team started, Herod Agrippa I (grandson of Herod the Great) had James killed in order to gain favor with the Jewish authorities who strongly opposed Christianity (See Acts 12:1-2).

Jericho (Good News 37:34-42)

For those unfamiliar with Jericho, this name is normally pronounced JER-i-koe. This is one of the names that must be present in the main body of the translation.

In Good News 2:16, this city is mentioned as the home of a woman (Rahab) in Jesus' ancestry.

In Good News 22:26, this city is mentioned as the destination toward which a Jewish businessman was traveling when he was attacked by robbers and left for dead. (This man was then rescued by a Samaritan businessman.)

In Good News 37:34, this city is the site where Jesus healed a couple of blind men. Matthew and Mark say that Jesus was leaving Jericho when he met and healed these men. Luke says that Jesus was approaching Jericho. This paradox is easily resolved by knowing more about Jericho in New Testament times. At that time a new city of Jericho had been built by Herod the Great, and the old site was just a small village, but both were referred to as Jericho. Jesus was on the road between these two.

In this same incident, Matthew mentions two blind men while Mark and Luke mention only one (and Mark calls him the "son of Timothy"). Again, it's not important how many blind men were there or what their names were. It's likely that the man called the "son of Timothy" was well-known to early Christians, while the other man may have been much less well-known. It's not hard to suggest reasonable explanations for why Mark and Luke didn't bother mentioning the second blind man.

In Good News 37:43, this city is mentioned as the home of a tax collector (Zacchaeus) who climbed a tree in order to see Jesus and who then gave his life to the Lord.

Jerusalem

For those unfamiliar with Jerusalem, this name is normally pronounced Jeh-RUE-suh-lem. This is one of the names that must be present in the main body of the translation.

Jerusalem was established as the capital of Israel and the location of the temple by King David. In New Testament times, it wasn't the political capital, but it was certainly the religious center of Judaism because the temple was there. Because of its religious significance, Jerusalem was also an important political center.

The streets of Jerusalem were narrow, and there weren't a lot of places for a large group to gather. The palaces of different officials were located in different parts of the city. Pilate's was close to the temple, because if trouble started, that's where it was likely to start. Herod's was on the eastern side near the outer city wall. The location of Caiaphas' palace isn't certain, but the best available information puts it in a southern part of the city. When it comes to the place where Jesus was crucified, there's just not enough information in the Bible to be certain, except that it was near the road just outside the city walls.

Jesus and Divorce

In Good News 9:47-48 and Good News 23:26-35 we find Jesus saying that a man who divorces his wife for any reason other than sexual infidelity causes her to be sexually unfaithful (adultery). There's no way of telling whether Jesus meant that sexual infidelity justifies divorce or whether he was simply saying that you can't cause someone to be sexually unfaithful (an adulterer) if that person already is. Either way, Jesus is opposed to divorce. Jesus went on to say that if either of two divorced people were to marry someone else, he or she'd be sexually unfaithful in that act. The point here is that in many cases—perhaps most cases—divorce was seen as a means to marry someone else. In such cases, divorce is just an excuse for legalized sexual unfaithfulness. Ideally, Jesus would always want couples to find a way to reconcile.

The reason Jesus said that a man who divorces his wife causes her to commit adultery is that, in that culture, it was almost impossible for a woman to get by on her own. There were certainly exceptions to this, but they were rare. Thus, if a man divorced his wife, the only good option for that divorced woman was to find another man to be her husband. But God isn't impressed with human documents, so although the husband may have provided a certificate of divorce, Jesus was saying that God would still consider the marriage vows as binding.

And the principle applies to more than divorce: God isn't impressed by human legal documents when it comes to marriage. When a couple start having sex, God considers them married (1Corinthians 6:16). For God, marriage licenses aren't the issue. God has designed us so that when we start having sex, a bond forms (this has been demonstrated scientifically), and breaking that bond creates pain. So when you break or weaken that bond by having sex with another person, that's a case of letting selfishness lead you to hurt someone else. Such selfishness is the very heart and soul of sin.

A movie called Love Story had a line in the script repeatedly that said, "Love is never having to say you're sorry." That may sound good, but it's not true. Any love that lasts decades is a love that's eager to say, "I'm sorry," whenever one mate hurts the other. And the forgiveness aspect of Christian love is necessary for a truly successful marriage.

However, there are cases where, although these teachings against divorce are still true, divorce would be justifiable by the standards Jesus taught about Christian love. For example, if one spouse is truly abusive either to the other spouse or to the children (or both), the standard of Christian love would dictate that, both for the sake of children and for the sake of the abuser, the marriage should be dissolved and the abuser should be reported.

Every case is different and must be treated in light of God's standard of Christian love, with the final understanding that divorce, while it's always wrong, can be the lesser of two evils. And divorce isn't the unforgivable sin—God's grace covers this sin just like it covers any other sin common among humans. There are other sins Jesus condemned much more strongly than divorce.

We, as humans, tend to think of sexual sins as worse than other sins, but that's not supported in Jesus' teachings. Too often, the Christian team has marginalized divorced people as if they were a special class of sinners. We're all sinners in need of God's grace and forgiveness, and there's nothing in the Bible saying that divorce is worse than the other sins we practice daily. Divorce is certainly not God's desire, but once it happens, we as Christians, in Christian love, are to do what we can to help both partners deal with the aftermath in a way that will bring the most honor and the least dishonor to God and his team.

Jesus and Temptation
The Wilderness Temptations

In considering Jesus' temptation in the wilderness (Good News 7:1-7), we shouldn't imagine that Satan tempted Jesus by coming to him as a demon with a pointed tail and a pitchfork. We don't know how Satan presented himself, but if it had been obvious to Jesus that he was dealing with the devil, the temptation wouldn't have been real. There are many cases in the Gospels where it's clear that Jesus operated as a human with limited knowledge, even though the God who knows all things was present with him. It was only as a human experiencing the limitations of humanity that he could be tempted in all ways as we are (Hebrews 4:15). Jesus had to fight the battle of living a sinless life without special privileges that would give him an advantage Adam didn't have.

The First Temptation

Let's imagine a kindly man meeting Jesus in the wilderness and striking up a conversation, expressing concern for Jesus' obvious condition after more than a month without food. Now imagine that this man, who seemed so kind, began talking with Jesus. It wouldn't be surprising that Jesus' claim to be the Christ might come up. At a seemingly innocent point, the man might humorously point out that some of the stones there in the wilderness looked like loaves of bread, and then he might offer what would be presented as a helpful suggestion—as the Christ, why couldn't Jesus simply command the stones to be bread? In fact, the man might indeed have been a kindly and interested person through whom the devil found a way to attack. Remember, Jesus once referred to one of his leading disciples, Peter, as Satan (Good News 29:14). And while we generally think of Jesus' response to this temptation to turn stones to bread as a stern one, if Satan were using some unwitting and kindly man, Jesus' response may have been gentle.

Jesus' First Response

Jesus replied by quoting a passage from Deuteronomy 8:3 saying "'Man shall not live just by eating bread, but by every word that comes out of God's mouth.'" Jesus may or may not have realized at that moment that he was dealing with Satan himself, but he certainly knew that using his powers selfishly wasn't God's way, even in as small a thing as turning a stone into bread. Later, Jesus would do similar miracles to feed crowds of thousands of people, but in those cases the miraculous powers were being used for others, not for himself.

The Second Temptation

For the second temptation, again it's possible that the devil was working through the same seemingly innocent person or another similar person. It's possible that the devil maneuvered their conversation until the best way to communicate the ideas being discussed was to go to a high point of the temple to view the crowds of worshippers below. And it's possible that the devil worked the conversation around to the point that he could make this suggestion seem almost reasonable. "If you're really the Son of God and you want to get the attention of all these worshippers of God, why not just jump down and let them see the proof that you're who you claim to be when the agents of God protect you from any injury." And this time the devil even used a passage from the sacred writings (Psalm 91:11-12) to bolster his attack. An important lesson here is that, just because a person quotes from the Bible doesn't mean that person is on God's side.

Jesus' Second Response

Jesus provided a very simple answer from Deuteronomy 6:16. The point of this answer is that God operates on the basis of faith. He won't allow us to test him by demanding proof—we're not even to try. Those who want proof of God's reality won't find it in such tests. The best proof is found in getting to know him by serving him. He'll reveal himself, but not in ways that the world considers proof.

At least twice during Jesus' ministry (Good News 15:5 and 26:40) the Jewish religious leaders asked for proof of Jesus' right to do the things he was doing and to teach the things he was teaching, and Jesus could obviously have provided plenty of proof, but in each case he avoided the temptation to give them what they demanded. The truth is, no amount of proof would ever be enough for those who aren't on God's side, and those who are on God's side find plenty of proof in things the world would never consider proof.

The Third Temptation

For the third temptation, Luke's account clearly implies that this temptation involved a vision. In New Testament times, it's possible that some people thought that all the kingdoms of the world could be viewed from a really high mountain, but today we certainly know this wouldn't be physically possible. Note that this time the devil didn't bother trying to use anything from the sacred writings, and this time the devil was much more obvious in his attack. It's like he was saying, "You want to win the world? Then get with the program! Wake up! This world belongs to me! I decide who runs the show here. But I'll give you the whole thing if you'll just bow down to me."

Remember, Satan's a liar. He may indeed be the prince of this world, but I seriously doubt he'd have fulfilled his promise to turn these kingdoms over to Jesus. And even if he did give all the kingdoms of the world to Jesus, it would only be because Jesus worshipped him and he (Satan) remained the ultimate authority. Satan always represents his way as the easy way, but in the end it's never the easy way—not even close.

Jesus' Third Response

This time Jesus quoted Deuteronomy 6:13– only God is to be worshipped. No matter how much Satan offers us or how useful it might look in accomplishing Christian ministry, what he offers is always a lie. And while the previous two responses Jesus gave might have been gentle responses, this one was clearly a harsh response. Satan had revealed himself for who he is, and Jesus forcefully expressed his rejection of everything Satan had to offer.

(Luke has the second and third temptations in opposite order, but Matthew's order seems more reasonable, so that's the order followed in this translation. The exact order wasn't an important issue to biblical authors in many cases—the important point was to communicate the reality of the events, not the order in which they occurred.)

Other Temptations

Those three temptations Jesus faced during his time in the wilderness were certainly not the only temptations Jesus faced. Hebrews 4:15 tells us that Jesus was tempted in every way that we're tempted. He was tempted by pride, by greed, by lust, by apathy, and by every sin that tempts you. Probably the strongest temptation he faced, based on things he said, was the temptation to avoid the cross. Good News 40:37 shows Jesus struggling with the cross shortly after raising Lazarus from the dead. In Good News 40:41 Jesus spoke of his crucifixion with an "if," showing that he did indeed have a choice and that there was a temptation to avoid the cross. And in the garden he asked God to find another way (Good News 46:7). He knew that the cross meant going to hell for people who'd never appreciate what he'd done, let alone accept him as Lord. We need to thank God daily that Jesus didn't succumb to that temptation.

Jesus and the Law

During his earthly ministry, Jesus repeatedly told people to live by the Law of Moses (see Good News 12:3; 20:63-65; and 30:1-4, etc.), but he also made it clear that he'd come to bring a drastic change to the purpose and role of that Law. Over and over he challenged the letter as opposed to the actual spirit of that Law. (See Good News 11:15; 13:53-54; 25:12; 40:1-7; etc.)

In Good News 9:28-30, Jesus said that nothing in the Law of Moses would lose its force until everything in that law had been fulfilled. However, in Good News 9:29 Jesus said that he'd come to bring that very fulfillment or fuller meaning to the Law. Then starting at Good News 9:34 Jesus did give fuller meaning to the messages brought by Moses and the prophets. At points he even turned what they said around completely, arguing that what they taught was wrong in light of the fuller understanding of the overall message that he was bringing. (For example, see his discussion of the Old Testament teaching of "an eye for an eye and a tooth for a tooth" in Good News 9:55-61 and his teachings about divorce in Good News 9:47-48 and 23:25-31.)

There's a very important implication here. If we refuse Jesus' teachings that give the fuller meaning to the Mosaic Law and the writings of the prophets, then every part of that law down to the smallest stroke of a pen still applies to us. It's only in accepting Jesus' new way of living that the old law is fulfilled and no longer applies as law.

Everything in the Law is replaced by the commandments to practice Christian love toward God and toward those in need. And for those who do this, there's no longer any penalty for breaking the law, because as long as we maintain our faith in God, he provides his grace to cover all our sins. We don't earn his forgiveness by what we do, but we make ourselves acceptable by our attitude. With God, it's always about our hearts being surrendered to him.

In Galatians, Paul wrote to emphasize this aspect of Jesus' teachings. He made it very clear that Christianity isn't about laws and rules. He even made it clear that any attempt to deserve salvation based on living up to such laws and rules is a rejection of Christianity, and that such a rejection of Christianity would actually remove a person from God's covenant of grace. The problem with laws and rules is that our faith is in ourselves and our ability to meet some standard, but we can never even come close to meeting God's standard, so our faith must be in God, not in ourselves.

Jesus as the Logic

Many Christians are familiar with the fact that John's Gospel uses "*logos*" to apply to Jesus' divine nature—a word that's often translated as "word." This is a very important passage, but we can't really understand this passage fully unless we understand something about the cultural background that shaped how John used this term.

Many pagan scholars in New Testament times held that every noun represented a supernatural ideal, and things in this world were appropriately called by a name based on how closely they resembled that supernatural ideal. For example, they would maintain that there was some supernatural ideal horse, and that any animal on earth called a "horse" would be called by that name because of that animal's resemblance to this ideal horse. Some Jewish scholars had also picked up on this idea, and the idea had, to some degree, permeated the culture of the Roman Empire.

It's also important to remember that John was writing about sixty years or more after Jesus' resurrection. Jerusalem had been destroyed. Judaism was struggling to find an identity without the temple. Meanwhile, Jews had become a minority among Christians because so many pagans were accepting Christianity. So the ideas John used at the beginning of his Gospel would've been familiar to many Christian leaders at the time he wrote—they'd come out of the pagan world where these ideas were common.

It's also important to understand that the word "*logos*" actually had a range of meanings besides the literal meaning of "word." These other meanings included such things as "reason" and "logic." (You can see the link between the Greek word "*logos*" and the English word "logic.") So by using this term, John was saying that the ideal supernatural reason and logic behind this creation existed as an eternally inherent aspect of God and that this "reason" or "logic" had come into this world in the person of Jesus Christ. (Remember, God is spirit. This "reason" or "logic" was an integral part of that spirit.) In other words, every aspect of God that deals with this creation, everything we could hope to understand about God, was present among us in Jesus Christ.

In Good News 43:34 we find Jesus saying, "There's much more to God than just what you've witnessed in me." But most translations quote him as saying, "The Father is greater than I." That translation is a valid translation of the words, but it too often implies a separation between Jesus and the Father that's inconsistent with what Jesus taught elsewhere. Too many people get the impression that Jesus was saying that he was in some way a lesser God. The other way of understanding these words, which is just as valid, is that Jesus was saying that those aspects of God that had nothing to do with his mission or this creation weren't present in him. If they had been, no human would've been able to survive meeting him. But every aspect of God that we could possibly comprehend was present in Jesus Christ. He was God with us in every way that we could stand. He's not another God or a lesser god.

We could compare this to a video conference call with someone we've never met. During the call, we'll probably see the person's face and hands and some of his or her upper body, but we'll say that we saw the person—even though there's much more to this person than what we experienced in that call.

This should remind us of Moses' experience with God (Exodus 33:18-23). What Moses experienced wasn't another God or a lesser god. He experienced the real one true God, but that God, in his mercy and love, only revealed enough of himself that Moses was able to survive the experience. Jesus came to bring that same experience to all who'd put their faith in him. Unlike Moses' experience, God did this through a human body so that many people could experience his presence.

The pronouns in the section of John's Gospel about Jesus as the Logos refer to God, but specifically to that aspect of God that dealt with anything that had to do with this creation. The idea is that there's much more to God than what we could ever know or understand from our perspective in this creation, but everything we could comprehend of God—every aspect of God that had anything to do with our creation—is included in what John called the "Logic"—that is, in Jesus himself. (See Good News 4:1-5.)

Jewish Elders

There are references in the Gospels to Jewish elders as leaders associated with those who opposed Jesus. Every town had elders. These were the older men in the community, and they exercised a great deal of authority over the political, economic, and religious affairs of the community. The elders mentioned in the Gospels were men who exercised similar authority in Jerusalem that influenced all Jews.

We don't have clear information about who'd have been included in this term. The official supreme Jewish authority was the Supreme Court (called the Sanhedrin or Council in many other translations), made up of seventy official members and led by the high priest. Those who were members of the Supreme Court would certainly have been referred to as "elders" in this sense. Yet there may have been others who would have been included in this title.

Jewish Feasts

According to Moses' law in the first five books of the Old Testament, there were three feasts that all Jewish males were supposed to attend at the temple every year. By New Testament times this wasn't possible for many Jews who were living in distant locations, but those who could (and who cared about trying to keep Moses' law) tried to attend as often as possible—especially for the great feast of Passover.

Passover / Feast of Unleavened Bread / First Fruits

The Passover is so important that it's sometimes called "the feast of the Jews." According to the Law of Moses, Passover is always to occur on the 14th day of the month Abib. (By the time Jesus was born, this month was called "Nisan.") On the 10th of that month each family was to select a lamb with no imperfections. The lamb was to be butchered shortly before sunset on the 14th ("at twilight"), and then the feast was to begin. The feast was to last into the night until the lamb had been entirely consumed. Anything that couldn't be eaten that night was to be burned before dawn.

Since sunset marked the beginning of a new day, the actual feast was on the 15th of Nisan. That day was a "Holy Convocation" (a day of rest or Sabbath), no matter which day of the week it was, because it was the first day of a seven-day feast called the Feast of Unleavened Bread, and the first and seventh day of that feast were both "Sabbaths." During this seven-day feast, no leaven of any sort was to be eaten or even to be in the house of any Jew. Eating unleavened bread commemorated how the Israelites left Egypt in such haste that there was no time to allow them to make bread with leavening—no time to let the dough rise. This Feast of Unleavened Bread was so closely associated with Passover that these two were both referred to as Passover, and that continues to be true today.

When the Passover lamb was butchered on the 14th of the month, some of the lamb's blood was to be spread around the door of the house, re-enacting the events of the night before the Israelites left their slavery in Egypt and started traveling toward the Promised Land. That night God sent an agent to Egypt to kill the first-born son of any family that didn't have the blood around the door, but to "pass over" the homes with the blood.

The Passover Feast is mentioned several times in the New Testament, but especially with reference to the events surrounding Jesus' arrest and crucifixion.

The Feast of Weeks

A feast called the Feast of First Fruits started on the first day of the week (Sunday) during the Feast of Unleavened Bread (Passover). Seven weeks after the Feast of First Fruits started was the Feast of Weeks, a summer feast. It would always start on the same day of the week as the Feast of First Fruits (Sunday), and it was always a special "Sabbath." The Feast of Weeks marked the end of the wheat harvest, celebrating the harvest season completed. Today Jews also link this feast with the giving of the Law to Moses at Mount Sinai.

Because there were 50 days between the Sabbath that started the countdown for this feast and the actual Feast of First Fruits, that feast came to be known in New Testament times as "Pentecost" (meaning "fiftieth"). And it was on Pentecost that the Holy Spirit came to the Christians in Jerusalem, and the Christian team first started with the immersion of over 3,000 converts.

This feast is mentioned in the New Testament only three times, the most significant of which is as the day when people were first encouraged to become Christians (Acts 2).

The Feast of Tents
This feast is sometimes called the Feast of Tabernacles or the Feast of Booths and it occurs in autumn as a feast of rejoicing. The feast commemorates the time the Israelites spent wandering in the wilderness before they entered the Promised Land. During this feast, all Israelites are to make "tents" to live in for seven days, simulating the structures the Israelites lived in during their wilderness wanderings. The first day and the eighth day are to be "Sabbaths"—days when no work is permitted.

This feast is mentioned only once in the New Testament as a feast Jesus attended one time (though Jesus probably attended this feast every year). (See Good News 32.)

Jewish Marriage Customs
In biblical times, each area or community might establish its own normal practices, and there'd always be exceptions. What's in the Bible falls into two categories: 1) If it deals with what happened (as in the case of Joseph and Mary), we can be sure that we have an accurate account of what happened and that what happened was generally consistent with what would normally happen at that time and that location given the circumstances described. 2) If it deals with a description of marriage customs (as in the case of stories Jesus used in teaching), we can be certain that the customs described were consistent with what would normally happen at that time and in the location where Jesus told the story, but not necessarily in other communities. (Of course for kings, the customs were whatever the king decided.)

Typical New Testament Jewish Culture
In New Testament Jewish culture, before the marriage, there was a contract or agreement that had cultural significance as binding as the actual marriage. Ending such a marriage contract required a divorce proceeding, even if the couple hadn't yet met each other. The length of time between signing the contract and completing the marriage varied based on a couple of factors:

One factor was the age of the prospective bride and groom when the contract was signed, because the contract might be signed when both the prospective groom and the prospective bride were small children or even infants, or it might not be arranged and signed until they were of marriageable age. Of course, in the former case there'd be years between the contract signing and the actual marriage, while in the latter case the time could be very short.

A second factor in the time between signing the contract and the marriage was the bride price. The contract typically specified that the groom would pay two amounts, one to the bride's father and one to the bride. By New Testament times, the payment to the bride's father was generally a nominal amount. The amount to the bride was generally the larger amount, and that payment became the bride's own property.

Marriage in the mid-teen years was more the rule than the exception, and in such cases the groom's payments to the bride and the bride's father were often provided by the groom's parents. If the groom had to provide the payments himself, it might take a groom a few years to gather enough money to make the payments. During that time, the contract remained binding, but the marriage would be delayed.

Women had little or nothing to say about who they'd get as a husband. Dating was unknown, and it wasn't unusual for a woman to meet her husband for the first time at the marriage ceremony. From the Bible, we can't tell if Mary had met Joseph before their marriage.

Typically, when the groom was ready to complete the marriage, he'd travel to the bride's home with some of his companions. The bride's friends would be there, and the two groups would have a party while the bride and groom formalized their union and shared their first night together. Then the whole group would travel to the groom's home—the bride's new home—and the party would continue for days. It was this kind of party that Jesus and his disciples attended with Jesus' mother in Cana (Good News 6:15-22). (It's possible that the marriage they attended was for one of Jesus' siblings.)

Mary and Joseph
Mary was bound by a contract to marry Joseph at the time she was told that she'd have a baby. (See Good News 1:15-16 and 2:1-3.) Living together and sexual relations were both strictly taboo at this stage, but the contract was binding. The wording in the Bible implies that Joseph was mature beyond what we'd normally expect of a teenager. Most girls were married in their teen years, so as a virgin, Mary was probably still in her teens, though it's possible that both we past their teen years because the marriage had been delayed while Joseph earned enough money for the required payments. Mary's trip to visit Elizabeth by herself (even if there were companions while traveling) fits a little better with that scenario. And Mary's immediate willingness to have this baby could also be because she was passing the age when her friends were starting their families.

In any case, as soon as Joseph learned of the origin of Mary's baby, he arranged to complete the marriage contract. Since the Bible tells us that they only went to Bethlehem because of a registration requirement, Joseph must have had at least a temporary residence established in Nazareth or somewhere close to Nazareth where they began their lives together.

A King's Wedding Feast
One of Jesus' stories (Good News 13:18-32) tells of a king who organized a wedding feast at his palace. The interesting thing in this story is that the king, having instructed his slaves to bring in everybody, good or bad, then found a man who wasn't wearing a wedding garment, and he had this man evicted. From the story, it's obvious that the man knew he'd be expected to have a wedding garment and that he had no excuse for not having one. And it's also obvious that those listening to Jesus saw no difficulty with this scenario. From historical documents, we know that at least some kings provided the wedding garments for all guests. That would fit the story very well. (In telling this story, Jesus might have had in mind an actual event in a nearby area that had made the rounds of local gossip.)

Teenage Girls and a Wedding Procession

Another story (Good News 40:16-25) tells of some young women (probably teenagers) waiting for a groom to take them to join in his wedding feast. In the story, these girls would've been friends of the groom or his family. The girls apparently expected the wedding procession not long after sundown, but for some reason the procession was delayed. Since the groom in this story controlled who could enter the gate at the end of the procession, this must have been the procession back to the groom's home. In the story, the groom's home had a wall around it with a gate for the entrance, which would've been normal for a middle-class family. Once the groom and his companions entered, the gate was shut and locked, and no one else was allowed in. That closing of the gates was the real point of the story. For God's kingdom, when the gates finally close, there'll be those who want in, but there'll be no more opportunity to get in.

Jews and Samaritans

The animosity between Jews and Samaritans was intense. Even secular Jews would often avoid contact with Samaritans as much as possible. No religious Jew would eat or drink anything provided by a Samaritan. (And most Jews maintained at least an appearance of being religious.) Both Jews and Samaritans claimed to be the true descendants of Abraham and the exclusive keepers of the true revelations given to Moses. To even offer a cup of water to a Samaritan or accept a cup of water from a Samaritan would imply an unacceptable level of friendship.

Samaritans were descendants of Israelites who'd remained in Israel when most Jews were deported to Babylon, and during that period they'd intermarried with non-Jews. While the exiled Jews were in Babylon, Persia conquered Babylon and some Jews moved to Persia. When those who'd been in captivity in Babylon and Persia returned to rebuild Jerusalem, the returning Jews rejected those who'd remained behind and intermarried with non-Jews. This led to deep resentment and even battles. If anything, the Jews considered the Samaritans to be worse than other non-Jews.

The Good Samaritan

In the story Jesus told to illustrate what Christian love is and what it does (Good News 22:21-35), a Samaritan saved the life of a Jew who'd been beaten and robbed. In our culture today, we can't appreciate the full meaning of that story unless we learn how much the Jews and Samaritans normally despised each other. The Samaritan who stopped to help a Jew had to know how Jews had mistreated his people. Some Jews held that helping a Samaritan woman in childbirth would be wrong, because it brought another Samaritan into the world. Yet this man was caring and generous in his help for a wounded Jew. He left retribution or vengeance to God, and he did what God wants all of us to do—he took care of the needs of this wounded man, even though he was a Jew.

Jesus and a Samaritan Woman

When Jesus met with a Samaritan woman near Sychar (Good News 24:1-38), she would've recognized his clothing as Jewish. It was certainly a surprise to even have him speak to her, let alone ask for a drink of water. In that culture, giving a drink of water was a sign of friendship. This Jew had just asked a Samaritan woman to be a friend. This was shocking on two levels. First, men didn't normally speak to women who were strangers. Second, Jews didn't ask Samaritans for anything if they could help it.

John the Disciple

John was the younger brother of another disciple named James. See James the Disciple for family information.

Historical records indicate that John was the last of Jesus' twelve closest disciples to die, living until about 60 years after Jesus' resurrection. He wrote five of the books we have in the New Testament: The Gospel of John, 1John, 2John, 3John, and The Revelation, and apparently all were written near the end of his life.

John the Immerser

The Date of John's Ministry

Luke provided several pieces of information to identify exactly when John's ministry began, telling who the rulers were in various places. Rather than list all the rulers that John listed (about whom most of us know nothing), since we now know that this description is for what we'd call 29 AD or very close to that, this translation just lists that year in terms we can understand today with the details in a footnote (Good News 5:1). The key piece of information is that John received his message from God in the fifteenth year of the reign of the emperor Tiberius. We know that Tiberius became emperor in September, 14 AD, so from September of 28 AD to September of 29 AD would be considered his fifteenth year.

This translation assumes that John's ministry began in the spring of 29 AD when weather would have been good for proclaiming his message and immersing converts and for people to travel into the wilderness to hear him, but his ministry might have started some months before that.

For those who might be interested, Luke says that Pilate was governor of Judea, Herod Antipas was ruler (tetrarch) in Galilee, Herod's brother, Philip, was ruler in areas known as Iturea and Trachonitis, and a man named Lysanias was ruler of an area known as Abilene. While there are unknowns concerning Lysanias, the others all fit well with this date.

John's Title

John became so associated in people's minds with the immersion that he practiced for converts that he came to be called "John the Immerser." (This translation uses the term "Immerser" rather than "Baptist" as the title people gave John. This has no connection to the doctrines of one Christian organization over another. Rather, it has to do with two things: 1) this translation's commitment to be an honest translation that carries the actual meaning of what was originally written in the books of the New Testament; and 2) the loss of meanings that are important if words aren't translated to communicate their actual meaning. See Baptize / Immerse above for more information on translation issues for this word.)

John's Message

The word "repentance" is generally used by other translators as the key to John's message, but in modern American culture, repentance is often thought of as regret for having done wrong (or as regret for having been caught doing wrong). The word normally translated as "repentance" actually indicates changing the focus of your mind. The idea John was teaching was that people need to change the focus of their lives from themselves and this world to God and his kingdom. Wherever this word appears, this translation emphasizes the need to turn one's life over to God. For more on this topic, see Repentance below in the Glossary.

Note that, like Jesus, John placed emphasis on doing good for others as the evidence of the life-change God demands. It's about giving a tunic to someone who has none or giving food to someone who has none. This caring love is the essence of who God is, and it's also what makes a person suitable for heaven, because that kind of caring love is what will make heaven a paradise. Note that when temple policemen (often translated "soldiers") asked John what they should do, John didn't tell them to stop doing their jobs; he told them to stop abusing their power as policemen in ways that would hurt others. Policemen are a necessary part of this world, and sometimes they have to kill as part of their jobs, but most of the time they do their job simply by being present. John told these policemen to avoid hurting others by abusing their authority. John's message to the policemen would apply to both soldiers and police officers today, since in New Testament times the soldiers had both roles.

One question we should ask when we think of John is this: "Is it the immersion or the life turned around that John taught as bringing forgiveness of sins?" As explained above in the Glossary under Baptize / Immerse, the word used here for immersion implies cleansing. However, if there's anything that the Bible is clear about it's that God isn't especially impressed by rituals as if they were some sort of magic. John made it very clear that people weren't candidates for his immersion unless they were truly changing their lives. By itself, immersion would do nothing.

God knows us. We as humans need something that physically marks the point when we turn from a focus on this world to a focus on him and his kingdom. We need to step across the line, and the symbol of being completely washed in water was the thing God chose to make the point that these people were truly making a commitment to turn their lives around.

However, this is John's immersion, and the New Testament is very clear that it isn't the same as Christian immersion (see Acts 19:1-5 for a clear example). The important point is that immersion, whether John's immersion or Christian immersion, if not accompanied by a changed life, is of no value to anyone and makes no impression on God. God isn't impressed by human rituals, and if a person who isn't turning his or her life around gets immersed, that person just gets wet.

Elijah and John

There's a prophecy in Malachi 4:5 that many Jews had interpreted to mean that Elijah the prophet would be resurrected in a very literal sense to prepare the way for the Christ. John properly denied that he was Elijah come back from the dead. If he'd claimed to be Elijah, it would've been hard to carry on his ministry. However, Jesus said that John did indeed fulfill this prophecy. John was the dramatic in-your-face wilderness prophet who came before the more sociable Jesus, just as Elijah was before the more sociable Elisha. Not that Jesus was never dramatic or in-your-face; he just had a much wider role to fulfill. John and his ministry have obvious parallels with Elijah and his ministry.

Joseph-Father of Jesus

Given his ancestry linking him closely with the kings of David's family, there had to be some special respect for people of Joseph's family. Joseph is described as "a good man" who, when he learned that Mary was pregnant before their marriage, "didn't want to make a public example" of her infidelity (Good News 2:1-2). While this isn't conclusive, the wording seems to indicate a more mature man, at least beyond his teen years.

The fact that he's never mentioned after Jesus' twelfth year and is clearly no longer living during Jesus' ministry is also an indication that he might have been an older man. Beyond the facts that he was a descendant of King David (Good News 2:7), that he had a reputation as a good man, and that he wasn't in the picture during Jesus' ministry, there's not much we know about Joseph. Even the idea that Joseph was a carpenter (which he almost certainly was) is based on Jesus being called "the carpenter, the son of Joseph and his wife, Mary" (Good News 8:6). (It was considered normal for the eldest son to follow in his father's occupation, but it's actually Jesus, not Joseph, who's described as a carpenter.)

In Jewish culture, the contract to marry was so binding that breaking the contract required an actual divorce, even though the marriage hadn't yet occurred. And under Jewish law, Mary could've been stoned to death as an adulteress because of the evidence of her pregnancy. Joseph was kind enough not to insist on stoning, but he wasn't about to marry some girl who was obviously having sex with another man—until God intervened.

The Bible doesn't tell us for certain, but the account reads as if Joseph arranged for the marriage to take place as quickly as possible after his vision (Good News 2:3-5). It may well be that he was eager to be the earthly father of the one who'd be God's Christ.

From the offering that Joseph and Mary brought to the temple (Good News 3:3), we know that Joseph wasn't wealthy before the visit of the eastern scholars. We don't know how much actual wealth these scholars brought or how much of it may have been used in the family's escape to Egypt and then in their return to Mary's hometown. Since it was the people of Nazareth who commented on Jesus being the "carpenter, the son of Joseph," it appears that Joseph worked as a carpenter in Nazareth (Good News 8:6), so it's likely the gifts of the scholars weren't enough to support the family indefinitely.

Judas: Two Disciples with the Name

There were two men named Judas among Jesus' twelve disciples and one of Jesus' brothers was also named Judas. One of the disciples was known as Judas the son of James, but we don't know anything else about him (Good News 14:3). Jesus' brother who was called Judas was probably the Jude who wrote the book of Jude in the New Testament, but we don't know anything else about him.

Judas Iscariot

The fact is that there isn't a lot we know about the Judas who betrayed Jesus (Good News 40:52-54). We know that he was called Judas Iscariot, that he was the son of a man named Simon (Good News 26:69), that he was the treasurer for Jesus' group and sometimes stole from their funds (Good News 37:54), and that he committed suicide after betraying Jesus (Good News 48:62).

The fact that Matthew records the death of Judas during his description of Jesus' trials doesn't mean that it happened at that time. It happened, but the Bible doesn't tell us exactly when it happened. It's likely that the whole process from the point when he realized that Jesus would be condemned until he committed suicide took at least two or more days, and it's also possible that he wouldn't have been completely convinced that Jesus would be condemned and crucified until Jesus was on the cross.

As for Judas' motives in betraying Jesus, many suggestions have been offered, but the one clearly indicated by the Bible is greed. Many have guessed that Judas thought he was going to force Jesus to establish his kingdom, and that's a reasonable guess—but only a guess. Remember, at the last supper the other disciples were still arguing about who'd be greatest when Jesus established his earthly kingdom, and even after Jesus rose from the dead, they were still expecting an earthly Israelite kingdom with Jesus as king (Good News 53:5).

But while the other disciples expected an earthly kingdom, they were willing to wait for Jesus, and apparently Judas wasn't willing to wait. When Judas realized that Jesus would be executed, he couldn't accept the loss of his worldly kingdom hopes, while the others still didn't lose their faith in God.

The very brief mention of Judas' death in Acts is obviously not the same as the description in Matthew, but there are no necessary conflicts. The two accounts were given in two very different contexts, and the fact that each emphasized things the other didn't mention isn't surprising. This translation suggests one way to blend them, but there have been other suggestions. It's even possible that Peter had some misinformation.

Judea and Galilee

Judea

For those unfamiliar with Judea, this name is normally pronounced jew-DEE-uh. This is one of the names that must be present in the main body of the translation.

The areas of the Roman Empire dominantly occupied by Jews included Galilee in the north, where Jesus spent most of his time, and the southern part of the Roman province of Judea in the south, which included Jerusalem. These two areas were both located between the eastern shore of the Mediterranean Sea and the valley of the Jordan River. The Roman province of Judea was about evenly divided between the southern half that was primarily Jewish (including Jerusalem) and the northern half that's referred to in the Bible as "Samaria." The New Testament refers to four men who ruled Judea: Herod the Great (who also ruled Galilee), Herod Archelaus (called "Archelaus" in the Bible), Pilate (the Roman procurator), and Herod Agrippa I. In the Bible, Herod the Great and Herod Agrippa I are both referred to simply as "Herod." See Herod and Pilate for more on these men.

Jesus was born in Bethlehem, which was a town in Judea south of Jerusalem, but during his ministry his trips to Judea were mostly to Jerusalem. There are two notable exceptions (the town of Bethany and a place along the Jordan River where his team were immersing converts), but each of these was along or near the normal travel route between Galilee and Jerusalem.

Jesus also made a stop at the Samaritan town of Sychar which was technically in the province of Judea, but, as just mentioned, the Bible refers to that area as Samaria. In the Bible, any reference to Judea or Judeans wouldn't include the area of the Samaritans.

Galilee

For those unfamiliar with Galilee, this name is normally pronounced GALL-li-lee. This is one of the names that must be present in the main body of the translation.

Galilee is the name of a section of land that was in the northern part of what had been the Kingdom of Israel when that kingdom existed. It was primarily populated by Jews in New Testament times. Both Galilee and Judea were parts of the Roman Empire and subject to the Roman emperor.

Galilee was the area where Jesus carried on most of his ministry. Nazareth, in south-central Galilee, was Jesus' childhood home, and Capernaum, on the north shore of the Sea of Galilee, was Jesus' base of operations for his ministry.

Much of Jesus' ministry was done on the shores of the Sea of Galilee. This inland sea or large lake formed most of the eastern boundary of Galilee. At around 700 feet below sea level, this lake is the lowest freshwater lake on earth.

Judeans / Jewish Authorities

For those unfamiliar with the word "Judeans," this name is normally pronounced jew-DEE-ans. This is one of the names that must be present in the main body of the translation.

What the New Testament calls Judea was roughly similar to the kingdom of Judah that had been ruled by King David's descendants after Solomon's death. Since Jerusalem and the temple were in Judea, the top Jewish authorities were there, including the high priest, the chief priests, the elders of the nation, the leaders of the Pharisees and Sadducees, and the leading scribes and lawyers.

To understand how the word "Judeans" is used in the New Testament, think of how the word "Americans" is used in other parts of the world. Sometimes when people say that "the Americans" did this or that, they actually mean the political authorities in Washington did something. Other times when people say the same words, they mean a group of American citizens did something.

In the New Testament, many references to "Judeans" actually mean the Jewish authorities associated with the temple or the Jewish Supreme Court, and such references are translated as "Jewish authorities" in this translation. However, in other cases that same word has a more general meaning, referring to average Jewish people living in the Jewish part of Judea, and in those cases this translation uses the term "Judeans." (This term would never have been used for Galilean Jews or any other Jews living outside of southern Judea.)

There's a lot we don't know about how the Jewish leadership operated. We do know that the high priest was officially the top Jewish authority and head of the Jewish Supreme Court.

In other translations, the word "Judeans" is often simply translated "Jews," but that doesn't communicate the real meaning. Such a translation implies that all Jews were included in what the Bible says, but, as mentioned above, Jews in Galilee or any other non-Judean area were never part of such a reference. Such a translation also doesn't provide any distinction between Jewish authorities and average Judeans, though the context clearly indicates which is meant in almost every case. This translation attempts to correct that by referring either to "Judeans" (Jews living in the southern half of Judea) or to the "Jewish authorities," depending on the context.

Lamb of God (See Good News 5:32 and 6:1)

Too often the words "lamb of God" call to mind a picture of a fluffy white animal romping innocently through green pastures. In biblical times, this reference would've brought a very different picture to people's minds. Lambs were often used for sacrifices. Their throats were slit, the blood was drained, and then their carcasses were burned on the altar as a sacrifice for a sin offering, a peace offering, or as the lamb slain for the Passover sacrifice. Jesus was the lamb of God in the sense that he was God's final sacrifice for all the sins of the world. And one of the requirements for a lamb to be sacrificed was that the lamb had to be perfect. When Jesus was described as the "lamb of God," those words were expected to bring all of this background to people's minds. He was to be perfect, and he was to be sacrificed for the sins of the world. Like the Passover lamb whose blood protected the Israelites from God's agent of death, so Jesus' sacrifice would protect us from death itself.

The Languages of the New Testament

The New Testament was written entirely in Greek, but occasionally the writers used the letters of the Greek alphabet to communicate what was actually a Hebrew or Aramaic word. Most of the Roman Empire spoke and understood Greek, so the authors of the New Testament used that language, but since the authors of the New Testament were all Jews and most of the people they wrote about were Jews, from time to time they used Hebrew words (the language of the Jewish sacred writings) or Aramaic words (the home language of the Jews in New Testament times). Sometimes they immediately provided the translation of such a word into Greek, and sometimes they left it without any translation, assuming the readers would know the meaning. In this translation such words are translated into their nearest English equivalents, though sometimes there's a footnote mentioning the use of a Hebrew or Aramaic word.

In New Testament times, most people in the Roman Empire (including the Jewish people) typically spoke and understood more than one language. For the average Jew in New Testament times, Aramaic (a language closely related to Hebrew) was the language of the home, but the language of business—especially any business that involved foreigners—was Greek. And the language for religious activities, including any serious study of the ancient sacred writings, was Hebrew (though most Jews were more familiar with the Greek translation of these ancient sacred writings—a translation known today as the Septuagint—or with Aramaic paraphrases of these writings—known as the Targumim).

The form of Greek used by the authors of the New Testament was a form commonly used for everyday business. This was the Greek most commonly used and most generally understood throughout the Roman Empire. This translation intentionally uses conversational English, because that's the most commonly used and most generally understood form of English in America today.

The Law of Moses

The first five books of our Bible (Genesis, Exodus, Leviticus, Numbers, and Deuteronomy) are collectively known as "The Torah," "The Law," or "The Law of Moses" (also sometimes called the Pentateuch because there are five books). These books provide the history of the world from a Jewish perspective, starting with the first humans and continuing through the establishment of a nation made up of twelve tribes all descended from Abraham through Abraham's son, Isaac, and through Abraham's grandson, Jacob (also known as Israel). Because Jacob came to be known as Israel and because his twelve sons became the heads of twelve tribes, these tribes came to be known as the twelve tribes of Israel, and the whole group came to be known as Israelites. In these books we find the record of how these people grew to be a nation and how they pursued a national dream of a homeland in an area known as Canaan, a land that God had promised to the descendants of Abraham through Isaac and Jacob (Israel).

A large part of these books provides a record of laws revealed by God to a man named Moses. These laws are extensive and cover civil matters (such as theft, murder, manslaughter, etc.), religious ceremonial matters (proper sacrifices, the priesthood, religious feasts, etc.), and moral matters (adultery, divorce, family relationships, etc.). In the New Testament, references to "the Law" are almost always references to the laws recorded in these books as understood by the Jews in New Testament times. Sometimes the reference may be to all of the laws in general, but in most cases such references are more focused on the moral laws, and especially the Ten Commandments. There was no way that a pagan who was unfamiliar with the Jewish sacred writings would ever even try to keep the civil and religious ceremonial laws in the Law of Moses, but such a person might well seek to keep the general intent of the moral laws just because of human conscience and the human awareness that there's a God and that there'll be a day of judgment.

In New Testament Jewish culture, the religious Jews were divided into several groups, but the two dominant groups were the Pharisees and the Sadducees. Both were very conservative in their view of the Law of Moses, but the Pharisees held that some of what God had revealed to Moses had been passed down orally rather than in writing, and that these oral traditions were as binding as any part of the written law. New Testament references to "lawyers" are references to Pharisees who'd become expert in memorizing and interpreting both the written and the oral law. When Jesus talked about the traditions of the Pharisees, he was referring to these oral laws that the Pharisees considered just as binding as the written laws. Sadducees rejected the idea of anything added to the Torah. (See Jesus and the Law and Lawyers in this Glossary.)

The position of the New Testament writers is that the Law of Moses was in force until Jesus' resurrection, but that this Law has been replaced by faith and grace. In Good News 9:70-71 we find Jesus saying that the Law of Moses was the rule until John the Immerser came. From that time on, the transition to the gospel of grace was in work. In Good News 5:5 we find John's side comment about the Law of Moses being replaced by the grace and truth brought by Jesus. While Jesus generally observed the Law of Moses and even taught people to obey it during his ministry (see such passages as Good News 12:3; 13:9; and 22:21-24), he also made it clear that he'd come to give those teachings fuller meaning (Good News 9:28-71; 11:5; 40:1-7; etc.), and that this fuller meaning was a way of grace that depended on faith rather than law (See Good News 51:36).

Under the Law of Moses, a person's relationship with God was thought to be earned or purchased by sacrifices and by keeping the laws. The concept of Christianity (which is strongly implied throughout the Jewish sacred writings) is that what God really wants is for people to give their hearts to him and dedicate their lives to living as he's taught us. For those who do this, God's grace covers any failure even before the failure occurs, because Jesus' death has already paid the price. And Jesus made it clear that there's nothing that any of us could do to earn forgiveness of even one sin.

Lawyers

The lawyers were men who dedicated their careers to becoming experts in the five sacred writings of Moses known as the Torah (literally, "the Law"), which all religious Jews accepted as legally binding, as well as all the implications of those laws. In addition, these "lawyers" were almost always Pharisees who believed that Moses had delivered additional laws that had been passed down orally since Moses' time. These oral laws weren't to be written down, so these lawyers had to memorize all the oral laws and volumes of material interpreting and commenting on both the written and the oral laws. (These oral laws and the comments have since been written down, and they make up the writings known as the Talmud—a document of several volumes.)

These lawyers were generally considered the authorities on almost every aspect of life for Jews, because between the written law, the oral law, and the interpretations of those laws, practically any aspect of life was covered. While the scribes gained significant expertise in the Jewish sacred writings by copying these writings, the lawyers had to know all that the scribes knew and a lot more.

Jesus often condemned his adversaries for the fact that they let their traditions (the oral laws and interpretations of the written laws) interfere with what the sacred writings clearly taught about what God expects of us. This was especially true of Sabbath traditions, but it went much further than that.

There are two important lessons we can learn from what Jesus told these lawyers: 1) we need to continually examine our traditions as compared to what the Bible says that God really wants, because far too often we get so caught up in our traditions that we wind up working against God; and 2) we need to remember that legalism doesn't work—it didn't work then, and it doesn't work now. God isn't about picking legalistic nits, he's interested in our hearts and whether we're serious about serving him.

Lazarus

For those unfamiliar with this name, it's normally pronounced LAA-zar-us. This is one of the names that must be present in the main body of the translation.

There are two men named Lazarus mentioned in the New Testament. One was a beggar mentioned in one of Jesus' stories. (Good News 20:54-65. See the discussion of this man in the article on Hell above.) That Lazarus is mentioned only briefly.

The second Lazarus mentioned in the New Testament was a friend to Jesus (Good News 35:45-36:25). This Lazarus had two sisters named Mary and Martha, and they lived in the town of Bethany not far from Jerusalem. From what the Bible says, it appears that they were financially able to house and feed Jesus and his twelve disciples when they came to town. Bethany was on the main road from the Jordan valley to Jerusalem, located close to the top of the Mount of Olives, so Jesus would've passed through there fairly frequently on trips between Galilee and Jerusalem. We may reasonably assume that Jesus attended all three of the annual religious feasts mentioned in the Law of Moses as requiring all Jewish men to come to the temple, and most of these six trips a year probably went through Bethany.

Not long before Jesus' crucifixion, Lazarus became sick and died, and Jesus raised him from the dead after he'd been in the tomb for four days. The Bible tells us of others who were raised from the dead by Jesus, but none of those had even been in the tomb, so a skeptic might think they weren't really dead. Lazarus would've died of thirst in the tomb if he hadn't already been dead. Also, the other cases where Jesus raised people from the dead all occurred, as far as we can tell, in Galilee, far away from Jerusalem and the Jewish authorities. Skeptics among the Jewish authorities in Jerusalem could've argued that such reports were exaggerations. This resurrection took place just outside of Jerusalem, and people from the city started going out to meet Lazarus and hear the account of his death and return.

This miracle had such a powerful influence on the people of Jerusalem that the Jewish authorities, who feared what Jesus might do, seriously considered having Lazarus killed. The Bible provides no more information about Lazarus or his family after that time, but apparently Jesus' crucifixion shortly after bringing Lazarus back to life would've ended any talk of killing Lazarus.

Levites

For those unfamiliar with this word, it's normally pronounced LEE-vites. This is one of the names that must be present in the main body of the translation.

Jacob (also known as Israel) was the grandson of Abraham, and he had twelve sons who became the fathers of the twelve tribes of Israel. One of Jacob's sons was named Levi, and many years later God chose his descendants to be the priestly tribe for all the other Israelites. However, the actual priesthood was restricted to the descendants of Moses' brother, Aaron. When the Bible refers to priests, it always means the descendants of Aaron. Levi's other descendants had duties related initially to the tabernacle and later to the temple, but they weren't to have the duties of the priesthood. All Levites were considered specially consecrated to the Lord's service. See Priests / Chief Priests and Zachariah for more information about the priests.

Mary Magdalene

For those unfamiliar with "Magdalene," this name is normally pronounced MAG-duh-lean. This is one of the names that must be present in the main body of the translation.

We don't know a lot about Mary Magdalene. Her name appears just once briefly before Jesus' crucifixion to let us know that she was one of the women who traveled with Jesus and who supported his work financially. We know that Jesus cast seven evil spirits out of her (Good News 8:22). Today she might have been diagnosed with multiple personality disorder (also known as dissociative personality), which is an extreme form of paranoia. Even today, no one knows what causes this terrible condition, but it's hard for most of us to imagine what a relief it would've been to be healed.

Mary's surname tells us that she was either from or somehow associated with the town of Magdala in Galilee. Whenever the women around Jesus are named, if Mary Magdalene is mentioned, she's the first one on the list with only one exception. This indicates that she was probably a leader of these women.

After Jesus' resurrection, Mary saw him in the garden in front of his tomb and mistook him for the man in charge of the garden. Thinking of him as the gardener, Mary offered to take care of Jesus' body if he'd moved it (Good News 50:37-43). Her financial support of Jesus' ministry and her offer to take care of Jesus' body indicate that she was probably wealthy, and that may well imply that she was a widow.

We don't know how old Mary was or what Mary looked like. She's often depicted as being young and quite beautiful, but young women were rarely wealthy in that culture. It appears that when the women went to the tomb, Mary left first to find Peter. It's possible that she was some relative of Peter's. In any case, leaving on her own may be another indication that she was mature enough to have a strong sense of self-confidence.

There are some who've indicated that Jesus appeared to Mary before any of the other women, but that doesn't seem to be the case when we look at all four Gospels. The blended accounts indicate that the other women left the tomb shortly after Mary, and that Jesus met them as they were going to report to the disciples (not including Peter), while Jesus didn't appear to Mary until after she'd reported to Peter and John and then returned to the tomb.

Other than these things, there's not a lot we know or can even speculate about when it comes to this lady. She was obviously a dedicated follower of the Lord from the time he healed her, and even after his death she remained dedicated to him.

Mary-Mother of Jesus

There are at least 5 women named "Mary" mentioned in the New Testament, but this Mary is the best known. Having said that, we know very little about Mary.

The Announcement to Mary

The fact that she was a virgin engaged to Joseph probably means she was in her teen years since girls were normally married around their mid-teens, though the information in Jewish Marriage Customs provides a possible alternative. There's nothing in the Bible about her parents—even whether they were still alive. The fact that Joseph was probably an older man indicates that the betrothal was probably not arranged at birth since betrothals arranged at a child's birth were generally to children of the same age.

How did Gabriel look when he appeared to Mary (Good News 1:15-24)? In the Bible, God's agents are generally described (when they are described at all) as men dressed in bright white garments. But there were other times when these agents were mistaken for men, and the description in Luke's gospel seems to indicate that Gabriel just walked into the house without attracting any special attention from people on the street outside. The description of this event in the Bible doesn't fit with a dream—this was a real visit in daylight. Did Gabriel give off a special light like on some TV programs? Did his clothing shine once he was in the house? Did he announce his name and office as he did to Zechariah the priest? We don't know. But for some reason, Mary was ready to believe that he was bringing a message from God, and she was also ready to accept that message.

In Mary's response to Gabriel, she demonstrated awesome faith. Gabriel had just told Mary that she'd be pregnant before she was married. That necessarily carried a huge social stigma. Mary had to know that this wasn't going to be easy. People would gossip, and she probably understood right away that most folks wouldn't believe this story about an agent of God. And there'd have to be difficulties with her own family. The Bible account doesn't mention that she asked Gabriel anything about how to handle the reaction of others, not even Joseph, but she had to wonder how Joseph would take this. Mary just trusted God!

Mary's Visit to Elizabeth

If we assume that Mary was a teenager, she wouldn't have made the trip to Elizabeth by herself (Good News 1:25-31), but the Bible describes her visit with Elizabeth as if Mary didn't have companions who stayed with her at Elizabeth's home. (See Jewish

Marriage Customs for another possible explanation.) It's possible that she used the agent's words about Elizabeth as a means to convince her parents or guardians that she'd seen an agent of God, or else how could she have known that Elizabeth was pregnant?

The poem Mary wrote was obviously not a spontaneous burst of speech. It's likely she bubbled over with enthusiasm in her initial conversation with Elizabeth and that shortly after that, perhaps at the encouragement of Elizabeth, she came up with this poem. She may have written it down then (though literacy wasn't universal, and most women never learned to read and write), or she may have memorized it without writing it down, going over it from time to time when she recalled this period of her life. This is indeed consistent with what a teenage girl with her heart set on God might do when involved in something so good and so awesome. And it wasn't as if she started from scratch—she worked from a Psalm that would've been a favorite for many Jews, and she adapted that to express her joy.

But picture the scene: Mary came to Elizabeth's house, probably somewhat uncertain about how to share her news. Who'd believe her? But as soon as she spoke, Elizabeth confirmed her news without hearing another word from Mary. Now this teenage girl was bubbling over with the news and her excitement. Every Jewish girl knew that someday one of them would be the mother of God's Christ, and now Mary and Elizabeth knew that Mary would be that girl. It had to be so exciting to find someone she could share this with—someone who'd completely believe her.

Elizabeth greeted Mary as the mother of her Lord when they first met, so Mary must have become pregnant just after Gabriel's visit. That means that Elizabeth's son, John the Immerser, was only about six months older than Jesus. The wording in the Bible isn't really clear about the relationship between Mary and Elizabeth, but somehow they were kin.

Did Mary leave Elizabeth before or after John was born? The Bible doesn't tell us, but the timing would've been very close. It's hard to imagine that she would've left just before John's birth unless there were some compelling reason we're not given, but the reason may have been too many visitors and too much awkward explaining about her pregnancy, which by that time would've been showing.

Looking for Jesus

When Jesus was 12 years old, he upset Mary and Joseph by staying behind in Jerusalem when his parents and their traveling companions left for home after a Passover feast (Good News 3:22-29). There's not a lot we learn about Mary in this account, except that she reacted just as a mother might react today. When she said that she and Joseph had been searching for Jesus for three days, there's a good chance she was exaggerating a little and the first day was mainly spent in traveling away from Jerusalem with their companions, but that's not certain.

A Wedding Feast

Just after his immersion, Jesus went with his mother to a wedding feast (Good News 6:15-22), bringing some disciples with him. When the groom ran out of wine for his guests (a very embarrassing situation), Mary's eagerness to help indicates she was either related to or a very good friend of either the bride or the groom. In any case, the fact that she went to Jesus to help this couple indicates that she'd already seen him use his miraculous powers. Even though Jesus wasn't ready to start using his power publicly, he did what the Law of Moses said to do—he honored his mother by fulfilling her request.

Is He Insane?

At one point during Jesus' ministry, as he was attracting large crowds, Mary and Jesus' brothers came to where he was teaching to check up on him (Good News 17:25-26). They were afraid he'd gone mad. The Bible doesn't give any information as to why they may have had such concerns. It's possible that some of Jesus' opponents had given Jesus' family a deceitful report. We also don't know what Mary's role was in that visit. We know that at that time, Jesus' brothers hadn't put their faith in him, but was Mary with them because of her concern for Jesus or because of her concern for what his brothers might do?

At the End

The Bible tells us that at Jesus' crucifixion, Mary was present, and Jesus turned responsibility for his mother over to his disciple named John (Good News 49:18-19). That fact implies that Mary had been Jesus' responsibility for some time—probably since the death of Joseph. We know that Mary lived as part of John's household for the rest of her life, but we don't know where that might have been. When Jesus first called John to follow him, John was living with his parents in Capernaum. After Jesus rose from the dead, it appears that John and the other disciples stayed in Jerusalem for some time. Beyond that we have only ancient rumors.

We know that Mary witnessed Jesus' resurrection. We know that toward the end of his ministry she was a faithful follower, and that after his resurrection, his brothers became disciples (Good News 53:16). Did Jesus appear to his brothers after his resurrection? We don't know. There's much more we wish we knew, but that's all the Bible tells us.

There are other stories about Mary, but many of them are clearly fiction, and there's no way to separate the facts from the fiction.

Matthew (Levi) the Disciple

Matthew, Mark, and Luke all record the account of Jesus calling a tax collector followed by a feast at the tax collector's home and controversy about the guest list (Good News 8:45-51). The Gospel of Matthew names the tax collector "Matthew" while Mark and Luke use the name "Levi," but it wouldn't be at all unusual for a person in that period to be called by more than one name. Matthew (meaning "gift of God") was likely the name given to him by his parents, while Levi may have been a nickname given because he was born into the tribe of Levi.

Matthew sitting in a booth indicates that he wasn't one of the more notorious tax collectors who often collected more than was required, thereby amassing significant wealth. Capernaum was a fishing port, and there'd have been a standard fee or tax for use of the port facilities. Given his place in a booth near the shore, it's likely that collecting this tax was Matthew's job. This would've been a local tax used mainly to maintain local facilities, so he wouldn't have been hated as much as those who collected taxes for

Rome. We have no idea how many were doing this job in Capernaum or if Matthew's departure would've stopped the collection of the taxes until a replacement could be found, but like Peter, Andrew, James, and John, this tax collector wasted no time in following the Lord.

Since Matthew worked in Capernaum, he would've been aware of Jesus, but we have no word on how much he knew about Jesus. Clearly he knew enough to respond quickly when Jesus invited him to join his band of followers.

Having a feast in his own house indicates that Matthew (Levi) was fairly well off. Having other tax collectors and others locally viewed as "sinners" as guests suggests that, while Matthew was probably only involved in a tax focused on local needs, he was still associated in people's minds with the Roman authorities and therefore had to find his friends among those who were viewed with disfavor by the local folks of Capernaum.

Maturity / Perfection

In the Bible, the word for "perfect" is the same as the word for "mature" or "full grown." Translators know this, but most English translations get it wrong in some important areas. Perhaps the most important example of this is at the end of Matthew 5. In the latter part of Matthew 5, Jesus goes over several things to emphasize that God's way isn't about external and legalistic obedience, but about obedience from the heart. Then in the last verse he says something that's generally translated along these lines: "Be perfect, just like your Father in heaven is perfect."

The problem is that none of us can be perfect, and Jesus knew this. So this gives the impression that Jesus commanded his followers to do something that he knew they couldn't do. But when we consider that the word "perfect" can also mean "mature," the meaning of this verse changes dramatically. It's not a command to be perfect, but a command to grow up spiritually in God's likeness. (See Good News 9:69.)

In this translation, each passage where this word is used has been examined to determine whether the meaning in English should focus on perfection or maturity. In more than one case, the meaning chosen isn't the most common translation.

Miracles

The Pattern of Miracles in the Bible

When we read the Bible, sometimes we get the impression that miracles were common in biblical times, or that the stories have to be fiction because of all the miracles that we don't experience today. However, careful consideration of what the Bible records will give us a very different perspective.

To understand miracles in the Bible, we need to divide miracles into two categories: 1) miracles that are obviously miracles (couldn't be coincidence or chance occurrences) and that are witnessed by a significant number of people (not just one or a few); and 2) all other miracles (those that might be chance or coincidence and those that were only witnessed by a very limited number of people).

Miracles in the second category might occur from time to time with little note among most people. Anyone who heard of such a miracle might well be skeptical, and those who experienced such a miracle were likely to keep quiet about it to avoid ridicule from skeptics. For the period of time covered in biblical accounts, most of the time these category two miracles were the only miracles recorded in the Bible.

In the Bible, miracles that could be considered as in the first category are recorded as having happened only two times over a period of about 6,000 years.
1. When Moses brought a new, major revelation from God to the people of Israel, three things were true: First, there were many miracles. Second, many of these miracles were obvious and undeniably miracles. Third, these miracles were witnessed by many thousands.
2. When Jesus and his followers brought a new, major revelation from God to the entire world, four things were true: First, there were more miracles than ever before. Second, these miracles were more obvious than ever before. Third, these miracles were witnessed by more people than ever before. Fourth, these miracles were recorded by more witnesses than ever before.

There are a few cases that could be considered exceptions to this, such as during the ministries of Elijah, Elisha, and Daniel, but none of them would stand out as clear evidence of obvious miracles taking place in the presence of thousands of witnesses. A relatively small number of people would've witnessed these miracles, and most of them could've been explained away as coincidence or chance or inflated rumors. The point is, for a period of about 6,000 years, the vast majority of the time very few people witnessed even one obvious, undeniable miracle. But when God was delivering a new revelation, he sent obvious and dramatic miracles witnessed by huge crowds to make the point that this message was his message.

What that should tell us is that, while God is always in the miracle business, we should not expect a new set of category one miracles unless God sends an entirely new message, and since the message that came through Jesus and his followers says that it's the final message (unlike the message that came through Moses that specifically said that it wasn't the final message), we need not expect a new age of category one miracles. This evidence also says that if there's a claim of a new revelation from God, we should disregard it unless it's backed up by an impressive set of major miracles.

Were the Miracles Real?

But could the miracles be fictional accounts? We now know that the books of the New Testament were definitely written in the first 65 years after Jesus' resurrection—all but a very few within the first 35 years. If these accounts had been fiction, there should've been eyewitness accounts to deny the claims of the Christians, but no such accounts from that period have been found. It was only after the original eyewitnesses were all dead that people began to seriously challenge these accounts, and such challenges have never provided any real proof that the claims of the Bible are fiction.

So what about evidence in the Bible itself? The Bible reports that Jesus performed many miracles, but at least twice during his ministry (once in Galilee and once in Judea, recorded in Good News 15:5 and Good News 26:40) he was asked by the religious leaders to show them a sign, demonstrating his right to make the claims he was making, and in each case he refused. The immediate question must be, "how could these men ask for a sign if Jesus was performing so many miracles?"

Jesus absolutely wouldn't put on a command performance for some committee of leaders sent to investigate him and the claims being made about him. His focus was on the message—the miracles were a sideshow to make the point that the message was from God. Jesus repeatedly urged those he healed not to spread the word about being healed, because he knew that the more the focus got on the healings, the less it would be on the message. If the miracles became the main focus, the message would be lost.

In fact, these leaders who demanded a sign were doing exactly what Satan had done when tempting Jesus in the wilderness, and the same principle was involved in Jesus' response. You don't put God on trial—he won't submit to human tests. If you put your faith in him, he's happy to bless you with astonishing miracles, but for those who want to put him on trial, his response is the same one Jesus gave when men put him on trial—silence.

Besides that, Jesus knew that no matter how great a miracle he did for these leaders, they wouldn't put their faith in him and his message. They'd find some way to explain away any miracle or any number of miracles. When some of them were faced with overwhelming evidence of his miracles, they simply credited his miracles to Satan's power. So while the miracles Jesus did were clear, obviously powerful, and witnessed by many, he wouldn't show off for the authorities.

Toward the end of Jesus' earthly ministry, there were two important miracles that have to do with this:
1. In one case a man who was born blind was healed by Jesus, and this healing was carefully investigated by the religious authorities. Their conclusion was that they were facing a dilemma because they couldn't deny that Jesus had performed a major miracle. Their response was to try to keep word of this miracle from spreading. (See Good News 34:1-37.)
2. In the other case, Jesus raised a man named Lazarus from the dead. Lazarus lived a short distance outside of Jerusalem, and word of this miracle spread rapidly. People from Jerusalem were going to Bethany to meet this man and hear the testimony he, his sisters, and the people of the town provided. In this case, the response of the Jewish authorities was a plot to have Lazarus killed. (See Good News 35:45-36:25.)

Jesus held off providing such clear evidence until very late in his ministry. Then the religious leaders were finally reduced to blustering—the evidence was overwhelming. In almost all cases, it's God's way to operate by faith, not by proof—and there are very good reasons for this approach.

But the most telling case of evidence for the reality of Jesus' miracles occurred when he rose from the dead and the Roman soldiers at the tomb came to the Jewish authorities to demand a cover-up. The Jewish authorities could've simply reported these soldiers to Pilate so they'd be arrested and executed. But instead, the Jewish authorities bribed the soldiers to spread a ridiculous rumor that Jesus' disciples had come while the soldiers slept, had rolled away the stone from the tomb without waking the soldiers, and had stolen the body. It was obvious that even this story should've got the soldiers executed, but the Jewish authorities promised to intervene with Pilate if Pilate heard the story. (See Good News 50:1-12.)

Money in the Bible

What follows here is a description of how money values used in the Bible have been converted to values Americans in the early 21st century would understand better for this translation. None of the names for money items discussed in this article appear in this translation except in footnotes or in this article. In each case, the estimates are given in general terms rounded to a value easy to deal with, not trying to be exactly accurate. In biblical times, money was normally measured as a specific weight of a particular metal (bronze, copper, silver, or gold), so inflation wasn't a serious issue. The value of a coin would change as the value of the metal changed based on supply and demand, but these changes were relatively small.

Denarius

A denarius was a coin that was generally considered fair pay for a day's common labor. If we figure a typical day as 10 hours of labor at $10 an hour, that would be $100 for a day's labor (equivalent to a denarius). Throughout this translation, all money values used are based on this estimated value of a denarius done in 2016. If you want to update the estimated values to a different time period, this would be the basic value from which to work.

In Jesus' story of the two debtors (see Good News 22:4-15 and under Talent below in this article), the debtor who owed a smaller amount owed 100 denarii. Using the estimated value above, a hundred denarii would be equal to about $10,000. While this is a large sum, it's a debt that a person might pay if given time, and a tiny debt compared to the larger debt.

Mina (Pound)

Sixty minas were equal to one talent, which would make a mina worth almost 90 denarii (see Talent below in this article). As discussed below, the value of a talent in equivalent terms today would be about $500,000, so a mina would've been worth about $8,000.

Luke is the only book in the Bible that mentions minas. The mina is mentioned in a story Jesus told about a wealthy man who entrusted money to some of his slaves and later called them to account. Matthew and Luke each recorded a version of this story, but when Jesus told the version in Matthew, he talked about talents rather than minas. For Luke's story, the master entrusted ten minas, or about $80,000, to each slave.

In Luke's account, after mentioning the ten slaves, Jesus' story focuses on only three of them. One slave turned his ten minas into twenty minas, another had turned his ten minas into fifteen minas, and the third had buried his ten minas. Other than these items, the only real difference is that in Matthew's account the two successful slaves are made "ruler over many things," while in Luke's account the two successful slaves are made ruler over ten cities and five cities based on their success levels. The real difference between the value entrusted and the value rewarded is the difference between about $80,000 as compared to ruling ten cities or between about $40,000 as compared to ruling five cities, huge rewards for faithfulness in relatively small matters.

While it's not certain, it seems likely that the story as recorded in Matthew was a version Jesus used later in his ministry. That version amplifies some of the points Jesus was making, so this translation follows the account in Matthew where the two are significantly different. Jesus probably used this story several times, and no doubt he changed the details based on what he knew would best communicate to the crowd he was teaching at the time, but both biblical versions make the same points.

Because this translation follows the account as given in Matthew's Gospel, the mina isn't even mentioned in footnotes in this translation.

Mite

128 mites would be worth one denarius. Given the estimate of $100 for a denarius used above, a mite would've been worth about 75 cents. The mite is mentioned in the Bible only once, when a poor widow gave two mites to the temple treasury. This translation converts the amount given to about a dollar, which is close enough to get the point. (See Good News 40:13-15.)

Quadrans

Mark points out that two mites are the same as a quadrans. That would make a quadrans worth about $1.50. The quadrans was a coin used throughout the Roman Empire, so Mark used a reference to that coin to explain the value of a Jewish mite. Because the value of two mites is provided in terms we'd understand today, the quadrans isn't even mentioned in footnotes in this translation..

Talent

A talent was a measurement of weight, and in New Testament times in the Roman Empire, a talent was about 71 pounds. In the New Testament, except for one case in the Revelation where the word "talent" is used to describe the weight of hailstones, this word is used to describe a weight of gold or silver used as money. Other than the one reference in the Revelation, only Matthew used this term, and he used it in connection with two of Jesus' story illustrations.

In the New Testament, when "talent" is used to mean an amount of money the Bible never states whether it was a talent of silver or gold. Today the difference in value between these two metals is large, but in New Testament times the difference wasn't that large, with silver sometimes having a higher value than gold (though in the Bible the implication is that gold was generally more valuable).

In Jesus' story illustration of two debtors (see Good News 22:4-15), the debtor who owed the larger amount owed 10,000 talents. To put this in terms easier for us to understand, a talent in the Roman Empire was valued at somewhat more than 5,000 denarii. If we assume the value of a denarius as $100 as given above, then a talent would be worth about $500,000, so the 10,000 talent debt would be about equivalent to about $5 billion.

Jesus' point in that story illustration was that, just as a $5 billion debt is beyond any servant's ability to pay back, so our debt of sin and rebellion is beyond our capability to pay back. And since God's forgiven us such a huge debt, we should readily forgive those who owe us much smaller amounts.

In the other story illustration mentioning talents, three servants are given different sums of money: five talents to one, two talents to another, and one talent to the third according to the abilities of each to deal with such stewardships (see Good News 37:60-75). So using the same approach as above, these values were about equivalent to $2,500,000, $1,000,000, and $500,000—with even the smallest amount still very valuable, but with none of the amounts close to what the debtor owed in the story of two debtors.

In Jesus' story as he told it in Matthew's account, the first two slaves doubled the money entrusted to them, while the one receiving the smallest amount simply hid it in the ground. (See Mina above for the differences in Luke's account.)

When we see that the amount the last slave received was close to a half million dollars, we can see that even at a low interest rate, this man should've been able to get a valuable return on that much money, so his failure to at least invest it was inexcusable. Even given the values in Luke's account, $80,000 invested in New Testament times should've gained at a useful return.

Application to Heaven

In these stories about three slaves entrusted with money, the fact that the two who used their funds well were rewarded with far greater stewardships in each account. In the story as Jesus told it in Luke's account, the faithful stewards were rewarded by being made rulers over cities, not just villages or towns. Such a reward involved significant authority and the potential for far greater wealth.

An important point here is that faithful stewards are rewarded with even greater stewardships. Too many Christians view heaven as an eternity of nothing to do—in other words, eternal boredom. But Jesus' message is that there are great opportunities to be active, productive, and highly rewarded.

Moses

For those unfamiliar with Moses, his name is normally pronounced MOE-zes. This is one of the names that must be present in the main body of the translation.

When the twelve sons of Abraham's grandson named Jacob (also called Israel) were living, one of them (Joseph) was sold into slavery in Egypt. Through God's guidance, Joseph became a powerful ruler in Egypt during a time of famine. He was second only to the king, and was in charge of preparing for the famine and providing food for the country during the famine. Meanwhile, Joseph's family was suffering from the famine in their homeland of Canaan, and they came to Egypt to find food. Joseph arranged for the whole family to move to Egypt.

Hundreds of years later, the Israelite family had grown so large that the Egyptian rulers feared they might take over the country, so they enslaved these foreigners. During this time of enslavement, God raised up a man named Moses with the skills and knowledge needed to lead the Israelites out of Egypt, and he worked through Moses to bring them out.

Once the Israelites had escaped from Egypt, God gave Moses a set of laws that were to guide the Israelites as his special nation through whom he'd eventually bring a savior to the world. The most famous of these laws are the Ten Commandments, but there were hundreds of other laws. These laws established something the pagan world completely failed to recognize—that the God who created this world demands certain moral standards of the people he created.

By the time of Jesus' ministry, these Israelites were generally known as Jews, and they dominated a nation that was a very small part of the Roman Empire. However, most of these Jews had come to honor the laws God had given to Moses, though many of them got so focused on the tiniest legal details that they missed the real issue of caring love for God and for each other. It was this wrong approach to the law that Jesus fought against during much of his ministry. His goal was to replace this legalism with serious dedication to serving the God who personifies caring love, and his followers came to understand this.

The revelation that Jesus brought thus gave full and proper meaning to the law that Moses had received from God. The point wasn't legalistic obedience to earn salvation, but faithful service in order to be suitable for service in heaven. The Law of Moses still serves as a help to understand what God sees as right and wrong, but not as a path to salvation.

Nathanael (Nathan) (Bartholomew) the Disciple
When John immersed Jesus, he told his disciples that Jesus was the lamb of God. Some of John's disciples decided to find out more about Jesus, and one of them who was named Philip decided to bring one of his friends to Jesus. When Philip brought Nathanael to meet Jesus, Nathanael clearly didn't believe that Jesus could be the Christ. However, when Jesus mentioned that he'd seen Nathanael earlier while Nathanael was under a fig tree, Nathanael's attitude did a complete turn-around, and he declared his faith in Jesus as the Christ (Good News 6:7-14).

We don't know the details of what so dramatically changed Nathanael's perspective on Jesus, but it's obvious that Nathanael was very certain that whatever he did under the fig tree was private—that no one but God could've observed him. Some have speculated that Jesus was making a reference to a private prayer time Nathanael had under that fig tree. Those with enough wealth to do so generally had a walled area attached to the house for private family use. It's possible that Nathanael had a fig tree in such an area, and that he used the shade of that tree as a private place of prayer—a place only God would know about. That's only a guess, but something certainly convinced Nathanael to change his opinion of Jesus dramatically.

In this translation, in keeping with a policy of avoiding names that might be difficult to pronounce, this man is referred to as "Nathan." This is probably the actual name of the disciple called Bartholomew (which means "Son of Talmai").

Nazareth
For those unfamiliar with Nazareth, this name is normally pronounced NAZ-uh-reth. This is one of the names that must be present in the main body of the translation.

Nazareth was Jesus' hometown, the town in Galilee where he spent his childhood and lived until after his immersion by John the Immerser. In this translation, this name appears in the main body of the text a few times, but in most cases it's in the footnotes in keeping with the policy of limiting the use of names that might be difficult for some to pronounce.

Nazareth was in south-central Galilee, some distance from the Sea of Galilee. When Jesus was ready to begin his ministry, he traveled from Nazareth to the Jordan River to be immersed by John the Immerser. While he was with John, he met some of the men who'd later be part of his closest twelve disciples. At least three of these men were from an area on the north shore of the Sea of Galilee.

From the Jordan, Jesus traveled to the town of Cana, a short distance north of Nazareth in central Galilee, taking along some of his disciples. Since he'd not yet called the men who'd become his full-time followers, we don't know who these disciples were or how many there were. The reason for the trip to Cana was a wedding feast. Jesus' mother, Mary, was apparently either related to or close friends with the people involved in the wedding. It was during this wedding that the host ran out of wine and Mary called on Jesus to help. (It's unimportant, but it's possible the host hadn't planned on Jesus' disciples, and that's why he ran out of wine. It's also possible that this wedding was for one of Jesus' siblings.)

Following the trip to Cana, Jesus went home to Nazareth, and not long after that he was invited to speak in the worship center. However, what he had to say offended the people of Nazareth. They couldn't accept that this hometown boy was a true prophet of God—let alone that he was actually the Christ! Rather than rejoicing that the Christ himself was one of their kids, they forced Jesus to a cliff intending to throw him down to his death. Jesus managed to walk away through the crowd, but it was obvious that he wouldn't be welcome in his hometown. While Jesus had been healing people elsewhere, he was unable to do much for those in Nazareth because they refused to accept his message.

At that point, Jesus moved his base of operations to the town of Capernaum on the north shore of the Sea of Galilee. That was the home of at least five of the men who became his twelve closest disciples.

For the rest of his life, Jesus was known as "Jesus of Nazareth," but there's no indication in the Bible that he ever went back to his hometown. When he was crucified, the sign on his cross identified him as "Jesus of Nazareth, the king of the Jews." When the women came to the tomb after his resurrection, the agent of God called him "Jesus of Nazareth." But what a marvelous opportunity the people of Nazareth lost when they rejected him.

Nicodemus
 It's possible that Nicodemus came to Jesus at night (Good News 15:11) because one or both of them had such a busy schedule that this was the only good time for a private meeting. It's also possible that Nicodemus wanted to avoid being seen with this radical rabbi. It could be dangerous to be seen either by other members of the Jewish Supreme Court who wouldn't have approved or by the general public who might have taken this as a sign that the Jewish authorities supported Jesus' teachings. If Nicodemus were trying to avoid being seen, then Jesus' words may be seen as a rebuke—as if he were saying, "You can't be part of this kingdom by sneaking around. It's all or nothing."
 Nicodemus is described as "a member of the Jewish Supreme Court." This alone indicates that he was a wealthy and influential man. In addition, after Jesus' crucifixion, Nicodemus brought about 100 pounds of spices to prepare the body for burial (Good News 49:51). That's something that only a wealthy person could do.
 While there's no clear evidence of a relationship, some Jewish leaders mentioned in historical documents before and after this period were also named Nicodemus, and they may have been members of the same family.

Peter the Disciple
 Simon Peter was a leader among Jesus' disciples. He and his brother (Andrew) were the sons of a man named John and were fishermen on the Sea of Galilee. They were in partnership with James and John, the sons of a man named Zebedee, and Jesus called all four of these young men to be his disciples.
 "Peter" is a Greek term meaning "stone." "Cephas" is the Aramaic term with exactly the same meaning, and in the Bible, Peter is sometimes referred to as Cephas. In biblical times, the meaning of a name was generally considered more important than the sound of the name, so a person's name in another language might sound nothing like it would in that person's native language.
 Peter started out as "Simon." When he met Jesus, Jesus immediately gave him this new name. In American English, his new name would be "Rocky." In this translation, "Cephas" is always translated as "Peter" since American Christians know him best by that name. A footnote clarifies when the name "Cephas" is actually used.
 Peter was one of the three leading disciples. Within that group, he was the one most likely to speak or act before thoroughly thinking things through. We can see this in such things as his statement that his master would pay the temple tax without checking with Jesus (Good News 17:79-85), his words to Jesus when Jesus predicted his death (Good News 29:13), his offer to build three tabernacles when Jesus was transfigured and met with Moses and Elijah (Good News 31:13-19), his sword action when Jesus was being arrested (Good News 46:26-28), etc.
 From the information we have in the Gospels, it seems that Peter was often the spokesman for the disciples. This was the case when Jesus asked about a woman who'd touched him (Good News 16:29), when Jesus asked whether his disciples were considering leaving him (Good News 26:67), when Jesus asked who his disciples thought he was (Good News 29:5), etc. And of course, Peter was the main speaker at the feast of Pentecost when the gospel invitation was first proclaimed publicly.

Pharisees
 For those unfamiliar with this term, it's normally pronounced FAIR-uh-sees. This is one of the names that must be present in the main body of the translation.
 The Pharisees and Sadducees were the two dominant Jewish religious sects at the time of Jesus' ministry, though there were others. Pharisees and Sadducees were both strict religious groups, but their approach to the Jewish religion differed.
 The Pharisees accepted the Torah (the first five books of the Old Testament) as authoritative, but unlike the Sadducees, they held that, while Moses was the author of the Torah, he also received other revelations from God that were passed down only as oral tradition, and that this "oral Torah" was a living thing that should be interpreted and expanded by each generation. The Pharisees did accept the doctrine that there'd be a bodily resurrection, and they were generally more democratic than the Sadducees and more popular with the common people.
 However, while the Pharisees were more popular with the people, the majority of Jews were focused on their secular lives. Religion was an important part of their lives, but the dedication of the Pharisees was more than most people could find time for. The Pharisees never numbered more than a few thousand, and the Sadducees were an even smaller group, but these groups were highly influential in Jewish religious life.
 Jesus criticized both Pharisees and Sadducees, but he had more to say to the Pharisees than the Sadducees. One reason for this is that the Sadducees were largely concentrated in Jerusalem in the province of Judea, while most of Jesus' ministry was in Galilee. However, in spite of Jesus' criticism of the Pharisees, he did say that they carried on the work of Moses and that people should listen to them (Good News 13:9), but at the same time he warned his followers against acting like the Pharisees.

Pilate (See Good News 49-50)
 For those unfamiliar with Pilate, his name is normally pronounced PIE-lut. This is one of the names that must be present in the main body of the translation.
 Once Herod Archelaus (see Herod above in this Glossary) was removed from authority, the district of Judea was taken away from local rulers and governed by Roman officials for several years. Pilate was the fifth Roman to be the prefect of the province of Judea, which included what the Bible refers to as Judea and Samaria combined. (None of the other prefects is mentioned in the Bible.) After the experience of having Herod the Great's son, Archelaus, as ruler of this area, for many years the Romans decided they'd maintain control themselves—the Jews were just too fond of insurrection. Shortly after the Romans turned authority back to Jewish leaders, the Jews started an insurrection against Rome that ended with the absolute destruction of Jerusalem.

Pilate began his rule in 26 AD, three years before John the Immerser began his ministry, and he held the office of prefect for 10 years. The information on Pilate from sources outside of the Bible indicates that he was inclined to ignore the interests of the local population and to be harsh in his actions against any threat. It also seems that he wasn't well enough connected in Rome to feel secure in his position. In 36 AD he suppressed a Samaritan insurrection with such harshness that complaints from the local authorities resulted in him being recalled to Rome.

All four Gospels present a picture of Pilate as not wanting to execute Jesus. Based on what the Bible says, it's clear that Pilate's insecurity was an important factor in Jesus' crucifixion. He was willing to stand his ground until the Jewish authorities threatened to let Caesar know that Pilate had released a man who claimed to be a king. Pilate certainly knew that a careful investigation would show that Jesus hadn't been a threat to the Romans, but the authorities in Rome might not bother with a careful investigation. Rather than risk the displeasure of his superiors, Pilate finally agreed to have Jesus crucified. Given the chronology assumed in this translation, Pilate was recalled to Rome about two years after having Jesus crucified.

Poetry in the Bible

In America, most of our favorite poetry has some rhythm to the words, and generally lines of our poems rhyme. In biblical times, poetry involved rhyming ideas instead of words. There were several patterns for rhyming ideas. In some poems the poet would state an idea and then restate that same basic idea in different words. In other poems the poet would state an idea positively as true and then state its opposite as false. In still other cases the poet would state a pattern of ideas and then reverse the pattern in restating the same ideas in different words. And the variations could go on and on.

Many passages, and in some cases, whole books in the Jewish sacred writings were written in such poetic form. This served as a memory aid. Since reading and writings were specialized skills not available to most people, memorization was an important and often well-developed skill. People who listened to a speaker might not be able to quote the entire speech back word-for-word, but it wasn't unusual at all for people to be able to recount from memory all the main points and the basics of how the speaker dealt with those topics. Idea rhyming helped with that process.

In this translation, obviously poetic sections are heavily indented and organized in lines as associated with the poet's ideas. In some cases, the pattern used by the poet may not be obvious, but it's always there.

The Pool of Healing

A pool called Messenger Pool (shown as "the Pool of Siloam" in many translations, but "Siloam" meant "Messenger" or "one sent") is mentioned in Good News 28:3. In that passage there's a parenthetical comment in some manuscripts of the Bible about the water in the pool being stirred and the first person into the pool after that being healed. That comment isn't included in some of the most ancient manuscripts. Other manuscripts have the comment and add that an agent of God stirred the water. Based on the evidence found in the ancient manuscripts, John probably didn't include the part about the agent of God stirring the pool, but the rest seems to belong where it appears.

It's also obvious from the context of that passage that the part about the agent of God was probably a common belief among the Jews in Jerusalem. All the people at this pool who were suffering from various illnesses must've been at the pool for a reason.

It's likely that the first person into the pool would normally be someone who wasn't really very ill or disabled. Even if a person really needing a cure got in first, with all the people around the pool trying to be first in, it was probably hard to tell who really got there first, and someone who wasn't really that sick was probably credited with getting well. It's unlikely that this pool actually provided miraculous healings. In that period, verifiable healings would've attracted enormous crowds, and that doesn't appear to be the case here.

So this translation accepts the main account as true, but regards the part about an agent of God stirring the pool as an explanation added later based on something that at least some people in that area did believe.

Preaching / Proclaiming

"Preach" is one of so many words that we regard today as religious but that the authors of the Bible wouldn't have understood as particularly religious. This word meant to announce something as news. A news broadcaster would've been described as a "preacher." The job of a herald was to "preach" (announce) his message, whether that message was secular or religious. What we today generally refer to as "preaching" is actually more appropriately either prophecy or teaching. (See the article on Prophecies and Fulfillments below.)

Preaching (as used in the Bible) wasn't necessarily about speaking to a group. Preaching could be announcing the news to someone one-on-one, just as a herald might "preach" his message to a king in private.

Since this is true, all Christians have both the right and the responsibility to "preach" the gospel in the biblical sense of announcing the news to others who've not heard the message. Even those who can't speak at all can carry the message by hand signs or by writing or just by the way they live. In this translation, the verb normally translated as "preach" is translated by some word or phrase that better expresses in English what New Testament Christians would've understood.

Priests / Chief Priests

See the articles on Levites above and Zechariah below for more information about priests.

Priests

At the time of Moses, God chose the tribe descended from Jacob's son, Levi, as a special group to serve him. All men in that tribe were to serve God in special ways, but the descendants of Moses' brother, Aaron, were specifically chosen to be the priests of

Israel for all time. All male descendants of Aaron who were healthy were supposed to work in the temple as priests, but there were far too many priests for all of them to work there at the same time. Long before New Testament times, the priests had been divided into 24 groups or divisions. These divisions took turns serving in the temple. Each division would serve a week and then go home. Each division would serve two times each year, making 48 weeks. The Jewish year was made up of about 51 weeks, but there were three special feasts ordained by God for which all Jewish males were to come to the Tabernacle (later the Temple when that replaced the more portable Tabernacle), and all available priests were needed for those three feast times. Every few years an extra month had to be added to the calendar causing a year to have about 55 weeks. That extra month was treated as a repeat of the month just past, so while it's not known for certain, the priests who had served in that month the first time probably served again in the repeated month.

Except for the functions of the priests specifically mentioned in the New Testament, information on the detailed duties of the priests isn't important for understanding the message of the New Testament, and therefore such information isn't covered here. There are many sources for such information, including the Old Testament and especially the book of Leviticus.

Chief Priests

Chief priests are mentioned over sixty times in the Gospels and Acts, but there's not a lot of information available about them. The temple was a major operation and would've required a core group of priests who served full-time. The chief priests were certainly the priests employed full-time in the temple.

Most of the chief priests would've been Sadducees during New Testament times because the high priests and their followers were Sadducees, and they would've controlled who got to be full-time employees. The chief priests would also have been looked on as significant leaders of religious life for Jews—and for most Jews, religious life was the core of all life.

It's very likely that the high priest could rely on the support of the chief priests and their families in almost all matters. This would include the arrest and crucifixion of Jesus. It's very likely that the crowd outside of Pilate's headquarters calling for Jesus' crucifixion was made up largely of these chief priests and their families and friends.

Prophecies that the Christ would replace Judaism

One of the truly great values of the book of Hebrews in the New Testament is its emphasis on Jewish sacred writings that predicted the replacement of the religion delivered by Moses with a new religion delivered by a new champion. There were many such prophecies, and Judaism is the only religion with sacred writings that predict its replacement in this world. This Glossary doesn't attempt to cover all such prophecies, but it's appropriate to list some of the key prophecies here:
1. There'd be a new prophet who'd replace Moses as the primary authority (Deuteronomy 18:15-19)
2. There'd be a new priest who wouldn't be a Levite (Psalm 110:4; Hebrews 7:1-8:1)
3. There'd be a new covenant of the heart rather than law (Jeremiah 31:31-34; Hebrews 8:6-13)
4. There'd be a king forever descended from David (2Samuel 7:16)
5. There'd be a coming champion who'd be known as the son of God (Psalm 2:7; Hebrews 1:1-5)

Prophecies and Fulfillments

What Prophecy Is

In our culture today, we tend to think of prophecy as foretelling the future, but in the Bible that's not the real meaning. In the Bible, prophecy means a message coming "from divine inspiration and declaring the purposes of God, whether by reproving and admonishing the wicked, or comforting the afflicted, or revealing things hidden." In other words, prophecy is speaking a message as led by God's Holy Spirit (see 2Peter 1:21). In some cases, God inspired prophets to tell something about what would come in the future, but the bulk of prophecy in the Bible is God telling people how to live their lives daily for him. What we in our culture today call "preaching" is generally not preaching by the Bible's definition at all. If it's from someone being guided by God's Holy Spirit, then it's what the Bible would call prophecy. (Prophecy is also preaching when it consists of announcing the news of Christianity to those who don't know the message. See the article on Preaching above.)

What Paul wrote in 1Corinthians 14 makes it clear that prophecy isn't to be limited to professional leaders. In fact, in 1Corinthians 11:4-5 Paul told the Corinthian Christians how women should dress when prophesying in a gathering of Christians, demonstrating that it's appropriate for both women and men to prophesy in a Christian team meeting.

Some Christian leaders maintain that prophecy was a function of Christians in New Testament times, but that God's gift of prophecy is no longer available to Christians. Some point to 1Corinthians 3:8 as evidence that prophecy went away after the first century, but the context certainly doesn't support that claim. In Romans 12:6 Paul encouraged the Christians in Rome to prophesy. In 1Corinthians 12:10, Paul listed prophecy as one of the gifts God gives to Christians and in 1Corinthians 14:1 and 14:39 Paul encouraged the Christians in Corinth to seek the gift of prophecy. In 1Thessalonians 5:20, Paul wrote to the Christians in Thessalonica encouraging them not to despise prophecy. In 1Corinthians 14:3, Paul explained that prophecy is meant to build up and encourage fellow Christians. In 1Corinthians 14:29-31 Paul described prophecy as something that should be a normal part of a Christian team meeting, open to all Christians to participate. But from the way that Paul described prophecy, it's clear that what he was talking about was delivering a message that would encourage or teach, inspired by the guidance of God's Holy Spirit.

The Purpose of Prophecies Predicting Future Events

Any serious student of the Bible should quickly realize that with only rare exceptions, it isn't God's intent to tell us the future when he gives us prophecies that include future events. We're not meant to understand what the fulfillment will look like—we're only meant to understand that God knows. In 1Peter 1:10-12, Peter wrote about how prophets wanted to understand the very things they were prophesying, and they were told that they were serving another generation, not themselves. God didn't even tell them the real significance of their own words, so why should we expect God to tell us ahead of the right time? If God wants us to know something about the future, he won't make it hard to understand.

Over and over, we've seen that those who claim to know what the fulfillment of this prophecy or that prophecy will be are shown to be wrong. The religious leaders of New Testament times thought that they'd figured out the meaning of the prophecies of the Christ, but when the Christ came, he was so different from what they expected that they condemned him to crucifixion. Many claim to know exactly what the Revelation is about, but such claims are questionable at best. Those who claimed that the USSR was the great beast of the Revelation no longer want us to remember their words.

The Bible provides clear descriptions of prophecies that have been fulfilled, and every so often we get to witness additional fulfillments. That's when we know for sure what the prophecy was talking about. But for those that haven't been fulfilled yet, we need to simply accept that God knows what's coming, and that we don't need to know. We just need to know that he knows and then put our trust in him.

<u>Fulfillment versus Prophecy</u>

In the New Testament in general and especially in the Gospel of Matthew, there are quotations from the Jewish sacred writings that sometimes don't seem to fit when read in context. In fact, several really don't fit, and the authors of the New Testament certainly knew this, as did the people who read these books. The point of such quotations isn't that these were prophecies that were being fulfilled in the life and ministry of Jesus, but that events in the life and ministry of Jesus gave new and fuller meaning to familiar words from the sacred writings.

For example, in Good News 3:16 there's a quotation from Hosea 11:1 that says, "I called my son out of Egypt." The original passage talks of the nation of Israel as God's son being called out of Egypt. There's nothing in the passage to make the reader think this is about the Christ. But when Matthew wrote about Joseph bringing his family back from Egypt, these familiar words came to mind and were given fuller meaning.

Similarly, in Good News 3:18 there's a quotation from Jeremiah 31:15 that says, "A sound was heard in Ramah—weeping and anguished mourning. Rachel, weeping for her children and refusing to be comforted because they were dead." The original passage talks about the Israelites being taken into captivity. The people were brought to Ramah as a staging point before being taken to Babylon. Matthew's point is that just as there was tragic loss of life at that time due to an outside military power, so on a smaller scale there was tragic loss of life in Bethlehem due to the power of Herod (whom most Jews considered an outsider). The point wasn't that Jeremiah had predicted Herod's action, but that the familiar words from the sacred writings took on new meaning in what Herod did.

The Prophet

By New Testament times, prophecies of the Christ in the Jewish sacred writings had created a misunderstanding. The problem was that some prophecies clearly taught that the Christ would be a conquering king while others portrayed him as a suffering servant. One explanation popular in New Testament times was that the Christ would have a prophet who'd fulfill the suffering servant role while the Christ himself would fulfill the kingly role.

People asked if John the Immerser were "that prophet," and he denied it. We don't know if John understood that no such prophet would even exist. He did know that he wasn't that prophet.

People wondered the same thing about Jesus. He didn't seem to be the conquering hero that the Jews expected the Christ to be, but maybe he was the prophet.

As mentioned above in the article on Prophecies and Fulfillments, it's not God's intent to give us details about the future. It's only God's intent to let us know that he knows what's coming and he's got it under his control.

Repentance

Too often the New Testament use of the term "repentance" is misunderstood. Many Americans think of repentance as being sorry we did wrong or perhaps being sorry we got caught doing wrong. In most other translations, the word "repentance" is used a lot, but in most cases this translation replaces that word with the phrase, "a life turned around," or something similar.

This is another of those words that we think of as religious, but that wasn't a religious word in New Testament times. At its root it means "change one's mind," and it can apply to something as simple as a change of mind about which candy bar to buy. If you have your mind focused on a Milky Way bar, but at the last moment you change the focus to a Snickers bar you happened to see, that change of focus would be described as "repentance" by people living in New Testament times.

Of course, when applied to Christian conversion, this word refers to the change from a life focused on self and on the things of this world to a life focused on God and on the eternity he offers. This necessarily implies a whole different way of living. This change makes anything in this world, including one's own body, expendable in order to obtain that which is so much more valuable.

Repentance and faith have an important connection. When used with reference to salvation, repentance involves changing the focus of your life from yourself and the things of this world to God and the things of his kingdom. Faith is maintaining the focus of your life on God and the things of his kingdom (being faithful). Repentance is how you get to faith, and faith is how you maintain your place in God's kingdom.

Romans and Jews

Since the American Revolution, most Americans have never known what it's like to have an occupying military power in control (though southern states did have that experience following the War Between the States). The Jews of Jesus time knew what it meant, because the Romans maintained enough troops in the area to see that anyone attempting insurrection would be stopped quickly. Of course the Romans taxed the citizens of the countries they occupied, and those taxes were a constant reminder to the Jews that they didn't have the power to run their own country. To make matters worse, sometimes the tax collectors appointed by the Romans would overcharge people, and any interference with the tax collectors would be met with an armed response from the Romans.

Jews saw themselves as the chosen people of God, a holy nation, better than any other nation on earth. Having to accept Roman rule was galling. And any Jew who led a band of armed men against the Romans was considered a hero among the Jews.

The Romans brought education, culture, peace, and prosperity. There were always rulers, so for most people, Roman rulers were no worse than any other rulers, and in some ways they were better. But there were some territories in the empire that just wouldn't accept Roman rule, and the Jewish areas were in that group—especially Judea.

However, there were some Romans who found in Judaism a religion that made a lot more sense than any of the pagan religions of the empire. In the Bible, these people are referred to as "God fearers" or something similar. They wouldn't convert to Judaism, but they'd worship the Jewish God and even study the Jewish sacred writings. There's at least one case mentioned in the Gospels where a Roman military commander (a centurion) had used his own money to pay for construction of a Jewish worship center (Good News 12:8). In his case, the local Jews respected this commander and he liked the Jews—but that was the exception.

In 66 AD, the Jews started a serious rebellion against the Romans, and in 70 AD the city of Jerusalem was almost completely destroyed with over a million deaths in the fighting. In 136 AD the Romans crushed another Jewish insurrection and barred all Jews from living in Jerusalem. They were only allowed to enter Jerusalem for a period of fasting to commemorate the destruction of the temple by the Babylonians and then by the Romans.

Sabbath

The Law of Moses required Jews to keep the seventh day of the week as a special day in which no manual labor was to be done. This day was supposed to be dedicated to God and to passing on the message of God's revelations from one generation to the next. Because it was to be a day of rest from manual labor, it was called "Sabbath," meaning "rest." However, this same term was also used for any day of rest, especially a day of rest associated with some feast or ritual commanded by God. (In addition, it was used of periods of rest such as a "Sabbath year" when the fields were supposed to be allowed to rest for a year.)

It's hard to say how faithfully this was observed during biblical history. There were probably periods when the general idolatry of the people caused this practice to be neglected, but there are passages throughout the Jewish sacred writings (the Old Testament) that refer to the Sabbath, so we know that it was observed to some degree for most of Jewish history. By New Testament times, the Jews generally observed the Sabbath fairly strictly, especially in areas with Jewish communities. In Judea and Galilee, it would've been considered a crime to break the Sabbath rules that had been established. This was especially true among the Pharisees and their followers.

In Jesus' ministry, he often intentionally challenged the Sabbath traditions that defined in significant detail just what could and what couldn't be done on a Sabbath. The Gospels tell of seven specific cases where Jesus challenged Sabbath restrictions by healing someone on a Sabbath, and one other case where Jesus was allowing his disciples to pluck grain and eat it on the Sabbath (forbidden since this amounted to harvesting which was work).

In effect, the rules had taken something sweet that was meant to help people get to know God and turned it into something that could be harsh and even cruel. The controversy between Jesus and the Pharisees over what was or wasn't appropriate became enough of a focus that in at least some cases it appears that the Pharisees arranged to have someone needing healing attend worship on the Sabbath if Jesus would be present, just so they could criticize him for healing someone on the Sabbath. This infuriated Jesus. He'd consistently heal the person in need and then chastise those who criticized him for demonstrating God's love on a Sabbath.

For Christians, the Sabbath is no longer a requirement. In Romans 14:4-6 Paul specifically addressed this issue and said that, while it's fine for a Christian to observe one day as special, it's also fine for a Christian to observe all days as equally dedicated to God. There's no one day of the week that's "the Lord's Day." For a Christian, every day is the Lord's Day.

Observing a specific day as "the Lord's Day" has a tendency to cause some people to think that it's OK to live by God's rules on that day and then revert to their own rules on other days. That's clearly not what Jesus and his followers taught. If we observe one day especially dedicated to Christian team functions, that's fine, but we need to always remember that every day is the Lord's Day.

Sacred Writings

<u>The Meaning of "Scripture"</u>

The word "scripture" is another in our list of words that are thought of today as religious words but that weren't religious words in New Testament times. This word simply meant "writing," or "something written." Anything written was a scripture.

In order to talk about the sacred writings as a group distinct from other writings, the biblical authors either referred to the sacred writings as "<u>the</u> writings" (with a definite article) or included some wording in the context to make it clear that they were talking about the Jewish sacred writings. In the gospels, wherever this word appears as a noun, the context always makes it clear that the reference is to the Jewish sacred writings. So in this translation, the word generally translated "scripture" in other translations is translated "sacred writing" to better communicate what the authors intended, and a footnote points out that the literal translation is simply "the writing," but that the context makes it clear that the reference is to the Jewish sacred writings.

In America, the word "scripture" has come to be practically synonymous with the Christian Bible, so when we see that word in the Bible, we tend to think that it refers to the Bible itself. In fact, during biblical times, all books were scrolls. Pages of a book were glued edge to edge in a long strip, and then that long strip was wound onto a wooden spool. Scrolls are very hard to work with, especially if the content is very long. So in most cases, a scroll would contain just one of the longer books from the Bible. Shorter books might be combined on a single scroll, but no one scroll would contain all the books in the Jewish sacred writings (our Old Testament), let alone the whole Bible. And since the books of the New Testament were in the process of being written, references to "sacred writings" in the Gospels are always references to just the Jewish sacred writings, not the books of the New Testament.

It's worth noting that the verb for "writing" is the same word as the noun for "something written," and in the Bible, that verb is used for both sacred and secular writing. For example, when Pilate wrote the words to go on Jesus' cross, he told the Jewish authorities who wanted him to change the words, "What I've written, I've written" (Good News 49:17), which could be translated, "What I've scriptured, I've scriptured."

The Jewish Sacred Writings

While "the writing" or "the writings" would refer to the Jewish sacred writings, there's no official list of which books should be considered sacred and which should not anywhere in the Bible. Jews today think of their ancient sacred writings in three major categories: The Torah (Law), The Prophets, and The Writings. See the list.

Modern Divisions of Jewish Sacred Writings

The Law (Torah)	The Prophets	The Writings
Genesis	Joshua	Ruth
Exodus	Judges	1Chronicles
		2Chronicles
Leviticus	1Samuel	Ezra
	2Samuel	Nehemiah
Numbers	1Kings	Esther
	2Kings	
Deuteronomy	Isaiah	Job
	Jeremiah	Psalms
	Ezekiel	Proverbs
	12 Minor Prophets:	Ecclesiastes
	Hosea	Song of Solomon
	Joel	Lamentations
	Amos	Daniel
	Obadiah	
	Jonah	
	Micah	
	Nahum	
	Habakkuk	
	Zephaniah	
	Haggai	
	Zechariah	
	Malachi	

The Torah (sometimes called the Pentateuch) is absolutely the most sacred set of writings for Jews, and all religious Jews agree on the authority of those five books. After that come "the prophets," and then "the writings." While there's general agreement on which books should be included among "the prophets" and on the authority of those books, there's some disagreement about which books should be included among "the writings" and about how authoritative those books are.

In the New Testament, there are several references to two of these categories: "The Law" and "The Prophets," but the modern category of "the writings" is never mentioned.

Jews generally classify the Psalms and Daniel among "the writings" today, but from the use of those books in the New Testament, it appears that Jews at that time considered at least those two books to be as sacred as the other prophets.

The Bible provides no clue about the order in which these books should appear. For the most part, they were on separate scrolls and didn't appear as a single document.

The books in the Jewish sacred writings referred to most often in the Christian sacred writings were the Psalms, Isaiah, Deuteronomy, Genesis, Exodus, Leviticus, and Daniel in that order, with many other references to other books in the Jewish sacred writings.

Christian Sacred Writings

Peter wrote about some things Paul had written and grouped Paul's writings with "the other sacred writings" (2Peter 3:16). It's obvious that even in New Testament times, Christians considered such writings to be on the same level with the Jewish sacred writings. And it's obvious from the Christian sacred writings that those who wrote these books and letters were convinced that the message Jesus brought, while it was consistent with the intent of the Jewish sacred writings and with the God revealed in the Jewish sacred writings, took precedence over the Jewish sacred writings. The God of the Jews had come among us and told us how to understand and apply what he had revealed to Moses and the other prophets, and he had the authority to do that.

New Testament versus Old Testament

The Old Testament and the New Testament are absolutely linked together. The fundamental teachings of the New Testament about Christian love, faith, God, sin, righteousness, and such are also the fundamental teachings of the Old Testament. The God of the Old Testament is the God of the New Testament. He is spirit, and his spirit came among us without limit in the presence of Jesus the Christ. Jesus and his followers based their claim to be telling the truth on prophecies in the Old Testament, so if the Old Testament doesn't provide a message from God, those claims would have no value.

However, if there's one thing that's clear in the New Testament, it's that the Law God gave to Moses is no longer the authority for Christians. Before Jesus came, the Law was the guide, but that law was subject to all kinds of abuse. The New Testament clearly teaches that we're no longer under that law, so it would be entirely inappropriate for any Christian to use Old Testament teachings as the only support for Christian doctrines. If there's a New Testament teaching, the teachings of the Old Testament are not to be used to define what the New Testament teaches beyond what's clearly taught in the New Testament. Even the Jewish prophets who wrote many of the Old Testament books made it clear that what God wants is not legalistic obedience to laws, but rather dedication of your heart to serve him. As Christians, our faith in God causes us to do right far better than any law could ever do.

Christians have God's own Spirit as their guide. The New Testament is our source of information to judge whether what we're doing is consistent with God's will—it's the authority in such matters. But the ultimate guide for Christians is God's Holy Spirit. The entire Bible, as filtered by the New Testament, provides the standards by which we can judge whether a teaching is consistent with Christianity, because if it's not, it cannot be from God's Holy Spirit. But the Bible isn't a set of rules, and no set of rules could ever cover all situations. As Christians, we need to rely on God's Holy Spirit to guide us in following the principles of Christianity as revealed in the New Testament.

Sadducees

The Pharisees and Sadducees were the two dominant Jewish sects at the time of Jesus' ministry, though there were others. Pharisees and Sadducees were both strict religious groups, but their approach to the Jewish religion differed.

The Sadducees recognized only the Torah (the books of Genesis through Deuteronomy) as authoritative, and they insisted on a very literal interpretation of those books. Finding no clear teaching of resurrection explicit in the Torah, the Sadducees rejected any concept of resurrection. Note that when the Sadducees tried to confound Jesus with a question about the resurrection, Jesus used a quotation from the Torah to respond and show their error. He also insulted them when he said, "You don't know the sacred writings" (Good News 39:46).

In general, the Sadducees were the religious elite including chief priests and those closely associated with them. As a rule, they were wealthy and considered their wealth to be their reward for serving God and evidence that their lives were pleasing to God.

Satan / Devil

The word "Satan" has Hebrew roots meaning "Adversary." In a courtroom, the opposing attorney could have been called the "Satan." But among Jews, this word came to be used as a name for the spiritual being who is God's leading adversary in this world. And from Jesus' perspective, anyone who worked against God would be the tool of that spiritual power.

The word "devil" has Greek roots meaning a slanderer—someone who tells malicious lies or spreads malicious gossip about another. Again, over time this term had come to serve as a name for that same spiritual adversary to God. When Jesus spoke of that spiritual power as a liar and the father of lying, he used the word "devil" (Good News 33:32-34).

In this case we have words that started out without especially religious meaning, but that took on such religious meaning in biblical times. But in the Jewish sacred writings, sometimes it's difficult to tell if "satan" refers to the spiritual adversary opposed to God or if it refers to some human adversary. It's certainly used in some places to refer to human adversaries.

The Bible provides no clear information about the origin of the biblical Satan or why he's so determined to oppose God's ways. There's no information about how Satan came to have his own agents to help in his work. There are stories about Satan and his followers rebelling against God in heaven, and many people think those stories are in the Bible, but they aren't. A careful review of the very few passages that are thought to support that idea will show that there are other interpretations that are more likely.

The Satan or Devil of the New Testament is represented as a spiritual power who can work through people. The Bible provides no indication that he has any necessary physical form himself.

There's an apparent implication in the Bible that God allowed this Satan into his creation so that humans could experience the destructive nature of sin and learn to seek God's ways before God would bring them into his eternal paradise. The importance of this is to assure that those who reach heaven won't bring their rebellion against God with them. (Remember, sin is always treason—rebellion against God.)

Scribes

Here's another word we associate with religion when it wasn't really limited to religion in New Testament times. In the Bible, the scribes that are mentioned were those whose job it was to make copies of the sacred writings (as well as copy or write other documents). Because these men spent much of their careers copying the sacred writings by hand, they tended to become serious experts in what those writings said, and they were respected as such.

There were scribes in all the Jewish religious sects to write down and then copy any books the sect generated or maintained. Since the Sadducees accepted only the Torah as sacred writings, their scribes would've focused on those books, while the Pharisees would've wanted copies of the other writings they considered sacred (including books in our Old Testament other than the Torah and certain other books). In the New Testament, the scribes who confronted Jesus seem to be mainly associated with the Pharisees. There's also one case where scribes were apparently called into an examination of Jesus in order to record the official account of the proceedings (Good News 47:14).

Writing materials were very expensive in biblical times. A book like Matthew could take the skins from a whole flock of sheep to provide the "paper" on which to write. Professional scribes were trained in writing carefully; fitting as much on a page as possible while still maintaining clear letters that could be read easily. Copies had to be as exact and legible as possible, especially when copying any of the sacred writings.

Jesus taught with authority, and people were astonished. They were used to the scribes who always quoted this passage or that one in the sacred writings and the opinions of this rabbi or that rabbi as the authority for what they were teaching. Jesus taught on his own authority as the son of God. A scribe might refer to different passages or opinions that seemed to conflict with each other, but Jesus simply taught the truth he had from his Father. In fact, sometimes Jesus used his authority to contradict things written in the Jewish sacred writings (see the discussion of "an eye for an eye" in Good News 9:55-61 as an example).

Servants / Slaves

In English translations of the Bible, the word "slave" has often been translated "servant" or "bond servant," even though the meaning was well understood by the translators. In part this is due to sensitivity to the historical evils of slavery in England and America. But as a matter of faithfulness to the truth, when the literal word in the Bible is the word for a slave, not a hired servant, this translation is faithful to what the Bible actually says wherever possible. There is, however, one interesting case in the story of the prodigal son. In that story Jesus told how the elder brother called for a "boy" to tell him what was going on when the younger brother had come home and the father had organized a party (Good News 20:31). The word "boy" referred to some kind of young servant, but it could apply to either a hired servant or a slave, so in this case we can't tell whether this "boy" was a hired servant or a slave.

In New Testament times, practically any person with any amount of wealth would have at least one or two slaves, and a really wealthy person would have several. Many slaves were well treated, and it wasn't unusual for a wealthy person to have slaves in trusted positions. Some slaves owned other slaves. And in theory, everyone was a slave to the ruler of a country.

By law, if a master killed his slave, that wasn't considered a crime. In addition, a master could (and often did) use his female slaves for sex (see Exodus 21:7-11). A slave had no rights. And while, as already mentioned, there were slaves who were treated well and who held positions of great trust, many slaves weren't well treated, and many were worked to death in terrible conditions.

In New Testament times, the expectation was that a slave would do his or her job—everything assigned by the owner—with no expectation of thanks. Technically, it was impossible for a slave to do anything that the master would consider to be extra—more than what was expected.

Jesus used a story illustration about slavery in Good News 21:1-5 to make a very important point. We are, by our very creation, the same as slaves to God. He has the right to expect of us a life totally dedicated to his service. No matter how much good we might do, it all falls into the category of things that God created us to do and that he'd rightfully expect us to do. No amount of good deeds can ever earn us any credit with God. The good things we do are an absence of debits; they are never credits. And any failure to do the good things we knew we should do and could've done amounts to a debit. So while we can accumulate debits, we can never earn any credits. We're totally at the mercy of God's grace.

On the other hand, there were cases where a master would specifically allow a slave to earn money of his or her own. In those cases, there were times when such a slave could purchase his or her own freedom. And there were other times when a master would simply free a faithful slave. But this was always a case of generosity on the part of the master, and if he chose to do so, the master could change the arrangement at any time until he actually signed the document giving the slave his or her freedom. So the right to buy your freedom depended on the master's generosity. God's grace is the generosity that allows us to be free.

There are many ways that illustration breaks down, but the point Jesus was making is valid. You can't pay for God's forgiveness, you have to receive it as a gift. Anything you do to make yourself suitable to receive that gift has nothing to do with paying for that gift. (Of course for Christians, it's not what we do, it's our hearts surrendered to God—that's always been the case. But once we do surrender our hearts to God, we will naturally seek to do his will.)

Sin / Rebellion

Any form of rebellion against God is sin, and any form of sin is rebellion against God. The two are the same thing, and God takes rebellion very, very seriously.

In Good News 34:37, Jesus told the Pharisees that if they were actually blind to the wrong they were doing, they wouldn't be guilty of sin, but since they claimed to see the truth, their guilt remained. In other words, if they had a valid excuse for not knowing that they were doing wrong, it wouldn't have been rebellion, and they would've been innocent. It's not what a person does that's sin, it's the rebellion.

In Romans 7:7 Paul wrote about how he wasn't guilty of coveting until he came in contact with God's Law that told him it was wrong to covet. Again, doing wrong unintentionally isn't presented in the Bible as sinful. James wrote, "For the one who knows to do something good, and who doesn't do it, that's sin" (James 4:17). It's not rebellion if you don't know you're working against God. But as Paul said in Romans 1:18-23, the very creation in which we live provides a revelation of the reality and holiness of God. There are certainly some things we couldn't figure out just be observing the creation, but anyone who doesn't realize that there is a holy God must be intentionally closing his or her eyes to the truth.

So sin must involve either intentionally doing what you know God wouldn't want you to do or intentionally not doing what you know God would want you to do. Those are the two sides of rebellion.

Now, Jesus said that everything God ever told us could be summed up in two commandments: care about God with everything you've got and care about your neighbor as you care about yourself (Good News 40:3-4). When he said this, Jesus intentionally used a word for the caring love that sees the needs of others and seeks to help with those needs. (See Christian Love / Caring Love above.) God doesn't expect you to do what you can't do. He knows your limitations. But he does expect you to do what you can to help those in need. God doesn't expect you to give money to every person who claims to be in need to the point that you put yourself and your family in poverty, but God also knows when he's given you the ability to help. And the first line of help is absolutely free—it's prayer.

So, if you know this, every time you see a person in need and you choose to avoid that person or refuse to do what you know you could've done to help, you're in rebellion against God. You're a traitor to his kingdom because that's what he, as the King, has ordered as absolute policy in his kingdom. You vote for Satan to rule in this world rather than God, because that's exactly how Satan wants this world to run.

While we often think of apathy as having nothing to do with real sin, there's no worse sin than that. When Jesus told his disciples about the standard by which men would actually be judged (Good News 40:26-36), he said that those who'd be condemned weren't being condemned for what they'd done, but for what they'd failed to do. They were being condemned for their apathy. And if you say that there's nothing you can do, you're wrong. Each of us has the awesome power of prayer available at all times, and often God provides us with much more than we could use in order to empower us to help others in need.

The Jewish prophet, Micah, put God's requirements about as simply as they could be put. "He's already showed you as a human what's good. And what does God demand from you but to practice justice, love being merciful, and walk humbly with your God?" (Micah 6:8). To "practice justice" is simply to do what you know is right. To "love being merciful" has to do with forgiving those who hurt you and caring about those who are in need. And to "walk humbly with your God" has to do with always seeking God's ways. Who could find fault with that standard? Yet we turn against him and fail him daily.

Selfishness and the worldly focus it fosters are the things that lead us into rebellion against God. Indeed, selfishness with its focus on the things of this world is the heart and soul of rebellion against God. Jesus made it very clear that if your focus is on the things of this world, you can't hope to win in the end, because this world is scheduled for destruction. But if your focus is on God, you can't lose.

Son of Man and Son of God
Son of Man
In many translations, Jesus is quoted as calling himself the "son of man," often capitalized as "Son of Man." "Son of man" is a title Jesus used for himself frequently, and he used it to emphasize his humanity. While "son of man" is an entirely legitimate translation of the words in the Bible, in our culture today it can fail to communicate what Jesus intended. In the New Testament, it's clear that whenever Jesus used this phrase he was speaking of himself and he was emphasizing his human nature rather than his divine nature. So in this translation, wherever this phrase appears it's translated by a phrase like "I, as a human" in order to make it clear that Jesus was speaking of himself and that he was emphasizing his humanity.

The term "son of man" was fairly common in the Jewish sacred writings (the Old Testament in our Bibles), especially in the book of Ezekiel where God consistently referred to the prophet as "son of man." It was a phrase emphasizing the humanity of a person.

In most cases in the Jewish sacred writings, this phrase simply means "human," but there's one case in Daniel where the passage says, "I was watching in the night visions, and behold, one like a son of man, coming with the clouds of heaven! He came to the ancient of days, and they brought him near before him. Then to him was given dominion and glory and a kingdom that all peoples, nations, and languages should serve him. His dominion is an everlasting dominion that shall not pass away. And His kingdom is the one that shall not be destroyed" (Daniel 7:13-14 NKJ). This seems to be an obvious reference to the Christ as "son of man."

For Jesus, this phrase was his favorite phrase for himself, emphasizing both his humanity and his claim to be the Christ. Of course, God was always present in Jesus—Immanuel, God with us, but there were many times when Jesus wanted us to know that he lived as a man and that he dealt with the limitations and the temptations of humanity as a human. He suffered pain and passions just as we do.

Jesus knew that after his resurrection and ascension there'd be people who'd argue that he wasn't really human, but this would mean that he wasn't really tempted as we are and that he didn't really die as we do. Jesus considered it very important to emphasize his humanity. In all of the Gospels, it's clear that he did refer to himself as the unique "Son of God," but it's also clear that he referred to himself as a human much more often than as the Son of God.

Jesus was every bit a human, but God's Spirit was present in him without limit—present in a way we can't even imagine. (This would be like our experience of God's Holy Spirit within us, except that presence is far more limited for us because of our sinful nature.) Most of the time when Jesus used the phrase "son of man" he was emphasizing that what he was saying was true of himself as a human, but not necessarily true of himself as God's Spirit present with us. Again, he was emphasizing his human nature as opposed to his divine nature.

Son of God
However, though Jesus used the phrase "son of man" more frequently than any other to describe himself, he made it very clear that he was God's son in a special way that wouldn't apply to any other human or any created being. (See Hebrews 1 for more about

that.) While Jesus was very much a human in that he suffered the things other humans suffer and he was tempted just as all humans are tempted, he also had God's Holy Spirit in him in a way that no other human can even comprehend.

If we try too hard to understand this concept, we quickly get into areas where we may be making up answers that aren't supported by biblical teaching. Human logic isn't adequate to deal with such matters. There are, however, some things we can know from the Bible.

- We know from Jesus himself that God is spirit, not limited to any bodily form, so the divine nature of Jesus had to be spiritual, not physical. (See Good News 24:19.)
- We know from God's own words that we as humans cannot experience him in his fullness and survive, so we know that God's presence in Jesus was limited at least to a level that we could survive. (See Exodus 33:20.)
- We know from various passages that the whole creation was the work of that Spirit of God that was present in Jesus. (For example, see Good News 4:1-2, Ephesians 1:8-9, and Colossians 1:15-20.)
- We know that the God who gave the law to Moses was this same spiritual God who lived in Jesus. (Good News 4:1; Romans 13:10-11 as compared with Isaiah 45:23; 1Corinthians 1:30-31; Hebrews 1:10; and 1Peter 1:24-25 are all passages that make it clear that the God of the Jewish sacred writings is the same as the God who lived in Jesus.)
- We know that Jesus promised his disciples that God's Spirit would come to them and live in them, and that this Spirit would be his own spirit. (See Good News 43:25.)

Beyond that we don't need to know the details of how God works such things out, and speculation can be very dangerous. (See Sons and Fathers in Biblical Thinking for some insights into how people would have understood Jesus' claim to be God's son.)

Sons and Fathers in Biblical Thinking

Today we understand at least some things about eggs, sperm, and DNA. In biblical times, people knew nothing about such things. Biblical cultures were agricultural, and their understanding of human or animal reproduction was very different from ours. Farmers understood that seeds came from plants, and that a seed needed to be planted in the soil in order to get a new plant to grow. If the seed weren't planted, no new plant would grow. However, planting the seed wasn't the only factor. These farmers could see that the soil affected the plant. A seed planted in barren soil wouldn't grow. And the plant that grew from any seed would be affected by the fertility of the soil.

Using that information, people decided that having sexual intercourse was like planting a seed, and the woman's womb was the soil into which the seed was planted. The seed came entirely from the father—not from the mother. The mother's womb might affect how the seed grew, but the basic characteristics of the child had to come strictly from the father.

In this concept, a child was an extension of his or her father. In a sense, the child was the equivalent of the father. This led to the idea that rewarding or punishing a child was the same as rewarding or punishing the father (an idea sometimes incorrectly thought to be supported by biblical teaching).

In 1Corinthians 11:12 Paul said, "For as the woman comes from the man, so also the man comes through the woman." This is clearly consistent with the concept just described. Also, in Hebrews 7:9-10 the Bible says that in a way, even the tribe of Levi that collects the tithes actually paid tithes through Abraham, because Levi was still in Abraham's body when Abraham paid tithes to Melchizedek. Abraham was Levi's great-grandfather, but the concept described above explains this thought. Abraham's son was a direct extension of Abraham coming from Abraham, and in the same way his grandson and great-grandson also came from him through his son and grandson respectively.

Once we understand this concept, it gives new meaning to Jesus calling himself the son of God. In that culture it was like saying that he came out from God as an integral part of God. It did indeed make him the equivalent of God (Good News 28:17). It meant that he'd always been an integral part of who God is (Good News 4:1-5).

There's no way for us as humans to completely understand God or how his presence in Jesus and the presence of his Holy Spirit in us really works. It's just what it is. And we shouldn't expect to be able to take what the Bible says as a clear technical description. The Bible uses human language to communicate something that can't be fully communicated in human language. But what we can do is see that Jesus came from the one eternal God, that he is an integral and eternal part of who God is, and that knowing Jesus is the same as knowing God.

Supreme Court

Most other translations refer to this group as "the Sanhedrin" (a word with no familiar meaning for most Americans) or "the Council" (another word that doesn't carry a very clear meaning for most Americans), but this group were the ultimate court for all religious issues in Jewish life. And since all aspects of Jewish life were somehow related to the Jewish religion, this Supreme Court had authority in many areas that we, today, wouldn't consider religious. The word the Bible uses can actually mean any council or assembly of leaders, and while each town had its own such assembly, it's clear from the context that the use of this term in the New Testament almost always refers to the council of 70 or 71 Jewish leaders who ruled all Jewish people.

This group was subject to the Roman rulers, but they were still a very influential and powerful body, especially in matters of religion, with authority to maintain their own armed policemen (translated as "soldiers" in most translations) and to arrest, try, imprison, and punish those who broke their laws. Although they didn't officially have the authority to put people to death without prior Roman approval, the Romans didn't interfere with an execution as long as the execution didn't involve a Roman and there was no serious public disturbance because of it (see Acts 7:54-60).

The members of this "Supreme Court" were almost all opposed to Jesus, but there were some exceptions such as Joseph of Arimathea and Nicodemus. From what Paul wrote about voting for the death of Christians (Acts 26:10), he may have been a member of that Supreme Court before he became a Christian, though he would've been unusually young for that role.

Tax Collectors and "Sinners"

There are three different occasions where the Gospels mention tax collectors as associated with sinners. (All three are mentioned in Luke, two of these are mentioned in Matthew, and one is mentioned in Mark.) Obviously, in New Testament times, there was a strong tendency to associate tax collectors with sinners in general. Because of this, tax collectors generally had to find their friends among fellow tax collectors or those the community looked on as "sinners."

Matthew was a tax collector, and as just noted, tax collectors as a group were considered unfit company for the righteous. (See the article on Matthew under Gospels in the Glossary above.) Anyone who worked in the tax collection system in any capacity was seen as helping the hated occupying power—Rome. In addition, tax collectors were notorious for overcharging.

While Matthew was in a position that wasn't as subject to abuse as some positions, he was wealthy enough to have a feast in his own home with his friends and Jesus and his disciples as guests. The vast majority of Jews couldn't afford this kind of feast except possibly for the marriage of a child.

Matthew invited other tax collectors and people who were viewed as "sinners" as guests for his feast. This shows that, while Matthew was probably only involved in a tax focused on local needs, he was still associated in people's minds with the Roman authorities. Because of this, Matthew had to find his friends among those who were viewed with disfavor by the local folks of Capernaum—the "sinners."

Team / Church

The word "church" in the Bible actually means a team. Its root meaning has to do with being called out, but by New Testament times, it had largely lost this implication and was used commonly to designate any community sharing some common aspect, whether they were assembled together or not. The fact that it had a root meaning associated with being called out was just an added benefit as a word to identify God's team. Unfortunately, there is no English word for a team that shares such an implication. Some have translated this as "congregation" or "assembly," but those words imply a group that's physically located together. Christians are part of the team whether they're in a group of Christians or by themselves.

In our culture, a building owned by Christians for their meetings has come to be called "the church" when the biblical view is that it's the people who are the actual team. Rather than try to educate people to stop referring to a building as "the church," this translation uses the word "team," a word that carries the actual meaning of the biblical word that's been more commonly translated "church."

Today, we tend to think of "church" as a religious word, but in biblical times the word used in the Bible had no religious implications at all. In fact, there's one case in the Bible where this word is used of a large group of pagans who'd gathered to oppose the apostle Paul and his work.

Interestingly, the roots of the English word "church" actually do imply a building. These roots go to a Greek word meaning "the lord's house," with no necessary reference to God or religion. At the time that the Bible was first translated into English, the building owned by the church had come to be thought of as "the Lord's house" (with definite reference to God), which led to the use of the word "church" for that building, and in people's minds, the church was so centrally focused on that building that this word was also used to translate a New Testament word that more properly should have been translated to express the concept of a team.

Theophilus (See Good News 1:1-2)

In writing his two books (the Gospel of Luke and Acts), Luke introduced each with a brief note to a man he called "Theophilus." We don't know a lot about this man, but there are some interesting things that we do know and some things we can guess at based on what Luke said.

What we know for certain is that Theophilus was a relatively new Christian, that he was of pagan background, and that he was interested in knowing more about Jesus and about Christianity. There's no doubt about those things.

We don't know for certain what his name was. The name "Theophilus" means "One who loves God," and that could very well be his actual name, but it could also be a name Luke used to avoid exposing this man to criticism and persecution.

Based on what we know about publication of books such as those Luke wrote, this was an expensive undertaking. Just the materials would be costly, and the time required to do the work of writing meant the author had to have enough resources to supply his needs while he wrote the book. Generally, the author hired a professional scribe to do the actual writing, and that would've been another significant expense. So when someone financed the writing of a large book, often the author would start the book with some sort of greeting to the patron who provided the financing. That's almost certainly the case here, so we can be fairly certain that Theophilus was relatively well off financially.

In Luke's Gospel, he addresses Theophilus as "most excellent Theophilus." This is a title that might be used as a compliment for anyone with wealth, but it was generally reserved for Roman citizens of what was known as senatorial rank – in other words, the ruling elite of Roman society. That would fit well with Theophilus having the financial ability to support Luke's work as a writer. Theophilus was probably very well connected and may even have been part of the emperor's group of relatively close advisers.

Since Luke's second book (Acts) ends with Paul in prison in Rome, it seems to fit all the facts to suggest that Luke wrote these books while Paul was in prison. We know from the last verses of Acts that Paul was in prison there for at least two years, and that would allow time for writing these books. That would mean that these books were written about 62 AD while Nero was emperor but before Nero started persecuting Christians in July of 64 AD.

Paul was in prison awaiting trial before Nero. We don't have proof, but we can make an educated guess that Nero wouldn't have wanted to research the details of every case brought to trial in his presence. He'd probably assign a trusted adviser to look into lesser cases with the adviser having the task of telling Nero what decisions to make and why.

We do know that the book of Acts, while it presents many interesting things about early Christian activities, focuses mainly on who Paul was and what he did as a Christian missionary. We also know that in Acts, Luke emphasized that while Jewish leaders persecuted Paul, every time Paul appeared in a Roman court he was found guiltless.

Based on this information, it's quite possible that one of Luke's goals in writing Acts was to provide someone on Nero's staff with information to help get Paul released from his imprisonment. If that's the case, Theophilus may have been the person assigned to look into the case or he may have been in a position to influence that person. Beyond this, we don't have anything that gives us additional clues about this man.

Third Person Commands

Most English translations of the Bible quote Jesus as saying, "He who has ears to hear, let him hear." That translation doesn't really bring out the fact that this was a command to listen. English has no exact equivalent for this quotation and many others like it in the New Testament. It's actually a third person command, like saying "They listen!" as a command. That doesn't even make sense in English.

For this translation, these third person commands are changed to second person commands to communicate in English the force of what the Bible authors were saying. In this example, the translation would be "If you've got ears to hear, pay attention to this." The New Testament authors often used these third person commands, and wherever they occur, this translation uses this approach to communicate the force of the original words in a way that English readers can understand it.

Triumphal Entry (See Good News 38:4-26)

Traditionally, Christians celebrate a memorial of Jesus' triumphal entry into Jerusalem as "Palm Sunday." The Bible doesn't tell us what day of the week this event occurred, but if the chronology for Jesus arrest, trials, crucifixion, and resurrection presented in this Glossary is correct, it was more likely on Saturday.

John's Gospel mentions that Jesus attended a feast in Bethany "six days before the Passover" (John 12:1; Good News 37:50). This Glossary assumes that Jesus was crucified in 34 AD because the timing described in the Bible seems to require that the Passover occurred on a Thursday, and the only year that could fit with all the other details is 34 AD. If that's correct, then the feast in Bethany took place on a Friday. John's Gospel then mentions that the triumphal entry occurred "the next day" (John 12:12; Good News 38:4). That would put the triumphal entry on a Saturday, and there is some logic to that. If Jesus wanted to draw the largest crowd he could draw, a Saturday (Sabbath) when people didn't have to work would be ideal, especially since he planned to start his triumphal entry from Bethany, less than a Sabbath day's journey from Jerusalem.

Mark's Gospel makes it clear that Jesus went to the temple after entering Jerusalem, but that he only looked around on the day of the triumphal entry. It was the next day that Jesus returned to the temple to drive out the merchants and money-changers in the temple. (Mark 11:11-15; Good News 38:26-29). If the triumphal entry did occur on a Saturday, Jesus couldn't have cleansed the temple that same day since the merchants wouldn't be at work on a Sabbath. Cleansing the temple on Sunday would have made good sense, since the merchants would be back to work on Sunday.

There can be no doubt that Pilate was aware of what happened both during the triumphal entry and during the days after that event. The day of Jesus' triumphal entry, Pilate may well have made preparations for military action. The crowds following Jesus were vast, and if Jesus had planned to overthrow the Romans, with so many followers, he would have represented a serious threat. However, when he went to the temple to look around instead of immediately going to Pilate's headquarters looking for a fight, Pilate's fears would have been eased, and when he went back to the temple to drive out the merchants, Pilate may well have been very relieved. This may have influenced Pilate to try to release Jesus.

We know from archeology and ancient writings that the Romans kept a close watch on the temple since that was the place where political unrest was most likely to break out in violence, so Pilate would have known that Jesus spent the next week teaching in the temple and making fools of the Jewish authorities. It's no wonder that, after Jesus was arrested, Pilate had no desire to crucify him. He'd had a week of close observation to see that Jesus was a direct threat to the Jewish authorities, but not to the Romans.

Unforgivable Sin (See Good News 17:7-10)

Matthew, Mark, and Luke all wrote about an incident where some Jewish scribes who were of the party of Pharisees accused Jesus of casting out evil spirits by the power of Satan. In other words, they were saying that the power of God's Holy Spirit at work in Jesus was actually Satan. Jesus responded to this with a warning that, while people might be forgiven for lying about God or himself, if they lied about God's Holy Spirit as if he were unholy, there'd be no forgiveness. (This is why in our culture even today, people commonly use "God" or "Jesus" as profanity, but not "Holy Spirit." Jesus wasn't actually talking about profanity, but that's how this teaching has often been applied.)

The issue here is that reading about God in the sacred writings might lead to misunderstandings that would cause a person to call God evil (that has happened many times), and even meeting Jesus as a human might lead to some misunderstanding that would cause a person to say that he was evil, but actually coming in contact with God's Holy Spirit and calling him evil cannot be forgiven. And it's not clear whether Jesus was saying that God would refuse to forgive such a sin or whether he was saying that anyone who'd call the works of the Holy Spirit evil is so far gone that there'd be no hope of rescue.

Hebrews 6:4-6 describes a similar case where people who "were enlightened and have tasted the heavenly gift and have shared in the presence of the Holy Spirit" cannot be forgiven if they turn against God. They've experienced the very presence of God as his Holy Spirit within them and turned against him. There's nothing else God could do to reach such people.

This warning isn't for people who haven't really known God. It's for those who've experienced God's Holy Spirit in their lives. If, after actually experiencing the presence of God's Holy Spirit, they call God a liar or argue that his revelations aren't authoritative, they're certainly in danger of crossing this line. The sad fact is that supposedly Christian seminaries are the most likely place where young people with faith in God may be turned from their faith and wind up actually working against God.

No one can commit this unforgivable sin without first personally experiencing the presence of God's Holy Spirit. But to experience him in your life and then turn against him is the very kiss of eternal death. And it's not about backsliding or getting off course—it's about really turning against God and calling the experience you've had with his Holy Spirit an evil thing. No one does this accidentally or casually.

"The Whole World"

In the Bible, references to "the whole world" or words similar to that shouldn't be taken any more literally than when we use similar words today. When Luke wrote that "everyone in the province of Asia" had heard the message of Christianity while Paul was in Ephesus, he didn't mean that every single person in the province had heard the message. When Paul wrote that the faith of the Christians in Rome was talked of in "the whole world," he didn't mean that people in the Americas or Australia or even northern Europe or southern Africa or eastern Asia had heard. He didn't even mean that all people in the eastern regions of the Roman Empire had heard or that all people in certain provinces had heard.

When we say, "Everybody knows that....," we don't literally mean that every person knows. This is an idiom, and it may not even be true of a majority of the actual people. The same is true in the Bible. "The whole world" should be understood to mean "a majority (or at least a significant minority) of people in the world with which I'm familiar."

Why a New Translation?

There are so many English translations of the Bible today; you may wonder why anybody'd want a new one. Well, here are some of the things that are different about this translation, and it's these differences that provide the answer to that question:

1. All four gospels are blended into a single account. Read this one gospel account and you'll get everything from Matthew, Mark, Luke, and John. By reading all four gospels blended in this way, you, as the reader, can get a better, more complete view of Jesus' life and teachings.
2. Most translations today use words and grammar that are like "Bible-speak" to most Americans. This translation uses normal, conversational English.
3. In many cases, words that weren't religious at all in New Testament times have taken on so much religious baggage that the real meaning has been lost. In this translation, such words have been replaced with words or phrases that communicate the original ideas as written in the Bible.
4. Many of the names of people and places in the Bible are unfamiliar to most Americans. Most of these unfamiliar names aren't important in understanding the message, so, as much as possible; those names are only in the footnotes or the Glossary. For a few cases, a name had to be used even though it might be unfamiliar, and in those cases, there's a Glossary article including a suggestion of how to pronounce the name. (Nobody really knows exactly how to pronounce any of these names—there were no recorders back then.)
5. In this translation, dates are provided for the events surrounding Jesus' birth and his death. There's a great deal of controversy about these dates, and the actual dates don't really matter. These dates are provided to give the reader a feel for the flow of events. The dates have been selected based on a great deal of research. They are reasonable and informed guesses, but they shouldn't be considered part of the Bible message. If these dates prove to be wrong, that doesn't mean that the Bible is wrong.
6. In a couple of cases, honestly translating the meaning of something in the Bible into English words that are easy to understand may create problems with traditions we've held for hundreds or even thousands of years. This translation provides the honest meaning and a Glossary article to explain any issues.
7. This translation also includes the first chapter of the book of Acts, since that chapter is so necessary in completing the story of the life and teachings of Jesus. (A translation of the rest of the book of Acts is in work.)
8. In electronic versions, there are links to and from the footnotes and glossary articles.

<u>About Capital Letters</u>

In Bible times, the alphabet only had one set of letters, so any capitalization in a translation must be added by the translator. In this translation, common practice for American English in non-religious books is the rule. Additional capitalization requires the translator to make judgments about what people might or might not have been thinking when they used certain words, and this translation leaves such judgments up to the reader.

<u>About Footnotes</u>

This translation uses hundreds of footnotes to provide background information. In electronic versions, footnotes are done with links back and forth to simplify references.

Wind, Breath, and Spirit

In the Bible, the word for wind, the word for breath, and the word for spirit are all the same word. The three different concepts were understood in biblical times, but biblical cultures hadn't developed separate words for these three concepts. The result is that the translator needs to gather from the context which way to translate such words. When you're seriously studying the Bible, it can help to remember that a translator chose which way to translate this word, and you have every right to consider whether a different translation might bring out a valid meaning. Just remember, the meaning for the word must be consistent with the context of that passage and of the Bible as a whole.

A good example of this occurs in Jesus' discussion with Nicodemus. Jesus told Nicodemus, "The wind blows wherever it wants, and you can hear the sound it makes, but you can never know where it came from or where it's going. Those who are born of the spirit are like that—the rest of the world can tell they're there but don't understand where they're coming from" (Good News 15:16-17). Notice that in this passage this translation uses both "spirit" and "wind" as translations for this same word.

Understanding this triple meaning helps us understand some other things in the Bible. People often have difficulty understanding the difference between the biblical concept of a person's spirit and a person's soul. There isn't a simple answer that works in all cases, because there's some overlap in the intent of these words, but the fact that the three meanings given above all apply to one word probably indicates that "spirit" generally has something to do with a person's breathing, while the idea of a person's soul will not normally have that implication. The soul is the very essence of who a person is. If a person's body were to be completely replaced by another body, as long as the soul remained the same, the person would be the same person. The spirit may be an expression of the soul, but it's never that soul essence of the person.

When it comes to evil spirits or demons, this matter of three very different meanings for just one word may give us a clue to how people classified diseases as either physical or spiritual. Again, there's no line you can draw to say that the Bible always speaks of things on this side as the result of evil spirits and things on the other side as the result of physical illnesses. Anything that was obviously physical got classified as physical. Anything that didn't seem to have a clear physical cause might well be classified as the work of evil spirits. But just based on the word usage and a review of cases mentioned in the Bible, it's possible that one factor in determining involvement of an evil spirit might be some involvement of breathing, external attitude, or speech (which requires breathing). (Also see the article on Evil Spirits above.)

Priests Named Zechariah

There are two Zechariahs we need to consider here: Zechariah who became the father of John the Immerser and an Old Testament prophet named Zechariah:

Zechariah the Father of John the Immerser (Good News 1:3-12, 32-38)

The priest mentioned at the beginning of this translation as the husband of Elizabeth and the father of John was named Zechariah (some translations call him Zacharias). Don't confuse this Zechariah with the Jewish prophet who was also named Zechariah and who wrote the book of Zechariah. That prophet lived hundreds of years earlier, though the New Testament Zechariah was surely named for that prophet. From evidence in the prophet Zechariah's book and other places in the Old Testament, we know that the prophet was also a priest, just like this Zechariah. In fact, this Zechariah may well have been a direct descendant of that Jewish prophet.

For details on the Jewish priests, see Priests / Chief Priests in this Glossary. Zechariah was in the priestly division known as the Abijah Division.

At the time of Zechariah, the temple compound consisted of four courtyards and the temple building itself (see Herod's Temple above). The courtyards included 1) the outer courtyard known as the court of the nations (open to anyone), 2) the court of women (open to all Israelites), 3) the court of Israel (open only to Jewish men), and finally the inner court known as 4) the court of the priests. It was necessary to go through the court of the nations to reach the court of women, and through the court of women to reach the court of Israel, and then through that court to reach the court of the priests.

At the very heart of the temple compound within the court of the priests was the temple building itself, an extremely sacred area. Huge doors allowed access to the temple, but this access was only for selected priests. The temple itself consisted of two rooms separated by a huge curtain. The first room or holy place contained three pieces of furniture: a lamp-stand with seven oil lamps on its seven arms, an altar for burning incense, and a table where sacred bread was placed fresh each Sunday. The inner room was considered the Most Holy Place and only the High Priest was allowed to enter this room—and he only entered once a year. Twice every day a priest would enter the first room to offer incense to God. A priest would be selected by lot to offer incense each morning and each evening, and once he'd offered incense, he could never serve in that capacity again. Given the number of priests, it would've taken more than 25 years for all the priests to serve one time, and with continual addition of new priests, there was no problem having enough priests to accomplish this ministry every day. Some priests served a lifetime without ever having this honor.

Zechariah had served in the temple compound many times, but his service in the temple building itself was the first and only time. The Altar of Incense was next to the inner curtain that separated the Holy Place where Zechariah was from the Most Holy Place. On the other side of the curtain was God's place—the place of the Ark of the Covenant where God himself had met with Moses. (We don't know if the Ark of the Covenant was actually in the temple at this time—it may well have been lost or destroyed at some point long before this time—but this area was still considered God's area.) Incense was burned as a symbol of prayers being offered to God while at the same time, people outside in the temple courtyards were offering their prayers.

As a possible scenario, let's imagine that Zechariah was taking advantage of his golden opportunity to pour out his heart to the Lord about the child he and Elizabeth wanted so much, possibly even complaining to God about how faithfully they'd served God and how God hadn't rewarded this faithfulness with even one child. If that was the case, the appearance of Gabriel standing on the right side of the altar might easily have caused anyone to be terrified. This priest was supposed to be there to represent the people, the nation of Israel, not his own petty issues. And even entering this part of the temple was scary. Then the sudden appearance of this "man" would've left no doubt in Zechariah's mind that he was an agent from God with power to bring God's wrath down on anyone who displeased him.

Yet it's amazing how quickly we can go from fear of the Lord to skepticism. Given Elizabeth's age, it's not too hard to imagine Zechariah, who might already have been a little bitter in his prayers, replying with skepticism to this agent's promise of what seemed, from a human perspective, to be impossible. As for Gabriel, he seriously scolded Zechariah, but in his heart Gabriel was probably ready to break out laughing because he already knew how much joy this birth was going to bring into the life of this priest and his wife as well as many others.

It's interesting to note that in the Bible, the words Zechariah used that caused Gabriel to strike him mute are exactly the same as the words Mary used to Gabriel. The difference wasn't the words, but the attitude.

Zechariah, the Old Testament Prophet (Good News 13:33-70 – specifically verse 68)

The information above on the New Testament priest named Zechariah starts out with some information about this Old Testament prophet who was also a priest. But Jesus also referred to this prophet in a different context having nothing to do with that Zechariah.

Zechariah, the Old Testament prophet, was the son of Berechiah and one of the last of the Old Testament prophets. The Old Testament doesn't tell us how he died, but it's obvious from what Jesus said about him that he was murdered in the temple compound for having done right. In this conversation, Jesus mentioned Abel as the first righteous man in the Old Testament who was killed for having done right, and he mentioned Zechariah as the last of the Old Testament heroes who was killed for having done right. Jesus was telling the religious leaders of his time that their actions were making them share in the guilt for the murder of all the righteous people in the Old Testament.

Made in the USA
Charleston, SC
26 June 2016